GW01607460

From Cradle to Grave in a Fenland Town

Wisbech Photographed by Lilian Ream

Published by The Bluecoat Press, Liverpool
Book design by Michael March
Printed by Grafo, Spain

ISBN 9781904438960

Acknowledgements
We wish to thank the following for their generous help and support: David & Barbara Oliver, George Dunlop, Cambridgeshire County Council, The Hudson Foundation, The Robert Hall Charity and The Wisbech Society.

Many of the original negatives are in a poor condition and some of the photographs in this book reflect the fire and water damage, chemical deterioration and poor storage they have suffered. Rather than omit interesting photographs, it was decided to include them with their defects in part to highlight the extensive archival work still required to conserve this nationally important treasure.

Captioning the photographs has been hindered by the absence of any studio day books logging the negatives. The Lilian Ream Exhibition Gallery Trust welcomes any corrections or additional information that will help fill in any missing information.

Lilian Ream Exhibition Gallery Trust
c/o Wisbech Library, 5 Ely Place, Wisbech, Cambs., PE13 1EU
www.lilianream.org.uk

From Cradle to Grave in a Fenland Town

Wisbech Photographed by Lilian Ream

Compiled by Colin Wilkinson and Robert Bell

THE BLUECOAT PRESS

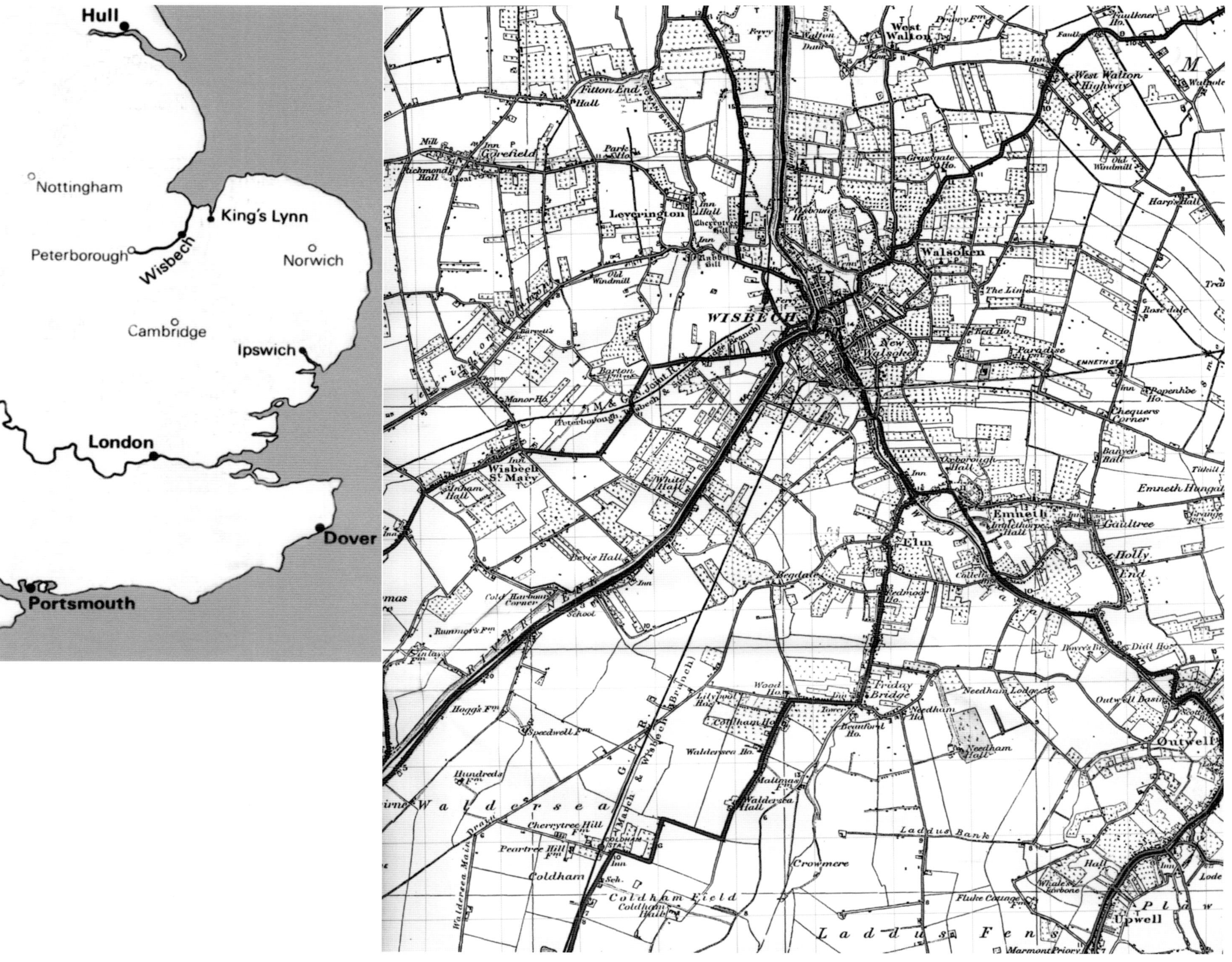

Hull
Nottingham
King's Lynn
Wisbech
Peterborough
Norwich
Cambridge
Ipswich
London
Dover
Portsmouth
West Walton
West Walton Highway
Fitton End
Hall
Gorefield
Leverington
Old Windmill
Walsoken
WISBECH
New Walsoken
The Limes
Rose dale
Paradise
EMNETH STA
Popenhoe Ho.
Chequers Corner
Banyer Hall
Harps Hall
Oxborough Hall
Wisbech St. Mary
White Hall
Emneth
Emneth Hungate
Gaultree
Holly End
Elm
Begdale
Bevis Hall
River Nene
Friday Bridge
Needham
Needham Hall
Outwell Basin
Outwell
Coldham Hall
Waldersea Hall
Waldersea
Hundreds Fm
Speedwell Fm
Hogg's Fm
Cherrytree Hill
Peartree Hill
Coldham
Coldham Field
Crowmere
Laddus Bank
Laddus Fens
Upwell
Marmont Priory

Contents

LILIAN REAM
WISBECH
TELEGRAMS: LILIAN REAM, WISBECH.
TELEPHONE: WISBECH 236.

FROM
Mrs. REAM,
Photographic Artist,
THE
Crescent Studio.
Branch Establishment
ALEXANDRA ROAD,
WISBECH.
Grandford House
March

FROM
LILIAN REAM
M.P.P.A.
Photographic Artist,
Crescent Studio
WISBECH.
Central Showrooms :
MARKET ST., WISBECH
Branches :
Alexandra Rd., Wisbech
Market Street,
LONG SUTTON.

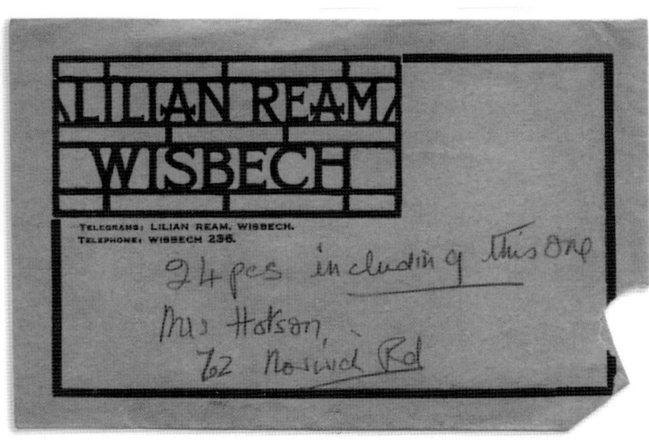

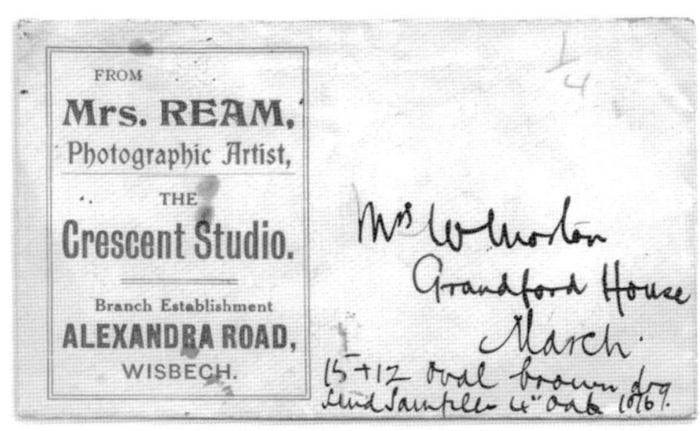

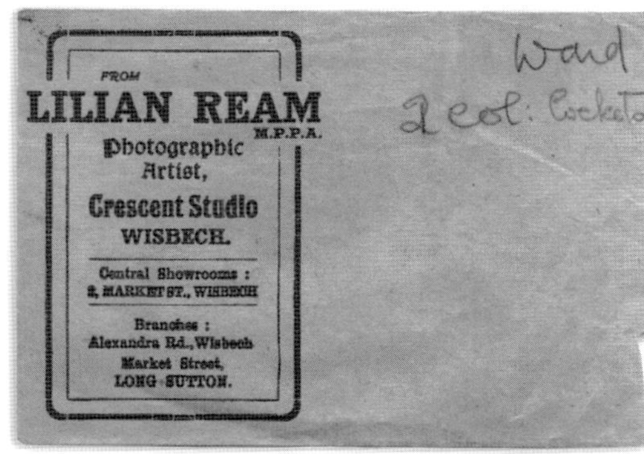

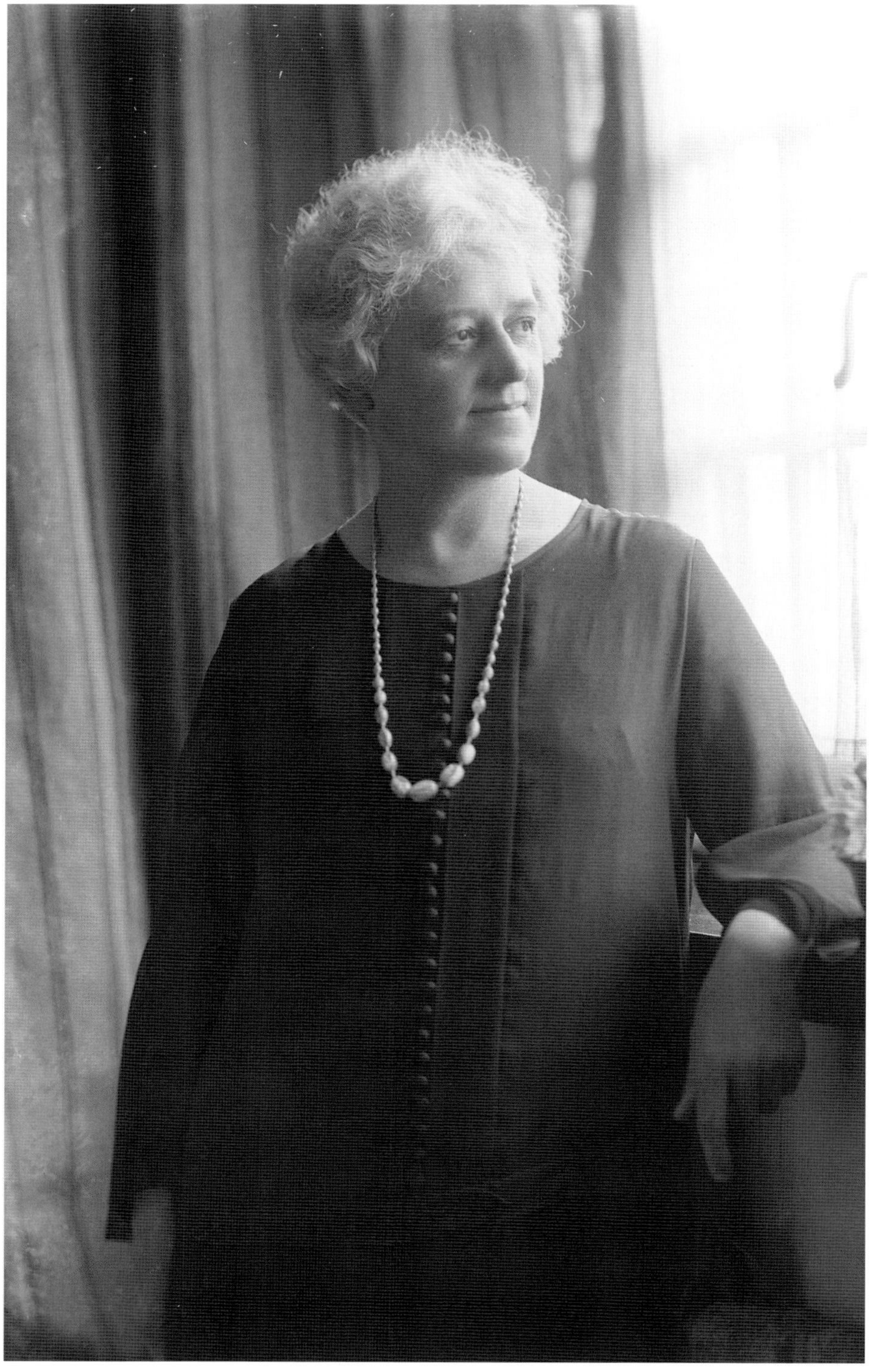

Lilian Ream poses for the camera, which must have been a daunting prospect for the photographer, late 1920s.

Introduction

I came across Lilian Ream's work by chance. As a publisher of photographic books about my home town, Liverpool, I was always on the lookout for new images. At that time, in the mid-1990s, auctions still provided the best source and I would regularly scan local newspapers for notice of future sales. In the *Daily Post*, which covered Liverpool and North Wales, I caught sight of an entry in a Colwyn Bay auction for several thousand glass negatives. For business reasons, I could not attend the sale but I telephoned and was given a brief description of the contents of the lot. For the first time, and totally out of character, since I had never bought anything unseen, I placed a telephone bid.

The following day I drove to the auction house to collect my winning lot. To my dismay, I was led to a pile of broken suitcases and collapsed cardboard boxes, all crammed with negatives in a clearly dilapidated state. Four thousand negatives take up quite a space and, when loaded in the car, the smell of chemical deterioration forced me to drive back with all the car windows wide open.

Back home, I opened the first leather suitcase and brushed away the dust and cobwebs of years of neglect. Most of the negatives were still in their envelopes, each with a pencilled name and negative number. Many were cracked or had sustained serious damage, including emulsion that peeled off at the touch – but most were in a viewable condition, perhaps saved from damage by being so tightly packed together. One by one, I placed them on a lightbox and began to realise what a treasure trove I had just bought, for here, in front of me, was the everyday life of a small market town in the Fens in the 1920s and 30s.

I selected out a hundred negatives and paid for them to be printed. Looking at the 10"x8" prints, I recognised there was a book worth publishing but I knew nothing about the collection and little about Wisbech. These were the days before the internet and information was not readily available. So I sat on the prints and negatives until an article in *The Times* (6 November 1999) reawakened my interest. Lilian Ream's old house at No. 4 The Crescent was up for sale (for £134,995) and the newspaper featured its sale with a short description of the pioneering photographer.

It has taken a further eleven years to get to this stage, during which time my admiration of Lilian Ream has grown. By reputation, she was strong-willed and fierce tempered but, as a woman in business in the early twentieth century, she had to have a forceful personality to succeed, especially in a small town where any weakness would be quickly exploited. As a photographer, her apprenticeship as a photographic artist had included every aspect of taking photographs, particularly portraits, as well as retouching negatives and hand colouring prints. This solid training may have lacked originality and spontaneity but it had all the groundings for a career as a commercial photographer.

Lilian Ream was no innovator, although Wisbech already had a strong photographic tradition. Valentine Blanchard, born in Wisbech in 1831, was an important early photographer, but it was the work of Samuel Smith that is possibly best remembered today. Sometimes called the 'father of documentary photography', Smith was a well-to-do builder and amateur scientist who was fascinated by the new invention of 'painting with light'. As a result, Wisbech has one of the finest records of its mid-nineteenth century development of any provincial town in Britain. Lilian Ream may have lacked some of Smith's innovative drive but she had the commercial acumen to create her own unique record of Fenland life in the first half of the twentieth century.

Ream's business was initially built on portraiture. In the days before mass camera ownership, there was a ready demand for studio portraits, particularly during the First World War when so many young men enlisted in the armed forces. Studio portraits had moved on little from its early days, with painted backdrops and staid room sets. For children, teddy bears and other toys were used to create the semblance of animation and Ream was not averse to taking her own children's Christmas presents to the studio for use as props.

As her business developed, the advantages of having a near monopoly of the commercial photography market in a small town paid dividends. The local newspapers regularly used her images and she quickly turned every small disaster and accident, every parade and fete, every shop opening and civic ceremony into a money-making opportunity. These were also the golden days of the photographic postcard, presenting another income stream to be exploited.

Above all, Lilian Ream realised the value of the group photograph. Unlike the later days of hand-held cameras and roll-film technology, the plate camera was a cumbersome piece of equipment that required each glass negative to be placed in a holder before exposure. Photographers had to be adept at taking the minimum number of plates, whilst, at the same time, trying to organise a group of people to pose in front of the lens. The successful group photograph was well worth the effort and could lead to multiple orders for prints. An outstanding feature of the Ream archive is the number of groups of workmen, school children, societies, churchgoers and so on. From rat-catchers to Primitive Methodists, masonic lodges to beauty queen contestants (with and without hats), rose queens to fruit pickers, Ream's camera was there to record them all for posterity.

In a contemporary setting, the work of American photographer, Neal Slavin, has interesting parallels. His 1976 book, *When Two or More are Gathered Together* concentrated on social clubs, professional societies, sports associations, and other gatherings of people. His work is, perhaps, a parody of the work of photographers like Lilian Ream but it is also a reminder of the shared interests and activities that take place in the workplace, school or social life. What Lilian Ream has captured is a rich seam of association between the people of this small Fenland area, which evokes both a sense of loss of a lost past and astonishment at the extent of activities that are revealed image after image.

Remarkably, Wisbech's population in 1931 was only 12,000. The photographs suggest a much bigger town, for every event is packed with spectators. Did anyone escape the seemingly ever-present lens, for the photographs include not only the comfortable middle classes but also rundown back-streets and children with holes in their clothes. One particularly poignant photograph is of the combined tea of the inhabitants of the workhouse and the almhouses (pages 172/3); a rare and haunting shot of the lives of the under-privileged that contrasts with the monocled James de Rothschild in his spats (page 126).

The Lilian Ream archive is, in my experience, the most comprehensive record of its kind in Britain. That it has survived fire, water damage, poor storage and chemical deterioration is a miracle. This book is, I hope, a fitting tribute to a great, pioneering photographer. I have chosen the title *From Cradle to Grave* because every aspect of town life was captured, however fleetingly. As a record of its times, the archive is indispensible. For those interested in fashion, transport, industry or civic life in general, there is a wealth of detail, and family historian tracing their roots will be unlucky not to find a relative amongst the thousands of faces. As a national treasure, the collection is too little known and, hopefully, this book will redress the situation and create a greater awareness of the importance of Lilian Ream's lifetime achievement.

Colin Wilkinson

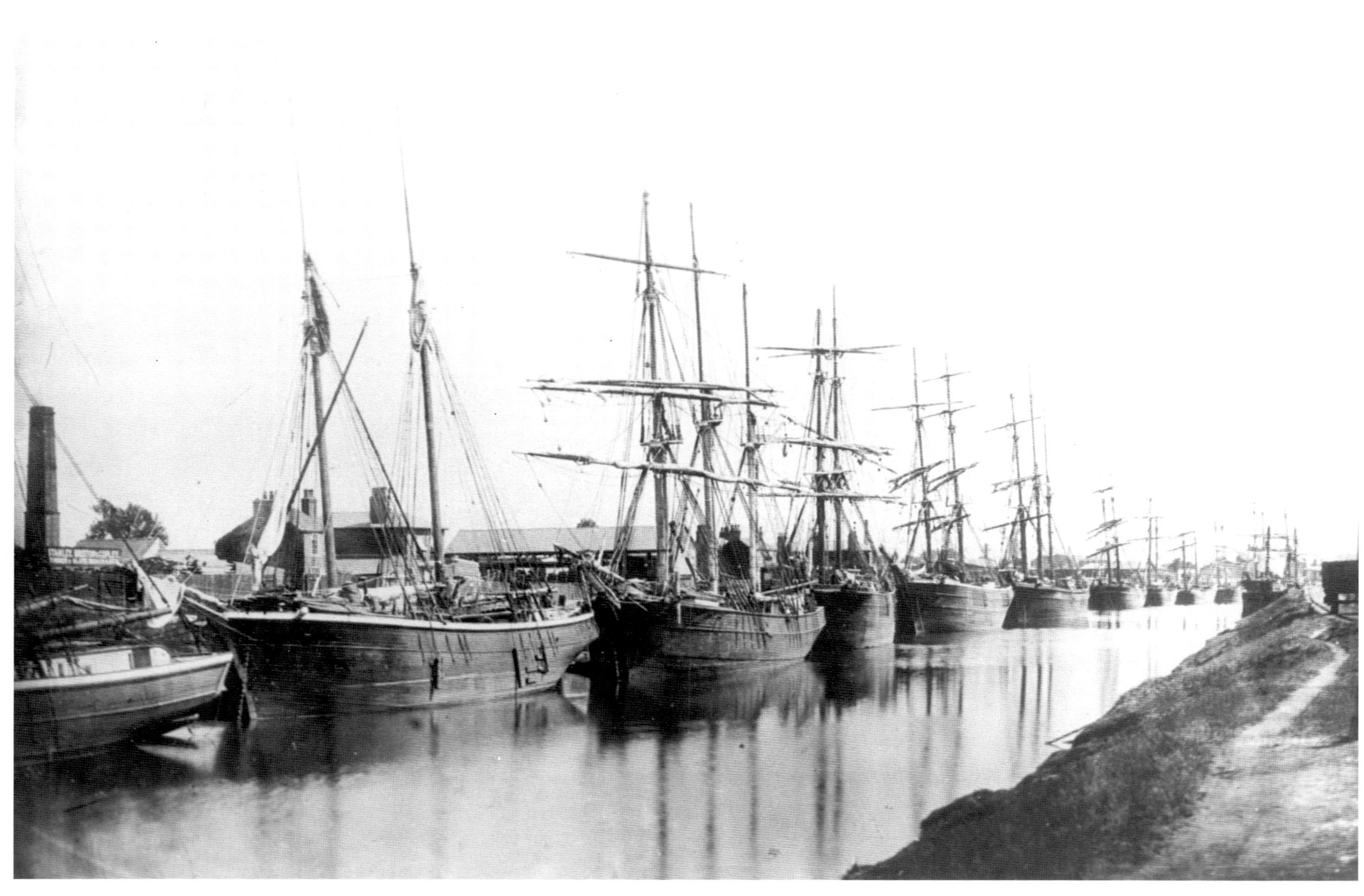

A fine array of sailing ships moored in Wisbech Port, c1880. As Lilian Ream's business expanded, she acquired many nineteenth century negatives, as well as producing copies of much earlier prints.

Wisbech

Wisbech is located around ninety miles to the north of London, at the coming together of the three counties of Cambridgeshire, Norfolk and Lincolnshire. Although several miles from the sea, Wisbech is the only port in Cambridgeshire. The town's former importance as an administrative and commercial centre is sometimes overlooked, prompting queries as to why the town is referred to as the 'Capital of the Fens'

Although there were undoubtedly earlier settlements at Wisbech, the first authenticated mention of the place name occurs in AD 1000 when it was one of several manors given by Oswy to the monastery of Ely on the occasion of his son, Ailwyn, becoming a monk.There are many theories as to the derivation of the town's name. There is the combination 'Ouze' and 'beck' referring to a beach near the Ouse. Alternatively you have the 'Wyse' and 'bec' theory which is a combination of the river Wissey and the Saxon name for a stream. In the 1660s local tradesmen issued several tokens that had a variety of spellings – Wisbidg, Wisbitch, Wisbich and Wisbech. In more recent years the interest in the town's name has centred on when it lost its 'a'. The use of the spelling 'Wisbeach' seems to have begun in the 18th century and there seems to have been a dual usage until the 1870s. At this time the Postmaster General and various railway companies were approached for their opinion and it was decided to lose the 'a'. One local wit asked whether, if the towns of Holbeach, Landbeach and Waterbeach were to drop their 'a', would Wisbech restore theirs!

After the conquest of William I, the Fens remained a troublesome problem for the new king and it was not until the betrayal and defeat of Hereward the Wake that the Normans could exercise any measure of control in this inhospitable and dangerous land. William's great survey of 1086, the *Domesday Book*, records 'Wisbece' as a modest vill (village) although substantial eel fisheries are mentioned. The following year the strategic importance of Wisbech was recognised by the Conqueror with the construction of a stone castle, which probably replaced an earlier timber and earthwork complex.

Wisbech's past wealth has been closely linked to the river and from mediaeval times up to the 18th century the town enjoyed periods of relative prosperity, punctuated by calamitous inundations that set the town's development back on its heels. The port too has seen similar ups and downs. When the Great Ouse, which flowed through the Well Stream, was diverted to King's Lynn around 1300, the silting of the estuary at Wisbech became a serious problem. However, with the cutting of Moreton's Leam, in 1478, the River Nene became Wisbech's principal artery to the sea and the town enjoyed a revival of its fortunes.

It was not until the early 18th century that the benefits of the large-scale drainage schemes of the previous century began to be felt. The subsequent prosperity of the district is praised in the Wisbech entry in the *Universal British Directory of Trade and Commerce* of the 1790s, which stated that the area had 'been in a most flourishing and productive state, the fields seem to laugh and sing with their superabundant produce'.

Before the coming of the railways, and later motor transport, the source of much of Wisbech's wealth stemmed from its port. Coal was brought in from North East England and timber from the Baltic. Ironically, the port's timber trade boomed during the 1840s and 1850s with the heavy demand for wood for new railway lines that were spreading across the country.

With the growth of the timber trade, a series of extensive wood yards were established in the port area along Nene Parade. Before mechanisation, men would carry the planks of wood direct from the boats into the yards using trestles to walk on. With the reduction in the trade few of the yards remain, although recently there has been a modest revival in timber imports.

With regards to exports, since the 18th century, the corn trade has been of prime importance to the mercantile health of the town. Vast quantities once passed through the town's markets – even more than London. Corn was shipped both around the coast of Britain and also to the continent. Large granaries were raised along Nene Quay and the west bank of the river from the bridge to West Parade. Of the few that have survived, most have been converted into flats. One of these was once occupied by H Friend, 'Metal, Feather & Skin Merchant'.

In the 19th century it was common to see thirty or more ships in the port at one time. They would moor right up to the town bridge in the sharp bend in the river beyond the bridge that was known as 'The Throttle'. Even in modern times, boats laden with oranges and bananas would come up to the warehouses on the west bank at the rear of the Old Market. However, with the opening of the Freedom Bridge in 1971, this became impossible. Now a busy road, Nene Quay was once an important unloading site in the port, the Corporation even going to the expense of constructing a crane and wharf in 1845.

When approaching Wisbech from Peterborough, either by road or river, the traveller, on passing through the industrial outskirts, is greeted by the wonderful prospect of the River Nene flanked by the North and South Brinks; the lesser Georgian and Victorian properties gradually give way to the more substantial houses of North Brink that are the core of what the architectural historian Nicholas Pevsner described as 'one of the most perfect Georgian streets in England'.

A market had existed on the left bank of the River Nene in Saxon times and as early as 1223 it had become known as the Old Market. This market became the centre for farming, fruit and horticulture and, in the past, sheep and cattle. The newer Market Place was formed just outside of the walls of the Norman Castle and dealt with locals' goods as well as those from outside the district. Originally there was only a market held on Saturdays but a second one was later introduced on Thursdays.

If the commercial significance of the town grew largely from the port, then its administrative importance stemmed from the Normans' recognition of Wisbech as being located at a strategic point where a castle could guard against incursions into the fenlands from the Wash. By the early 20th century, this was reflected in the town's status as a municipal borough, the administrative centre of the Wisbech Union, which also covered parts of West Norfolk; and a county court district.

As Lilian Ream's photographic business emerged and expanded in the first half of the 20th century it was well placed to record Wisbech as it developed through the Edwardian era, the Great War and the inter-war period. The firm was on hand to document Coronation and Jubilee celebrations, as well as major events such as the Wisbech Pageant of 1929 which was written and produced by the historian Sir Arthur Bryant. Any improvement to the town was photographed, with images regularly appearing in the local press. For instance, when the present town bridge was opened in 1931, this major construction project was recorded in the papers, using Ream photographs, from the first stages of the construction, side by side with the existing iron bridge, to the official opening.

During this period, the local fruit industry was at its peak and its many aspects were recorded by Lilian Ream. Seasonal workers from the East End of London were photographed on their arrival at Wisbech East Station and at the 'bunks' where they lodged on local farms whilst picking strawberries, raspberries, blackberries, apples pears and plums. Other aspects of the industry that were photographed were chip basket manufacturing, fruit transportation via the railways and fruit processing by such firms as Smedleys.

The photographs of Lilian Ream are an invaluable record of a market town at a time when it could be considered the equal of its neighbours Peterborough and King's Lynn; when it was a vibrant shopping centre serving town and district, and major public events and celebrations were frequent occurrences on the public calendar.

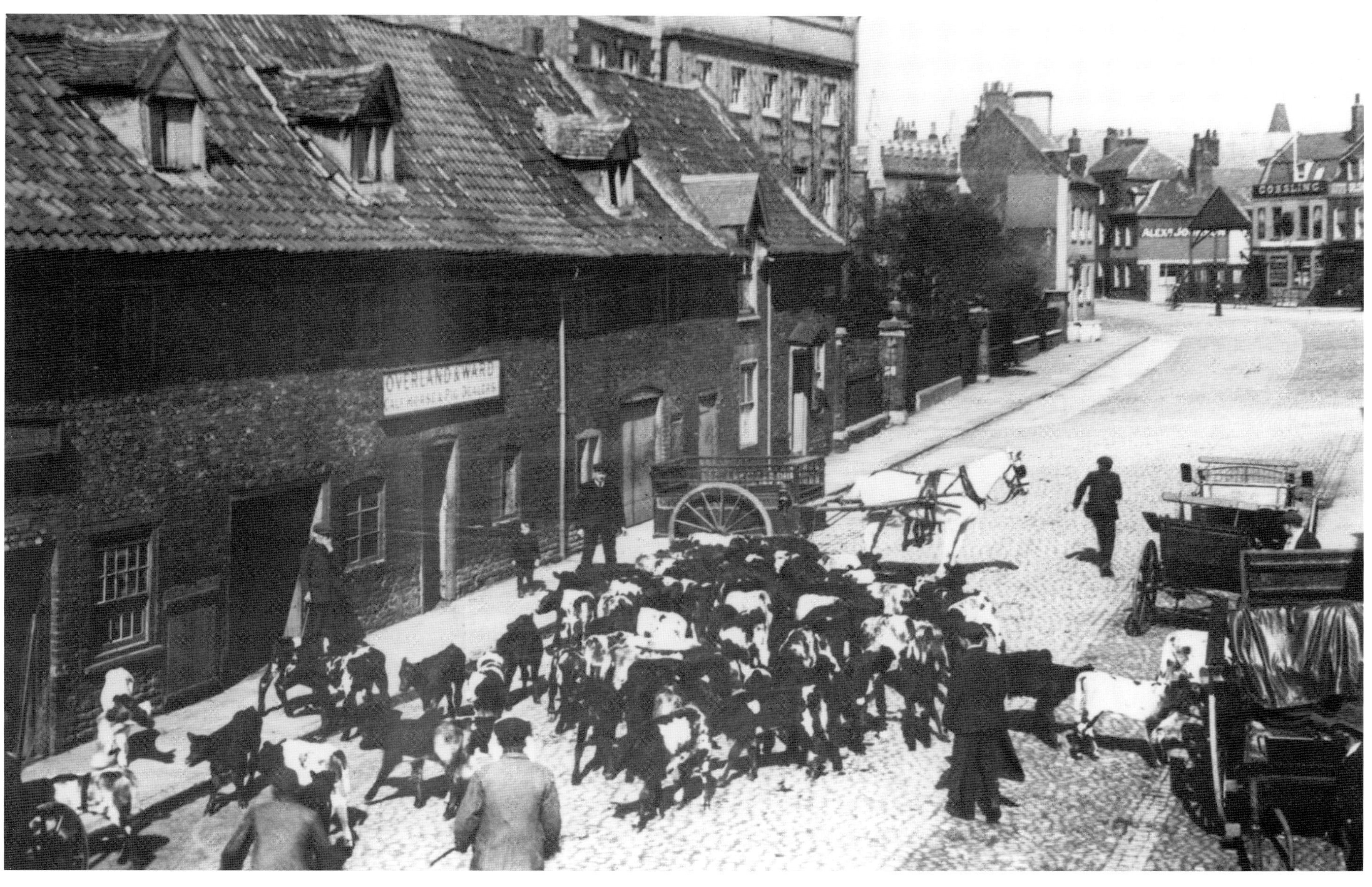

Chapel Road, Wisbech, c1910. Men attempting to 'coral' calves outside the premises of Overland & Ward, Calf, Horse & Pig Dealers, presumably in preparation for taking them to the nearby Cattle Market.

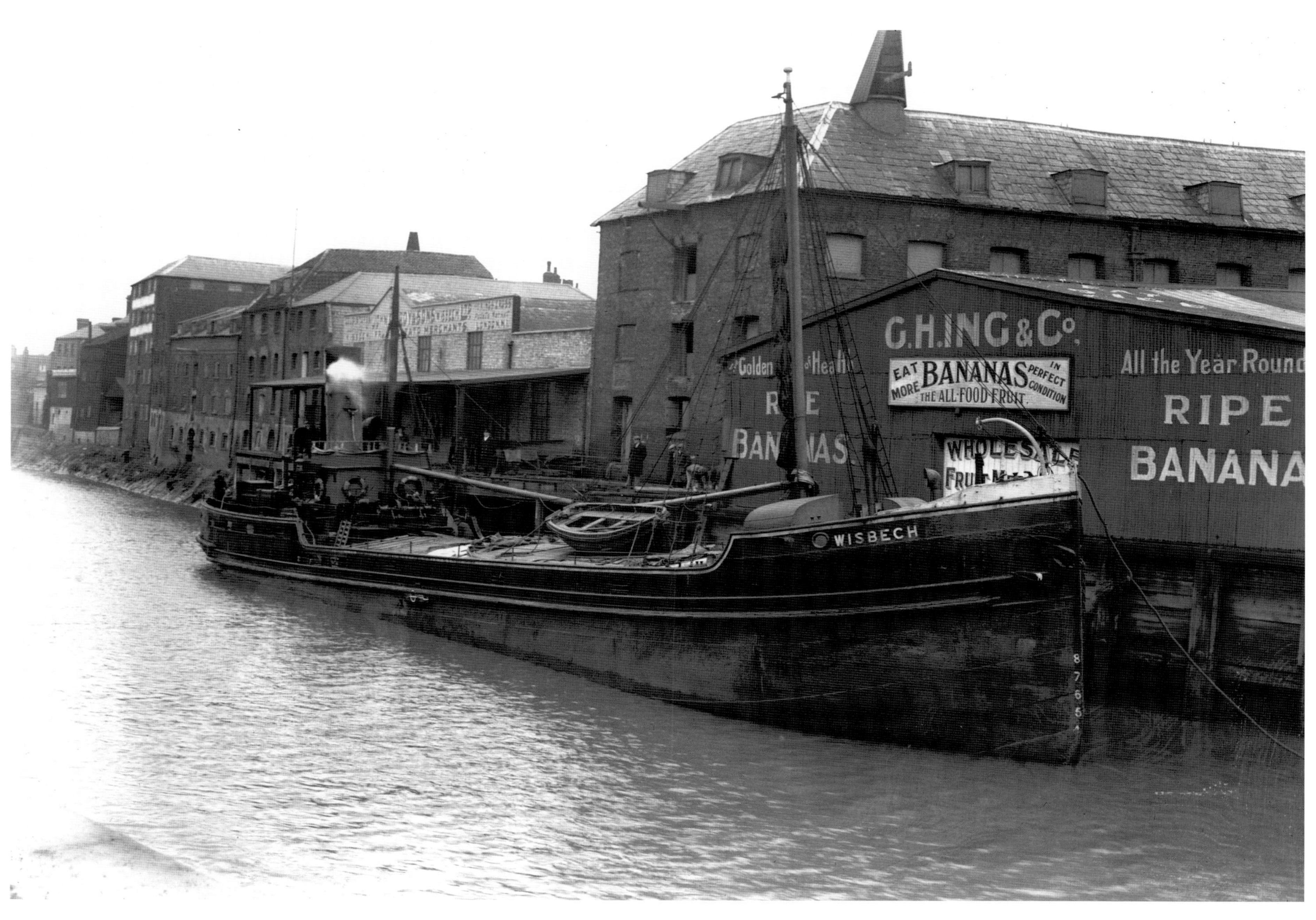

SS Wisbech moored at Messrs Gregory and Hampson's Wharf, February 1932. The Wisbech was a single deck steamer of 220 tons with collapsible mast and funnel; she was first of fleet of steamers which, in conjunction with river barges, linked Peterborough, Ely, Cambridge and Wisbech to the coast.

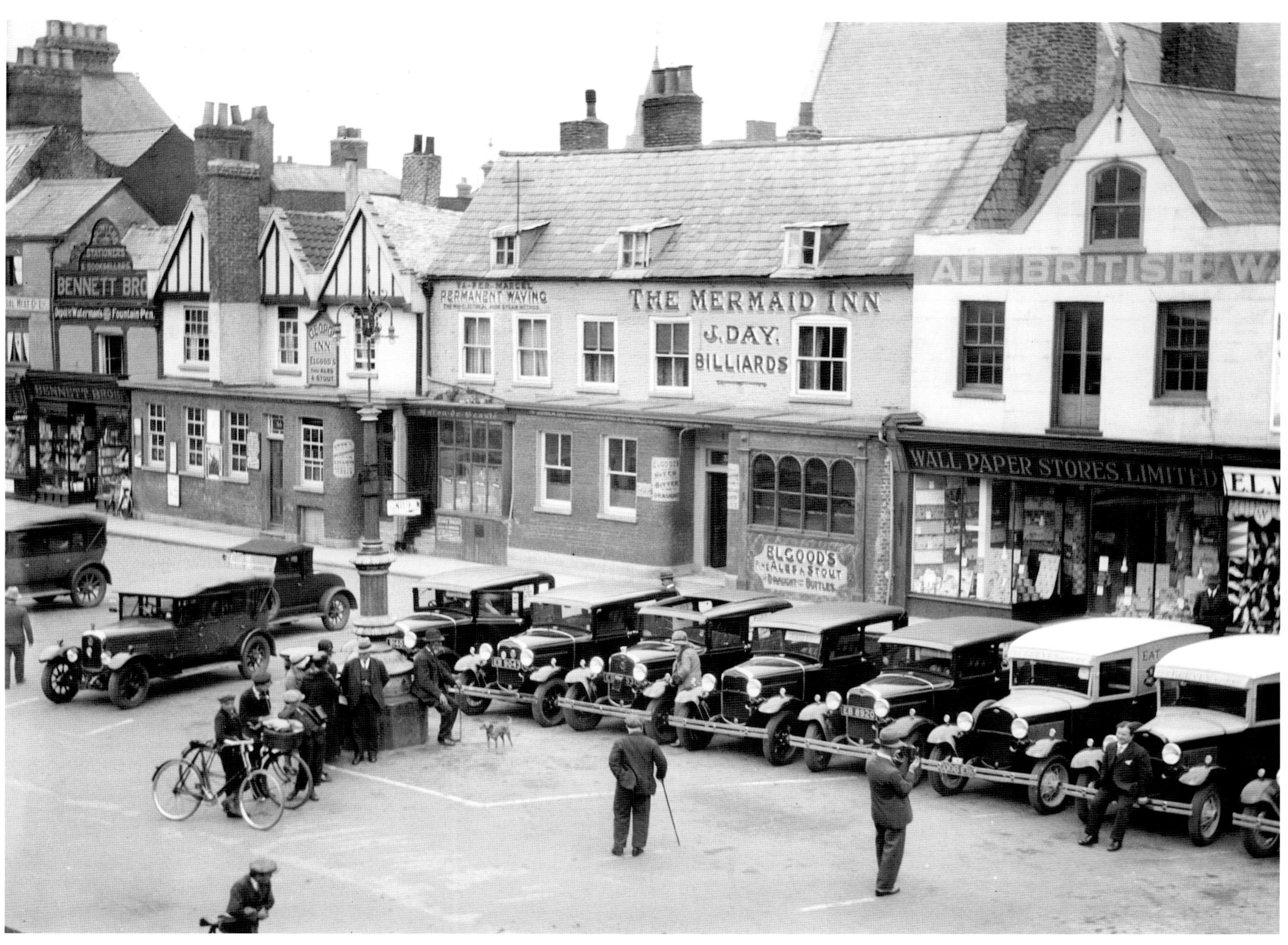

Wisbech Market Place in 1931. In the background are the George Inn and the Mermaid Inn two of the many inns and taverns that at one time flourished around the centre of town.

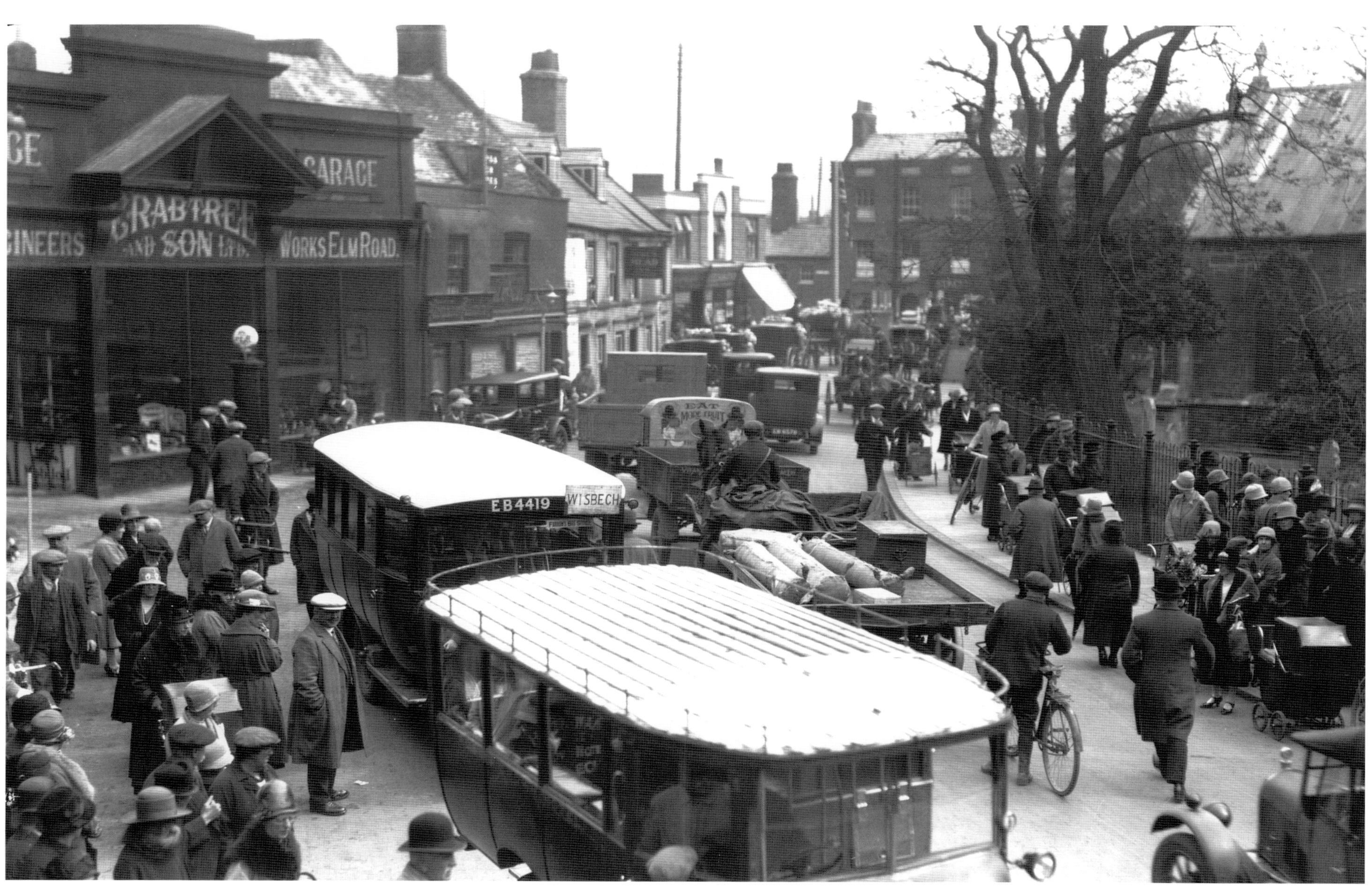

Church Terrace, Wisbech, 1928. Pedestrians, cyclists, horse drawn and motor vehicles jostle for space on the main road through the centre of Wisbech to Downham Market.

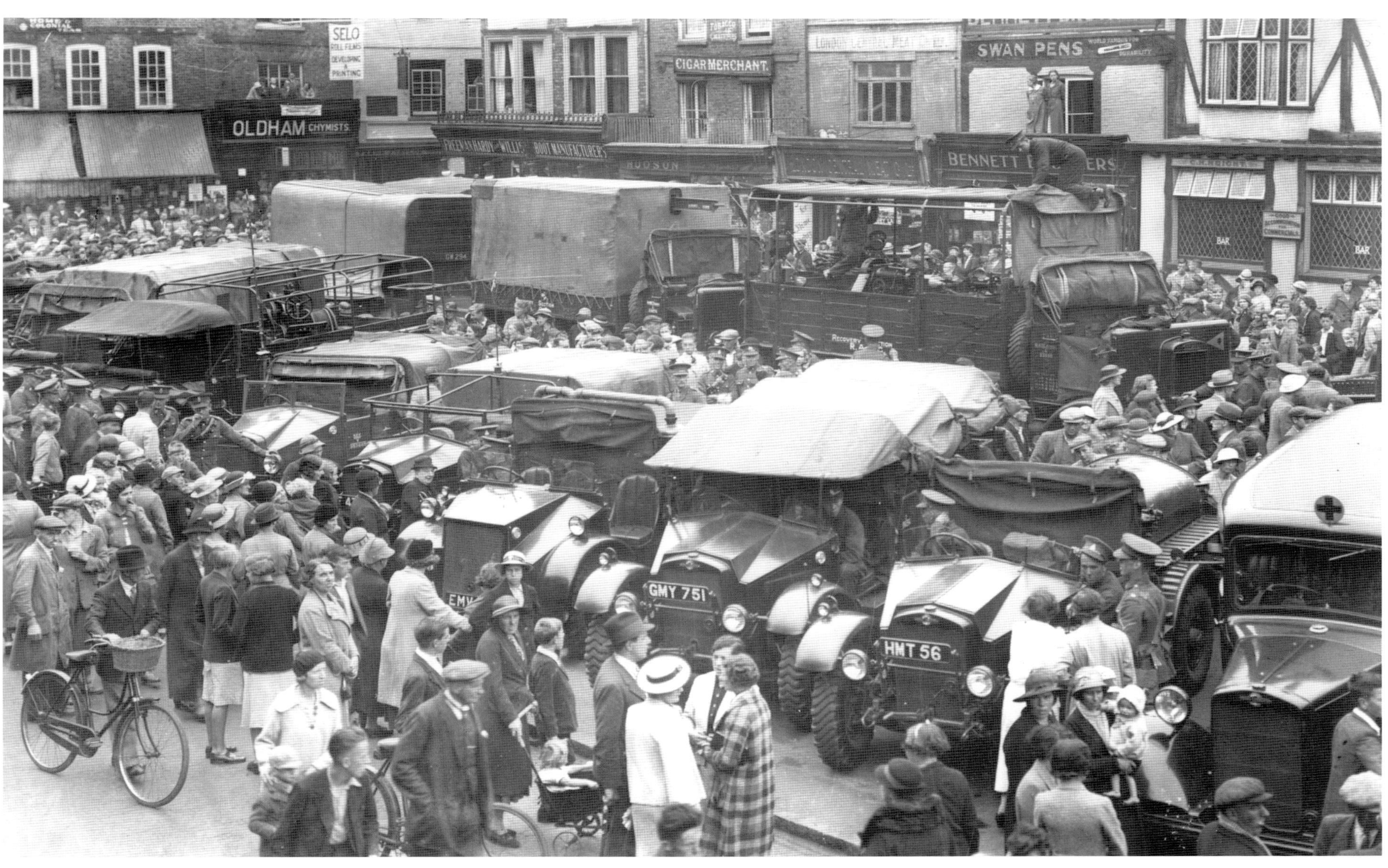

A display of a variety of vehicles of the Royal Army Service Corps on Wisbech Market Place between the wars. They range from ambulances to vehicles of the Recovery Section.

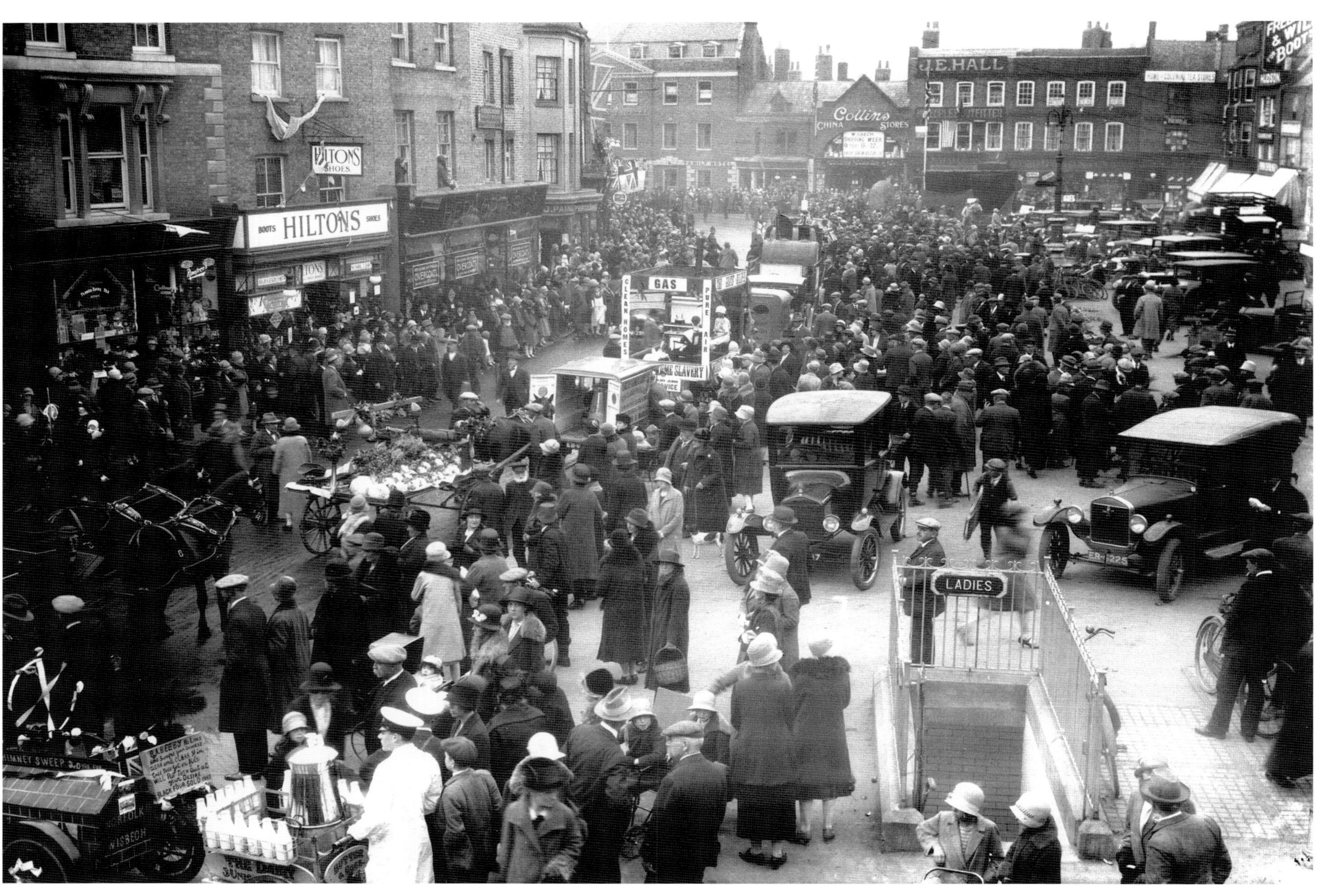

Shopping Week parade, Market Place, Wisbech, 1927. An opportunity for local traders to promote their businesses, this section of the parade includes displays of local produce and the benefits of gas in the home; whilst in the bottom right of the picture can be seen BA Beeby, Chimney Sweep of Norfolk Street.

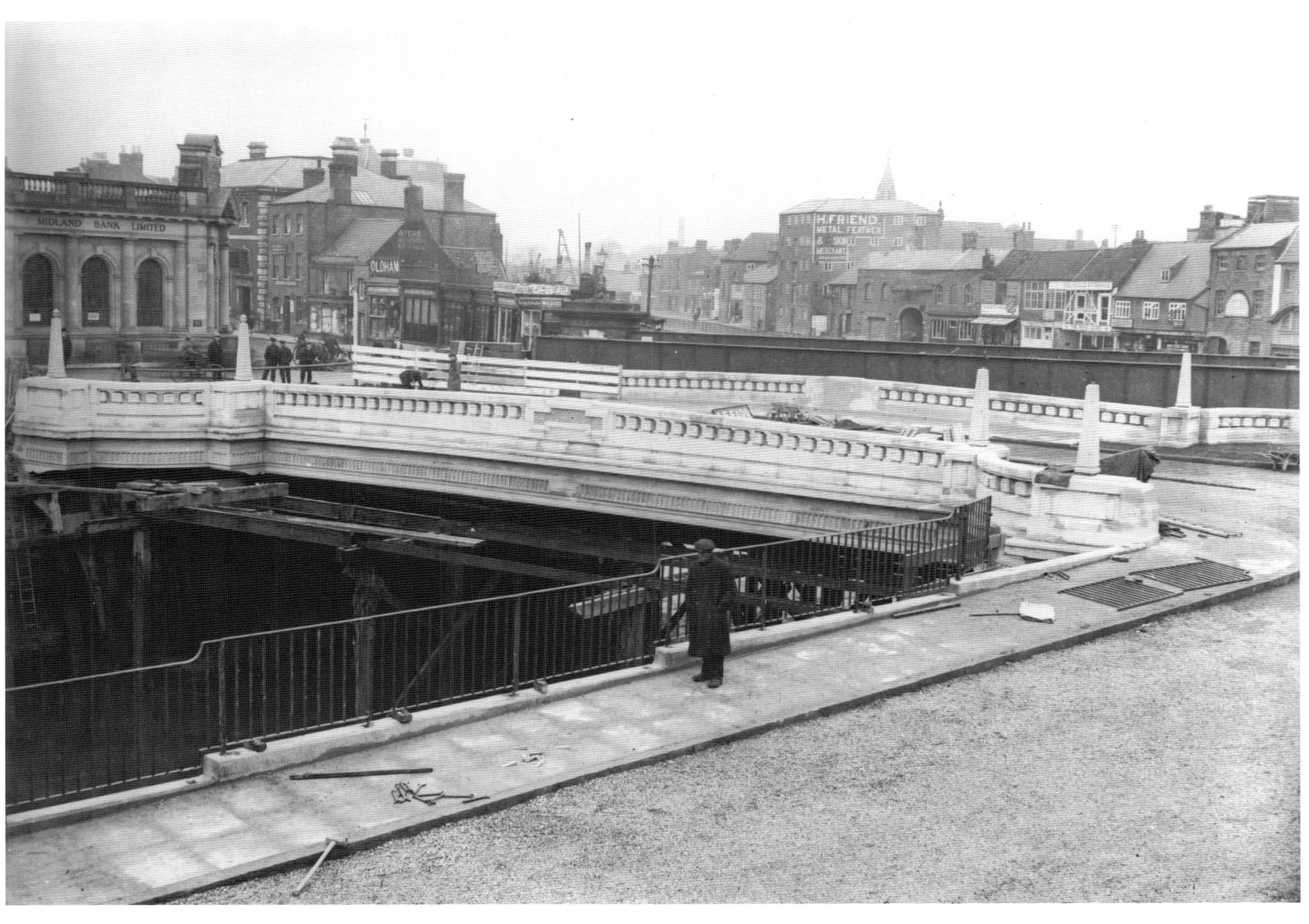

The new Town Bridge, nearing completion in early 1931. The bridge was constructed of concrete, with the upper parapets made by a local firm, Tidnams, who were pioneers in the use of pre-cast concrete.

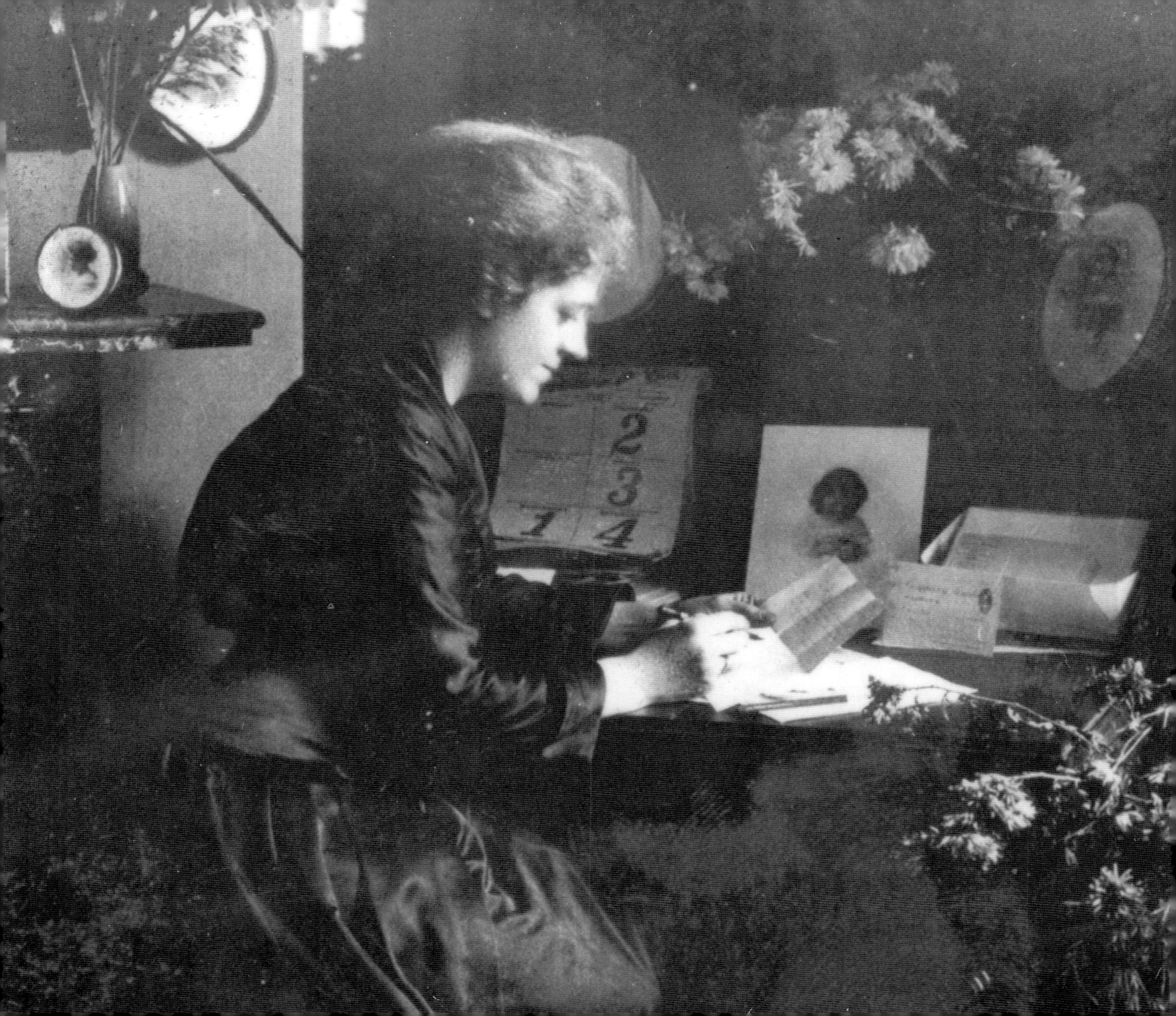
2
3
1 4

Lilian Ream

Lilian Ream was born in the village of West Walton, Norfolk, on 30 June 1877, the youngest daughter of a farmer, John Thomas Pratt and his wife Louisa. A precocious child, Lilian was educated at the private school run by Mrs Bradley at Wisbech Castle.

At the age of seventeen, Lilian became apprenticed to Alfred Drysdale whose photographic studio was situated in Lynn Road, Wisbech. Drysdale's studio had originally been started by Valentine Blanchard Junior, who had, on moving to Cambridge, sold the business to John Hinley; it was from Hinley that Dyrsdale acquired The Studio. Lilian remained with the firm through two more changes of ownership, firstly under Hardingham R Mehew and then with Leonard Smith, who was well known for his exploits as goalkeeper for Wisbech Town Football Club. Ream completed her training at the Borough Studio in York Row, which had been set up by John Kennerell around 1893. Prior to this he had had premises at 8 & 9 High Street, firstly as Beales & Kennerell and then on his own. The business was subsequently taken over by J Lawrence Brown and, by 1908, Lilian, now Brown's manageress, was made a partner in the firm.

The partnership proved to be a failure, at the core of which was a dispute over Ream's salary, and this led to her resignation. This was the background to a long and bitter rivalry between the two photographers.The split with Brown was formalised on 9 April 1909 after prolonged negotiations. Eight days later Ream launched The Crescent Studio at 4 The Crescent. The Reams lived on the premises and a studio with darkroom, changing and storage rooms covering a floor area of around 700 square feet was built in the garden. Before her split with Brown, there been had major changes in her personal life. On 25 January 1905, Lilian married Sydney Ream in the Zion Baptist Chapel, Victoria Road, and the newlyweds lived in the nearby Lonsdale Terrace. A couple of years later, their first child, John Roland Fosbrook Ream, was born; however, the role of housewife was not to Lilian's liking and she employed others to handle the domestic duties so that she could devote herself to her business ambitions. Whilst Lilian developed the fledgling studio, the family was supported by Sydney, a Saville Row trained tailor.

Whilst working with these late Victorian photographers, Ream had mastered the techniques of portrait photography focusing on the formal portraiture of individuals and groups with carefully composed backdrops, as recorded in the surviving carte-de-visites and cabinet cards of the time. During her time working with Brown, she had been introduced to the new format of the photographic postcard which was about to enter its golden age. Postcards were produced, not just with portraits, but general views and events relating to Wisbech and district. As newspapers started to include photographs in their issues, the *Wisbech & Isle of Ely Advertiser* and the *Wisbech Standard* became two of Ream's most important customers and it is mainly through this work that we now have such a fascinating photographic record of social and local history for Wisbech.

Added to her undoubted technical expertise, Lilian Ream had a formidable character and immense drive which she used to make the Borough Studio the pre-eminent photographic studio in Wisbech for over forty years. Although the Crescent had been the home of professional enterprises for many years, the intrusion of a photographic studio run by a woman caused some consternation. However, such prejudices gradually receded as Ream established herself as a photographer of quality who produced portraits for many local dignitaries.

By 1911, with the birth of the Ream's daughter Mary, Lilian's sister, Louie, had left London to take on the domestic responsibilities of the household, assisted by a nanny and other staff. These arrangements were further complicated by Lilian's parents moving in. This overcrowded existence was relieved during World War 1 when the Ream's purchased 5 The Crescent, which allowed the family to live in No. 5 and No. 4, formerly leased but now owned outright, was completely turned over to the business.

The Crescent Studio flourished and was based on high quality portraiture with such sitters as the local M.P. James de Rothschild, members of the Peckover family and local worthies such as the Mayor of Wisbech. Indeed, the firm produced the Mayor's official portrait annually from 1909 to 1971 and, on each occasion, the Mayor's official chair had to be manhandled from the Council Chamber across the Town Bridge to the studio.

During the War, whilst Sydney was away on service with Royal Naval Air Service, Lilian was finding it hard to cope with the rapidly expanding business and, in 1916, Roland and Mary went to live with Lilian's sister Millie in Hastings. This allowed Louie to help in the Studio along with

A young Lilian Ream in her studio.

Millie's daughter, Muriel. After Sydney's return, the domestic and business arrangements reverted back to the original routine.

Besides portraiture, Lilian Ream undertook outside work recording local events and weddings. More work was done for local companies who needed photographs for advertisements, catalogues or to record their premises, equipment and staff. The images taken provide a fascinating insight into the business and trading life of a small market town for over half a century.

Lilian Ream's business was now becoming the pre-eminent photographic studio in the district, whilst her great rival, J Lawrence Brown, was in terminal decline. Despite his financial difficulties, Brown would not sell the Borough Studio to his former employee and partner. When Brown ceased to trade, the premises were sold to a solicitor, Colonel Ollard, who converted the first floor to provide extra space for his business next door. As Ollard had no use for the ground floor, a chance arose for Ream to lease the Borough Studio – an opportunity which she seized with both hands.

Never one to sit back, Lilian continued to expand the business. She acquired a former branch of Jasper Wright's of King's Lynn, The Art Studio in Alexandra Road; this was run as a framing works under the name of The Burlington Studio. Further acquisitions included the Lynn Road Studio and the Imperial Photo Company at 50 Market Place. The latter was run by H Coates and Sons who were allowed to continue as publishers of topographical postcards. Another business, a craft shop, was bought in Market Street. After obtaining the freehold to the Borough Studio, Lilian developed the site to fulfil its potential. A new shop front was installed with a glazed arcade leading the customer into the main body of the shop. One half of the arcade was used by the studio and the other by MacBeth's ladies' outfitters.

When the new facilities – studio, workshops, dressing rooms, dark room and storage space – were completed, Lilian began to concentrate her businesses at the Borough Studio. The Market Street and Market Place enterprises were let and flats were created in No. 4 The Crescent, in 1928. The Borough Studio offered not only photographic services but also provided a wide range of craft materials. Whilst Lilian maintained her links with local businesses and cultivated new customers, Alan Midlane was employed as manager. His main asset was a calm disposition which stood him in good stead when dealing with his formidable and temperamental employer. Opening times for the Studio were from 9 o'clock in the morning to 7 o'clock in the evening four days a week, with one day half closing. On Saturdays, the Studio opened for an extra hour. The staff had expanded to include photographers, darkroom assistants, re-touchers, watercolourists and sales assistants.

Lilian's obsession with work led to her increasing detachment from her family. She even took negatives for retouching when on family holidays to Heacham. Unsurprisingly, her professional life led to a breakdown in her relationship with Sydney, soon after their silver wedding anniversary. The shock of separation, perhaps out of character, prompted her early retirement and she moved to 38 Upper Avenue, Eastbourne. Sydney and Roland lived above the Borough Studio whilst continuing to run the business. However, in 1935, after the marriage of her daughter, Mary, Lilian returned to Wisbech and took back control. By now, she was formally separated from Sydney, who moved into the White Lion Hotel until his death in 1950. Whilst the business continued to record in photographs major events, leisure activities, agricultural scenes and so forth, Roland Ream was beginning to develop his interest in cine films. Indeed, the firm had embraced cine films as far back as 1929 when they made a film of the Wisbech Pageant.

In 1949 Lilian Ream, then 72, decided to retire. A limited company was set up with Roland as Managing Director and Violet as Director and Secretary. Mr Midlane and three other staff received shares in the firm. With business settled to her satisfaction, Lilian retired to Eastbourne. She died on Sunday 20 August 1961, aged 84, and was interred in Walsoken churchyard. A formidable and remarkable woman of her generation, her legacy is a wonderful collection of images that provides a tremendous record of the people and history of Wisbech throughout much of the twentieth century

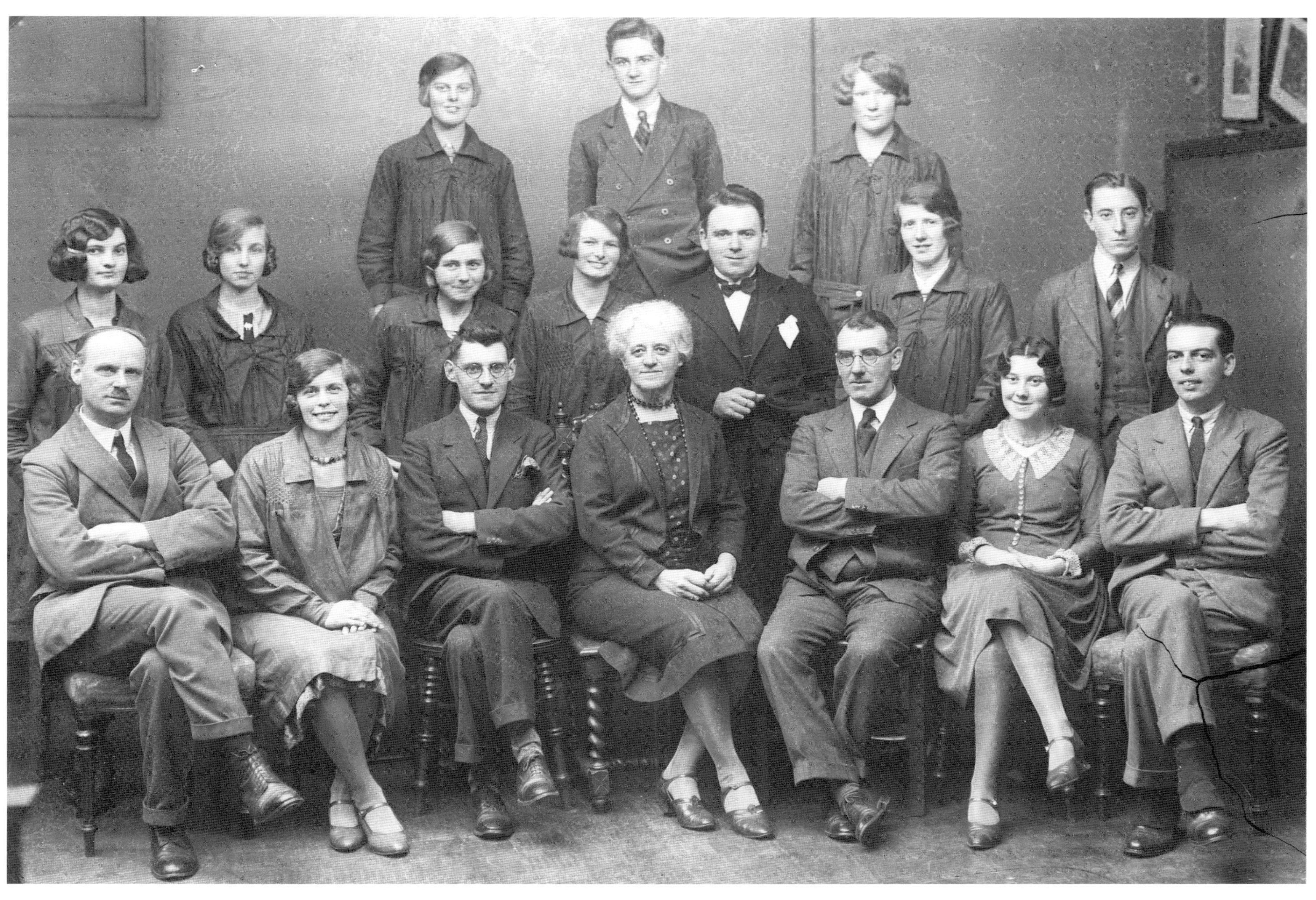

The Borough Studio staff in1929. Lilian Ream is sat next to her son Roland (left) and husband, Sydney (right). Mary Ream is sat next to Sydney and manager, Alan Midlane is front row, far left.

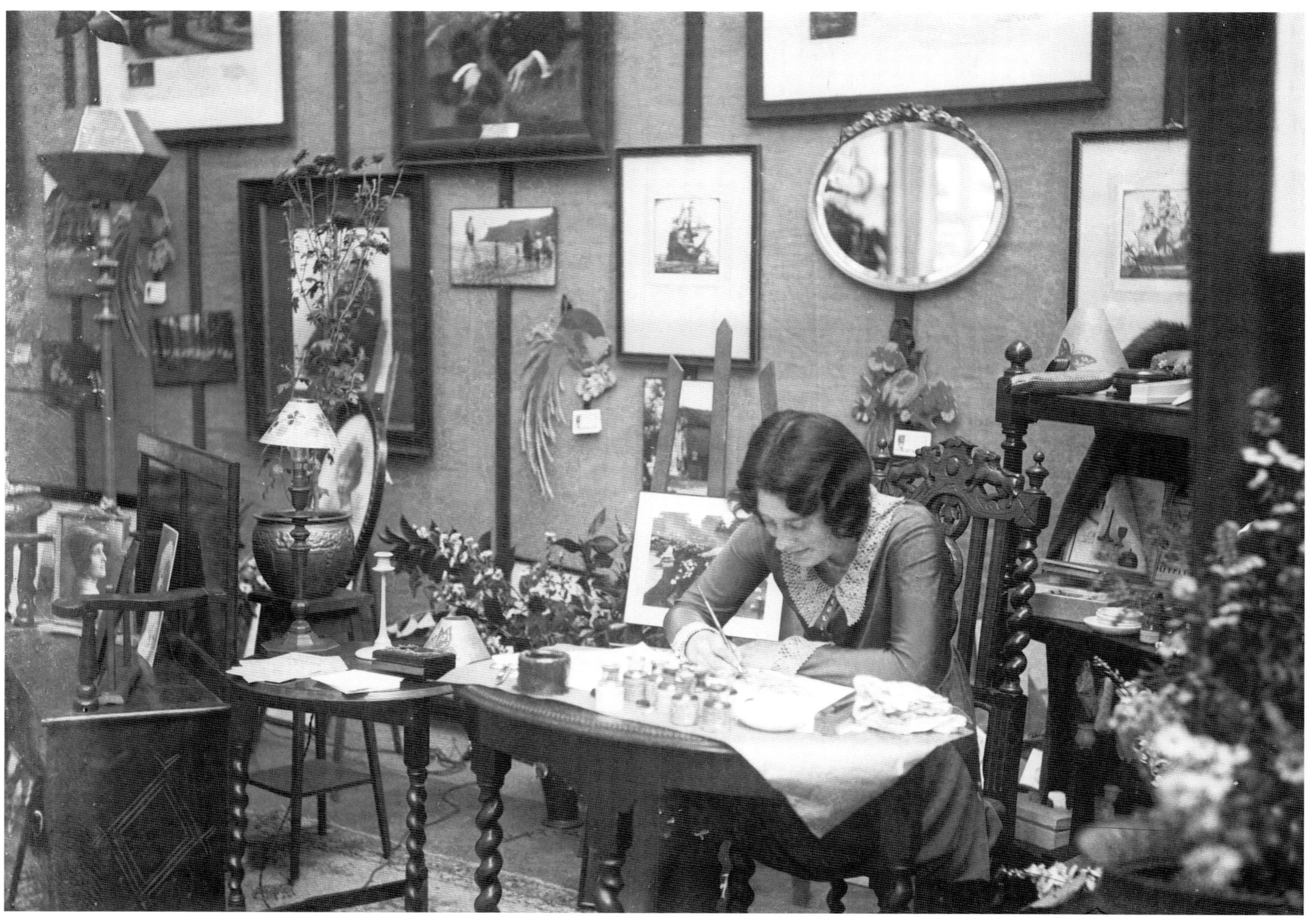

 Mary Ream hand tinting a photograph, 1929.

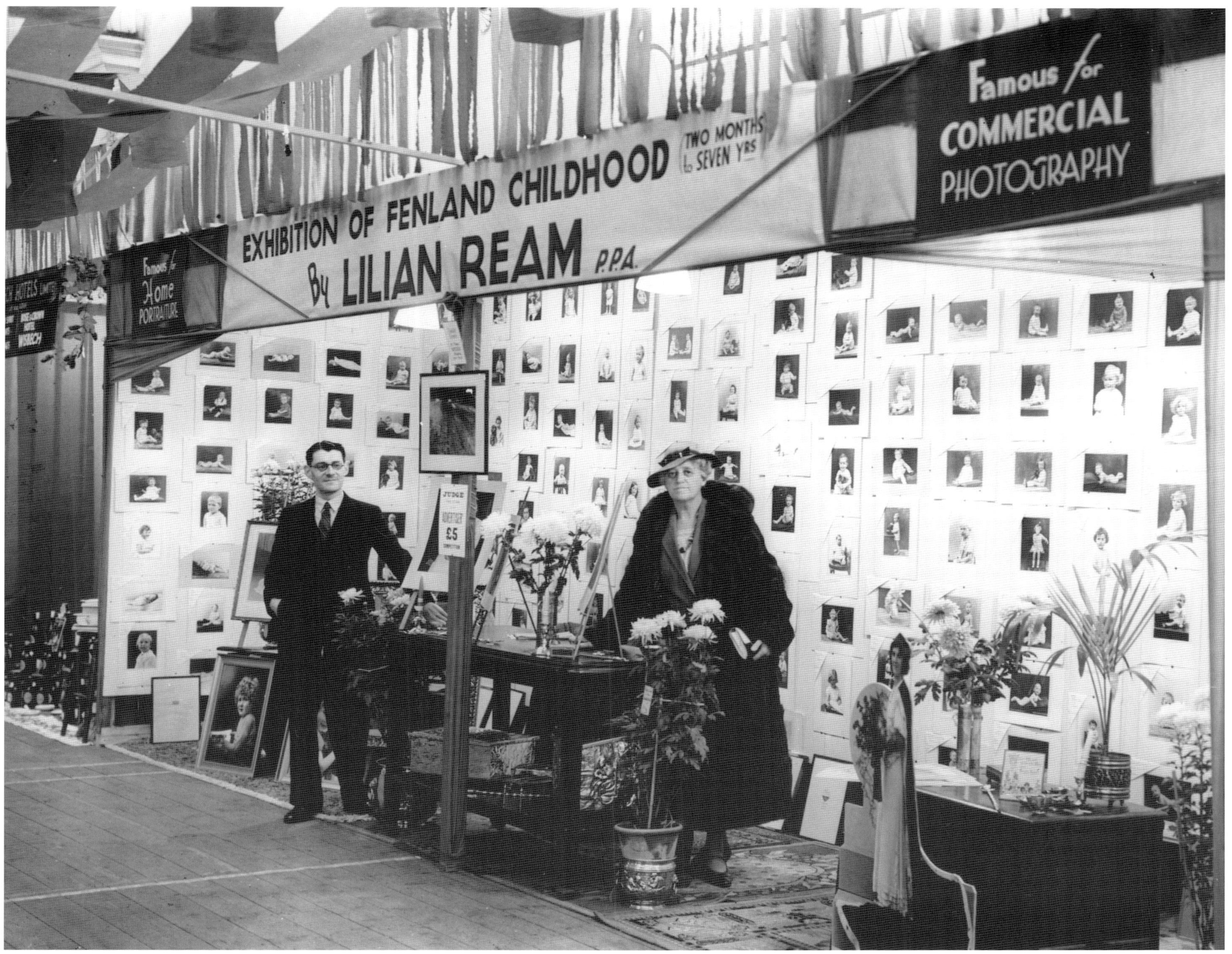

Lilian and Roland Ream at a trade exhibition advertising their portrait business.

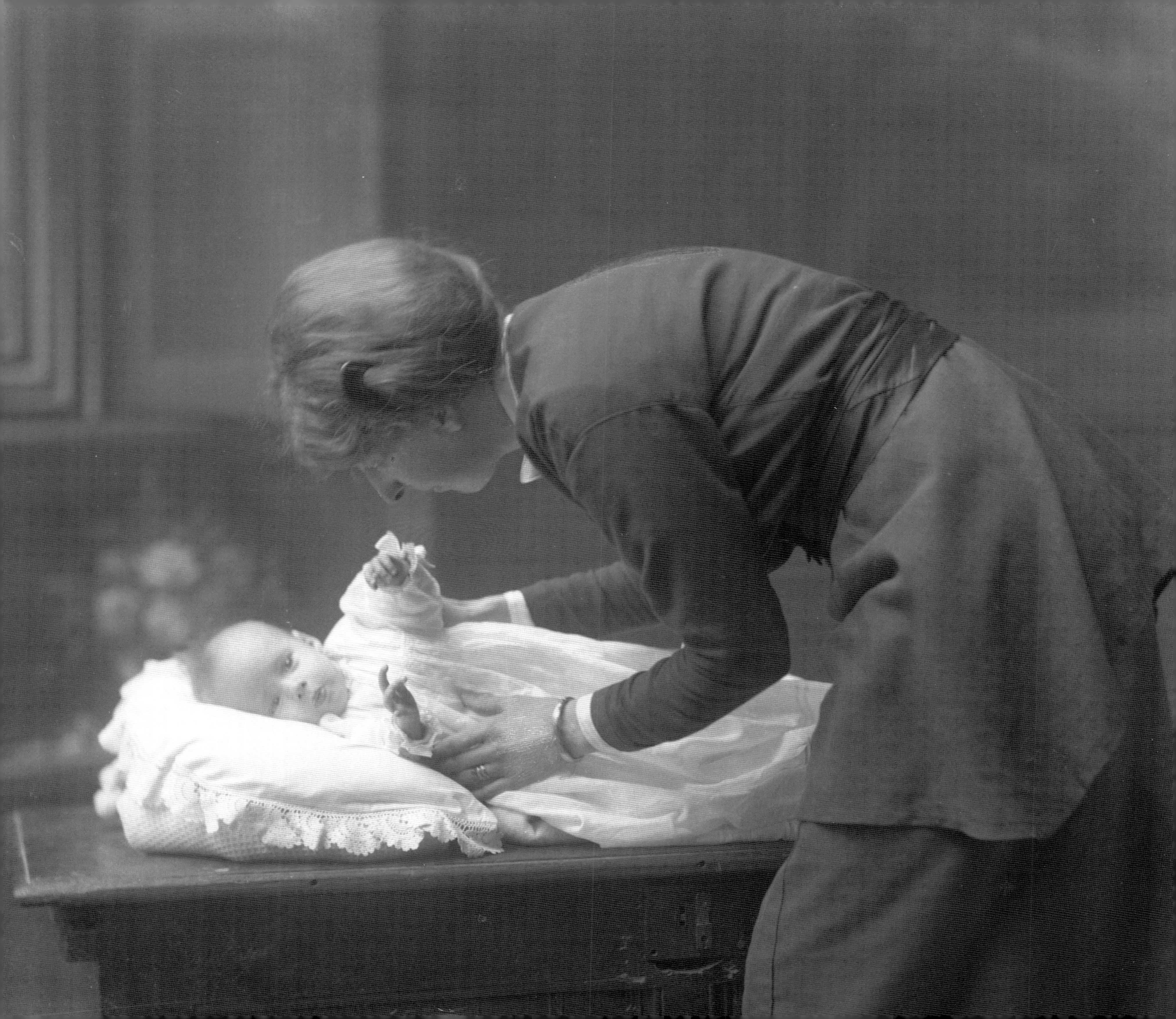

Childhood

Mother with baby, 1920s.

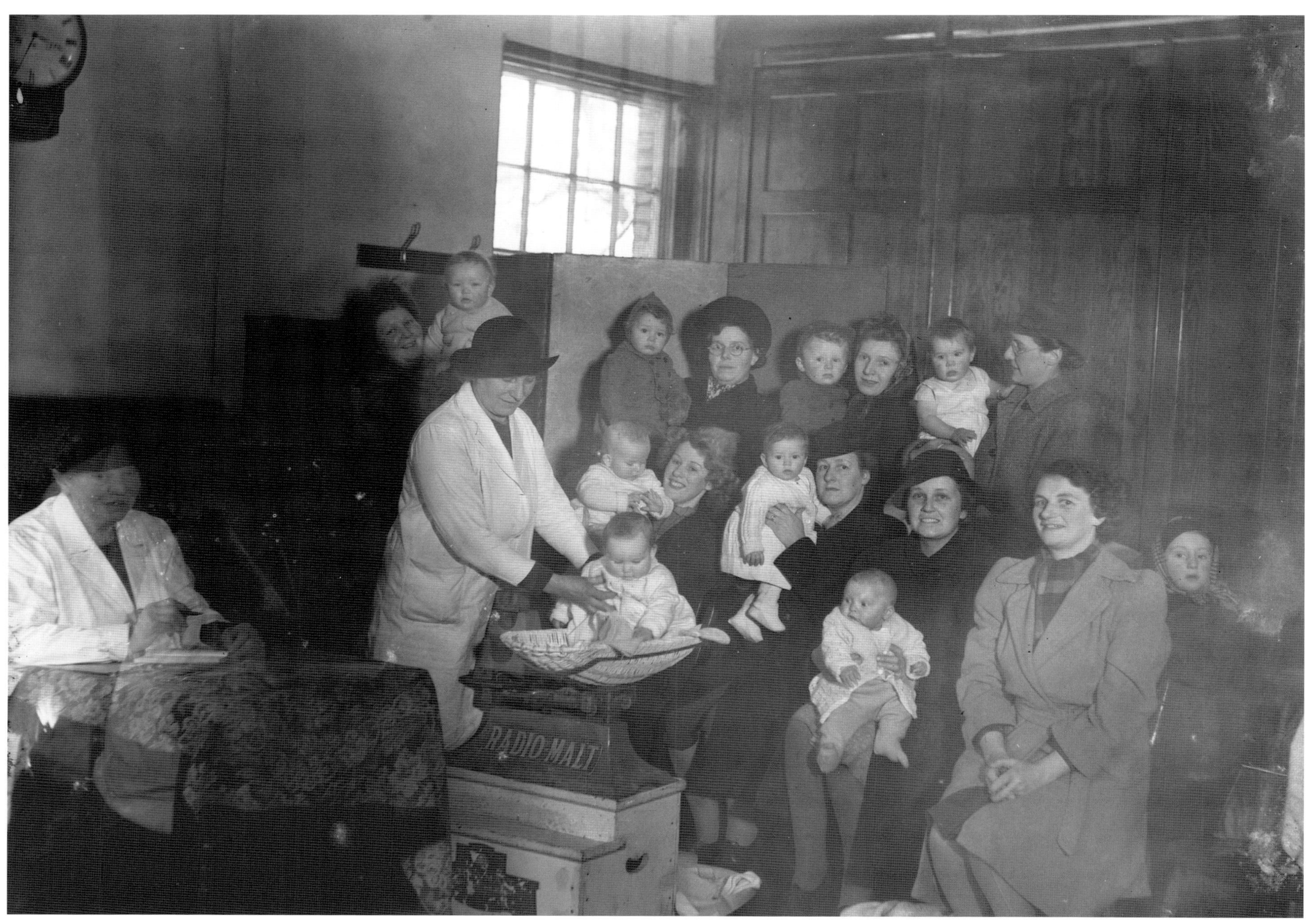

Weighing babies at the Infant Welfare Clinic, 1947. Regular weighing of babies helped to identify babies who were gaining weight either too rapidly or not enough. Note the weighing scales advertising Radio Malt, a malt extract preparation which was given to post-World War II children to help them gain weight.

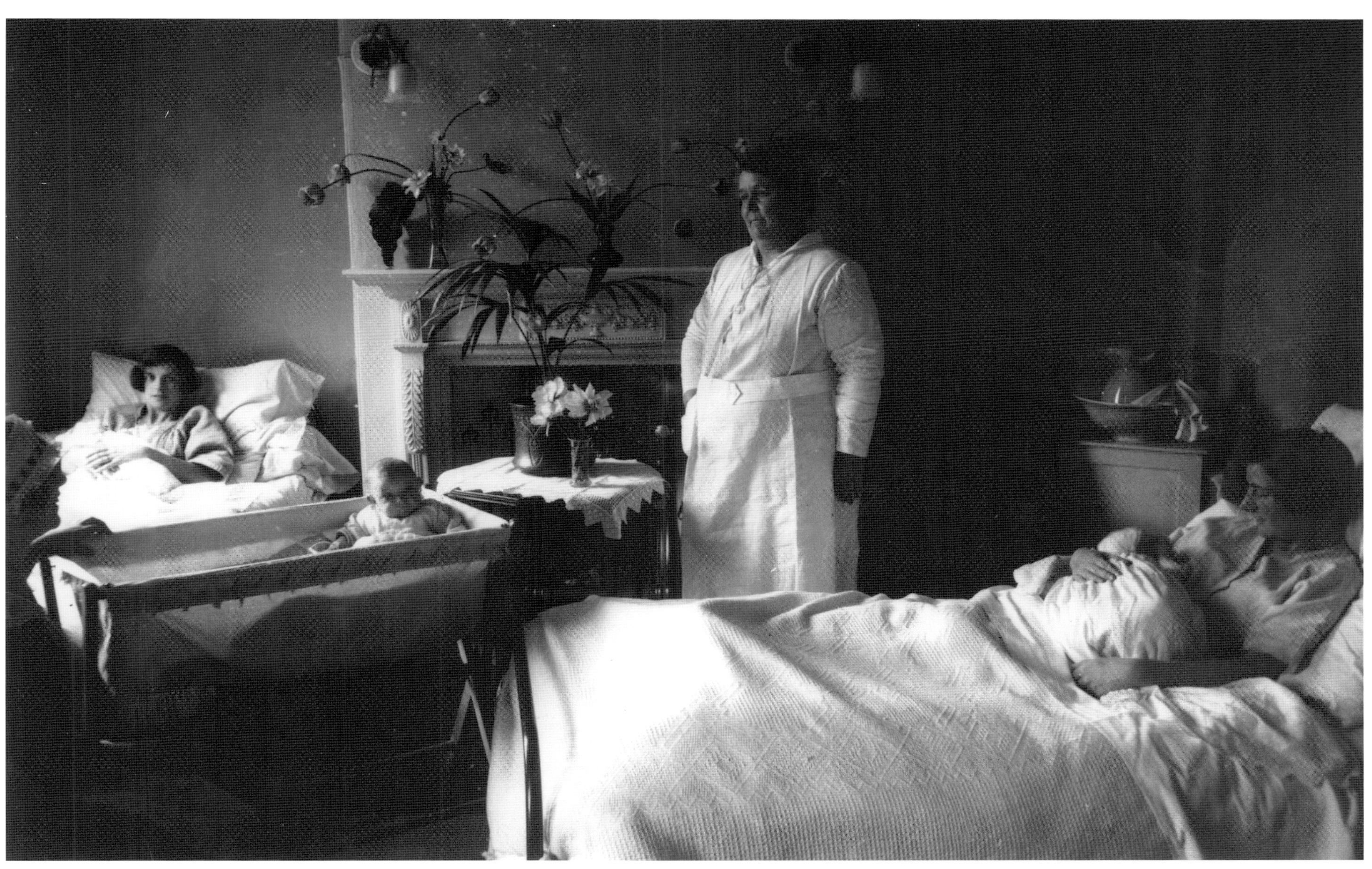

Mothers and babies viewed in a private maternity hospital, 1930s. This could be the private nursing home that existed in the Crescent next to Dr. Gunson's house.

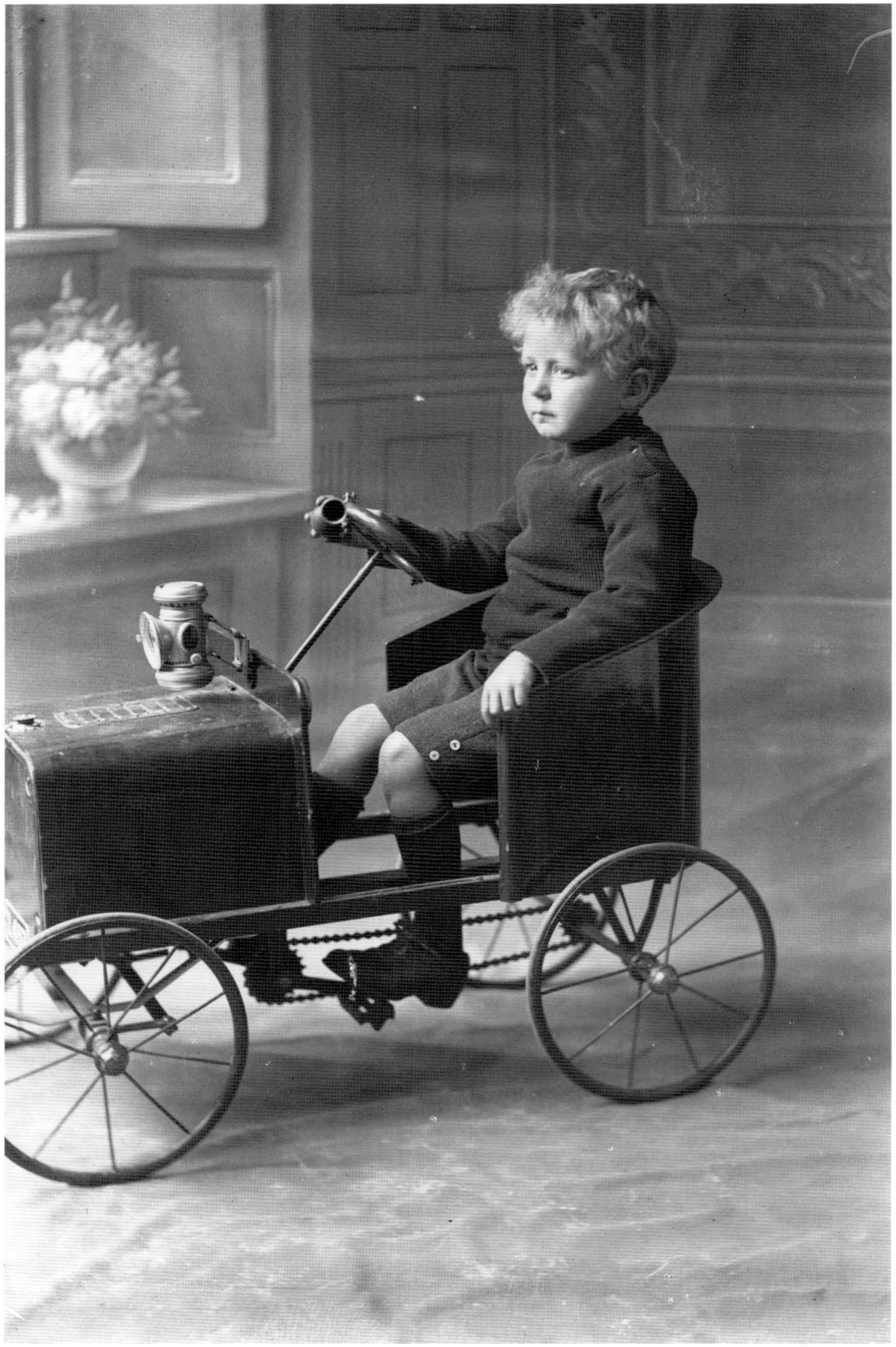

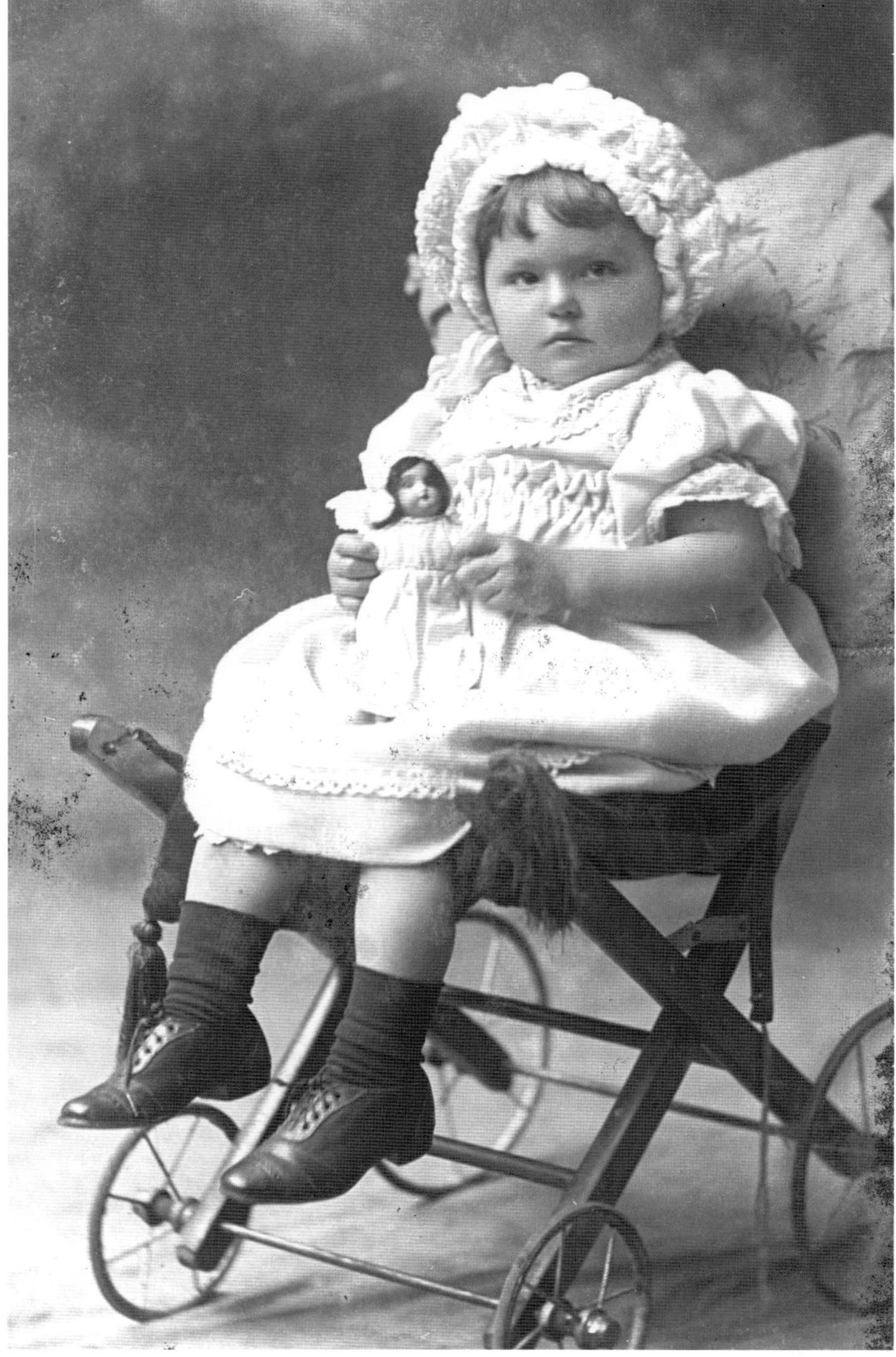

Master Frear poses in the Studio's pedal car, 1928.

Unknown sitter, 1920s.

Opposite. Girl with the Studio's toy pram and teddy bear, 1920s.

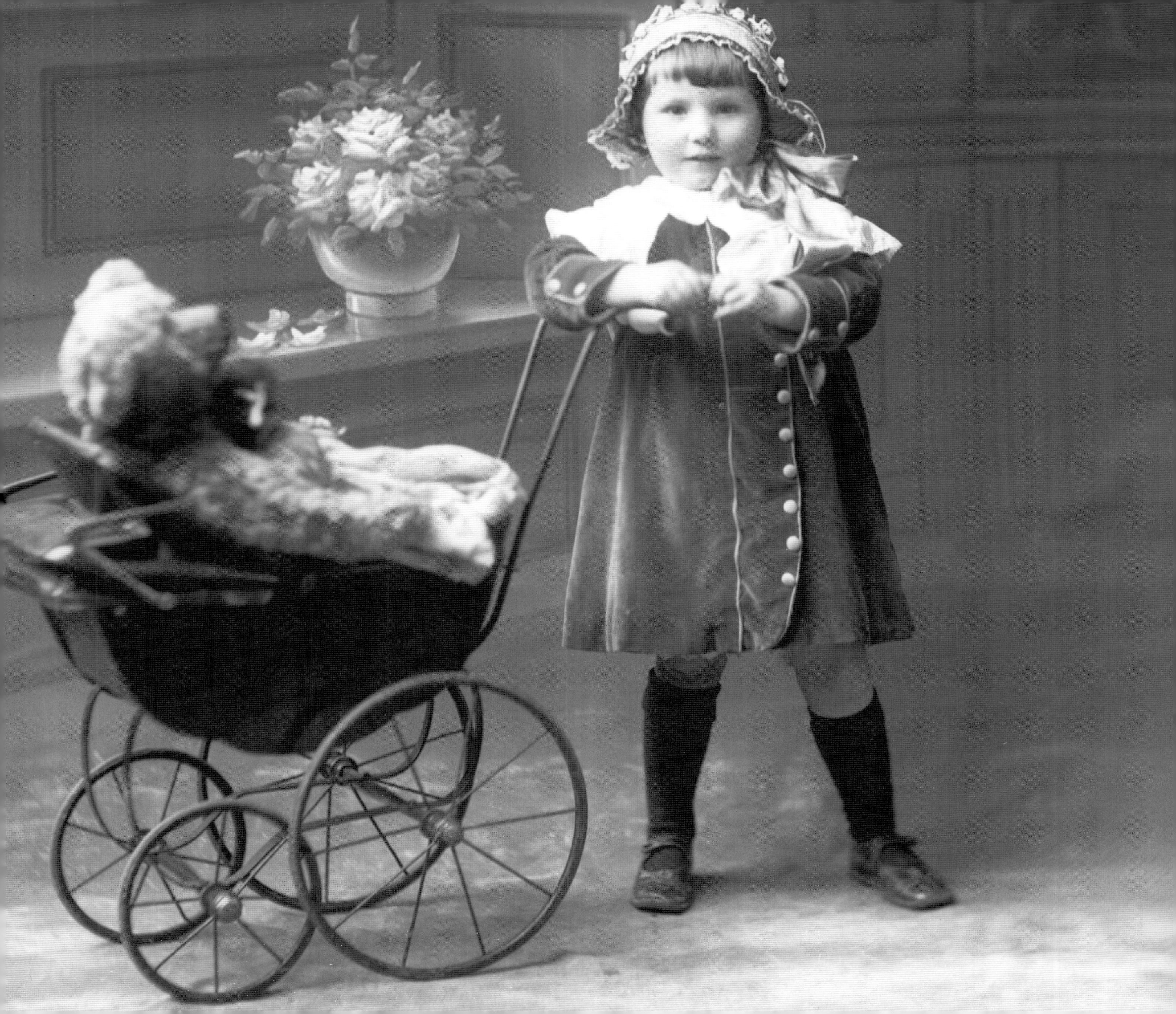

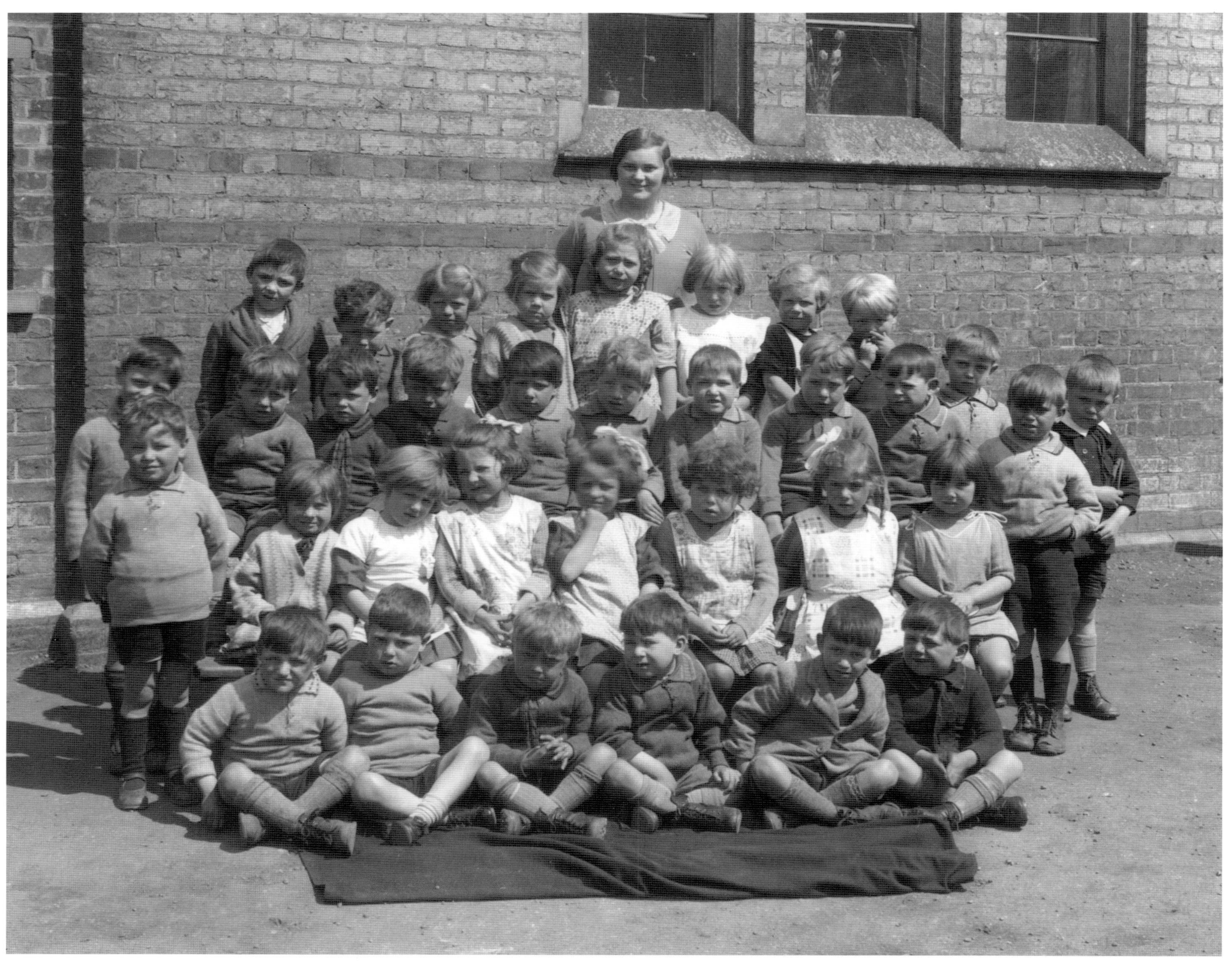

Children outside of the old Friday Bridge Infant School, 1920s.

Opposite. All the fun of the fair. The Mart, 1930s.

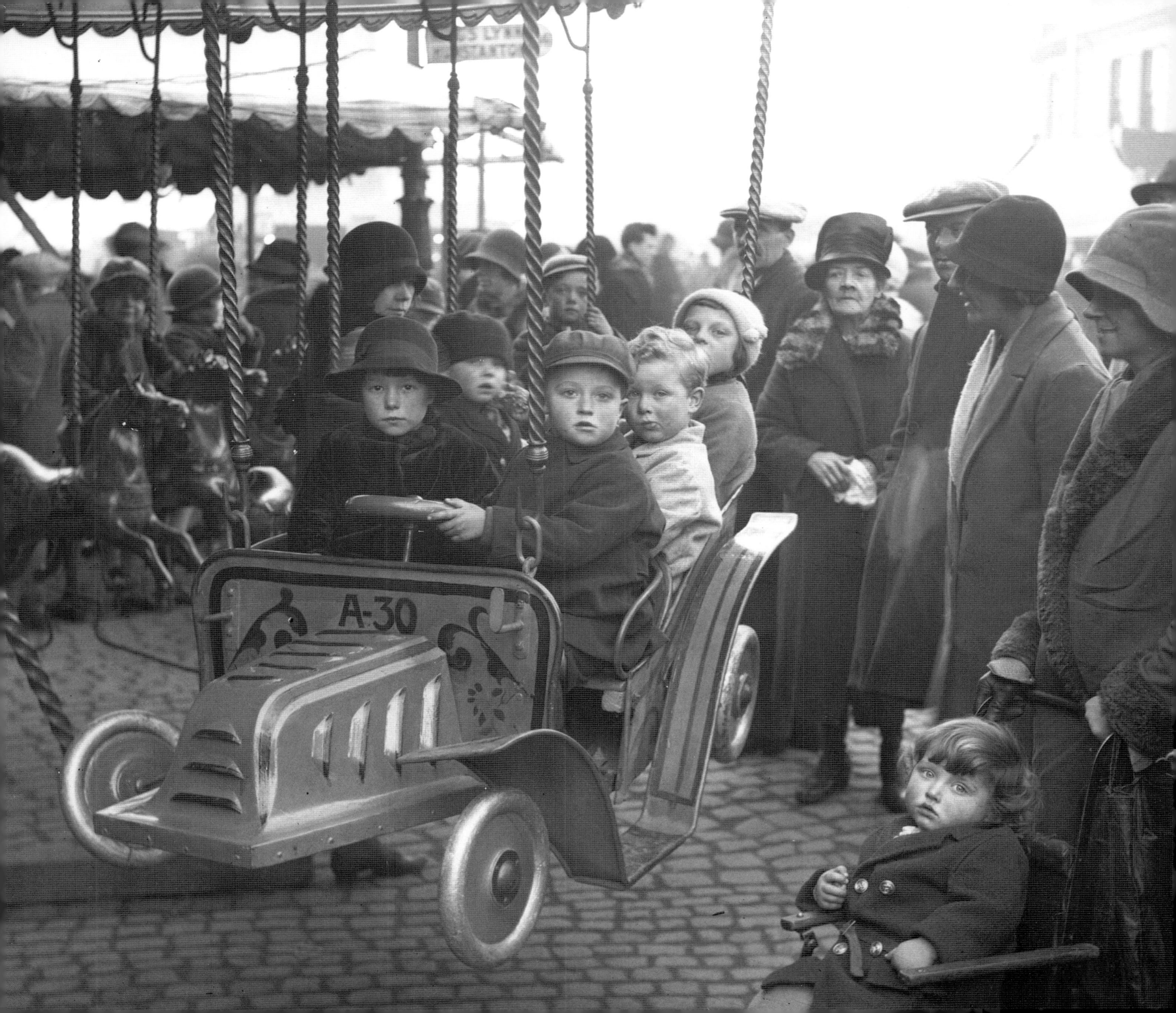
A-30

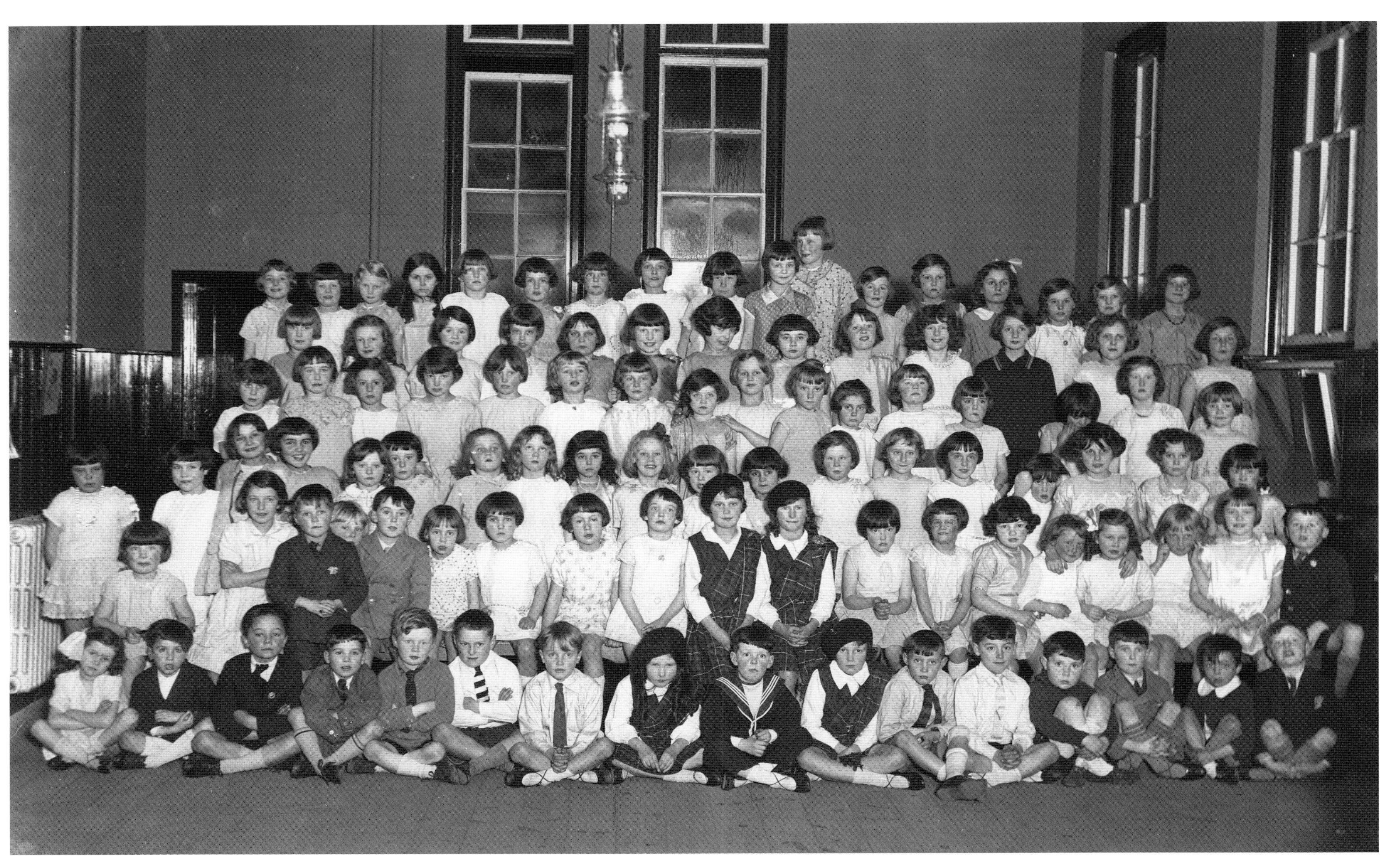

Pupils of Elm Road School, 1930s. The group of girls wearing tartan skirts and sashes suggest that Highland dancing might be on the cards.

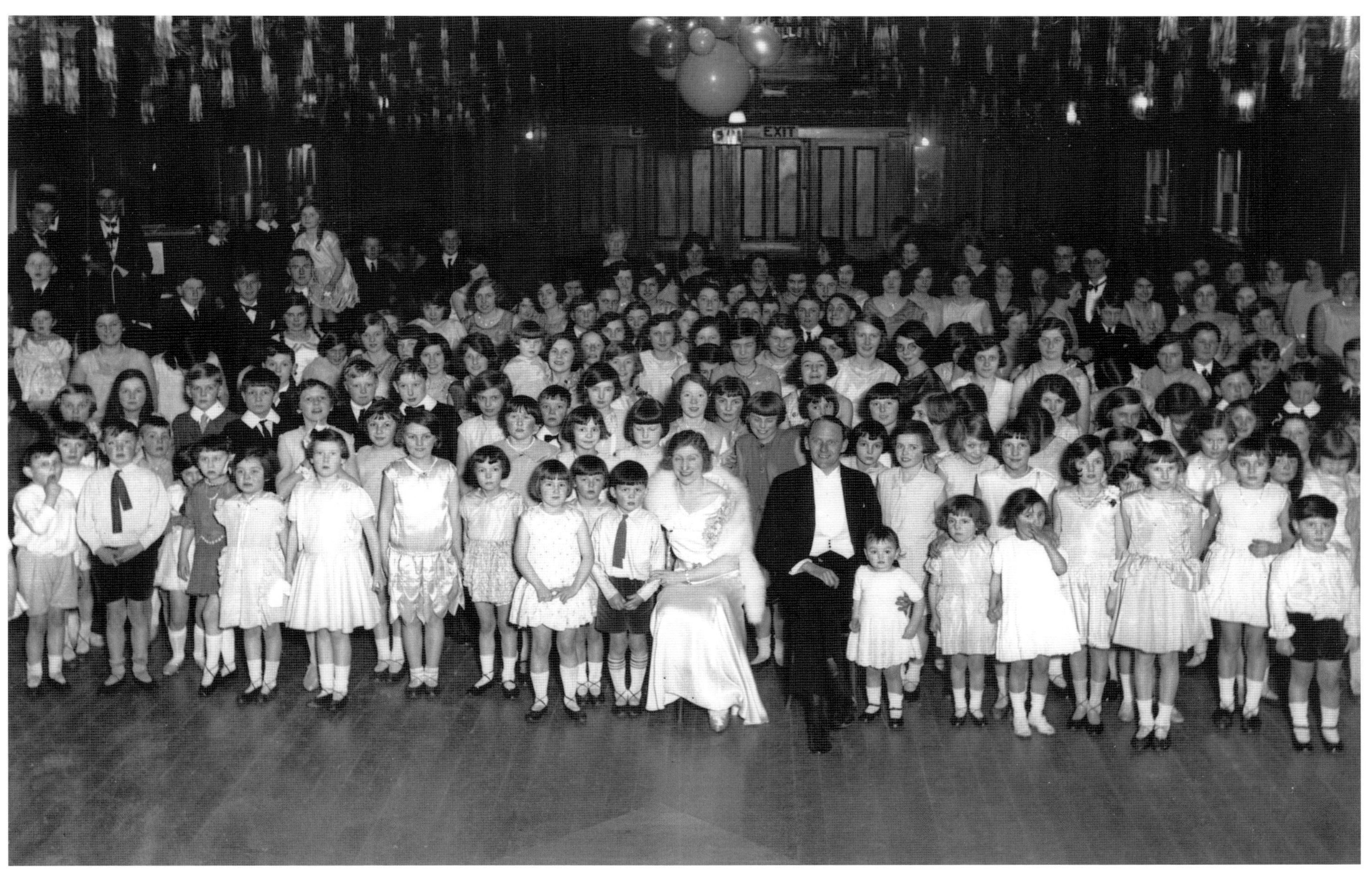

Children's party, late 1940s.

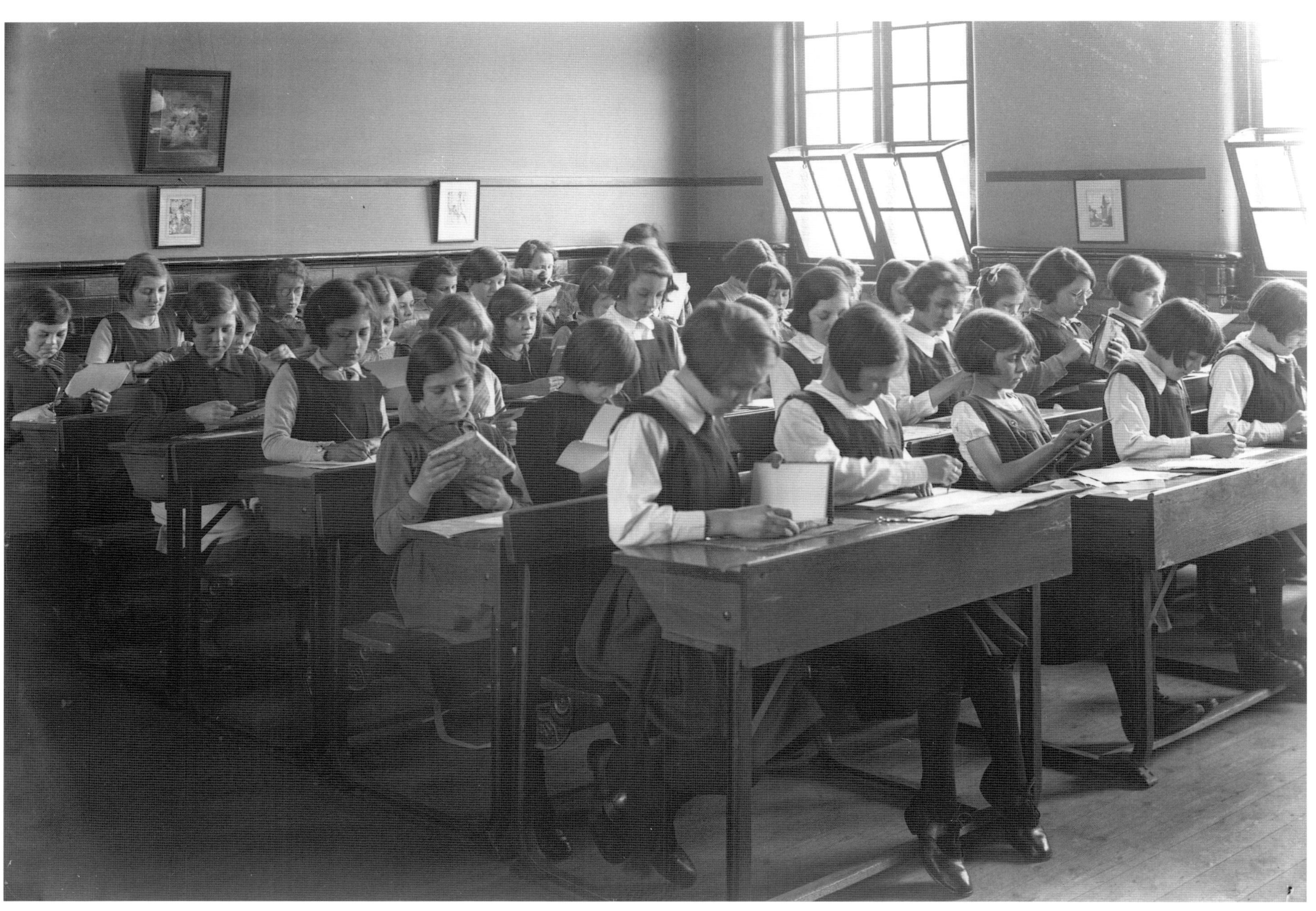

 The Queen's School, 1930s.

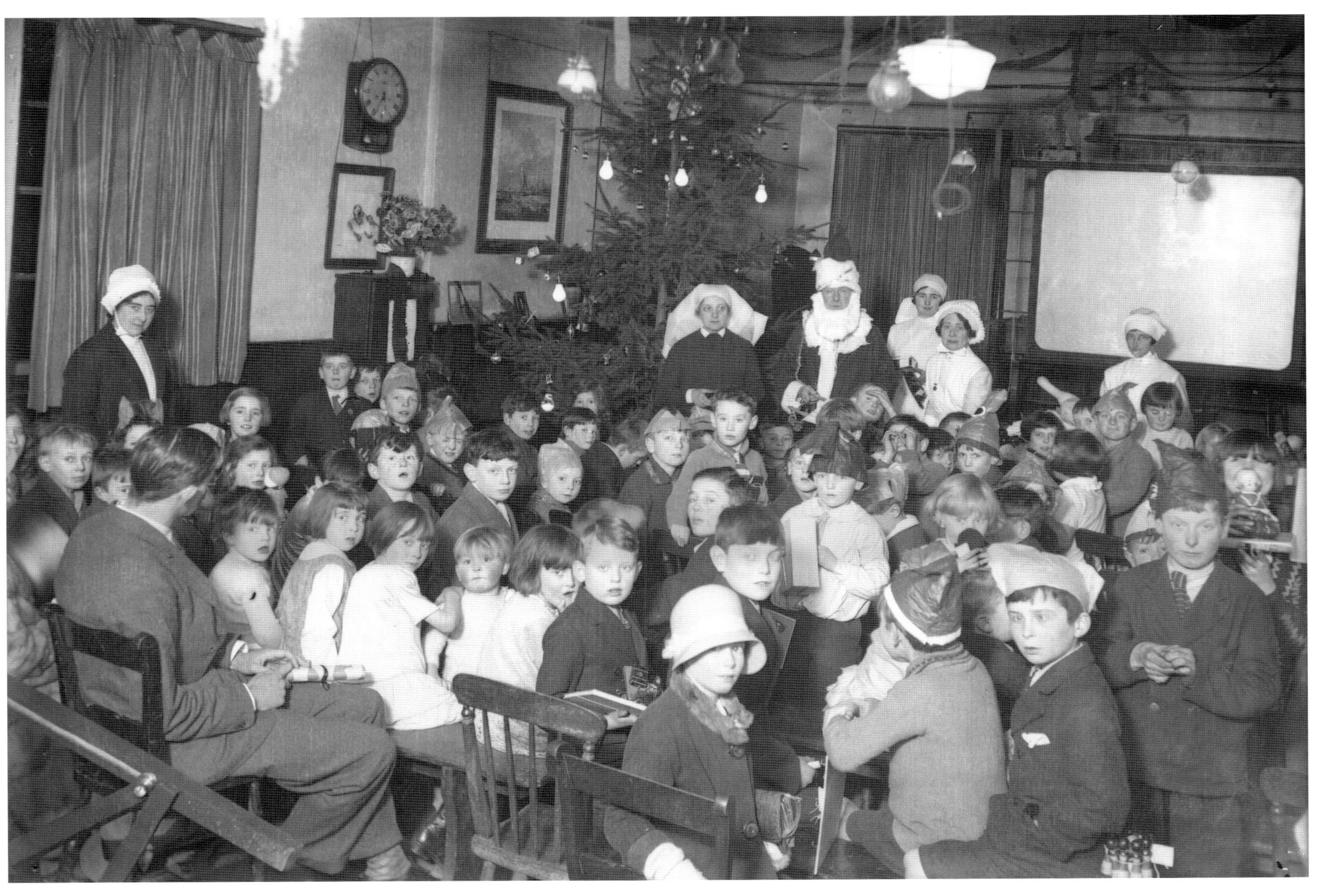

The Christmas Tree party in Park Hall given for children who had been outpatients of the North Cambs. Hospital, 30 December 1931. Beside the Matron is Dr Lucas in the guise of Father Christmas.

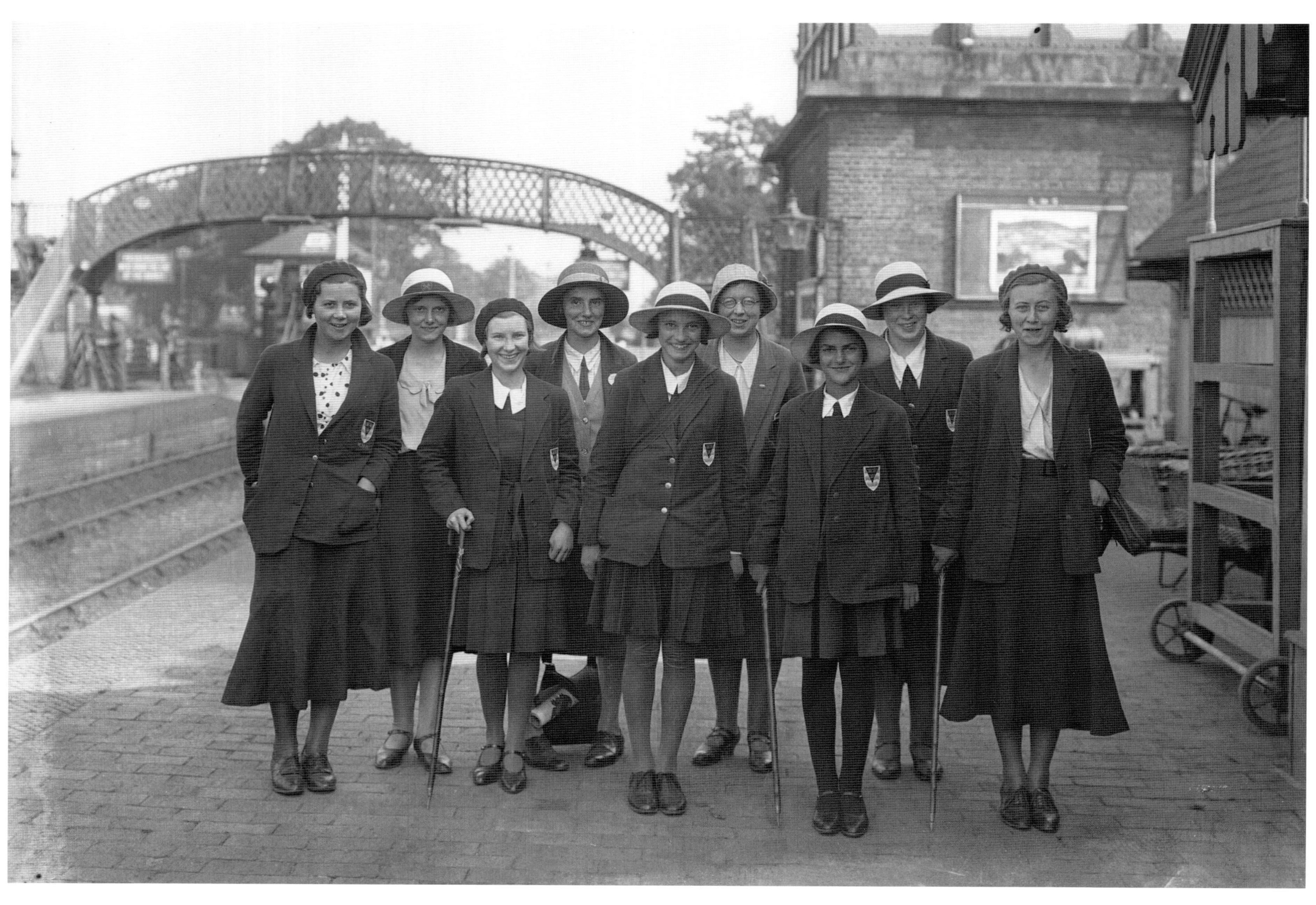

A group of Wisbech High School girls and teachers at Wisbech North Station, Harecroft Road, August 1932. The group had just returned from Geneva where they had attended the Summer School organised by the League of Nations; they are from left to right: Mary Holbourne, Mary Girling, Katherine Wardrup, Barbara Johnson, Vera Johnson, Mrs Tremayne (staff), Helen Hoyles, Mary Cook(?) and Kathleen Holbourne.

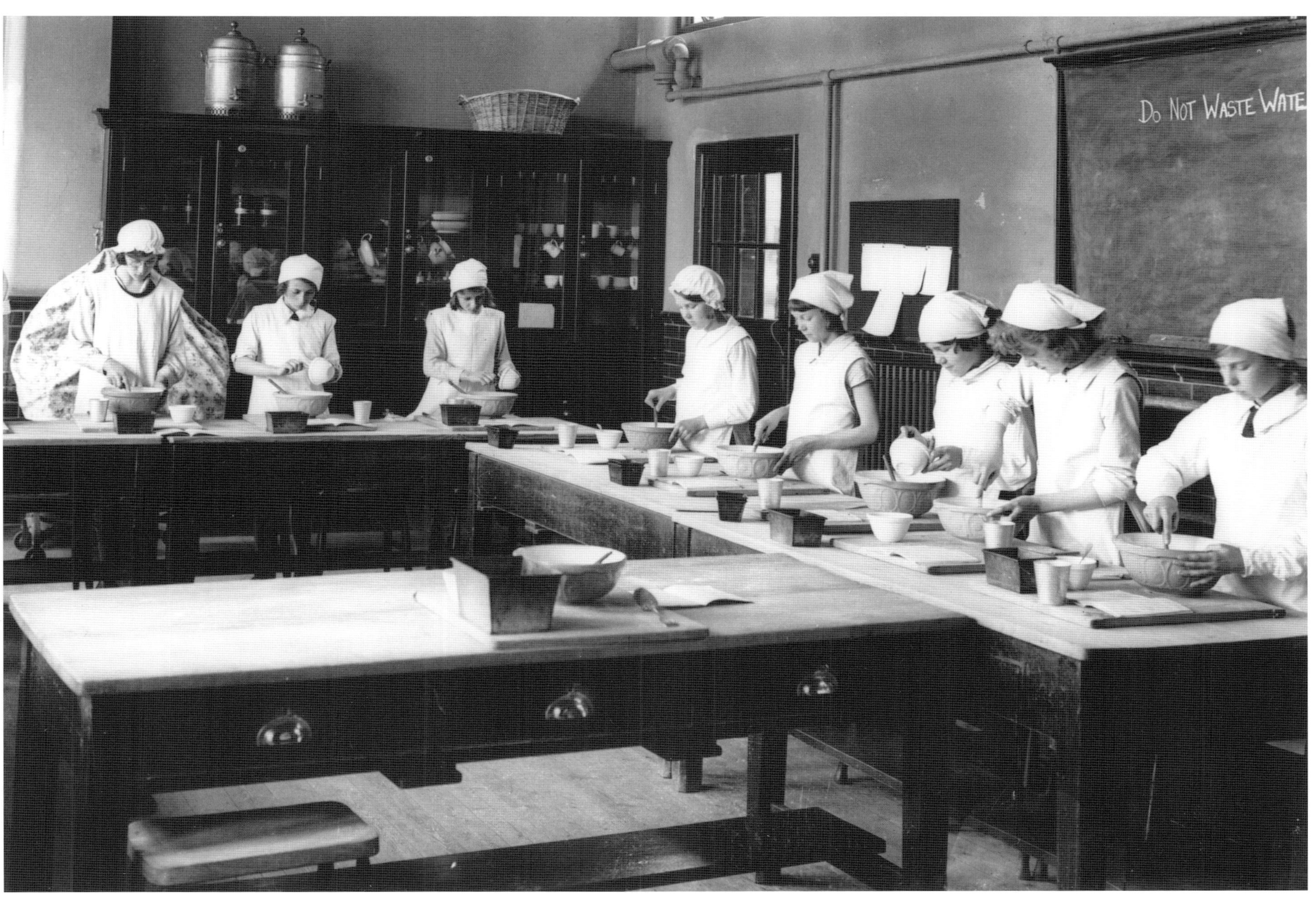

Domestic science at The Queen's School, 1930s.

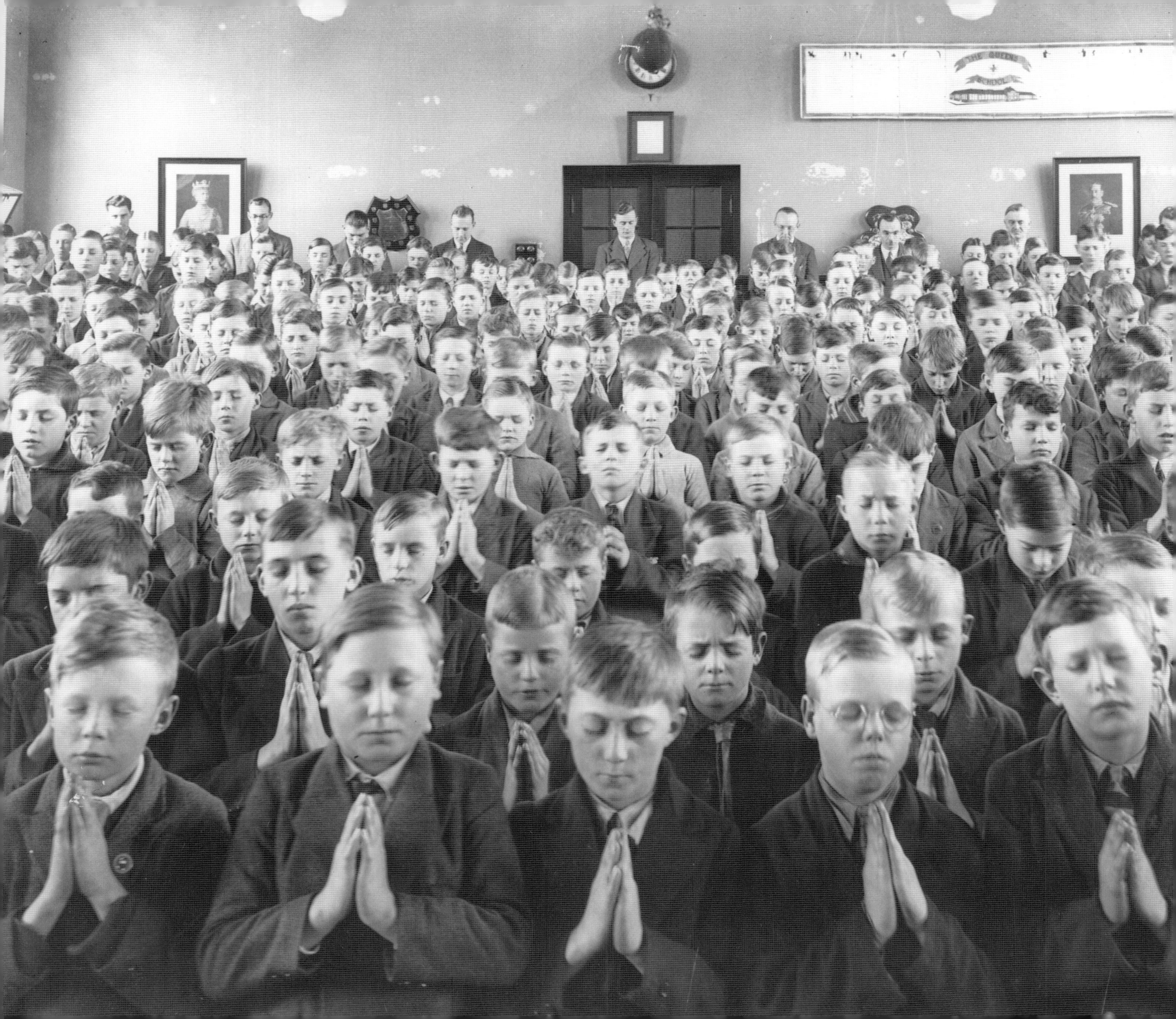
THE QUEENS
SCHOOL

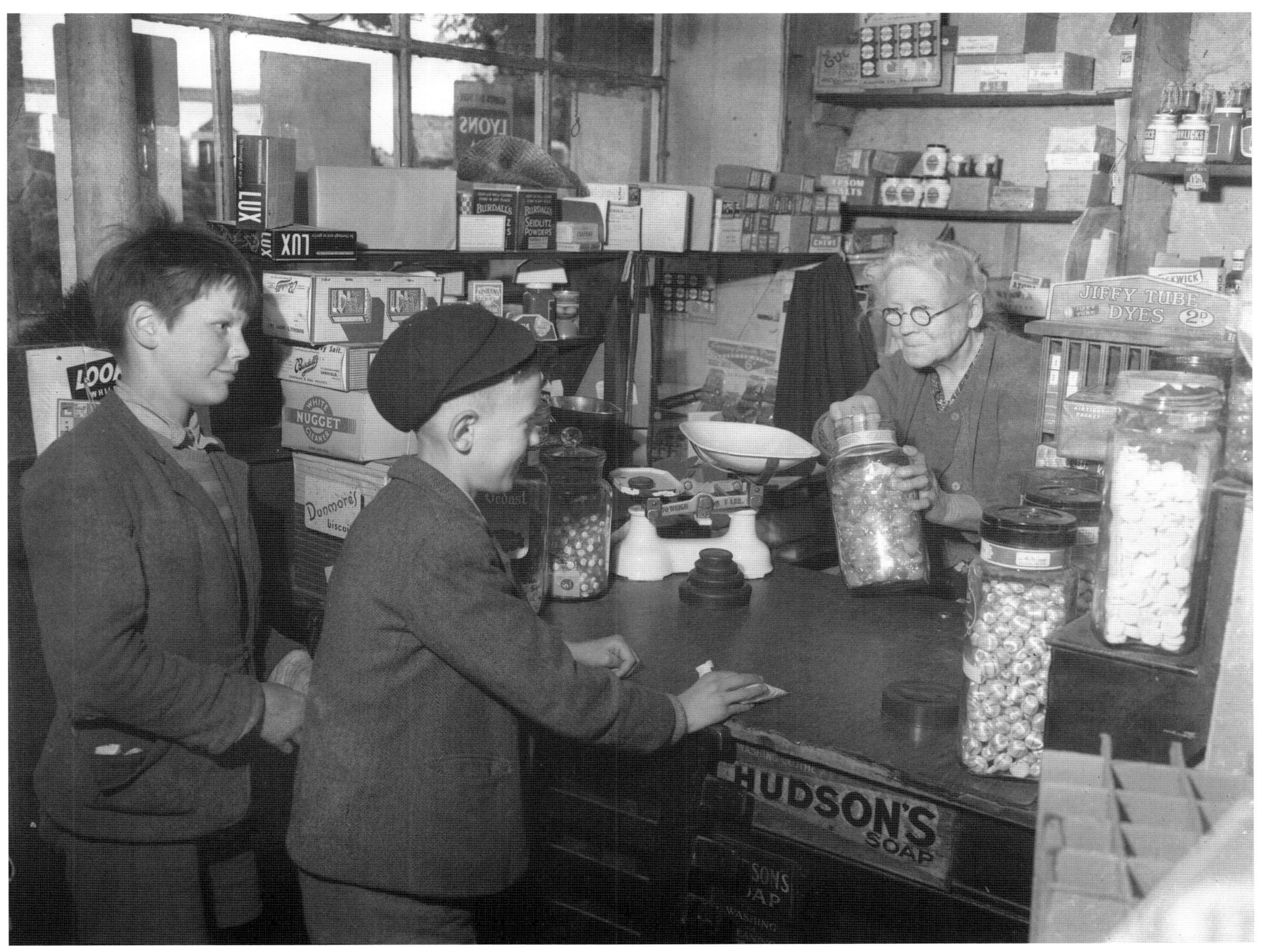

Smith's shop, Elizabeth Terrace, 1950s.

Opposite. Morning prayers at The Queen's School, 1930s.

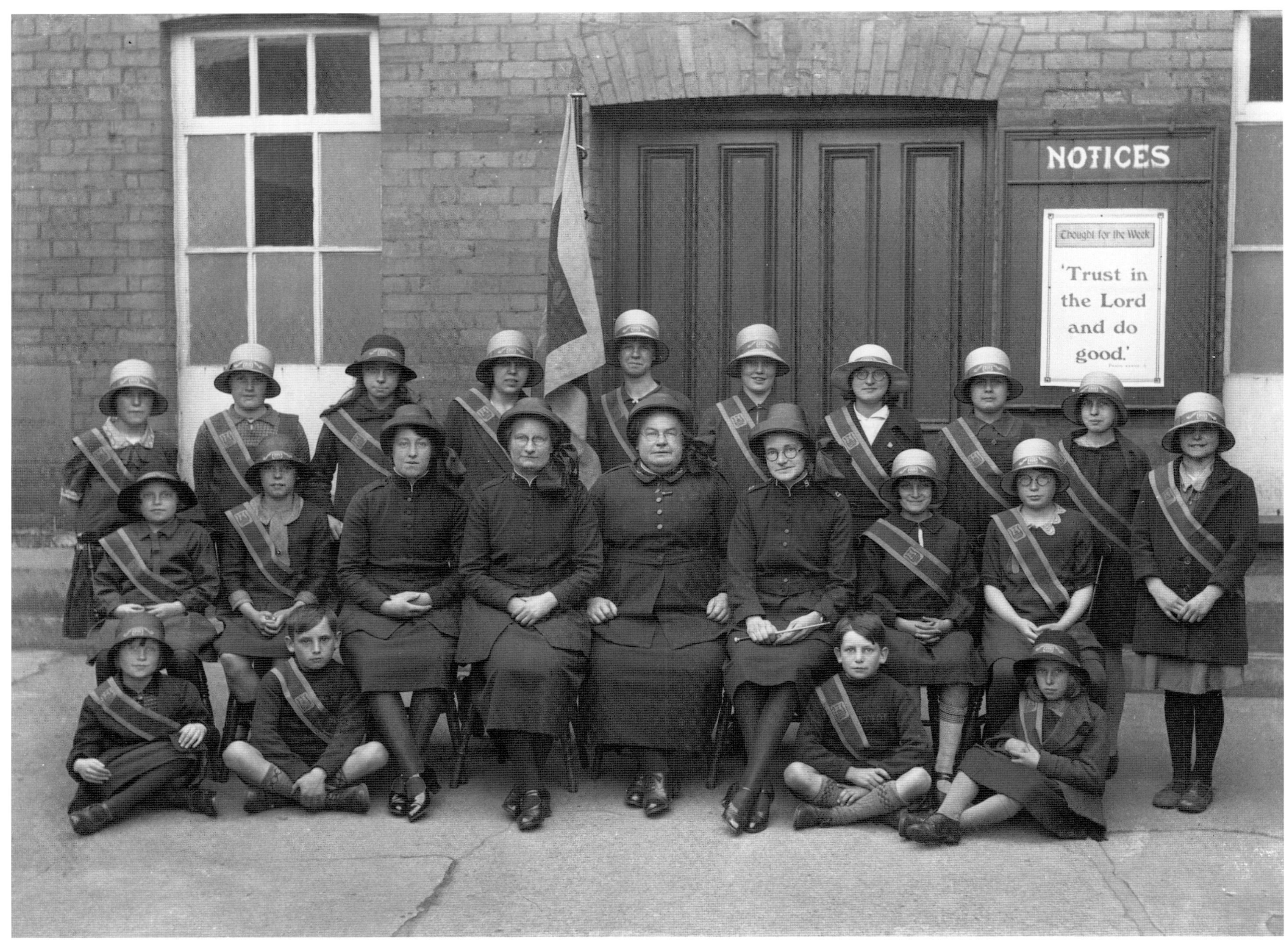

The Wisbech Salvation Army Singing Company outside of the Barracks in East Street, 1931. The group was also known as the Songsters.

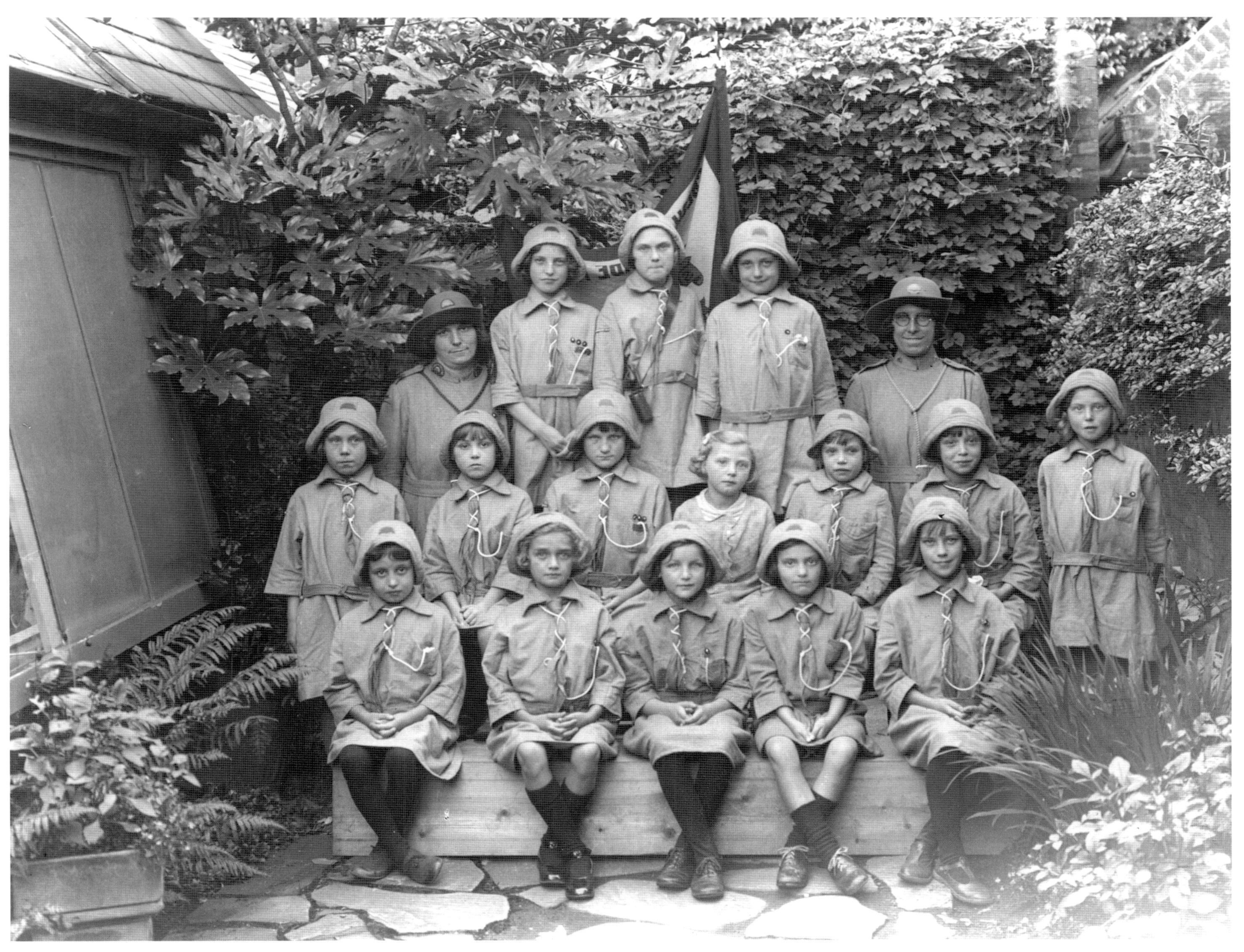

A group of 'Sunbeams'. Formed in 1921, the Sunbeams were junior members of the Salvation Army's Life Saving Guards for young girls. By 1959, both the Guards and Sunbeams were affiliated to the Girl Guide movement and became Guides and Brownies.

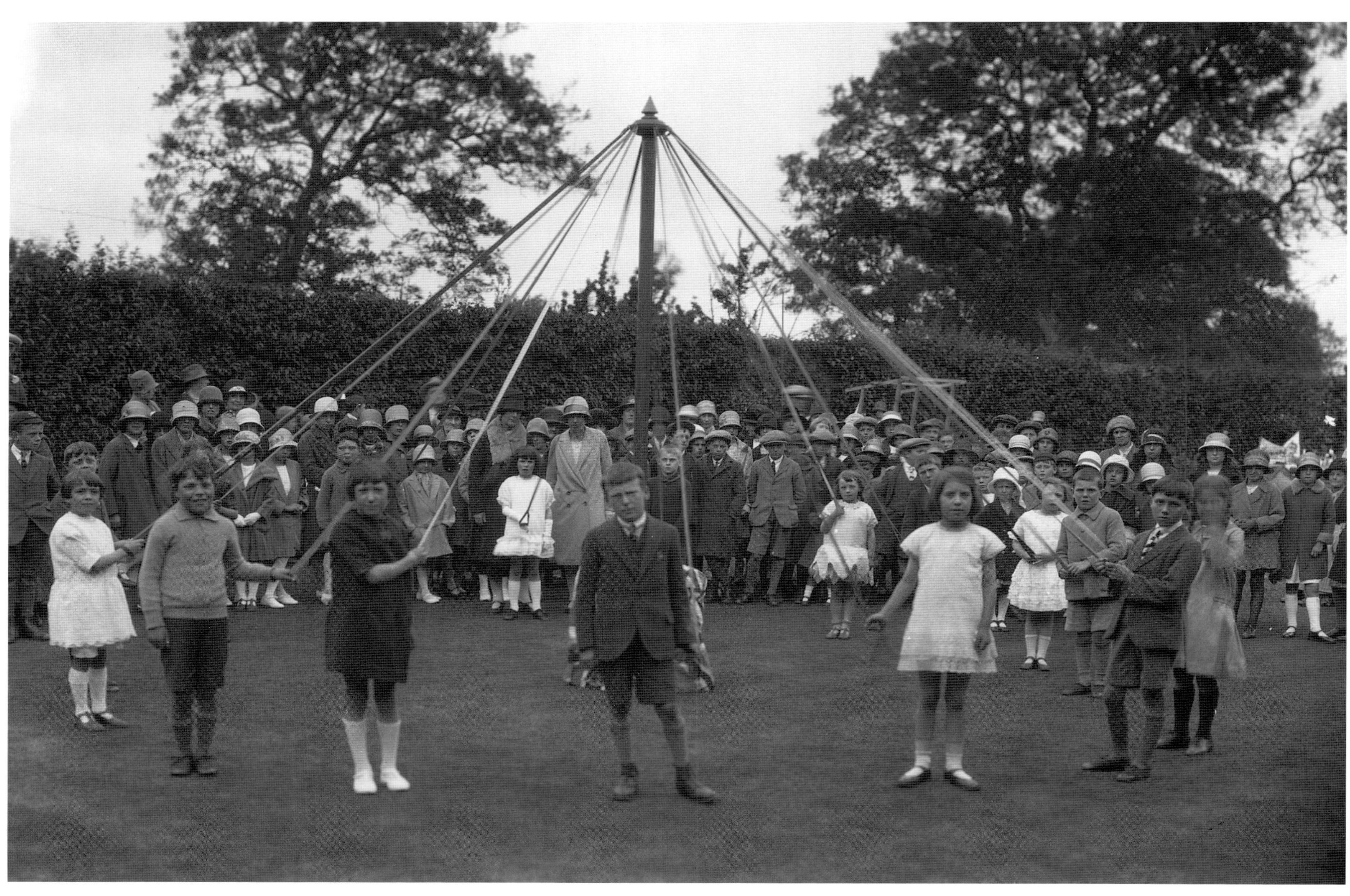

Maypole dancing by Leverington schoolchildren, 1920s. Events such as this were commonly celebrated in the local villages.

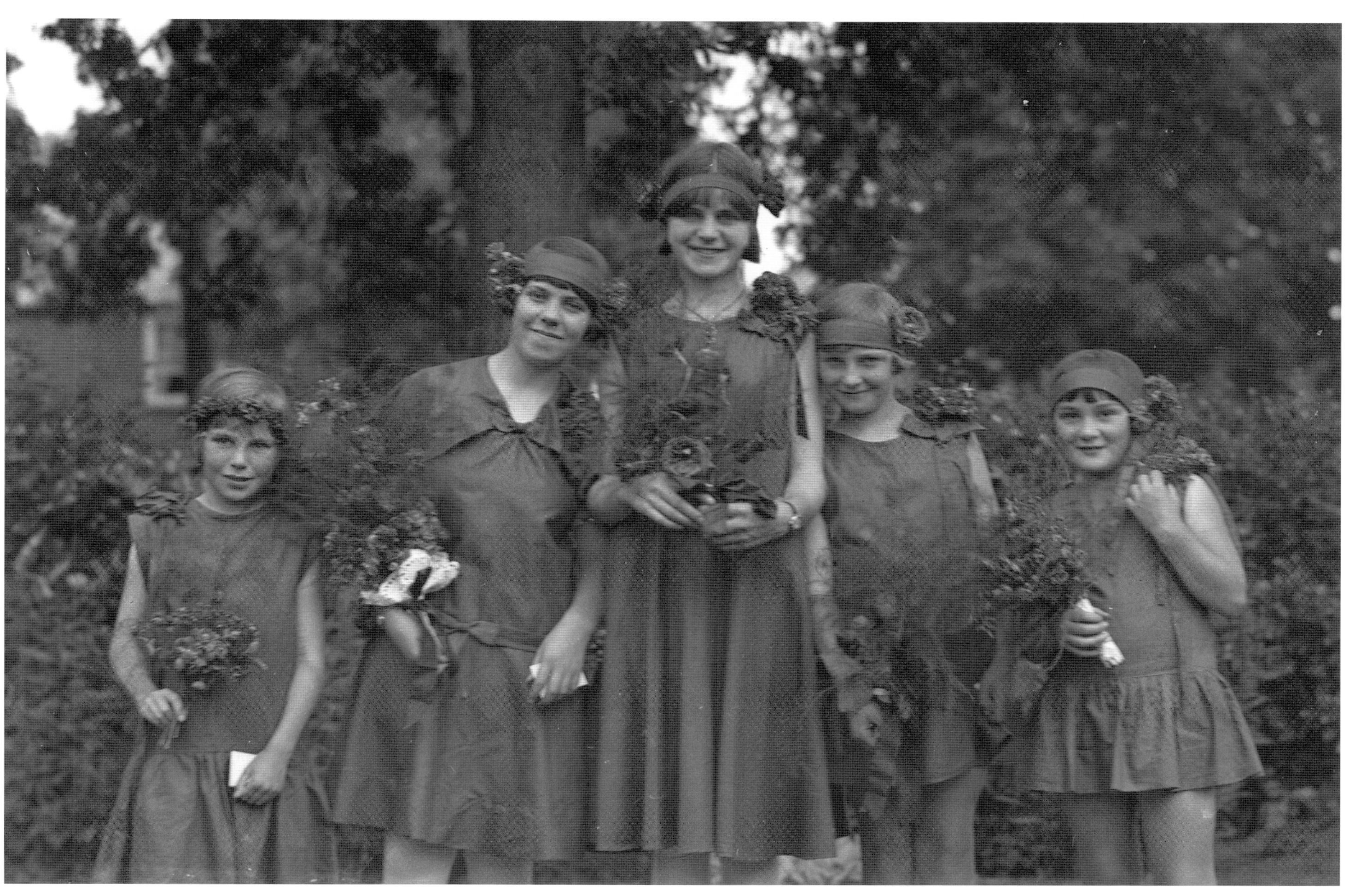

Girls dressed for Sutton St James Rose Festival, 1930s.

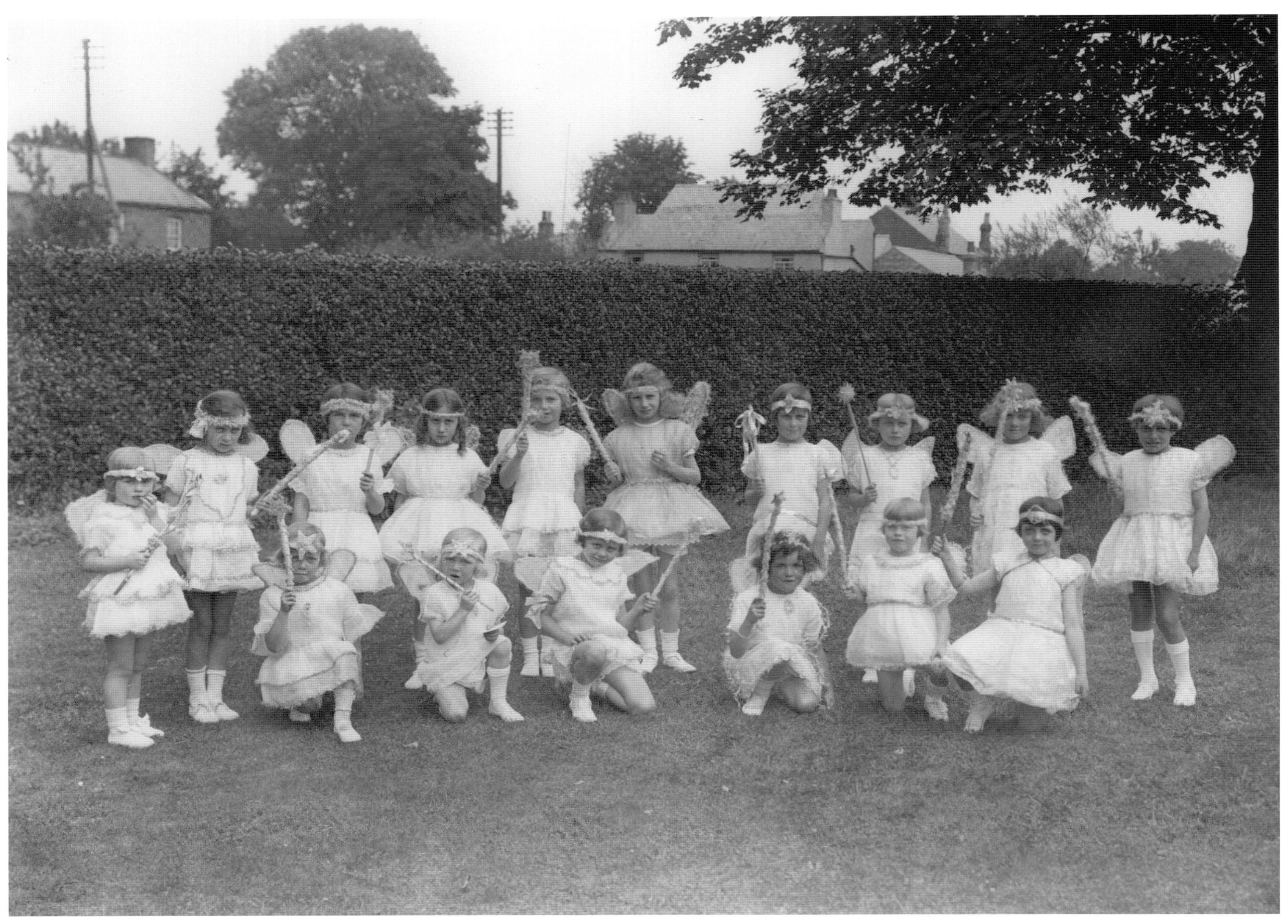

A charming group of young fairies photographed at the Rose Festival at Sutton St James, c1930.

Opposite. Sutton St James Rose Festival. The negative envelope is marked 'remove stand at back'. The rather crude retouching is quite evident.

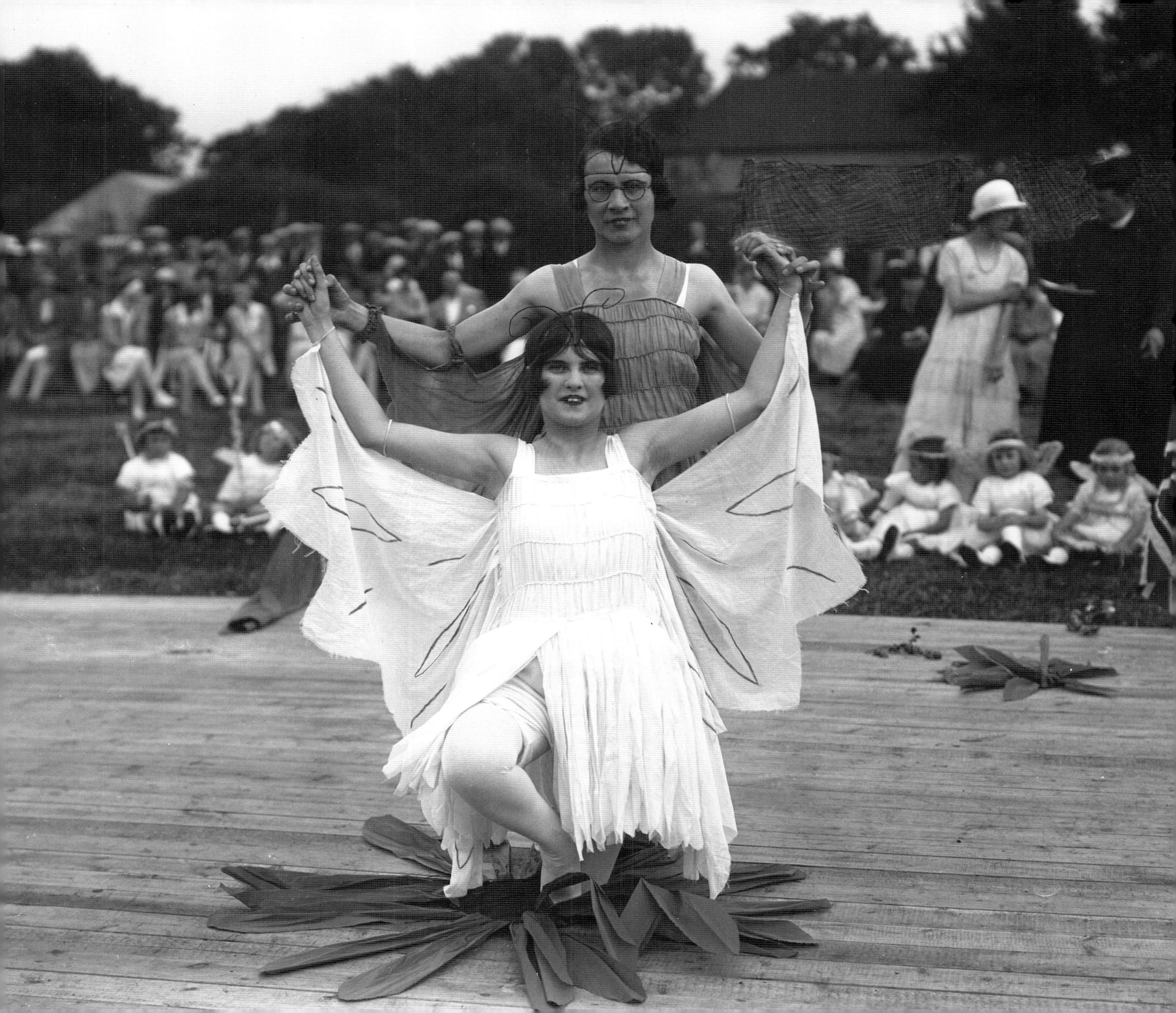

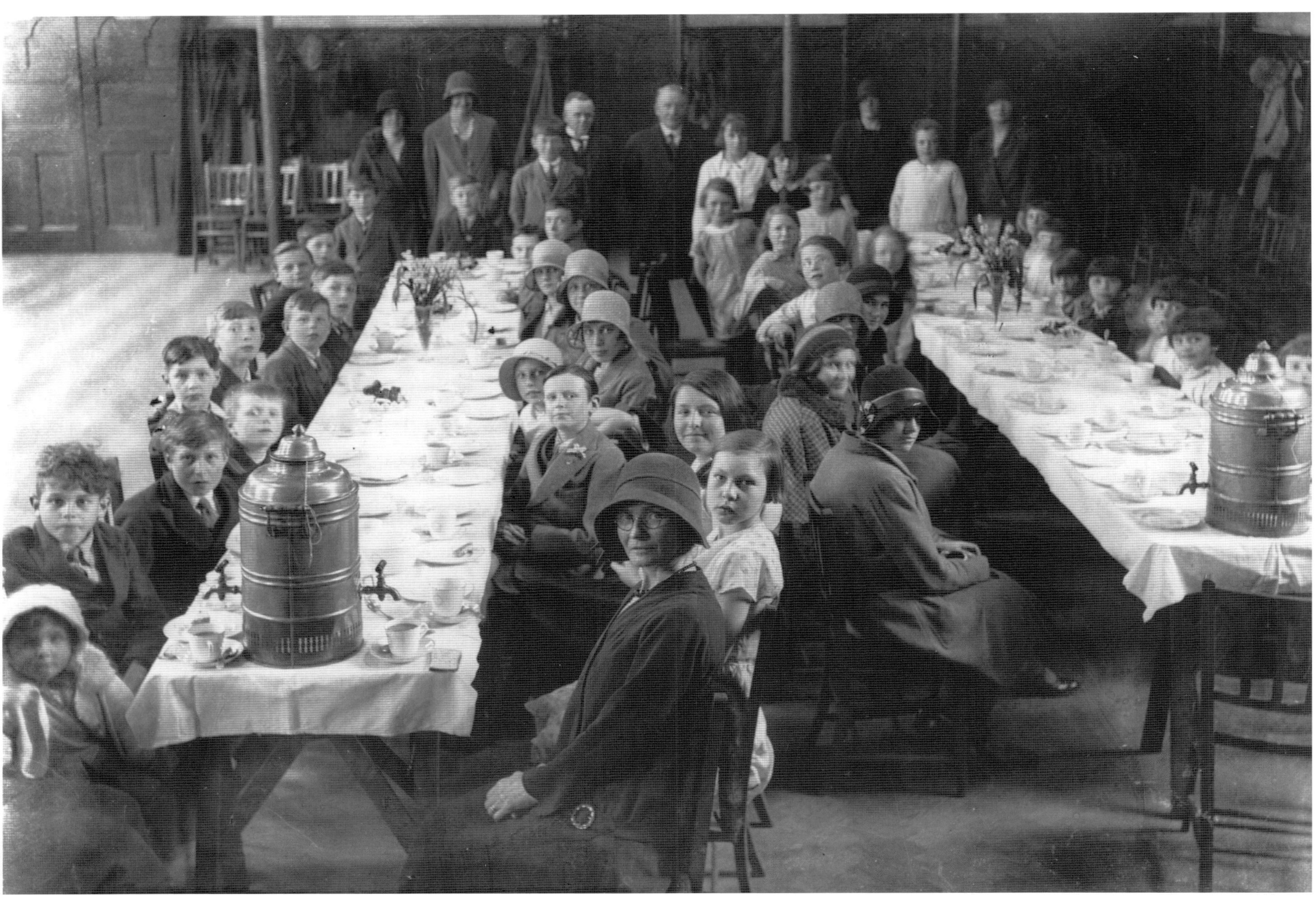

 Children enjoy a tea organised by Hill Street Baptist Church, late 1920s.

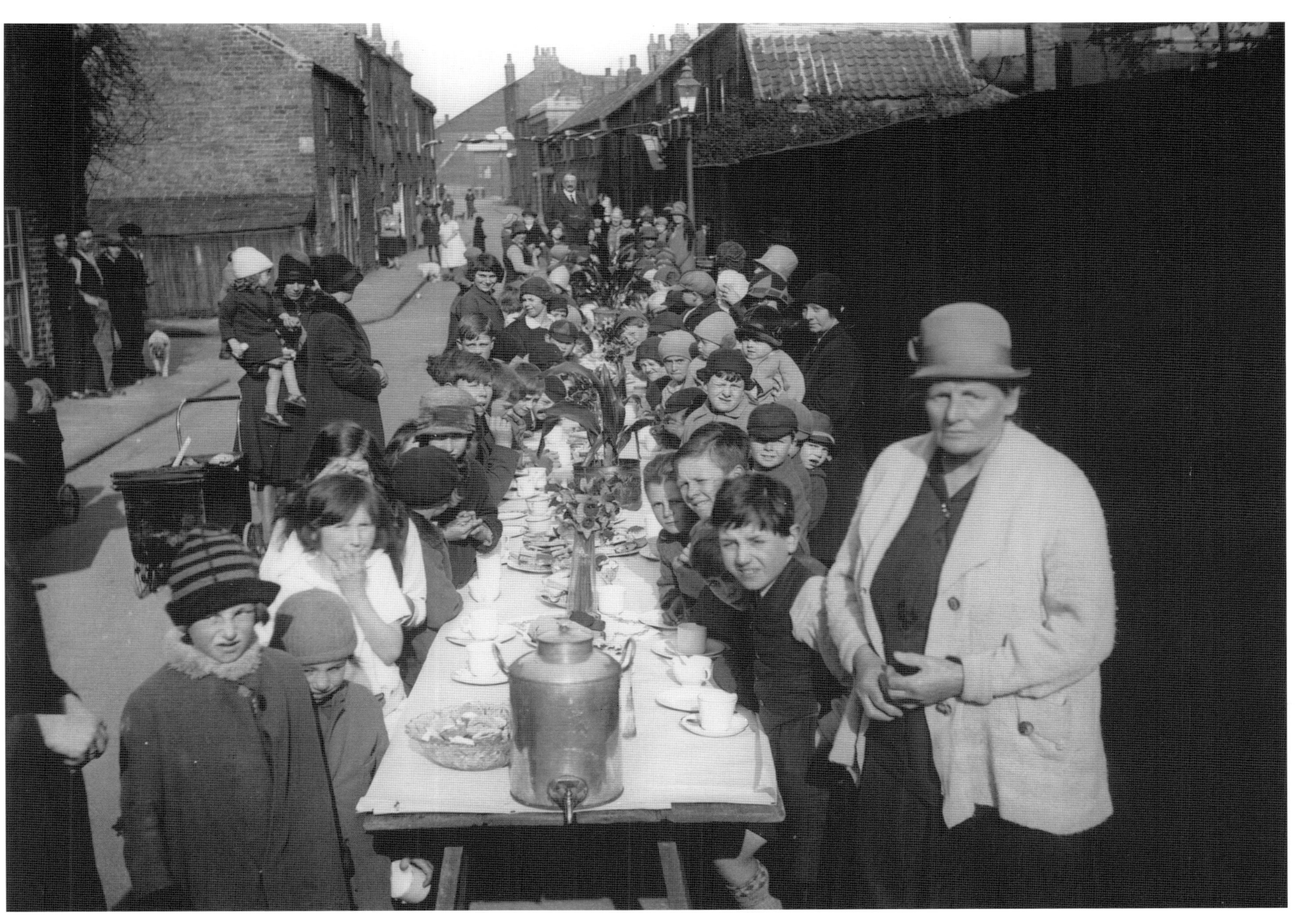

May Day celebrations in Sandyland Street, 1929. Activities included the crowning of a May Queen, a tea for the children, sports and a fancy dress parade.

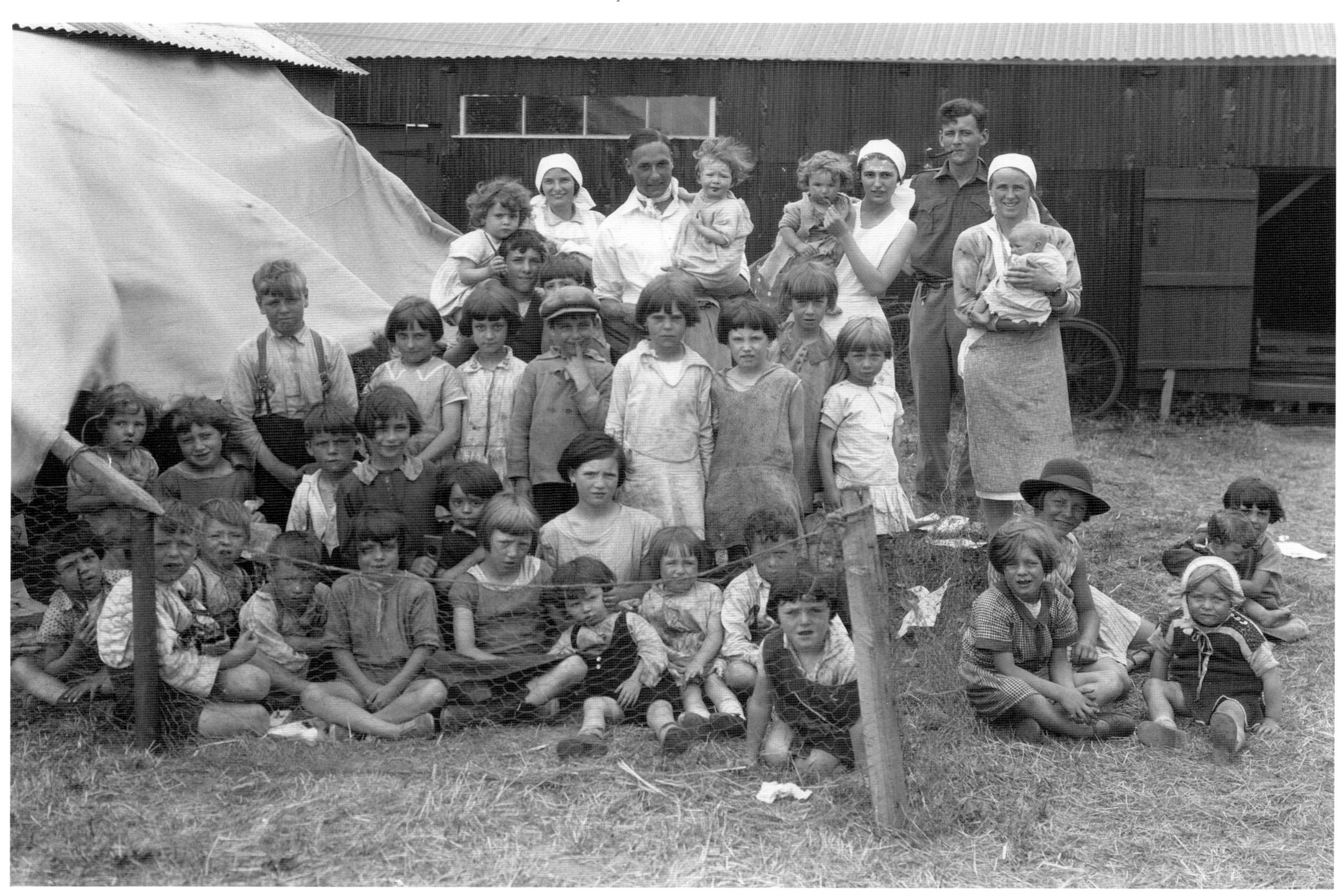

Above and opposite. Students from Cambridge University looking after the children of fruit pickers, c1930. The Cambridge Fruiting Campaign had been in existence since before World War I and aimed to provide crèches for the children, medical service and spiritual guidance.

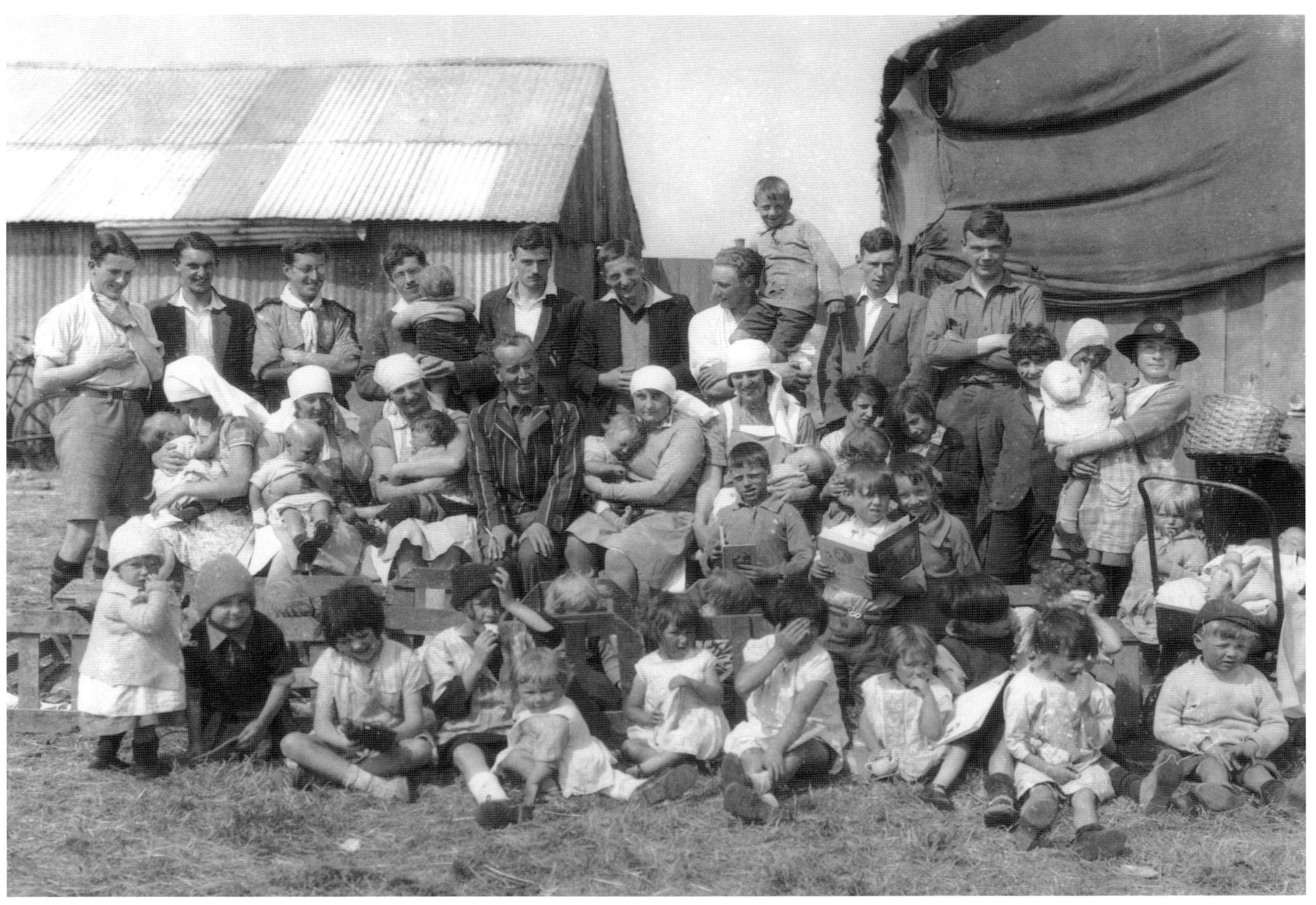

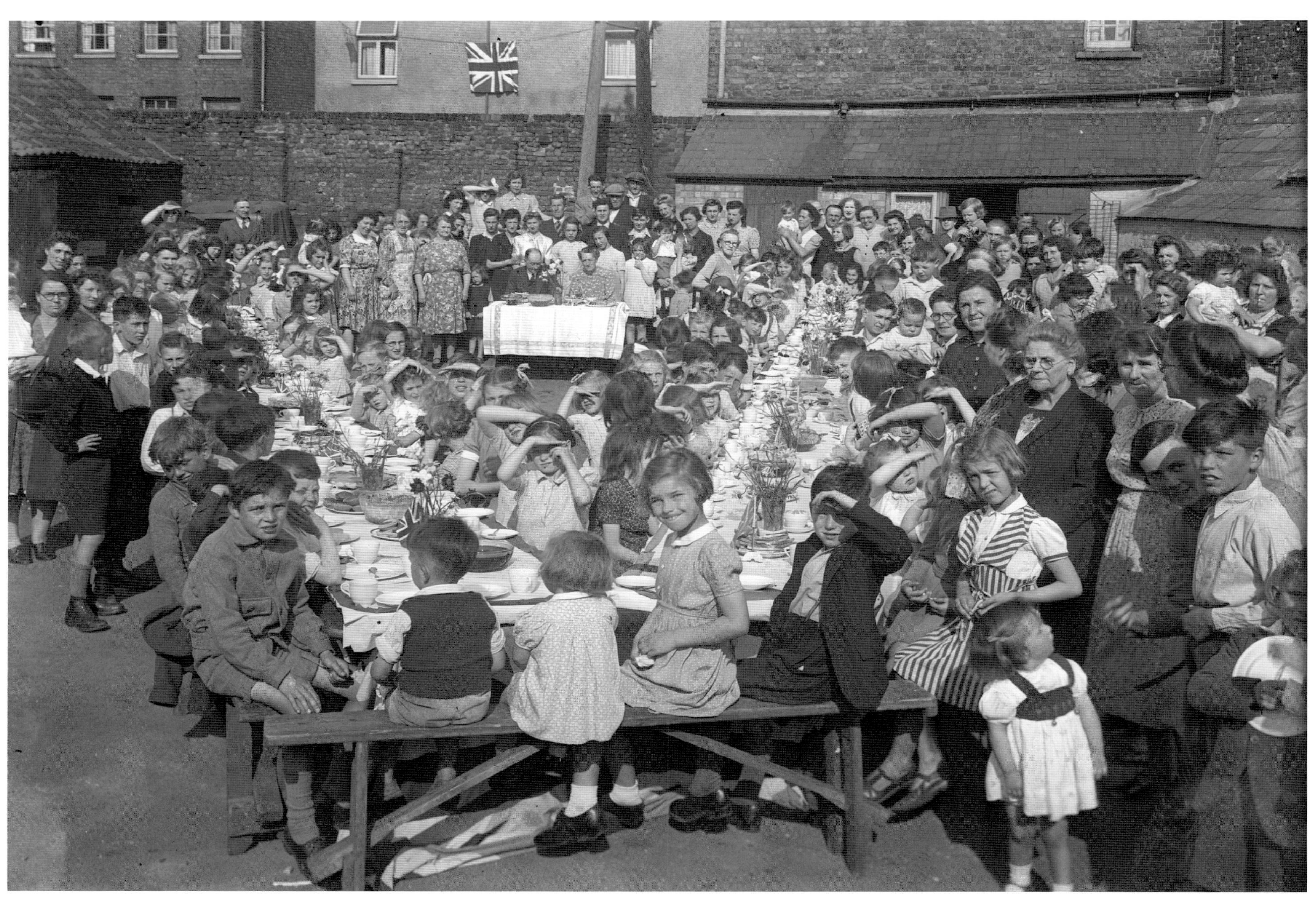

 V.E. Day party in the yard of the Dun Cow pub, Victoria Road, 1945.

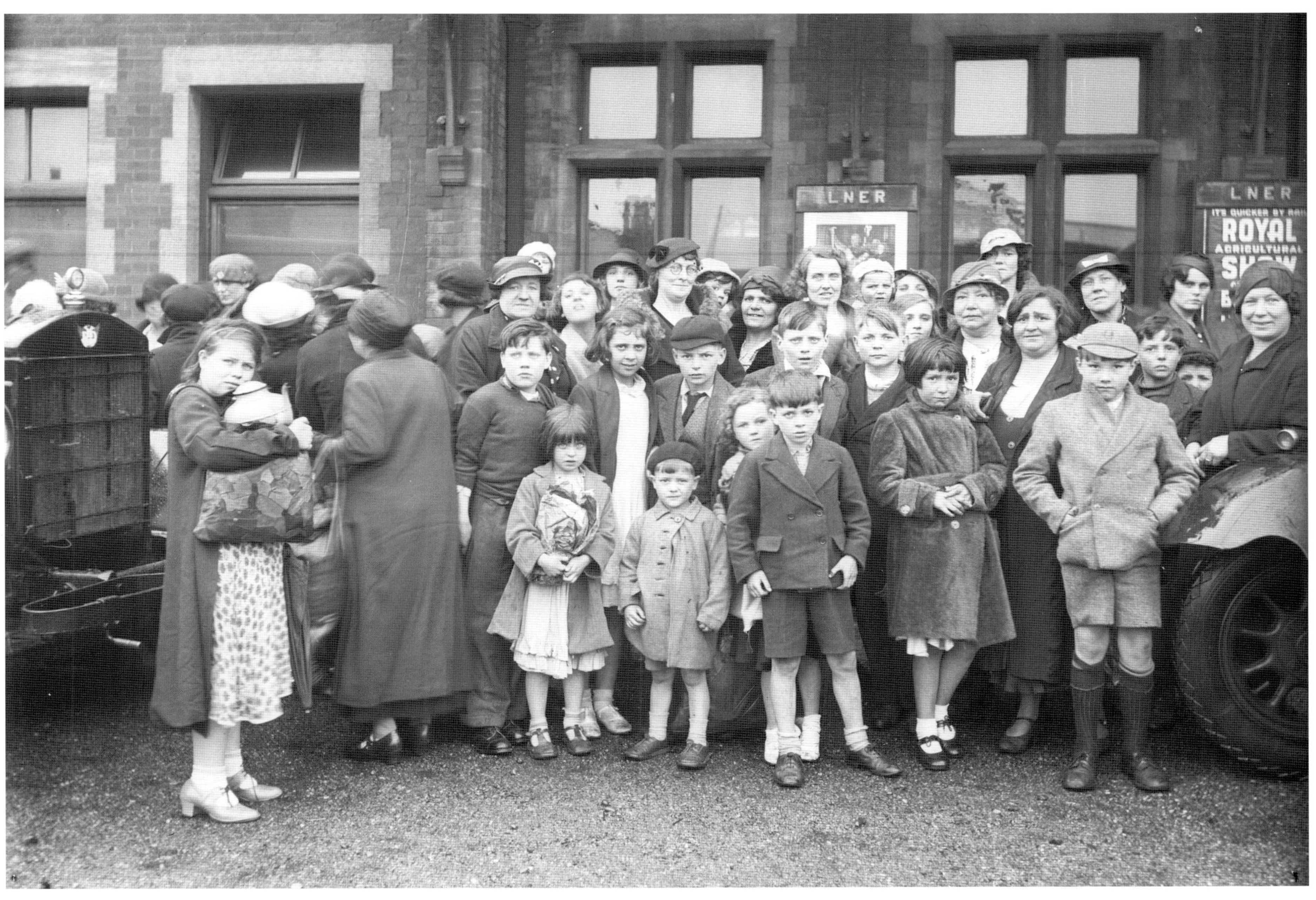

Fruit pickers from London at Wisbech East Station, 1934.

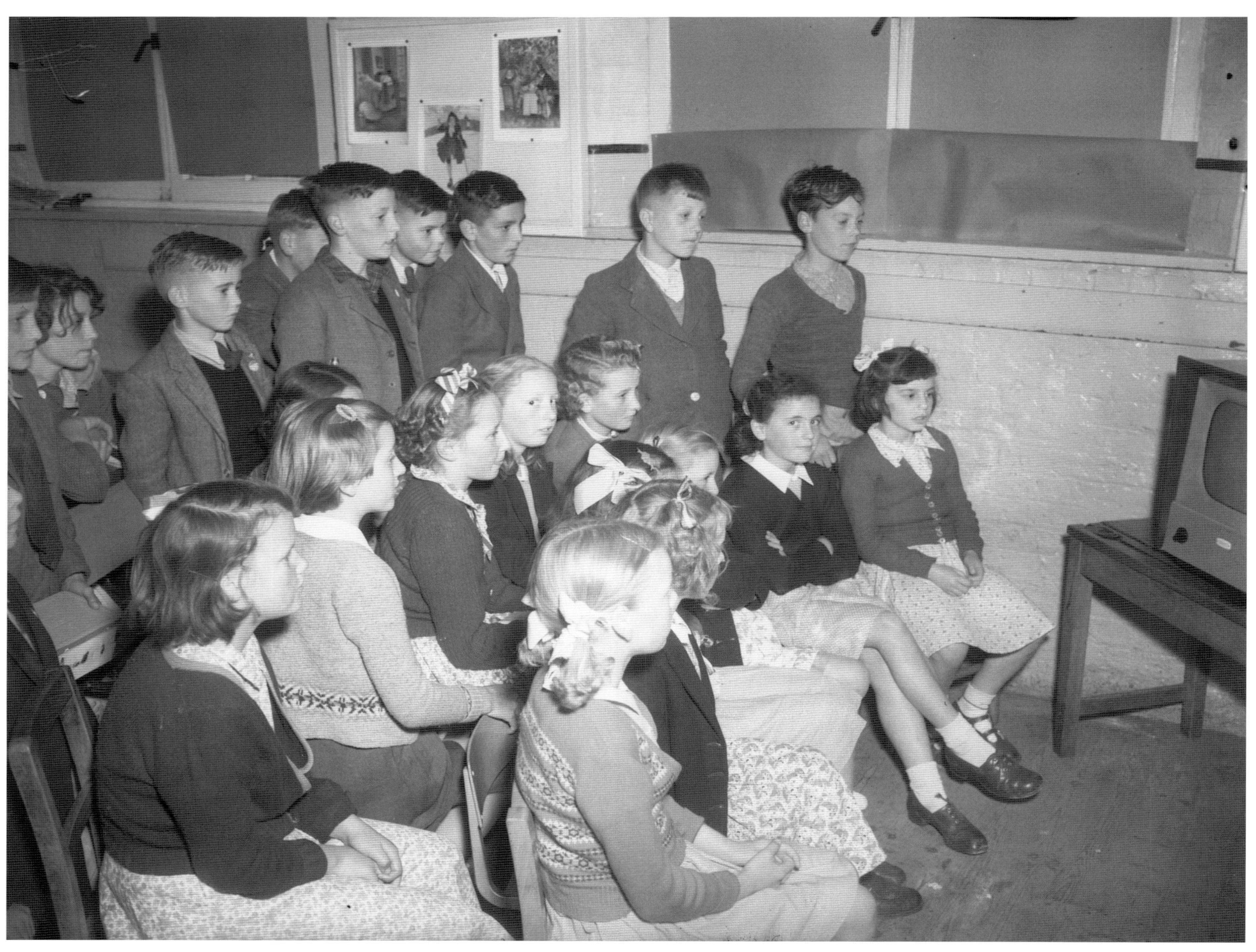

1953 and the dawn of the Television Age. The school children are probably watching the Coronation of Elizabeth II. Over 20 million people watched the event, for many their first experience of television.

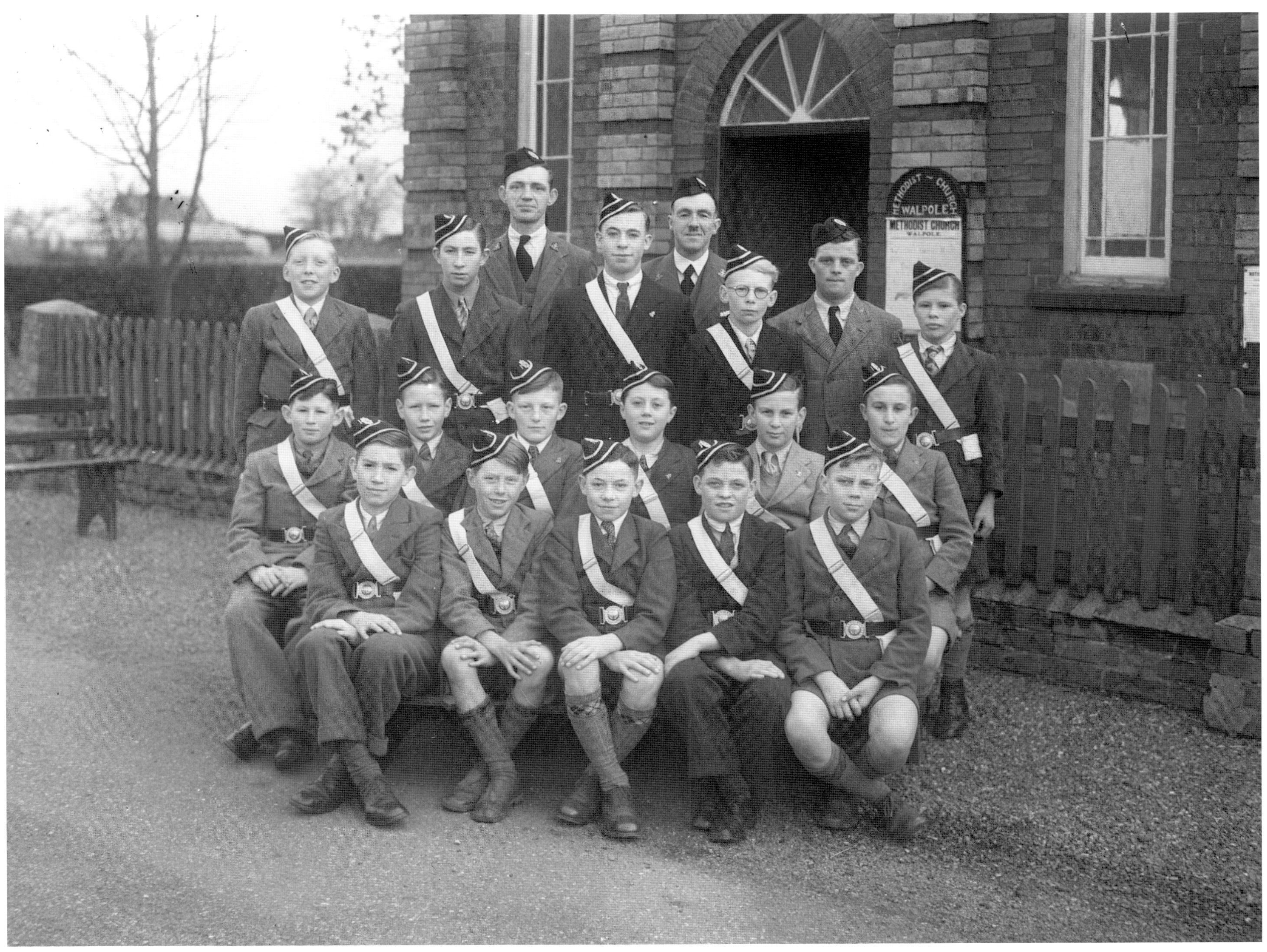

Boys Brigade, Walpole Methodist Church.

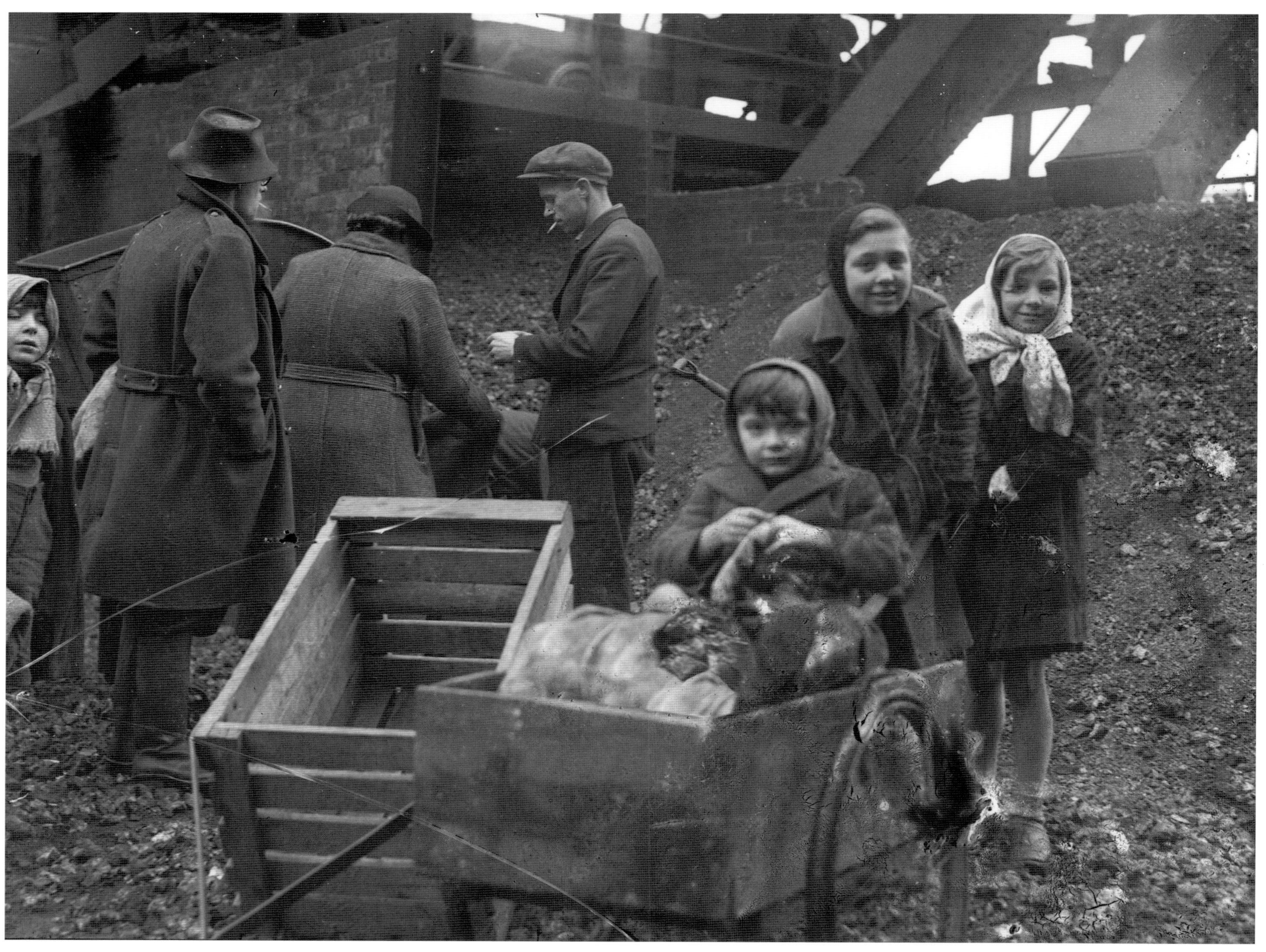

Adults and children, with improvised barrows, queuing to collect coke from the Gas Works in Chase Street. 1947. The harsh winter of 1946/47 brought fuel and food shortages, and, with the thaw and prolonged rainfall, widespread flooding.

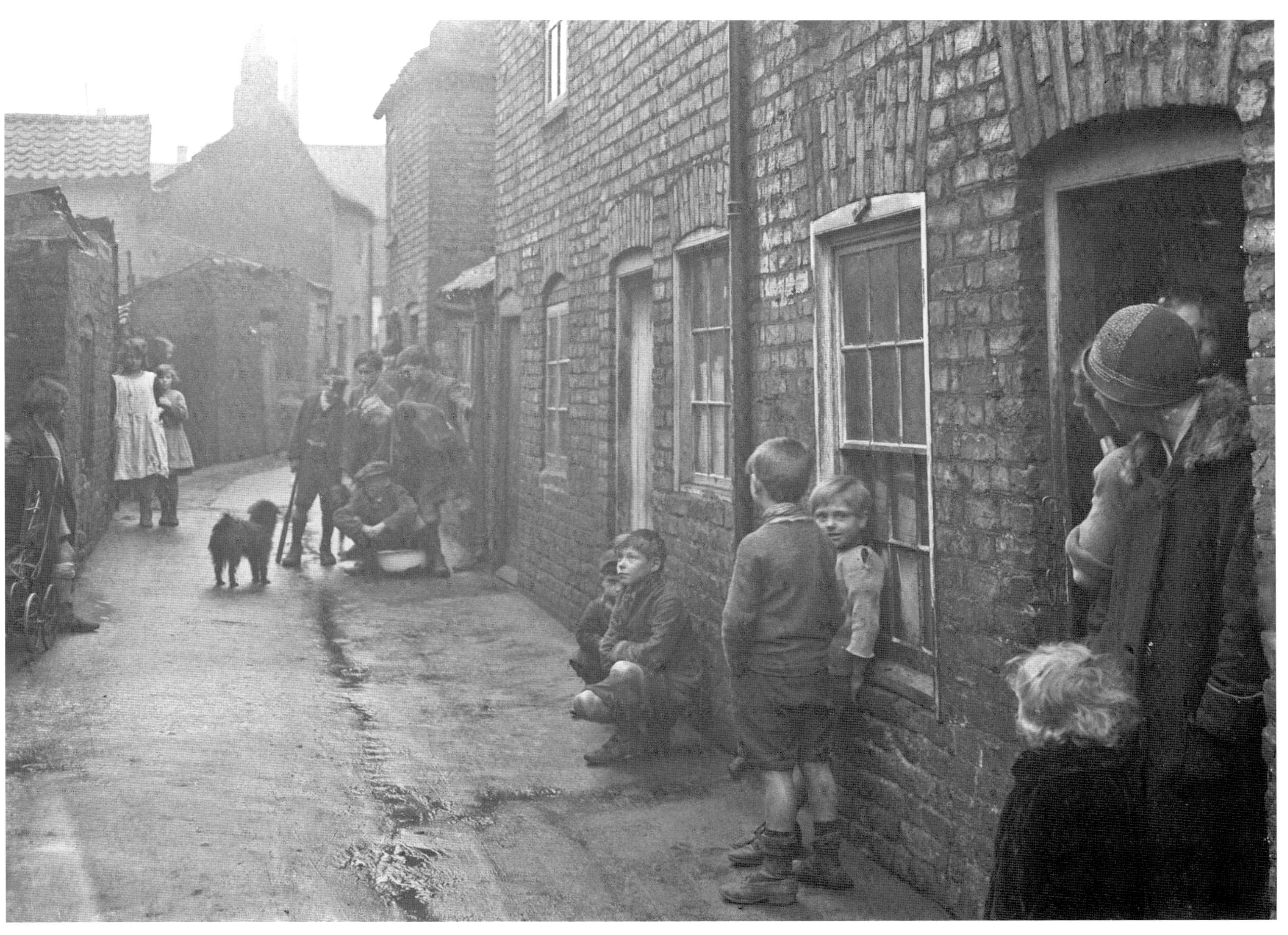

A view of a small passage leading to the Wisbech Canal, 1930s. Classed as slums, these overcrowded, two up two down houses were systematically demolished and their tenants transferred to the new housing estates that the Borough set out in such areas as Southwell Road and Bath Road.

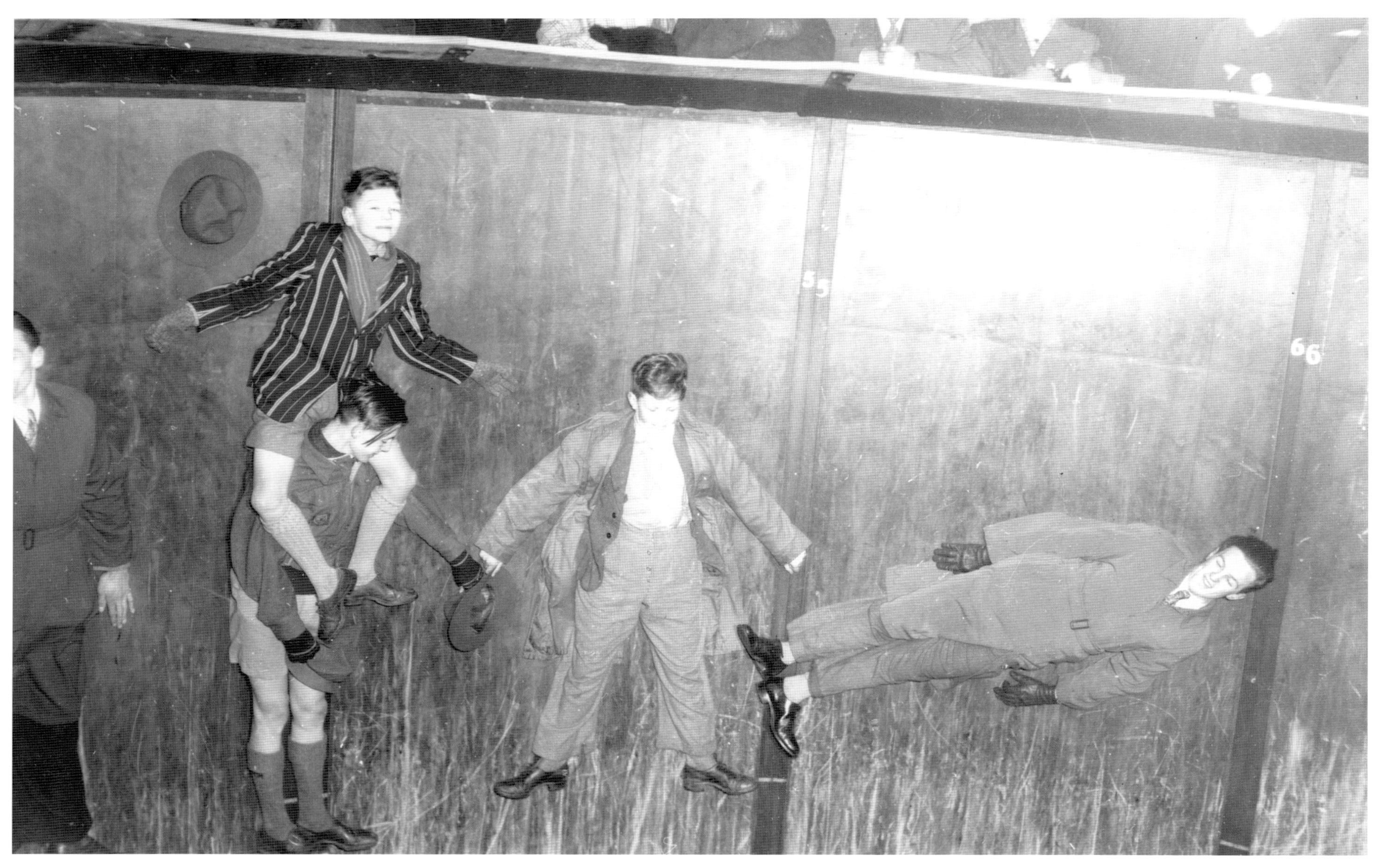

Boys enjoying the 'Ride-a-Wall' attraction at the Mart funfair in 1951. The large rotating drum pinned the 'riders' to the wall through centrifugal force, whilst the not-so-brave viewed the spectacle from the gallery above.

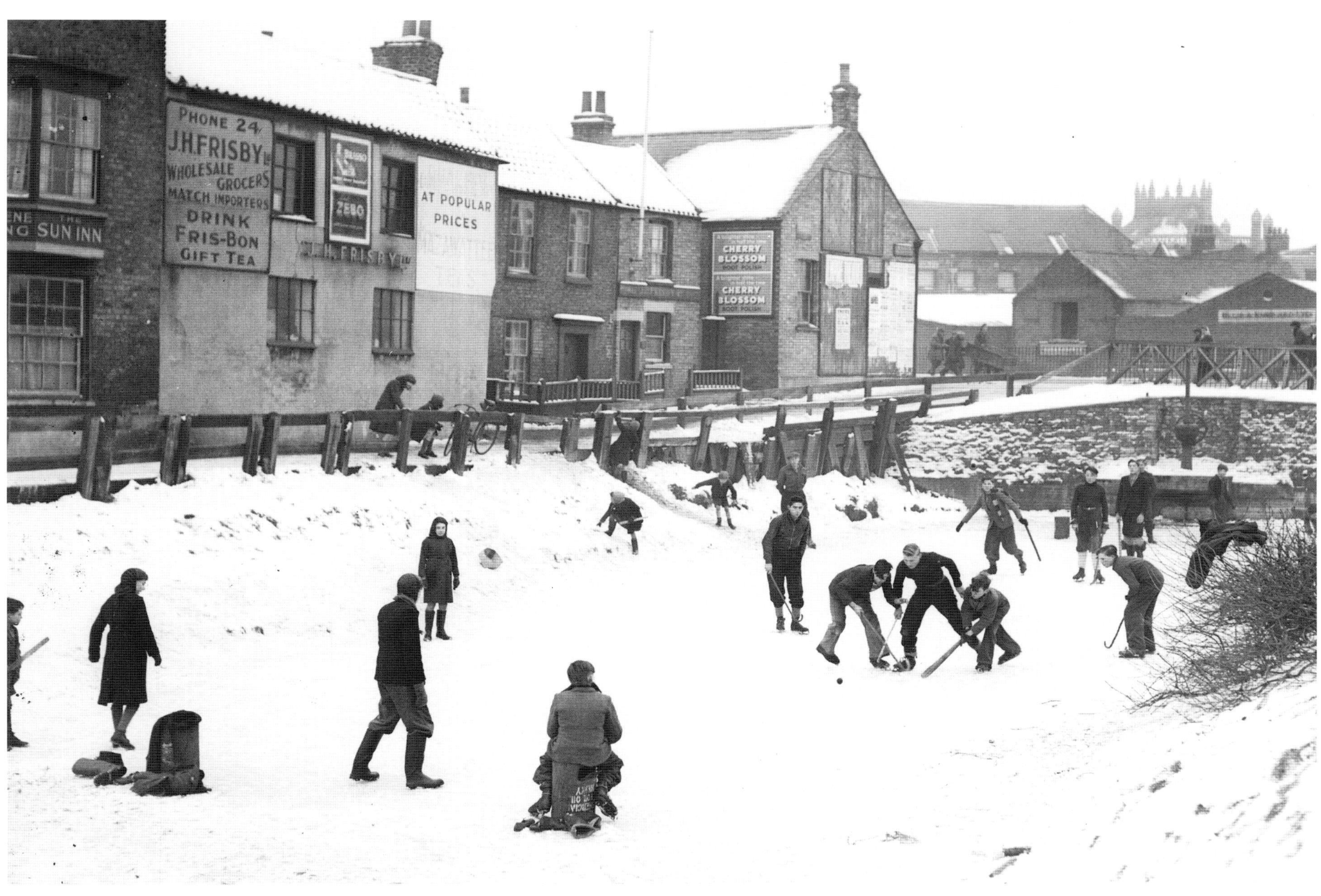

Like a Bruegel painting, the photograph captures the pleasure of a winter's day.

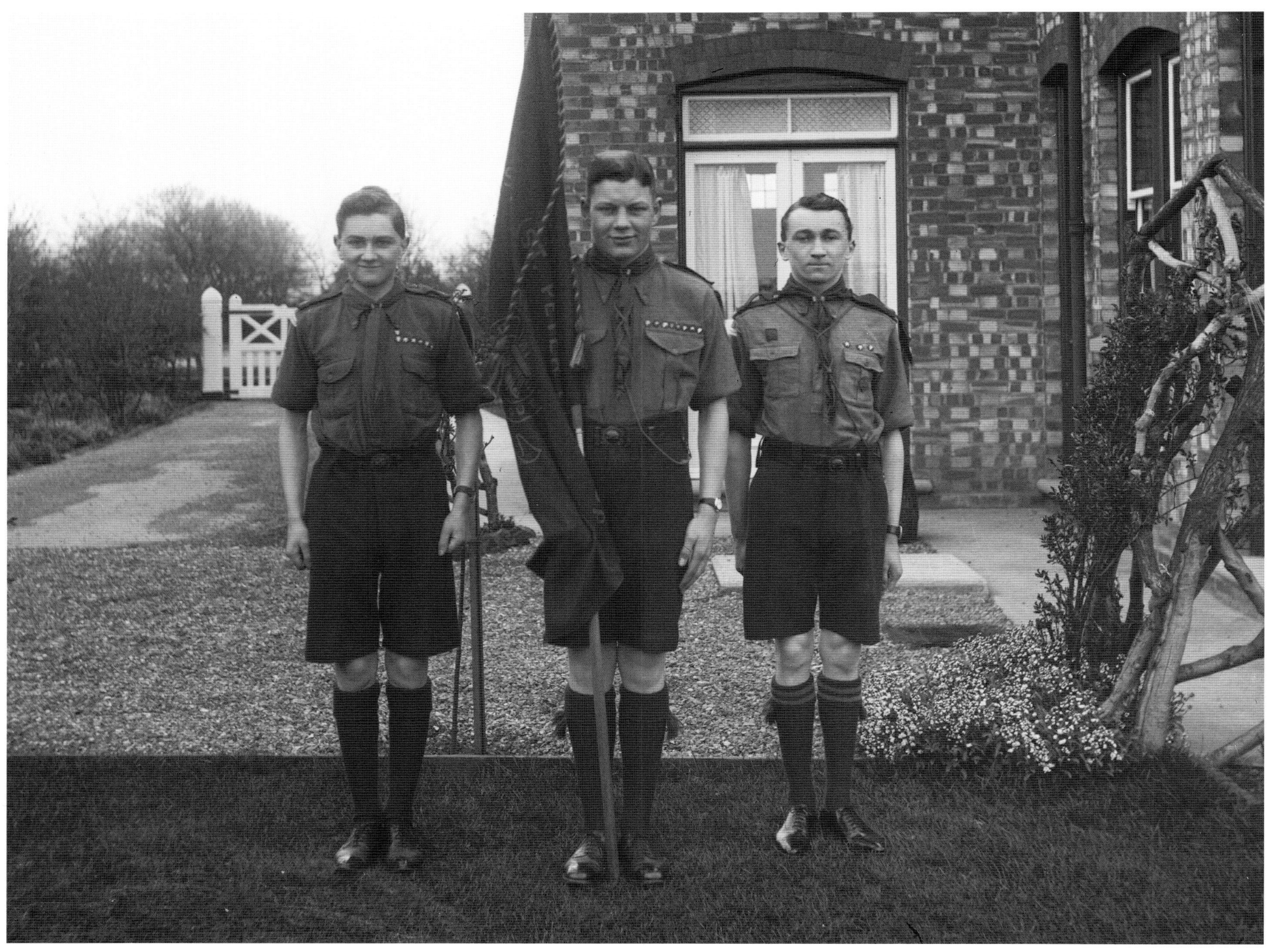

 Boy Scouts from St Peter's troop stand to attention, 1930s.

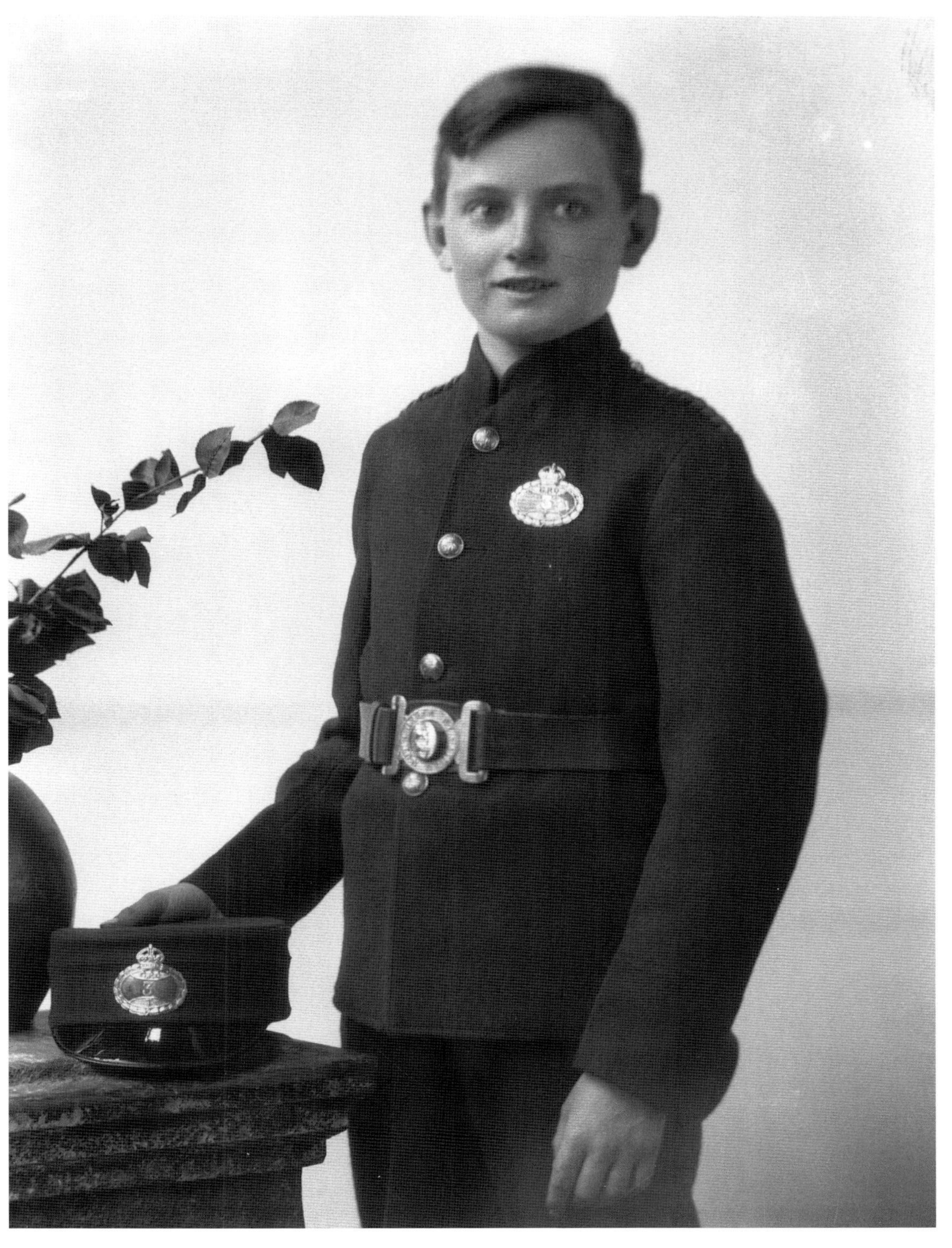

The end of childhood. A very young-looking Post Office messenger embarks on his working life, 1930s.

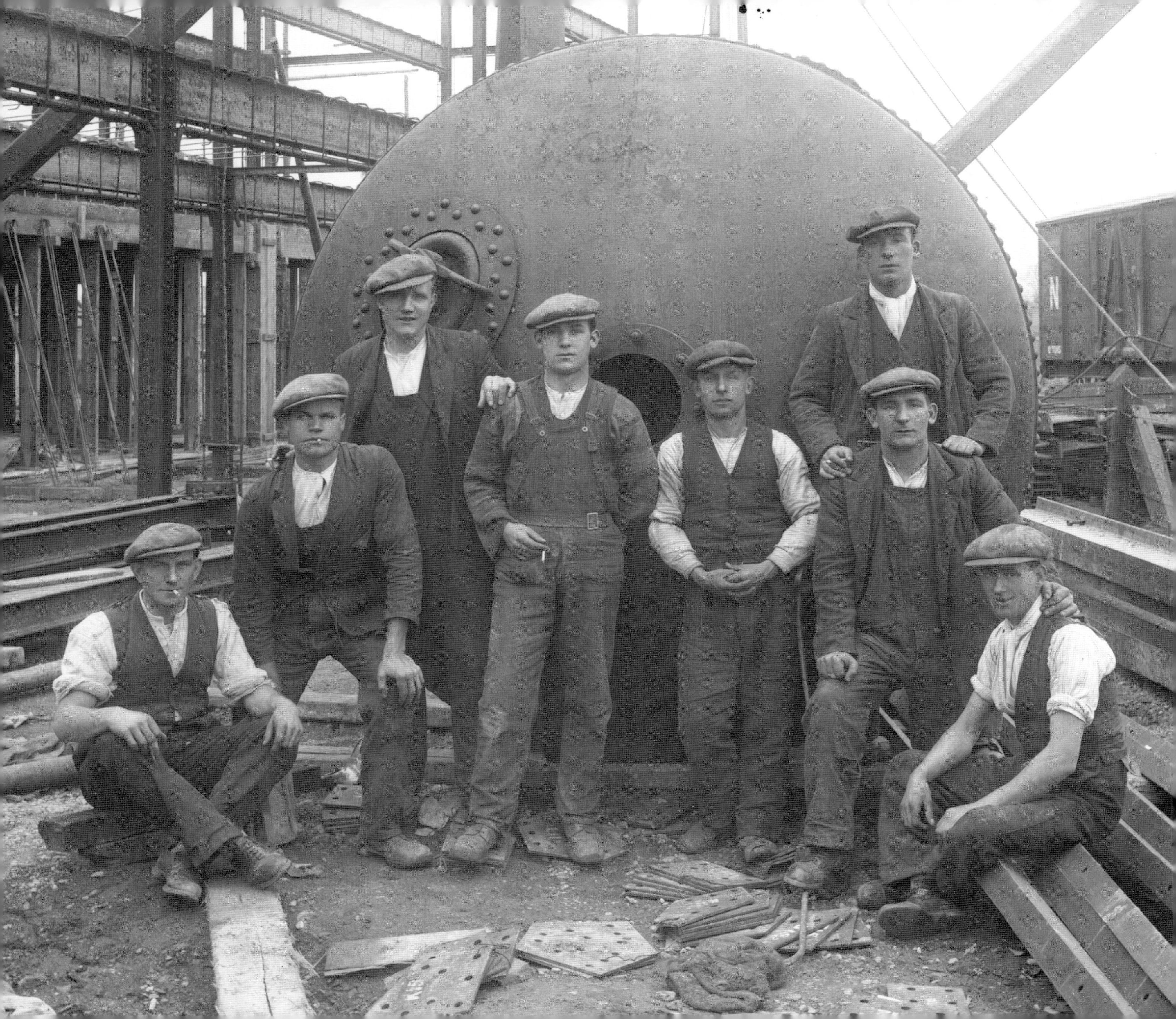
N

Work

Workmen having a break from working on a boiler at the National Canning Co. Ltd., Lynn Road, 1936. In the background is a truck on the harbour line that linked the port area to Wisbech East Station.

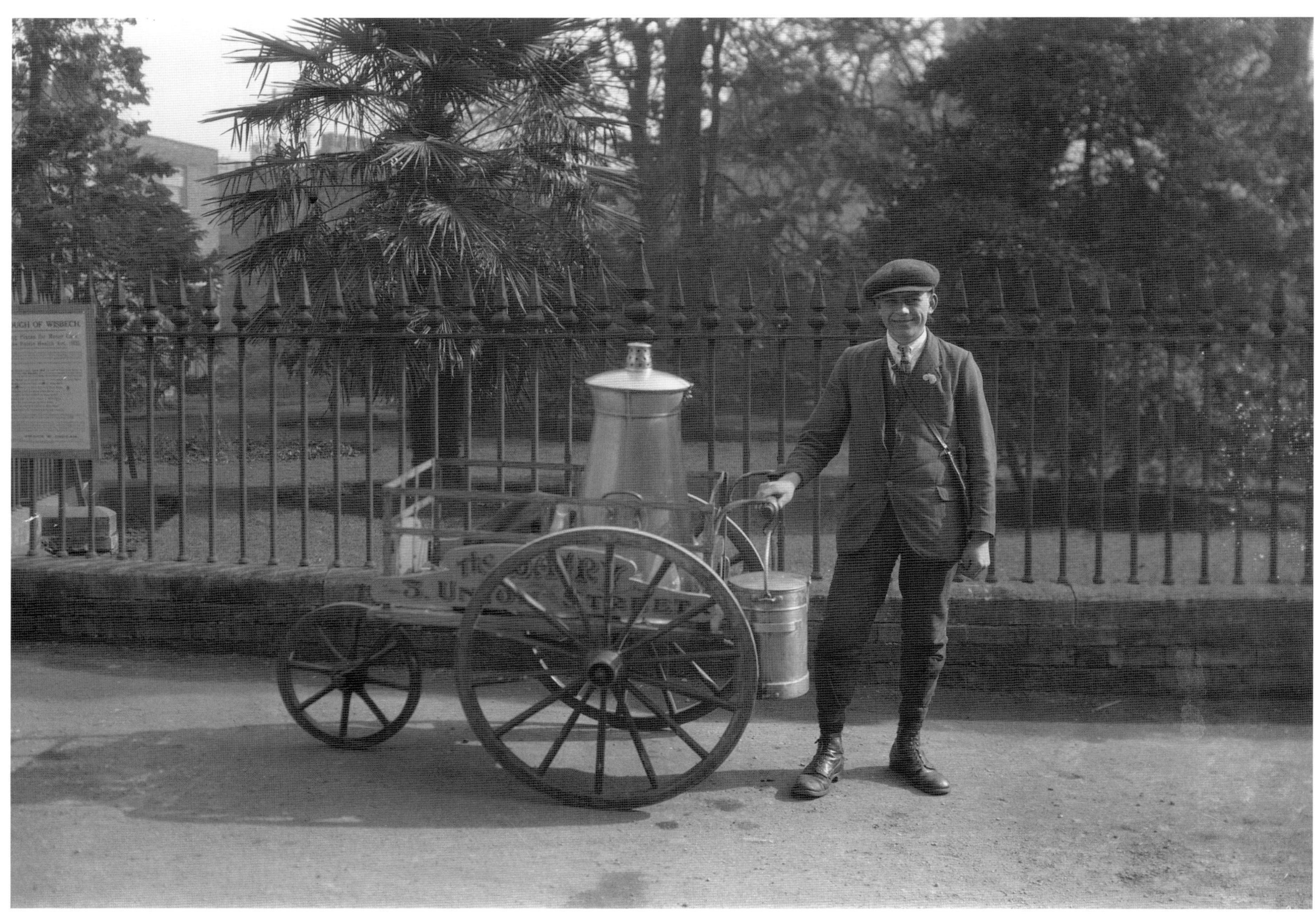

Milkman in School Lane, 1930. The dairy at 3 Union Street was run by the Wisbech Farmers' Dairy Co. Ltd.

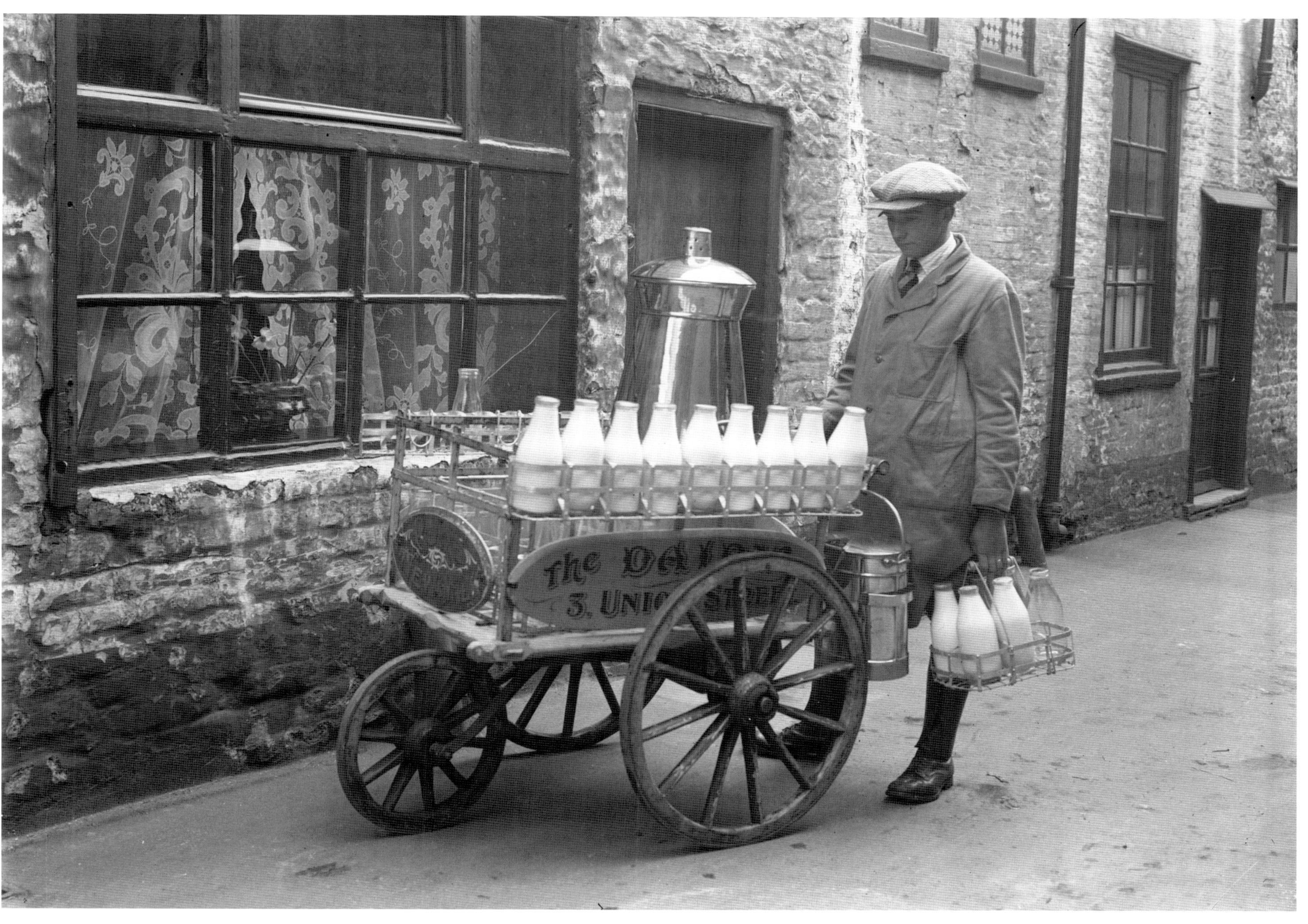

Milkman from The Dairy, 3 Union Street.

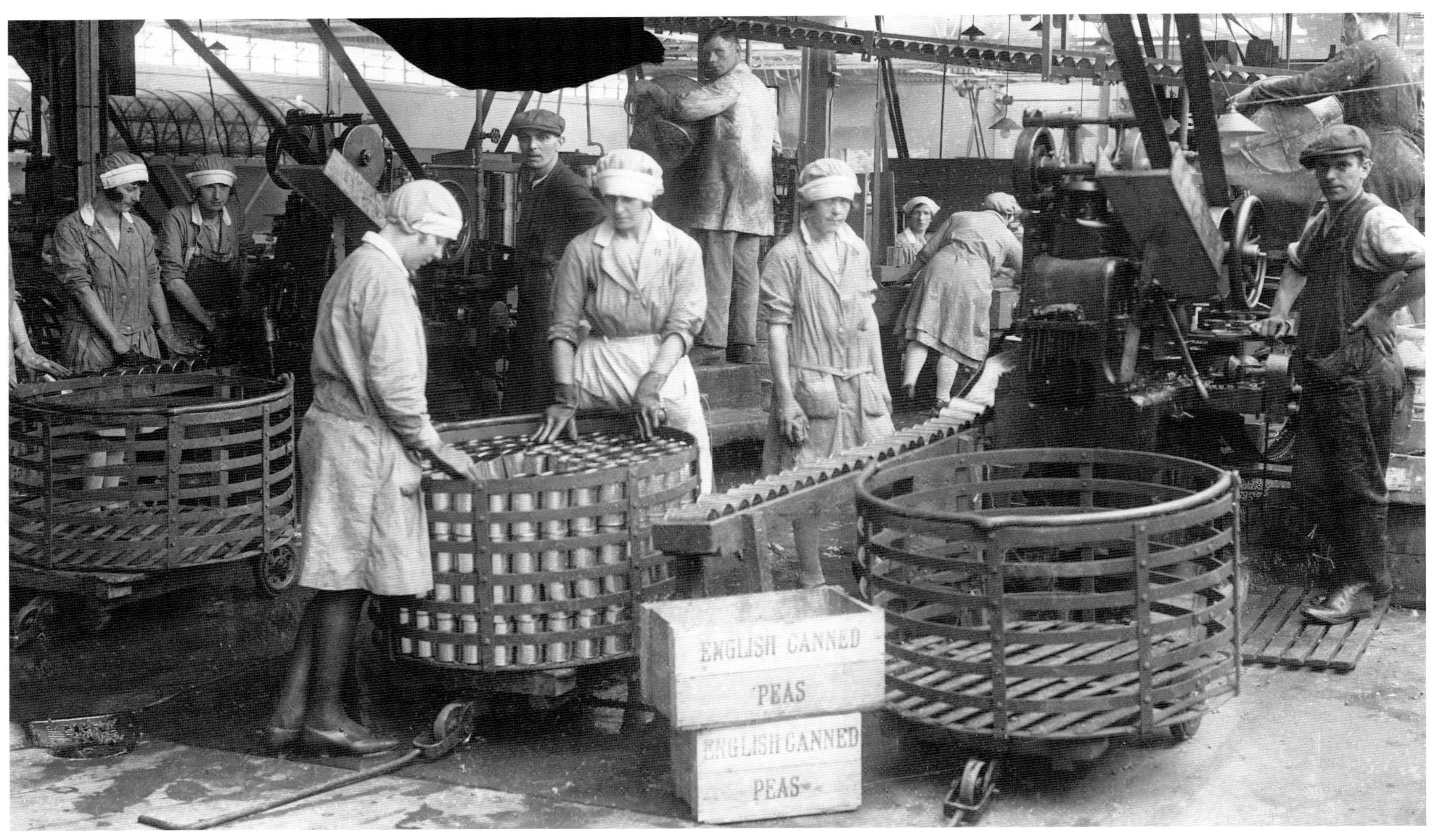

 Smedley's canning factory, 1931.

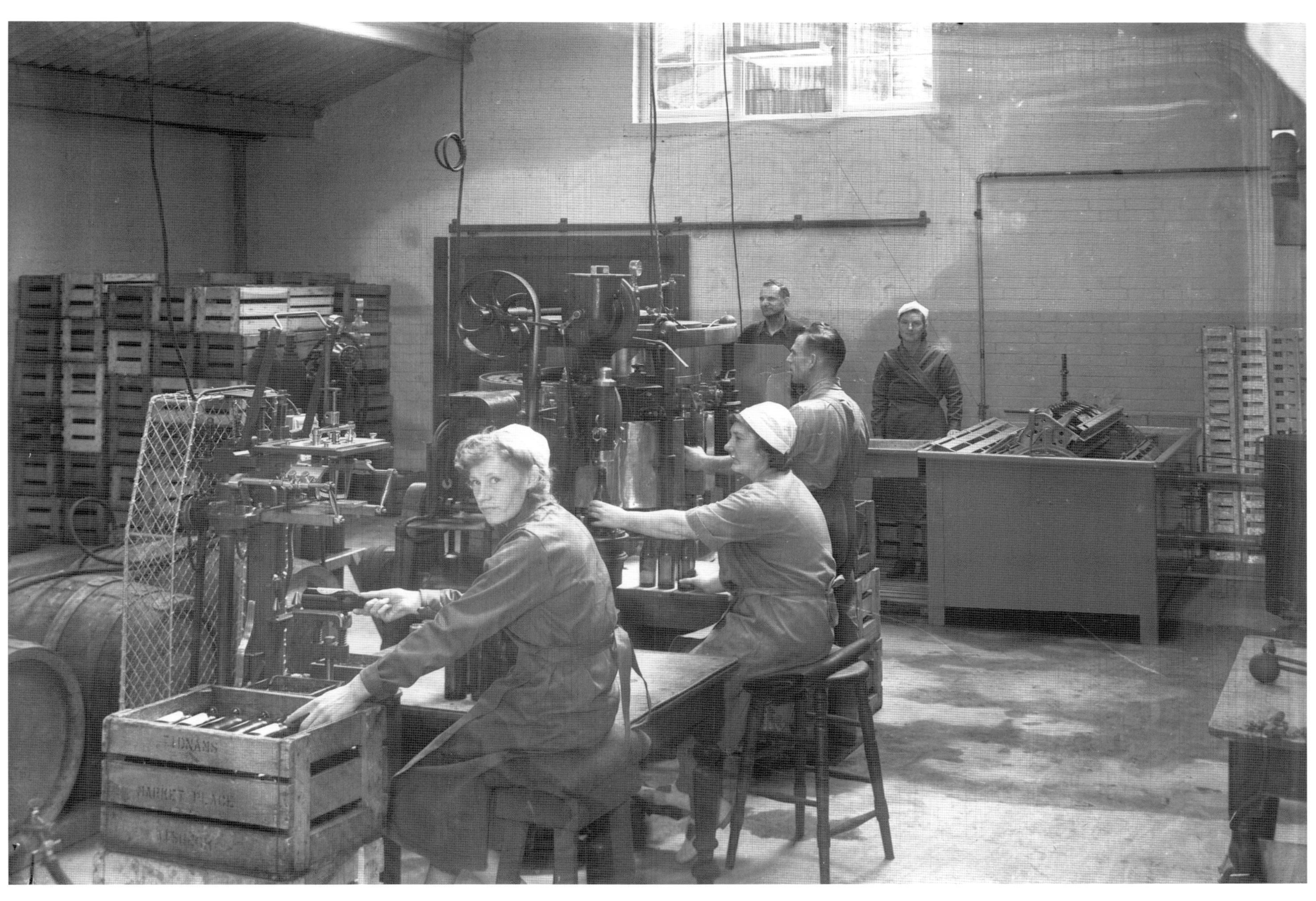

Tidnam's new bottling plant, 1949. Tidnam bottled beer, port and malt whiskey which were stored in their cellars at the Rose & Crown Hotel and under the Clarkson Memorial.

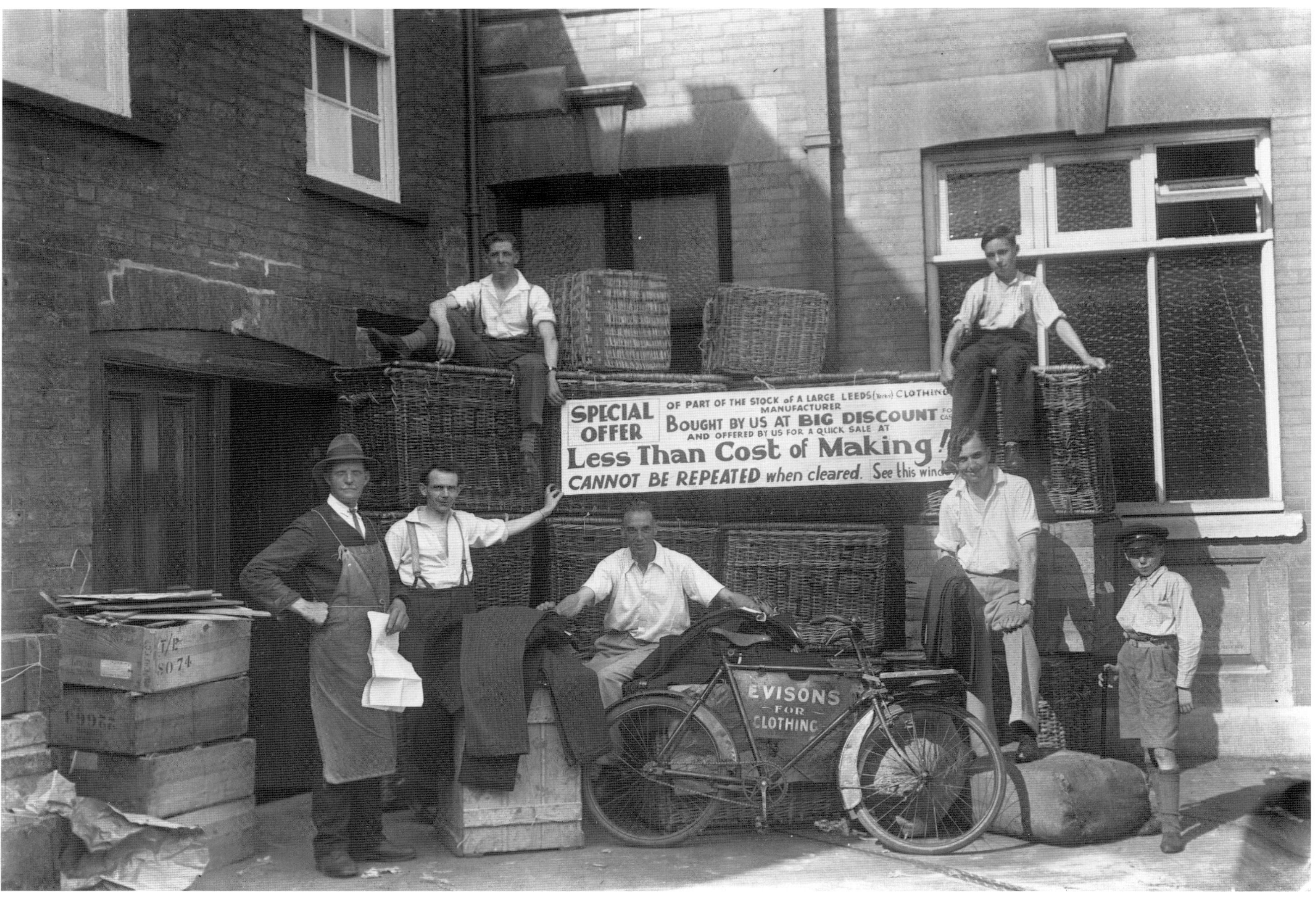

The staff of Evison's advertising their bulk stock of discount clothes bought from a Leed's manufacturer.

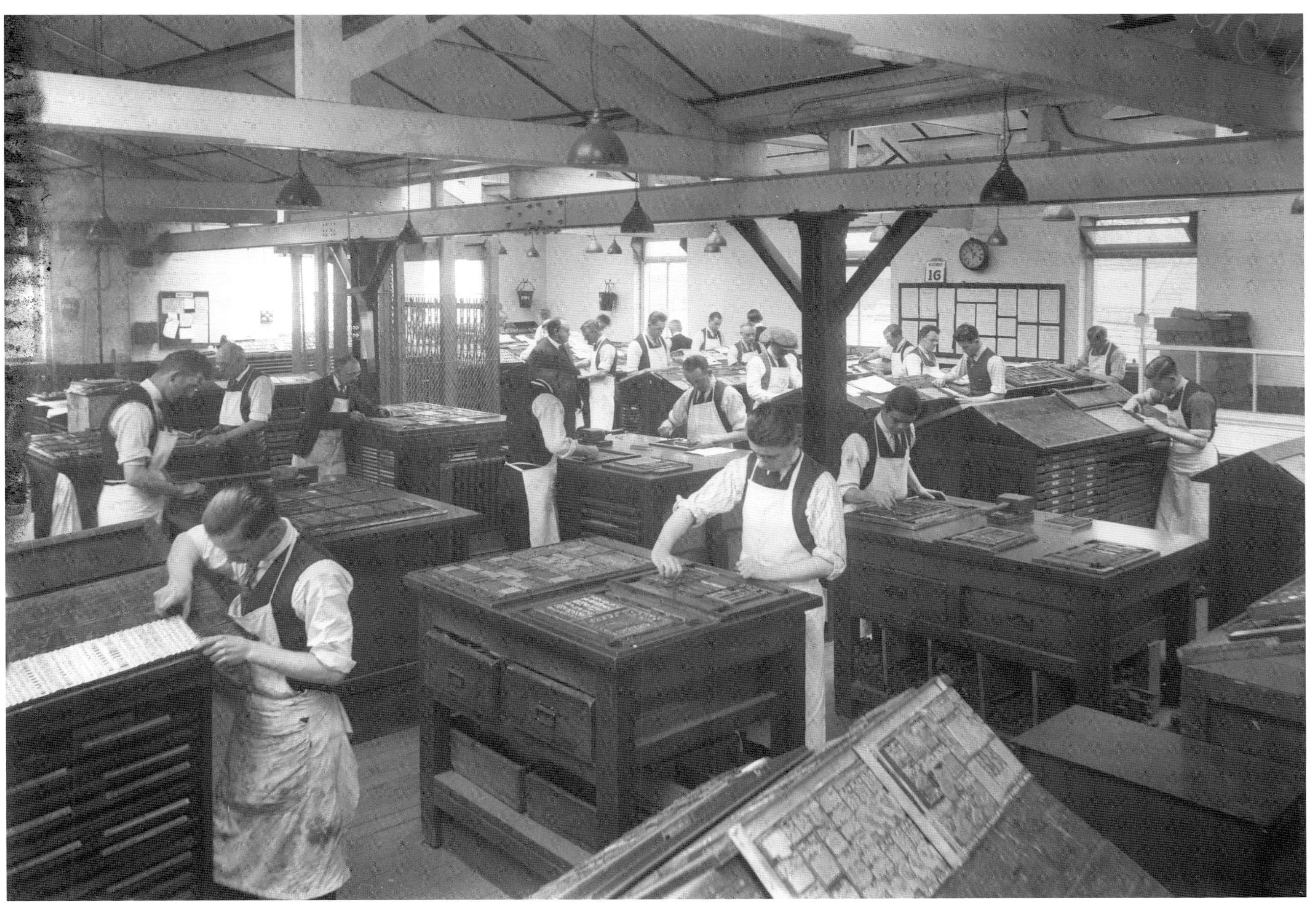

The composing room of Balding & Mansell, 1930. The firm were high quality printers who printed such important works as the *Catalogue of Printed Books* for the British Museum and the *Library of Congress Catalog.*

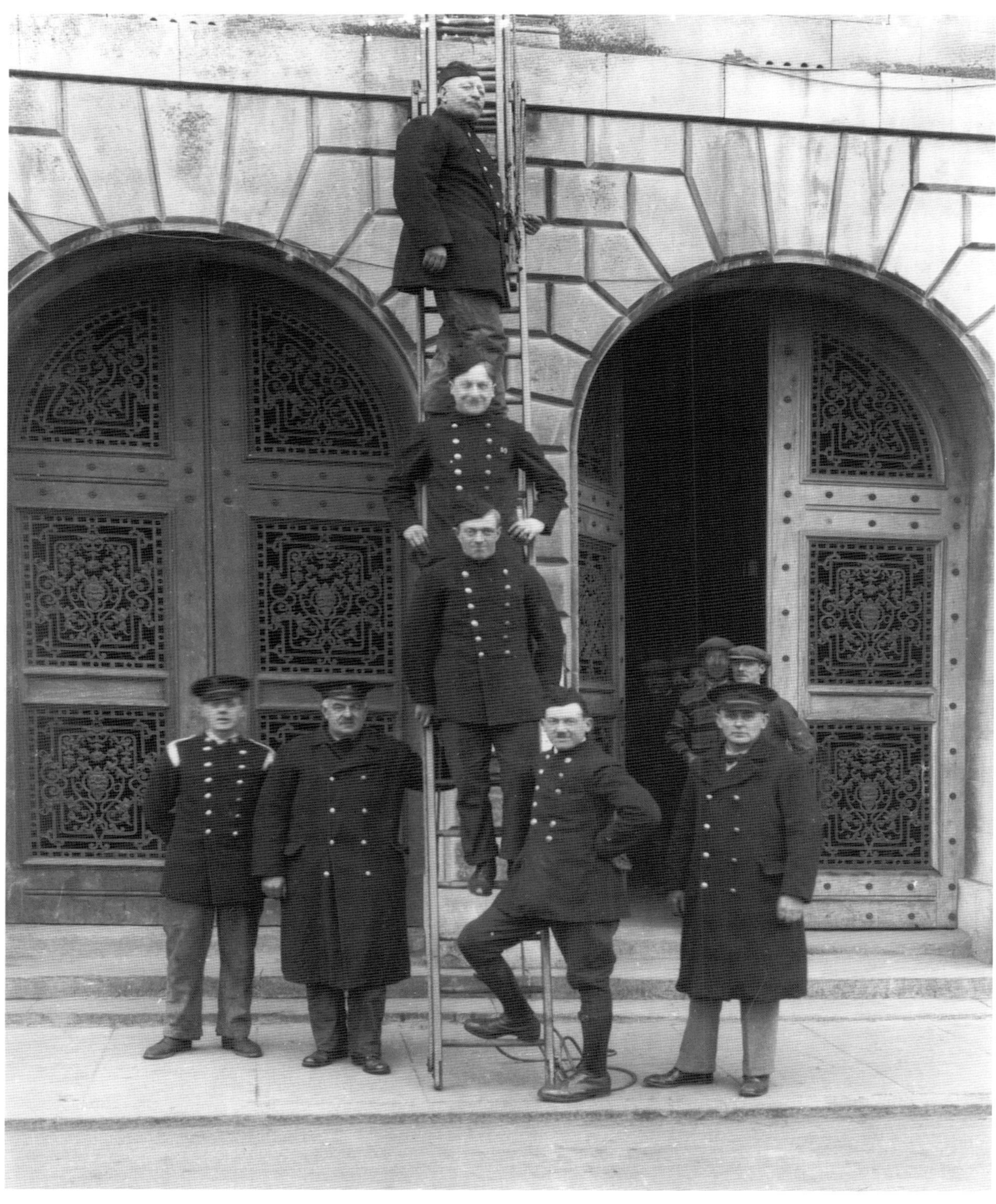

Firemen outside of the Corn Exchange are, second left, Bill Langford, and, proceeding up the ladder, L Humphrey, Jack Rippon, Percy Reed, 'Diver' Smith and, on the right, Capt. Friend, c1930. The Brigade frequently held public exercises around the Town, including firemen jumping out of the Corn Exchange's windows to be caught by their colleagues below.

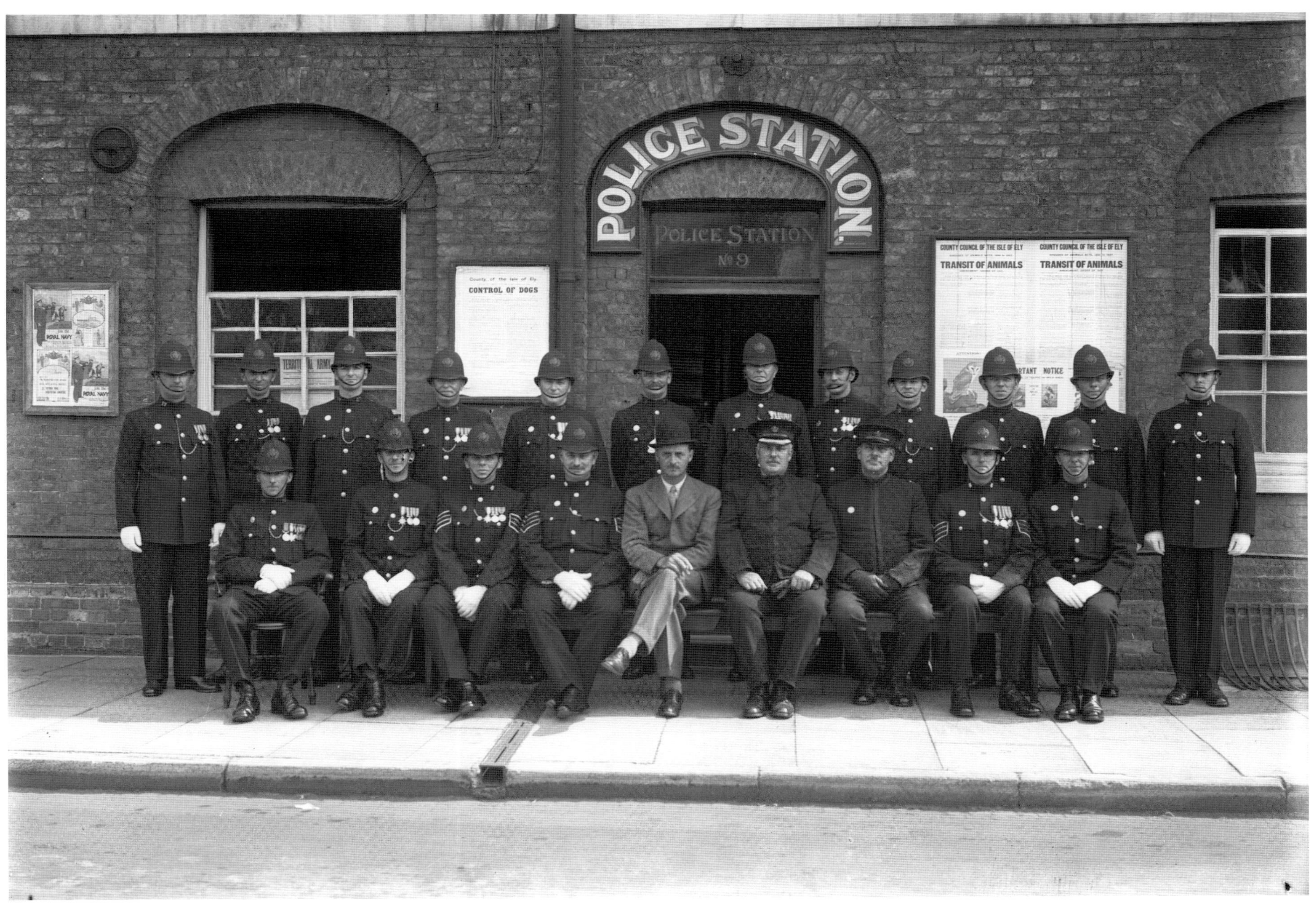

Officers of the Wisbech Division of the Isle of Ely Constabulary outside the County Police Station, 9 South Brink, 1934. The photograph was taken after the force's annual inspection. The officers are sitting (l to r): Pc Howard, Pc Kemp, Sergt. Moll, Sergt. Payne, the Chief Constable (Capt. J. Rivett-Carnac), Supt. FH Green, Insp. Bush, Sergt. Barwell, Pc Pegg. Standing: Pcs Everitt, Preston, Hall, Cracknell, Price, Hill, Lane, Ridgeway, Lubbock, Eagle, Stanton and Blackwell.

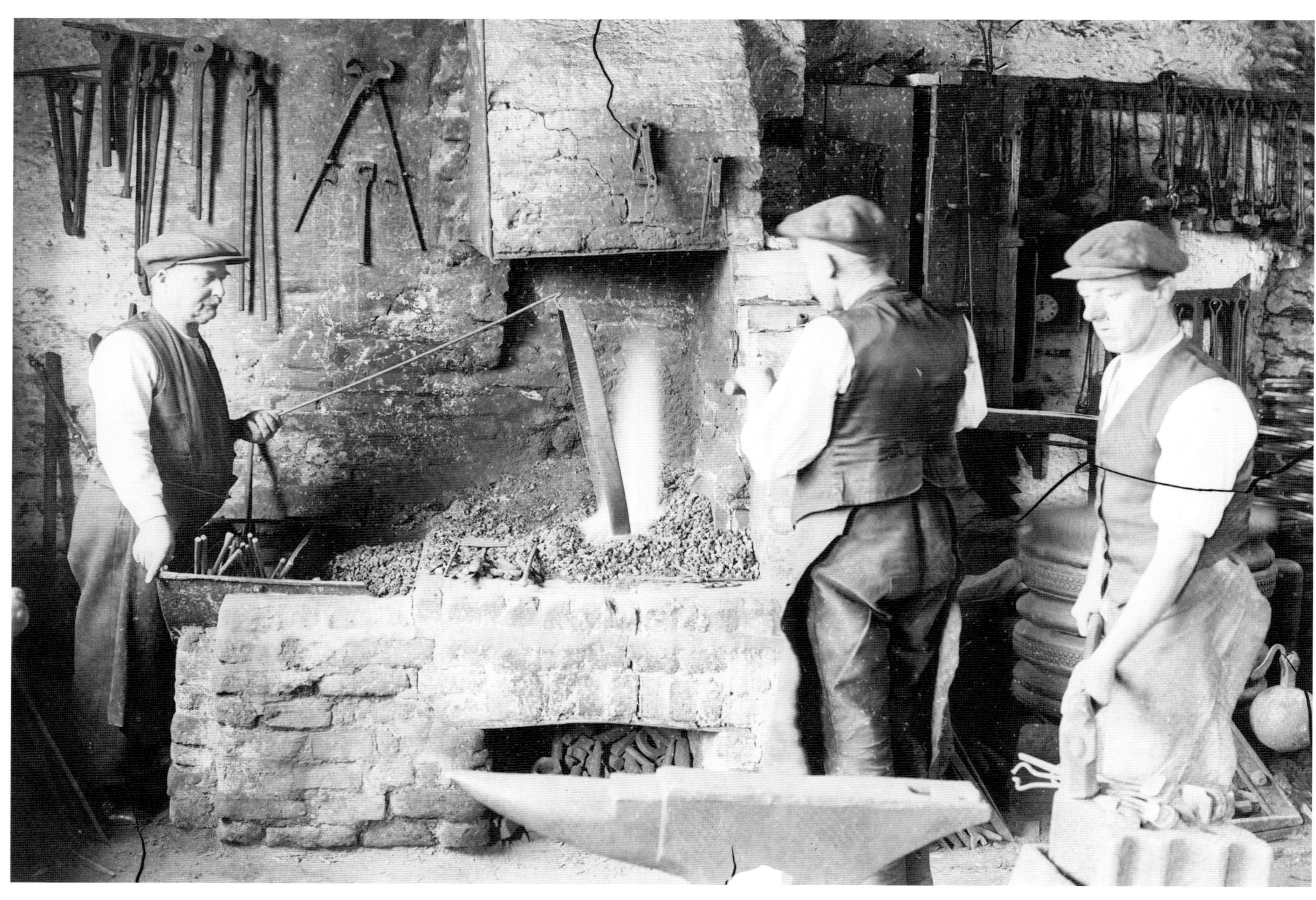

The blacksmith's forge of John H Martin at the Martin Works, Church End, West Walton, 1933. Mr Martin, on the left, and his men are at work welding a tyre for a wheel.

Opposite. Mr Riches, second from the left, a prolific rat catcher, with officials from Wisbech Borough Council, 1946.

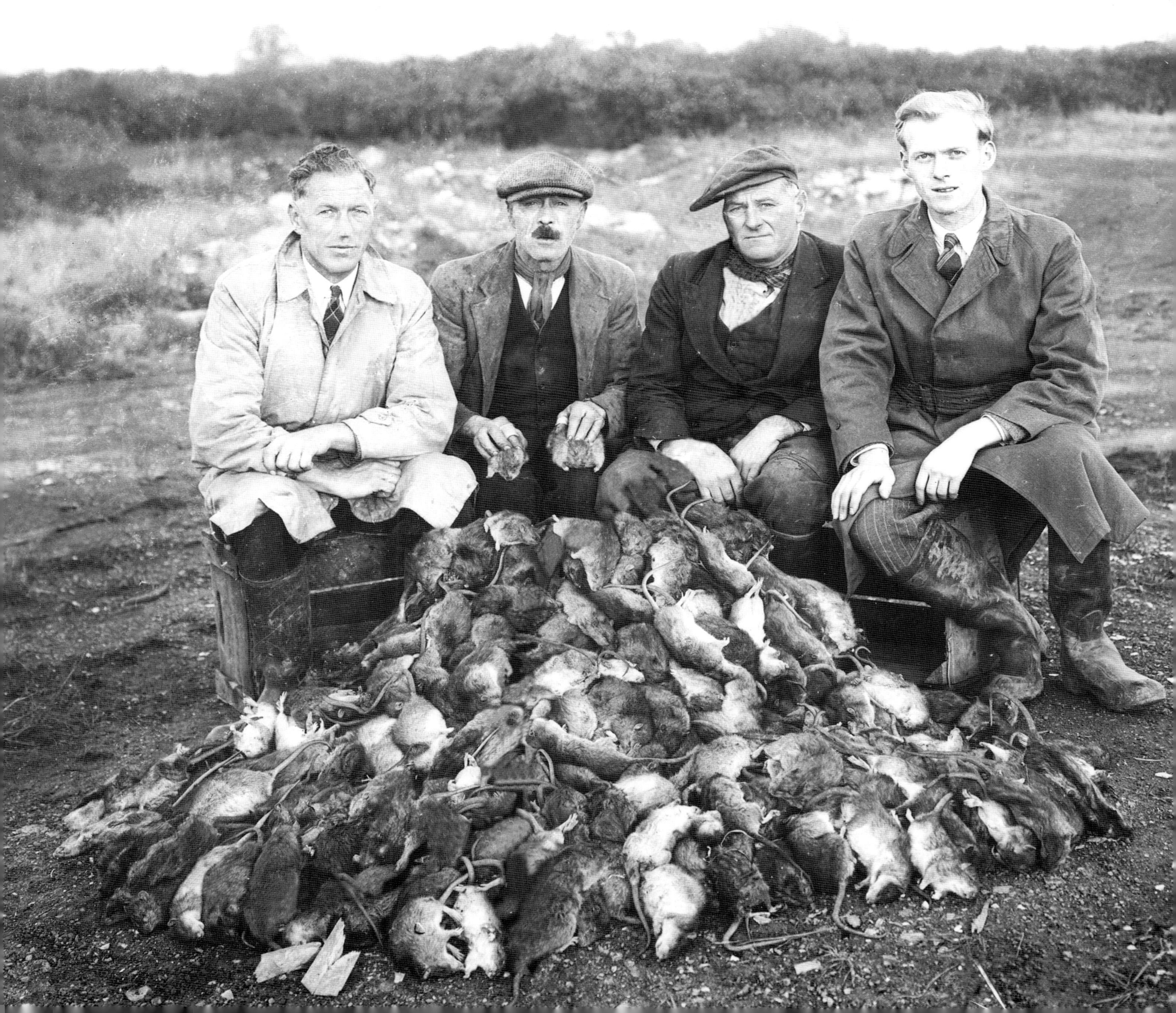

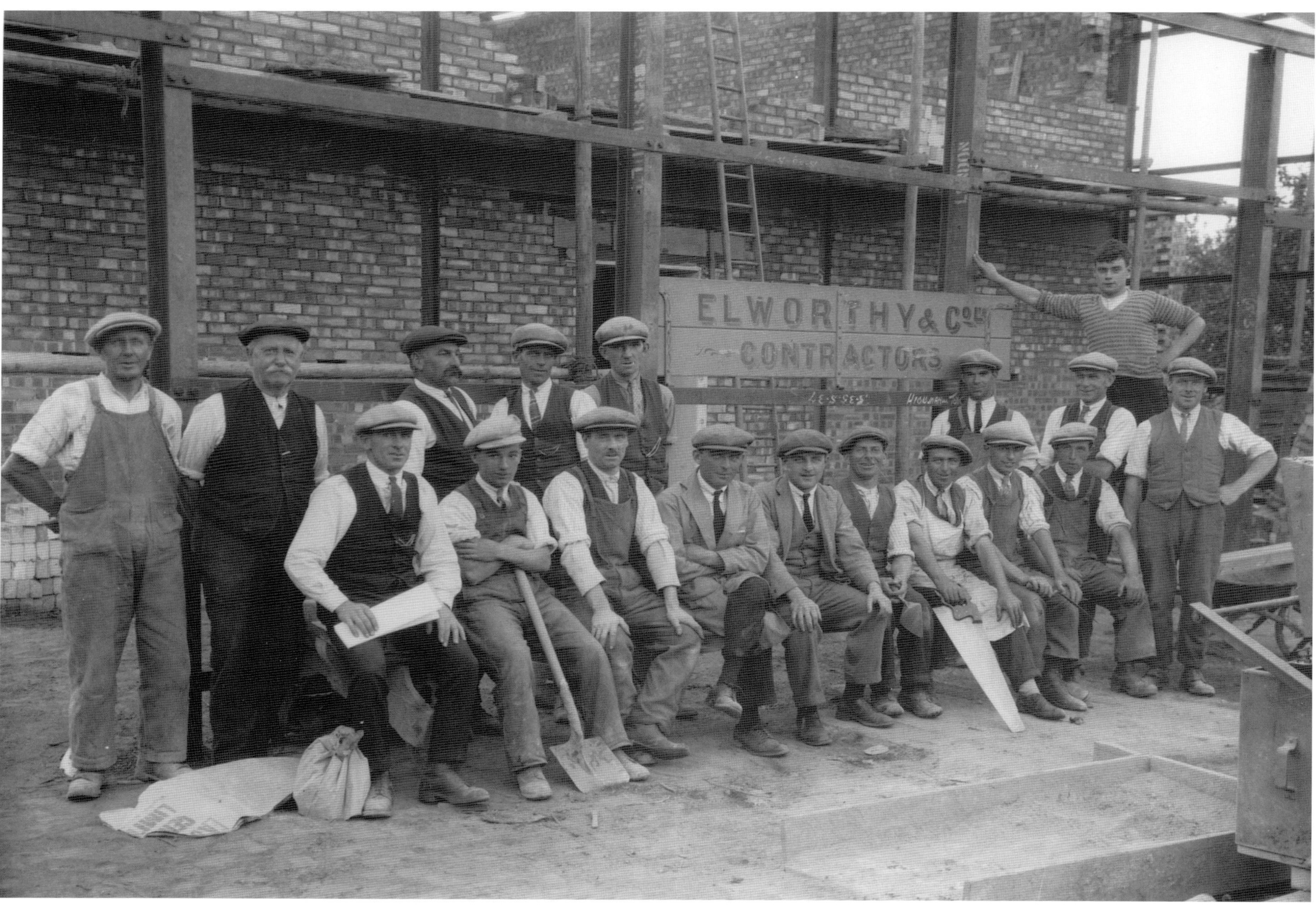

 Workers of Elworthy & Co., Builders, of Upwell, Norfolk, c1930.

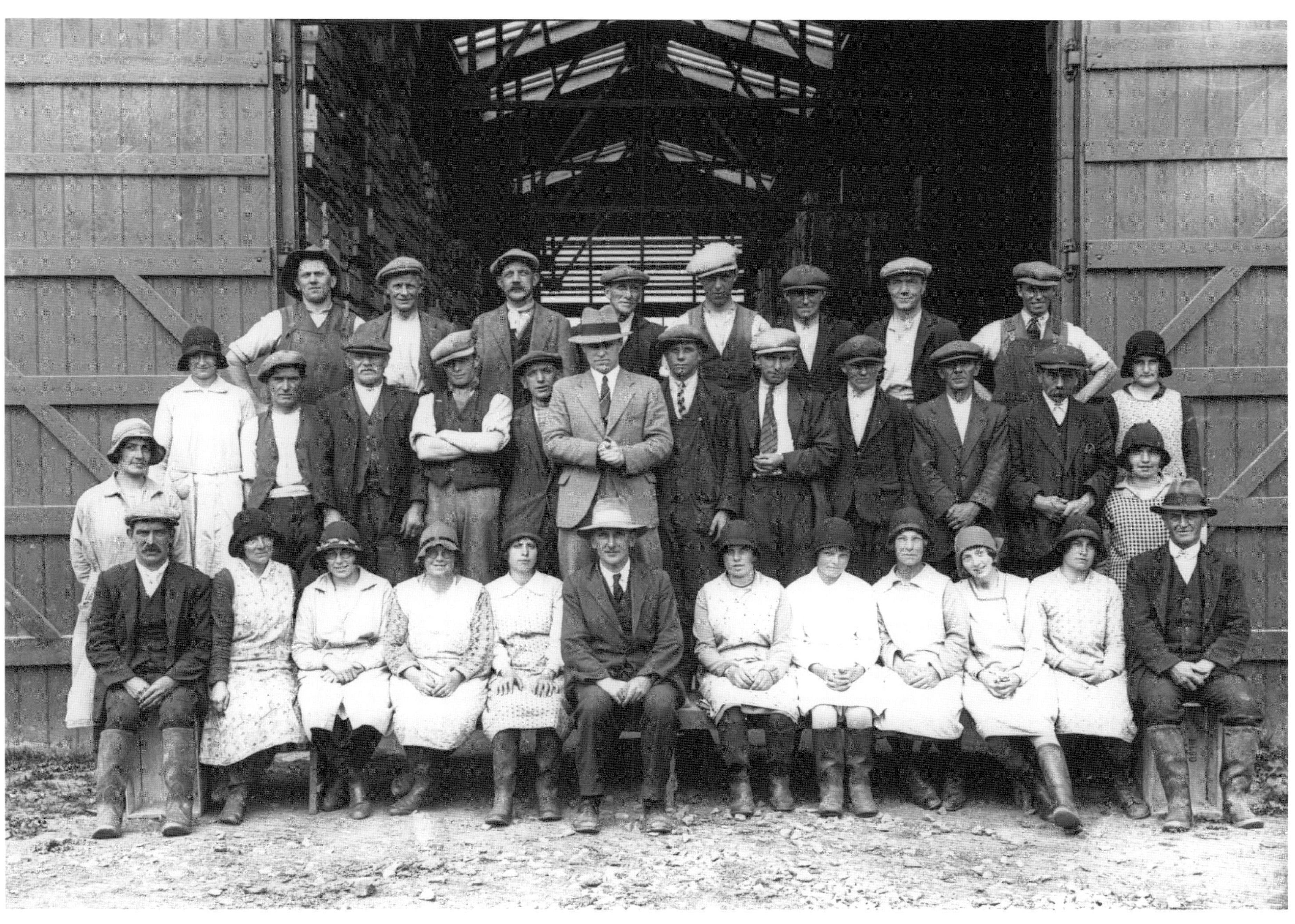

The workforce photographed in front of the sheds at Ayres Fruit Farm, Gosmoor Lane, Elm, c1930.

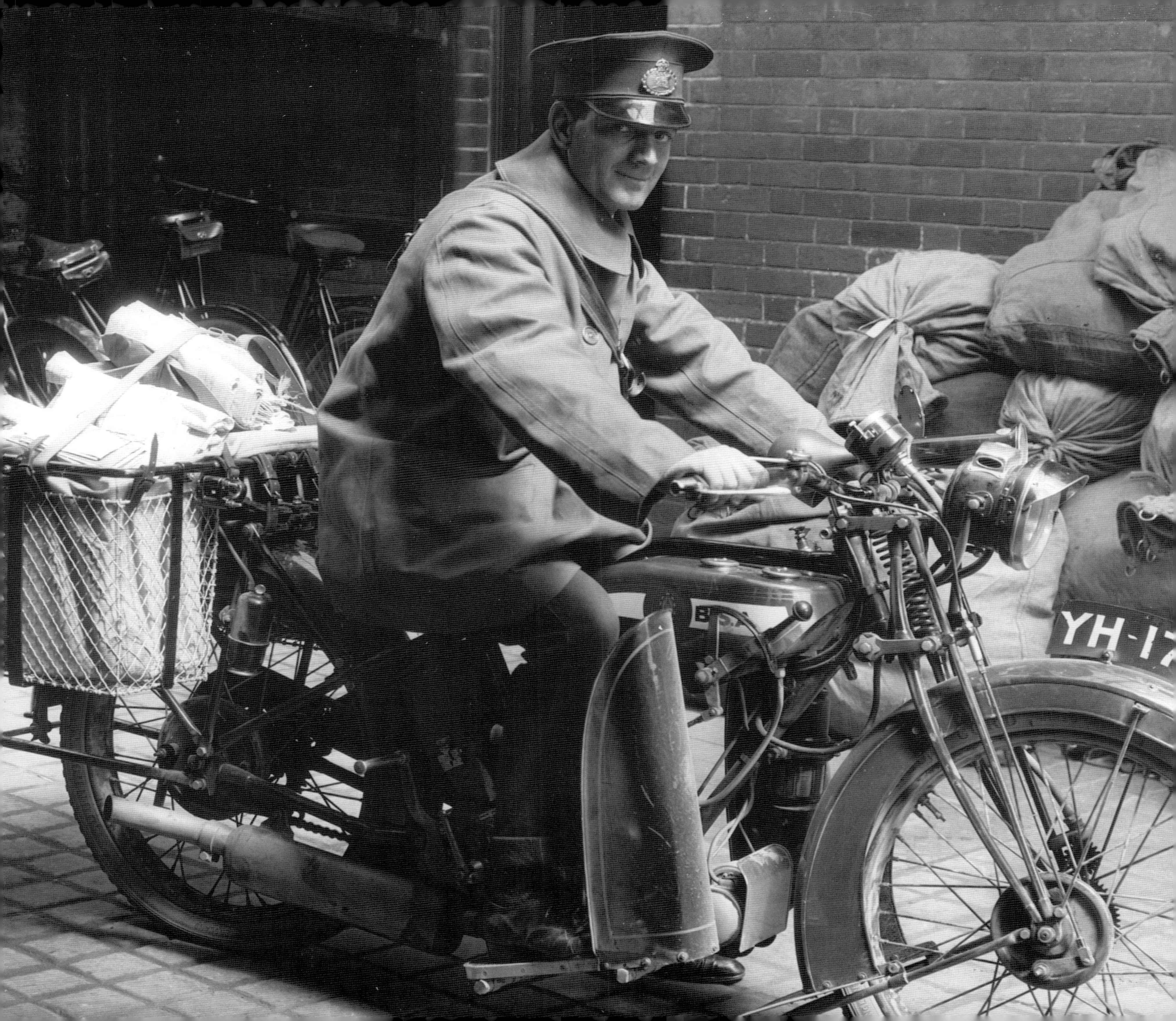
YH-17

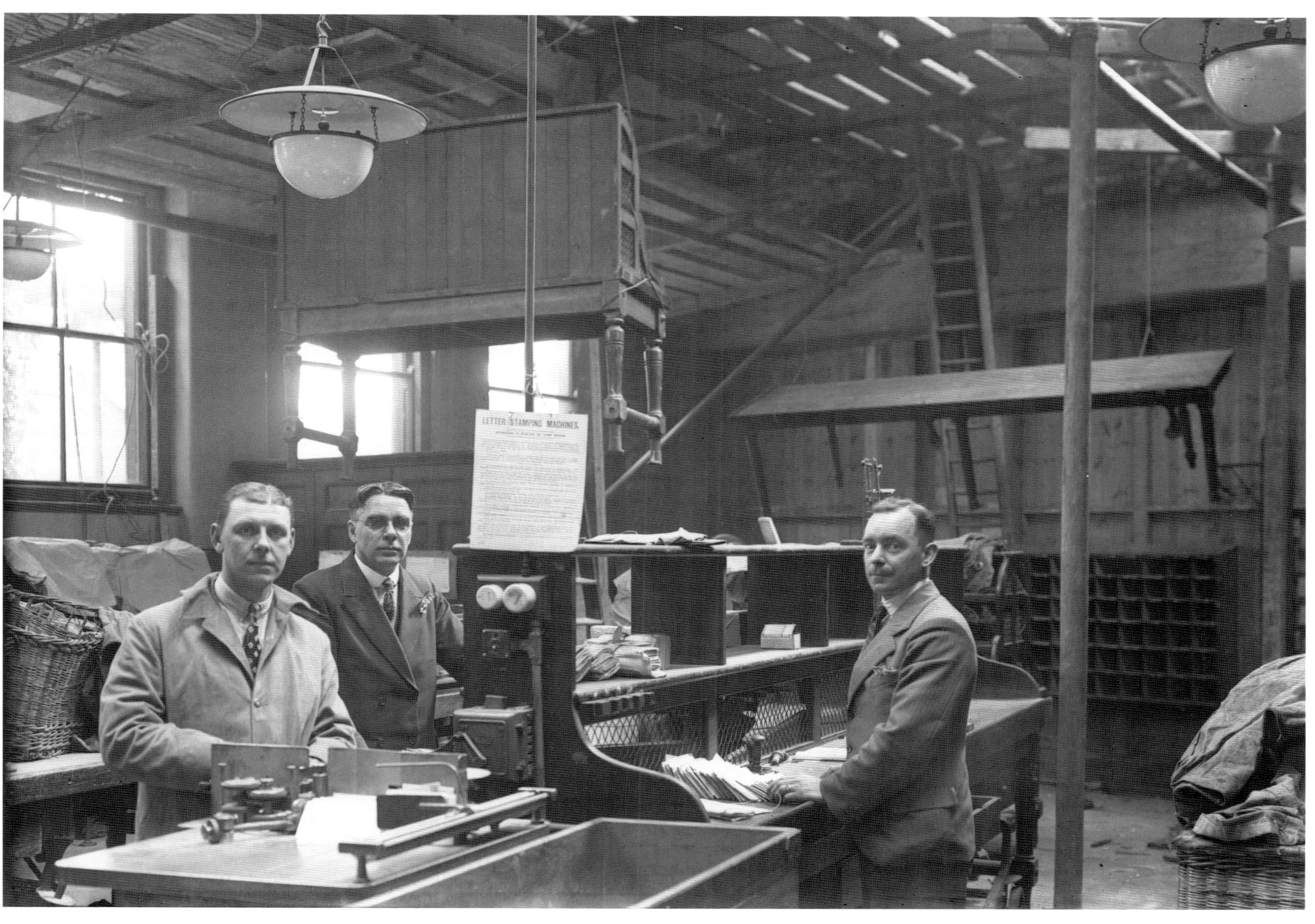

The newly opened sorting office, built beside the Main Post Office in Bridge Street, 1931. On the left is Harry Martin and in the middle is G Rutter, the Postmaster.

Opposite. Post Office motorcyclist c1935.

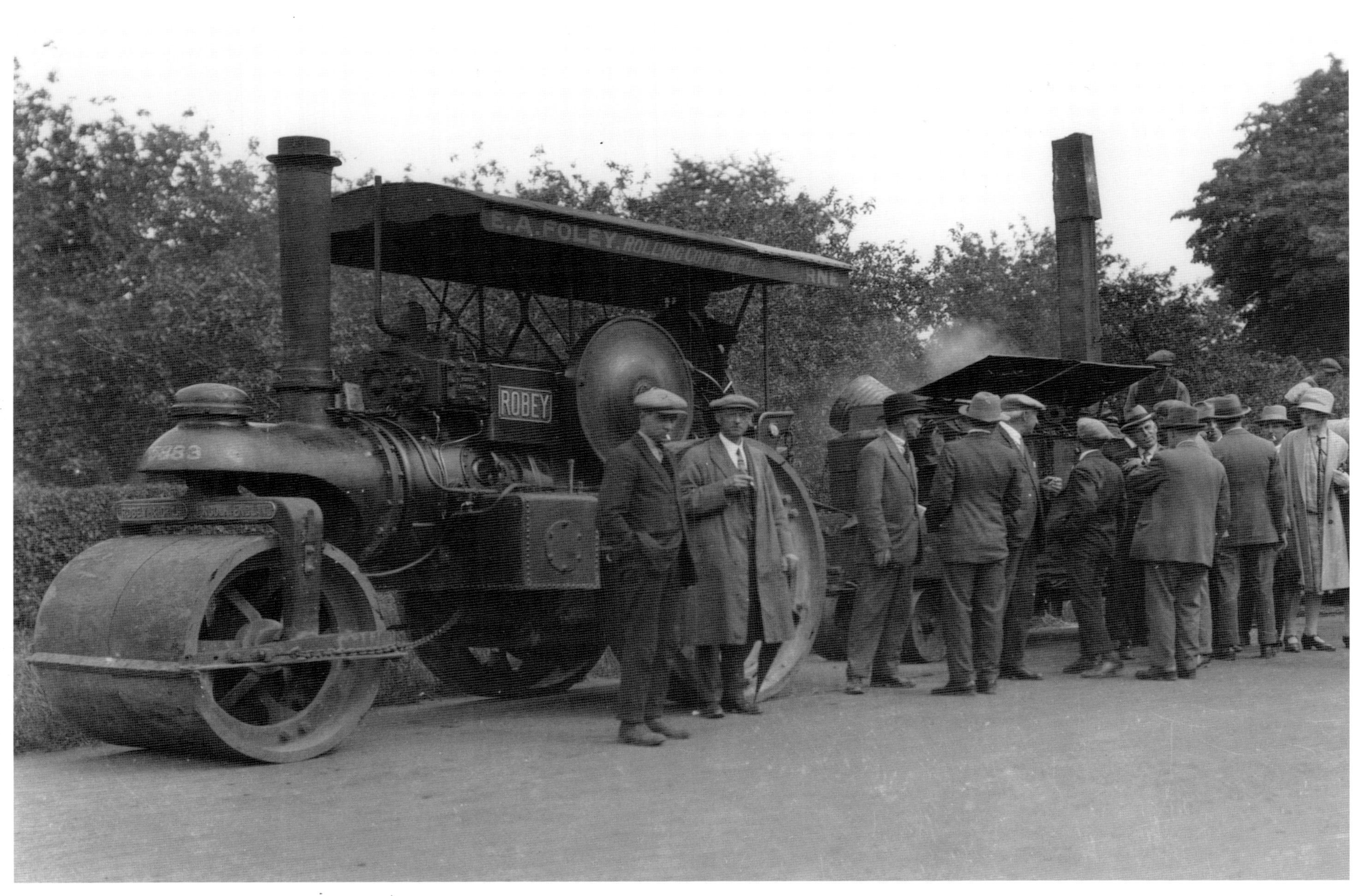

 A road roller of EA Foley Bourne, pulling a machine for laying tar and gravel, c1932.

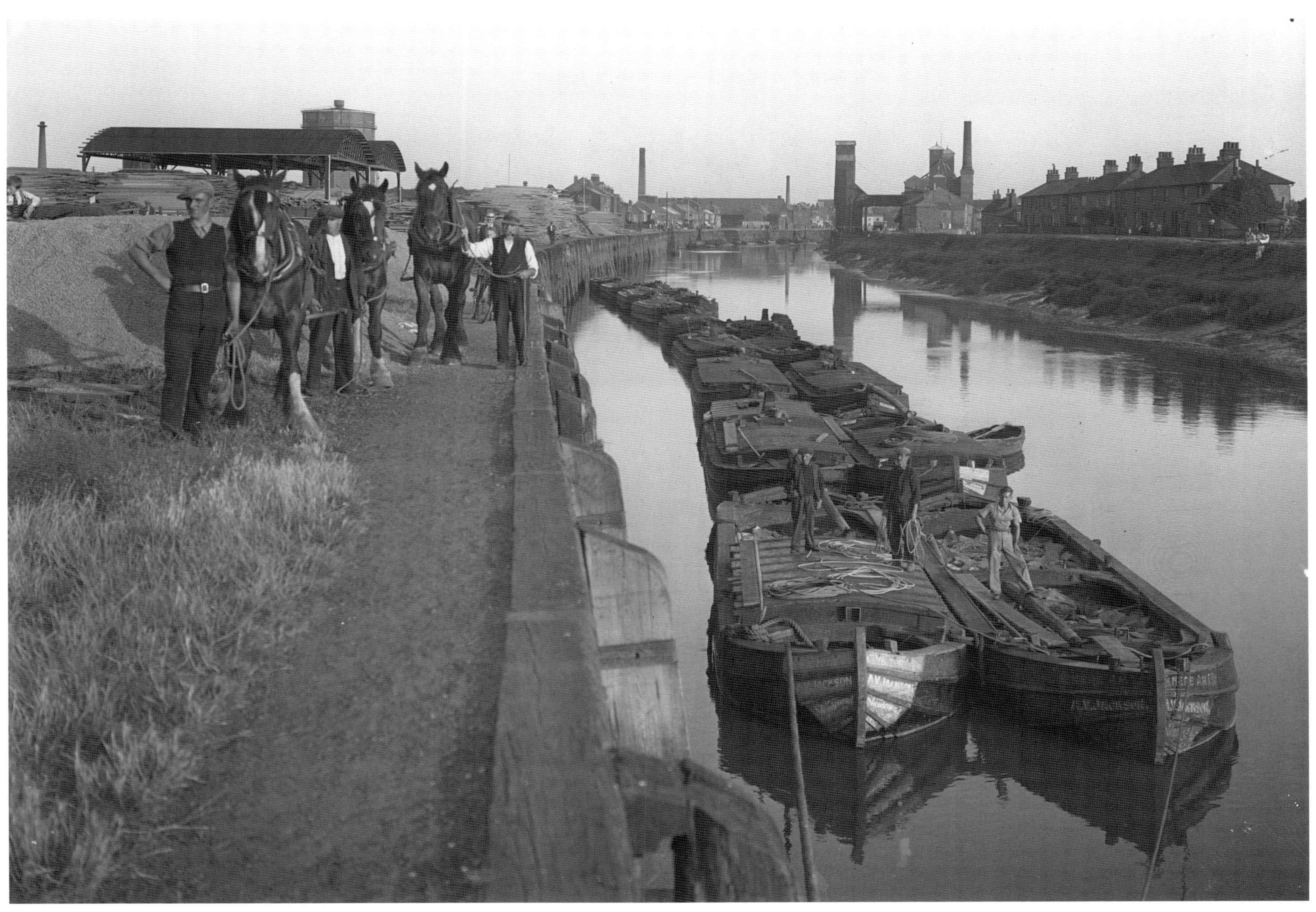

Horse-drawn barges being taken downstream, 1920s.

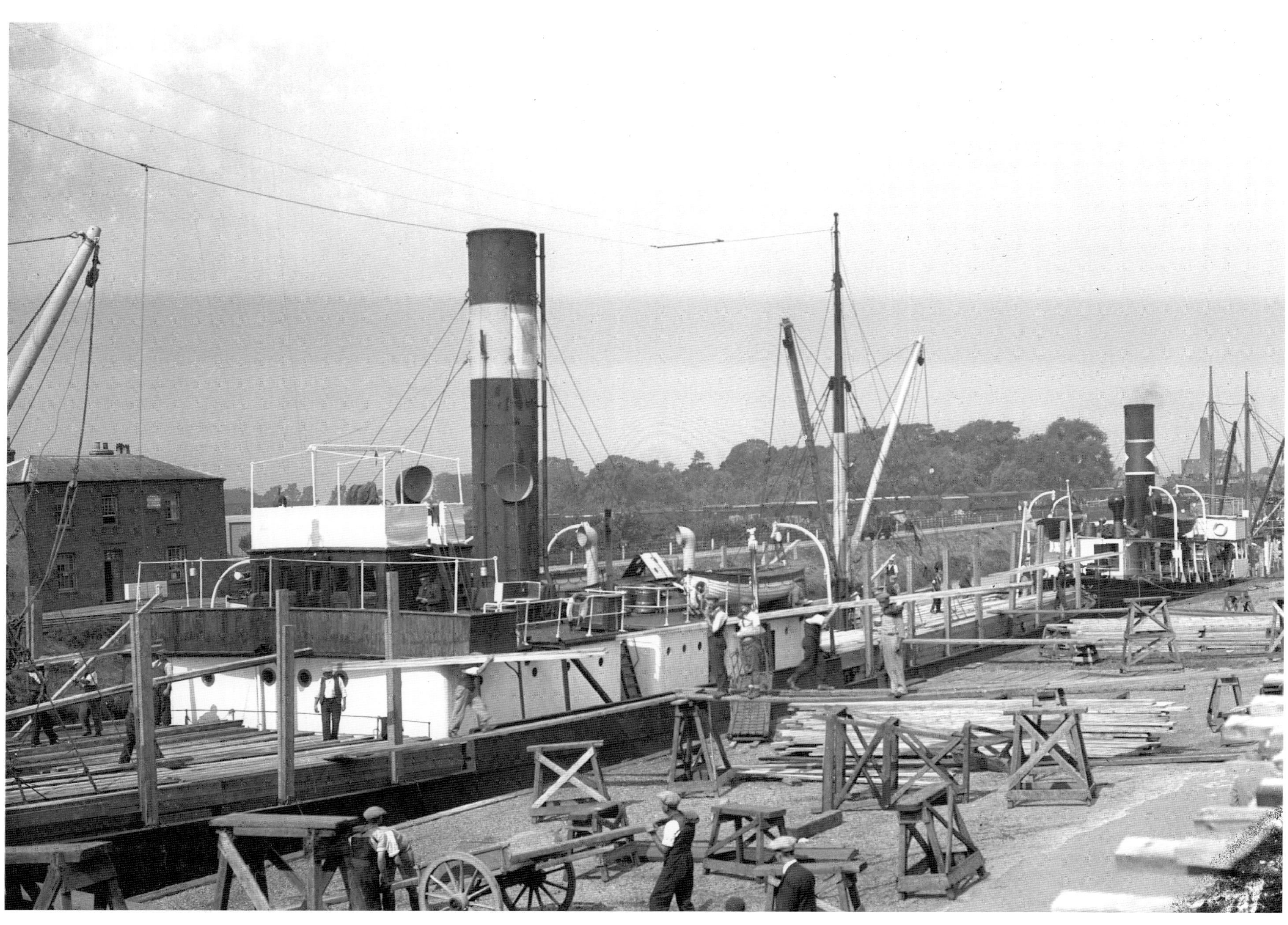

Unloading timber at Wisbech Port, 1932. Before the introduction of mechanisation, deal porters, as viewed in this photograph, would walk timber off the ships using trestles. Porters wore leather pads to protect their shoulders.

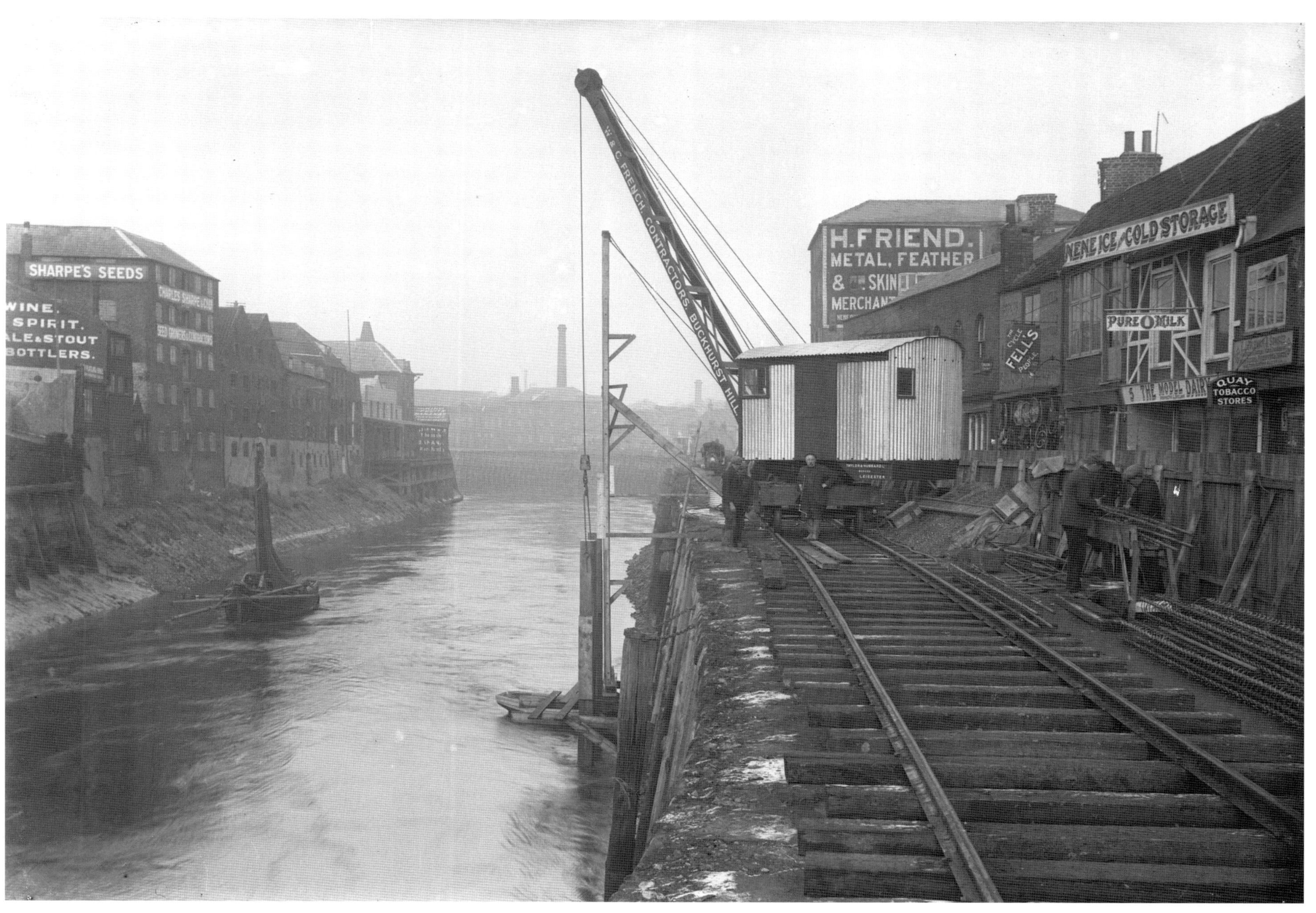

Piling works being undertaken by W & C French & Co. along Nene Quay, 1930. The work of strengthening the bank was a precursor to the building of the new Town Bridge in 1931.

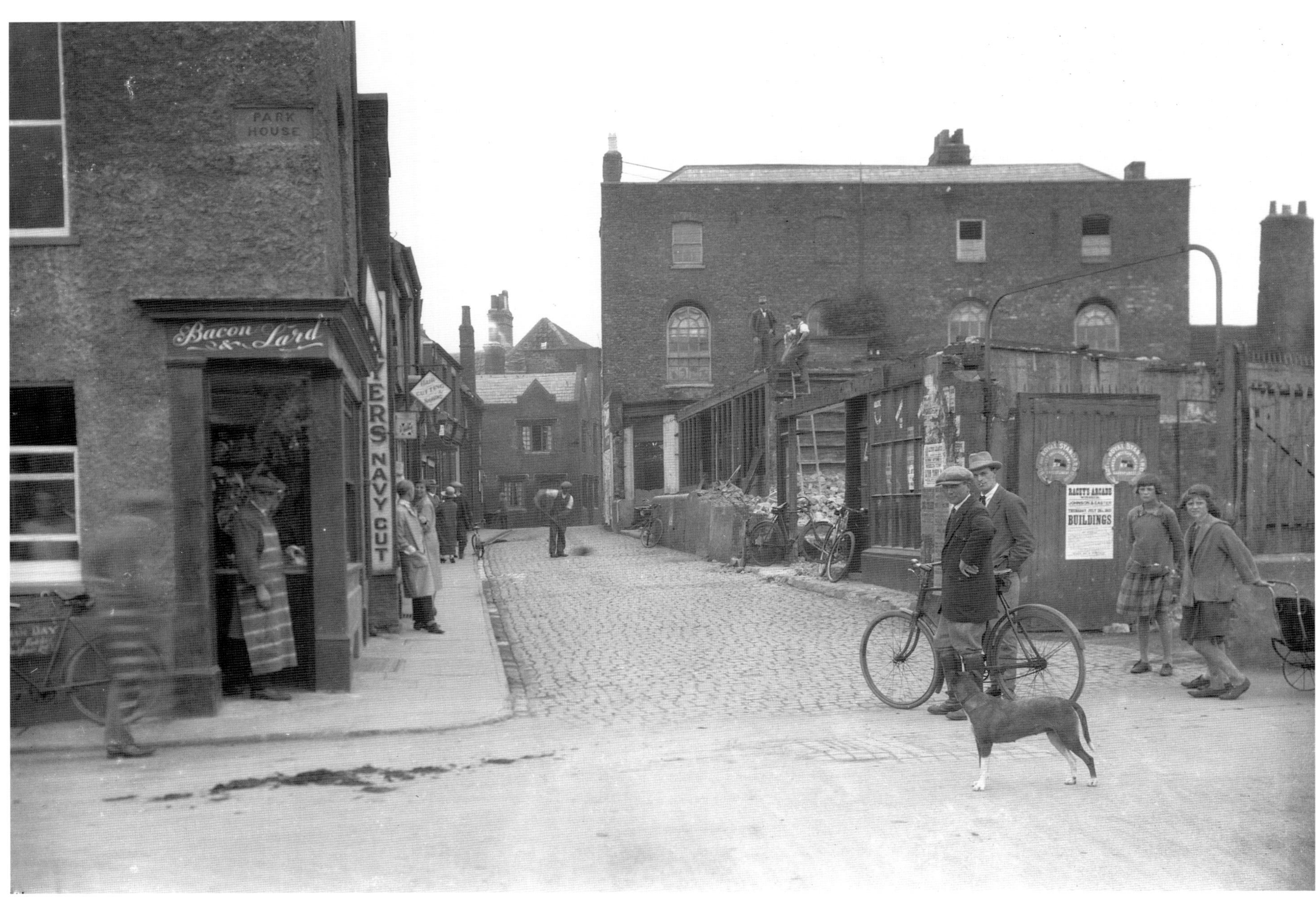

A view along Blackfriars Road, looking towards Racey's Arcade, which was in the process of being demolished to make way for the Empire Theatre, 1927. The Arcade, formerly known as Hill House, was once the home of Henry Leach, the first Mayor of Wisbech.

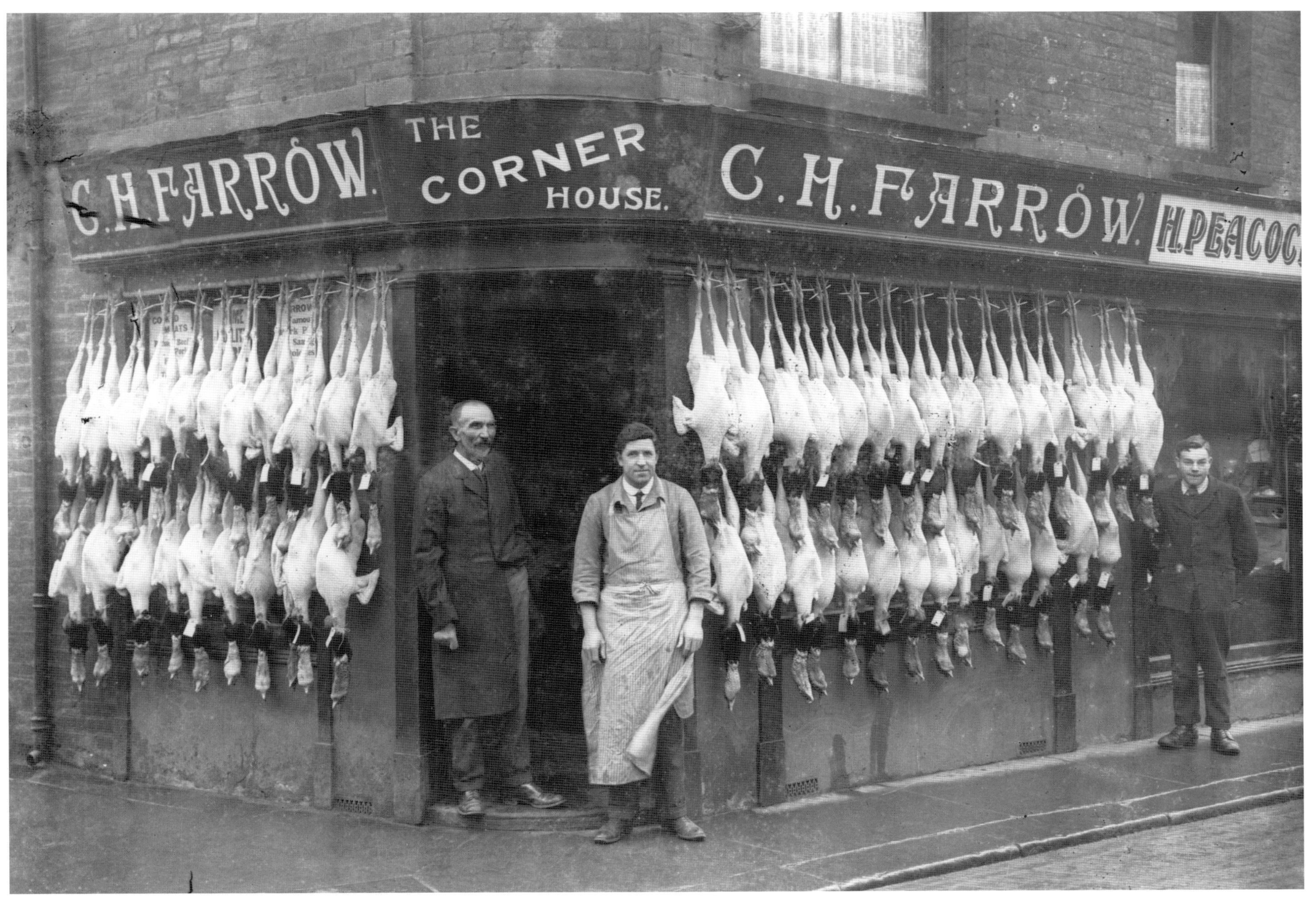

A magnificent display of turkeys at The Corner House shop of Clifford Hipkin Farrow, poulterer, 1 Union Street, late 1920s.

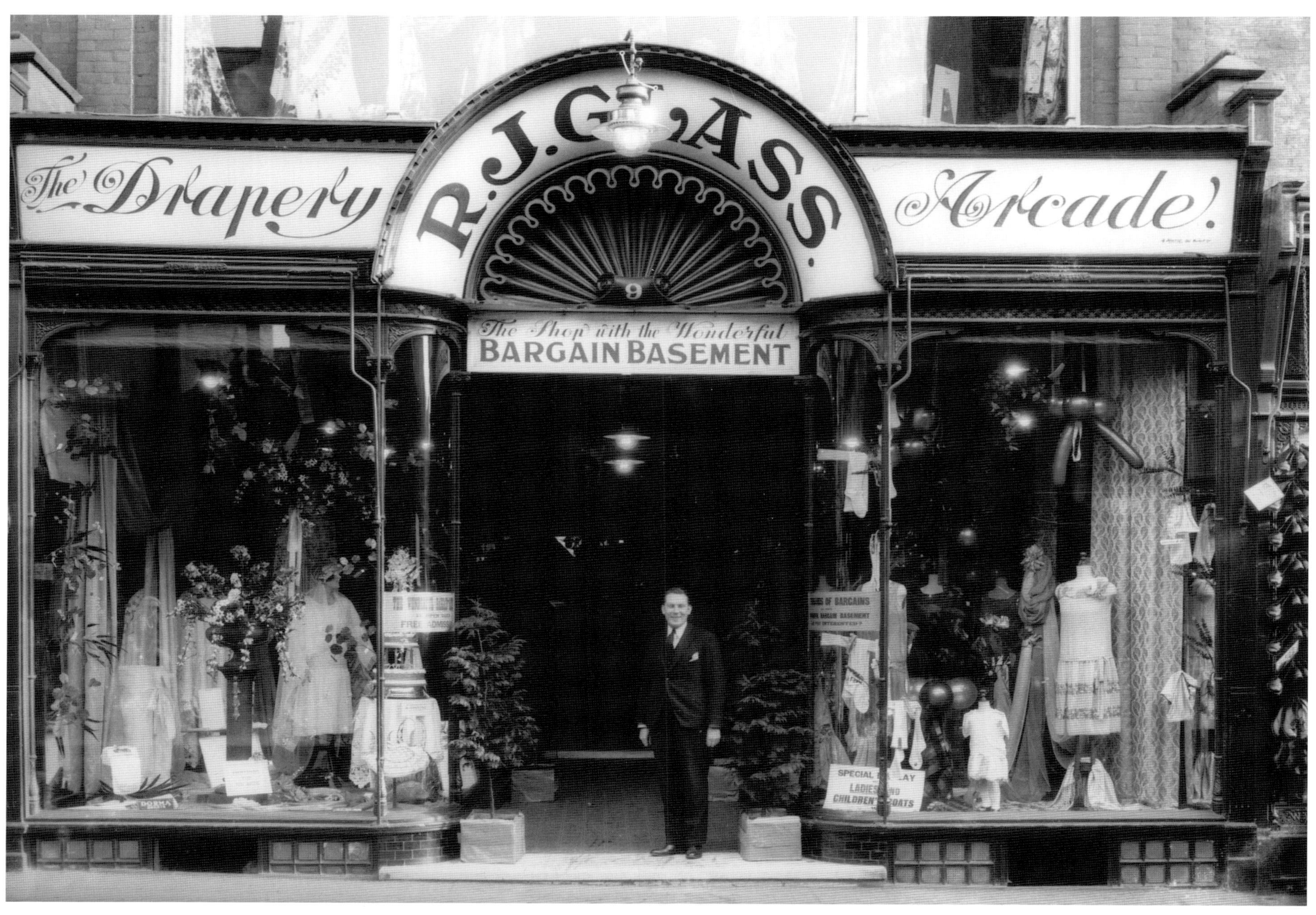

The drapery arcade of RJ Glass, 9 High Street, 'the shop with the wonderful bargain basement', 1920s. The business later expanded to incorporate number 10, before moving to the Market Place, with 9 and 10 being kept on by Glass as a home furnishings shop.

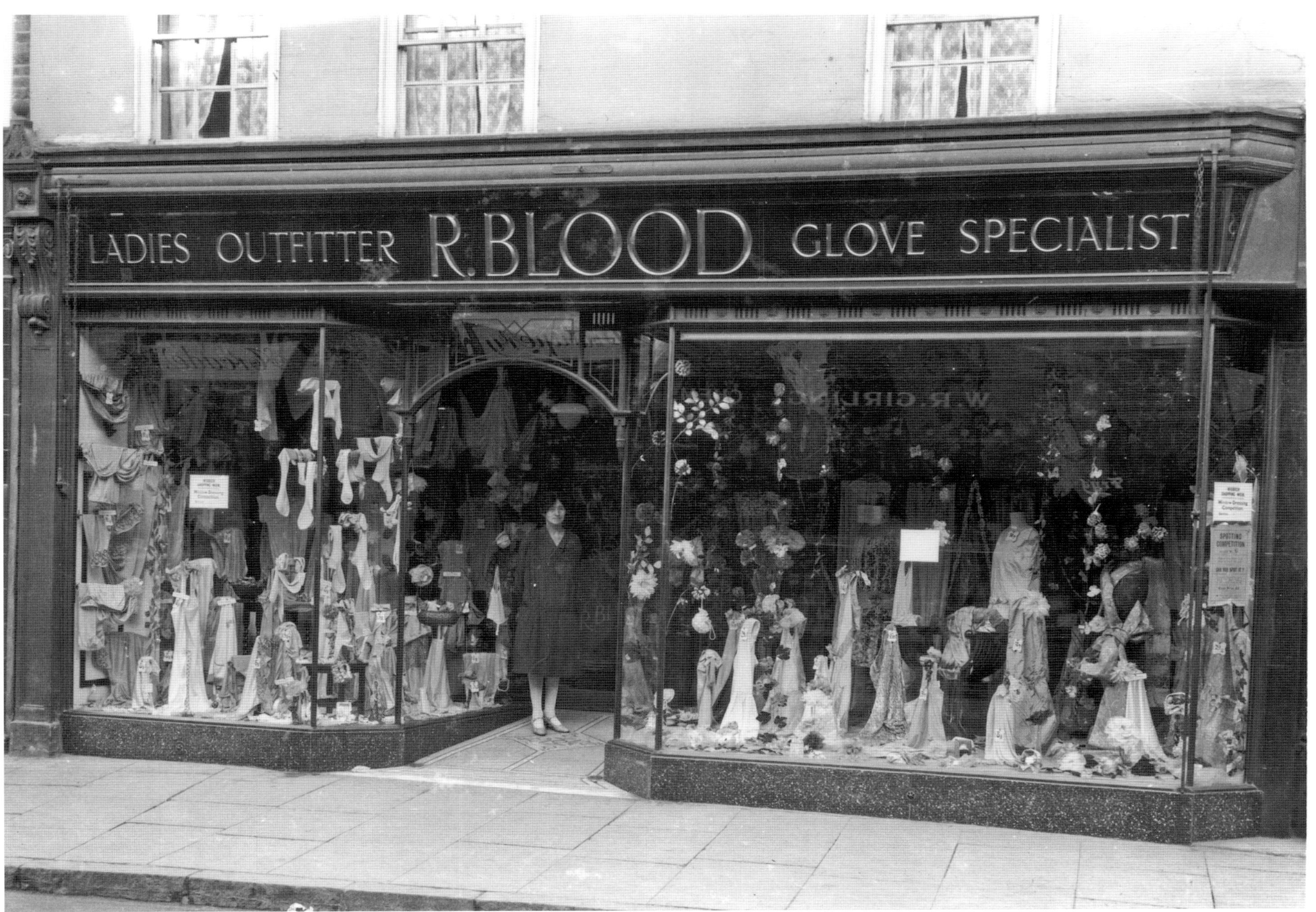

The drapers shop of Robert Blood & Sons, 28 High Street, 1920s.

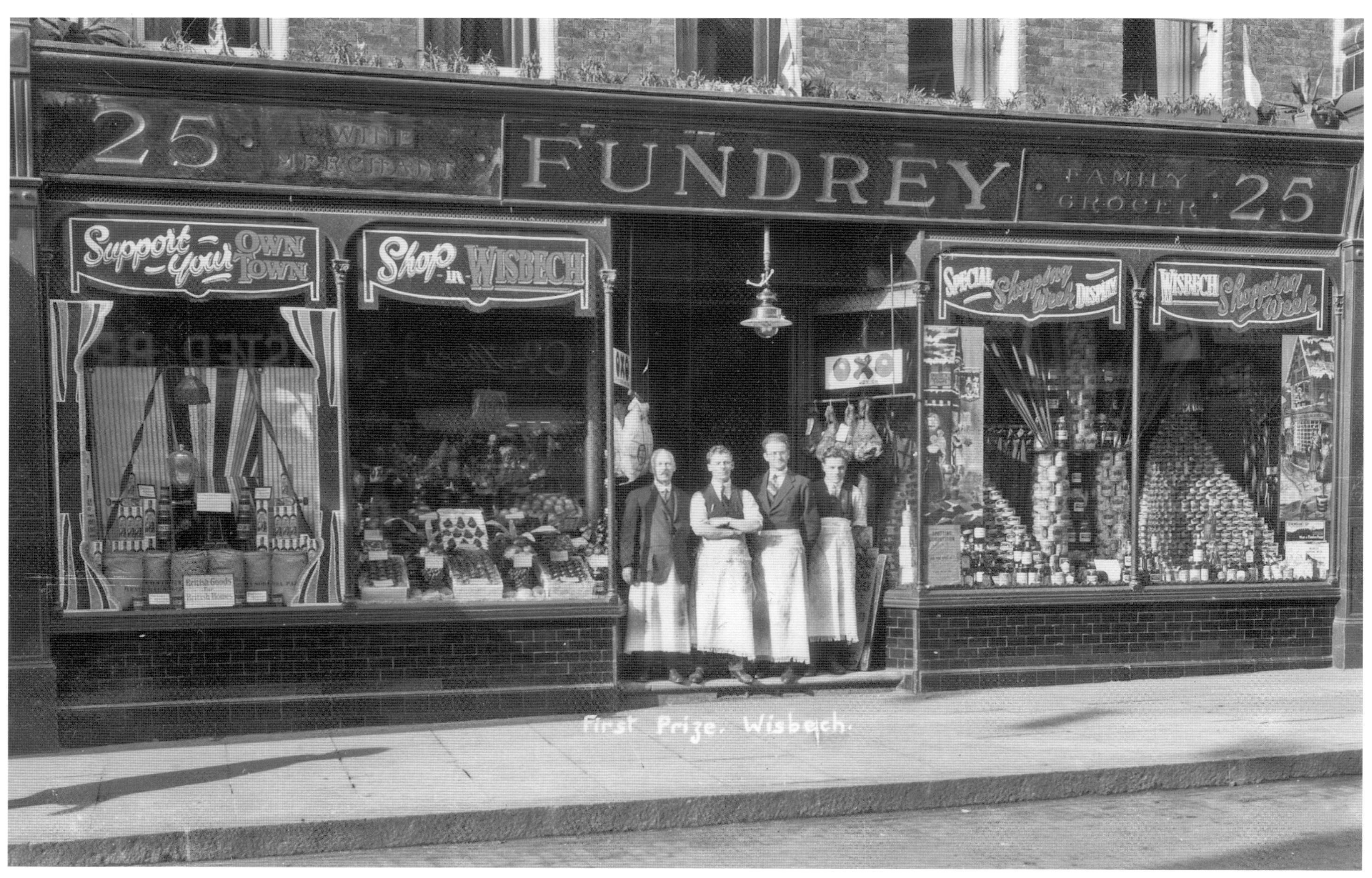

Walter Fundrey's finely set-out grocery shop at 25 High Street, 1930s. The caption suggests that the display won first prize during Wisbech Shopping Week.

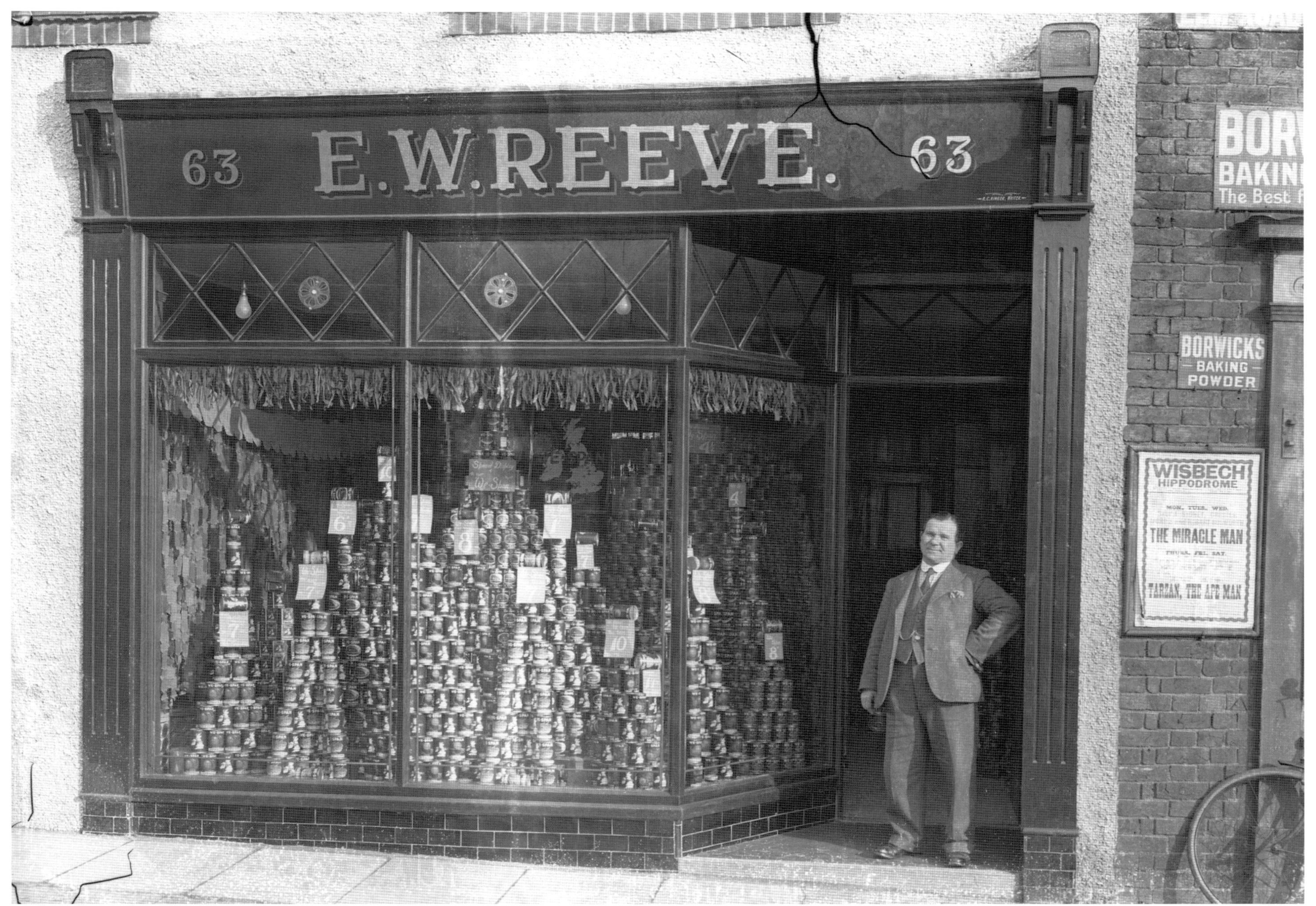

Edward W Reeve outside his shop in Norfolk Street with a display of We Span canned food, 1932. As well as a bakery at numbers 65 and 66, Reeve also had a antique shop at number 63.

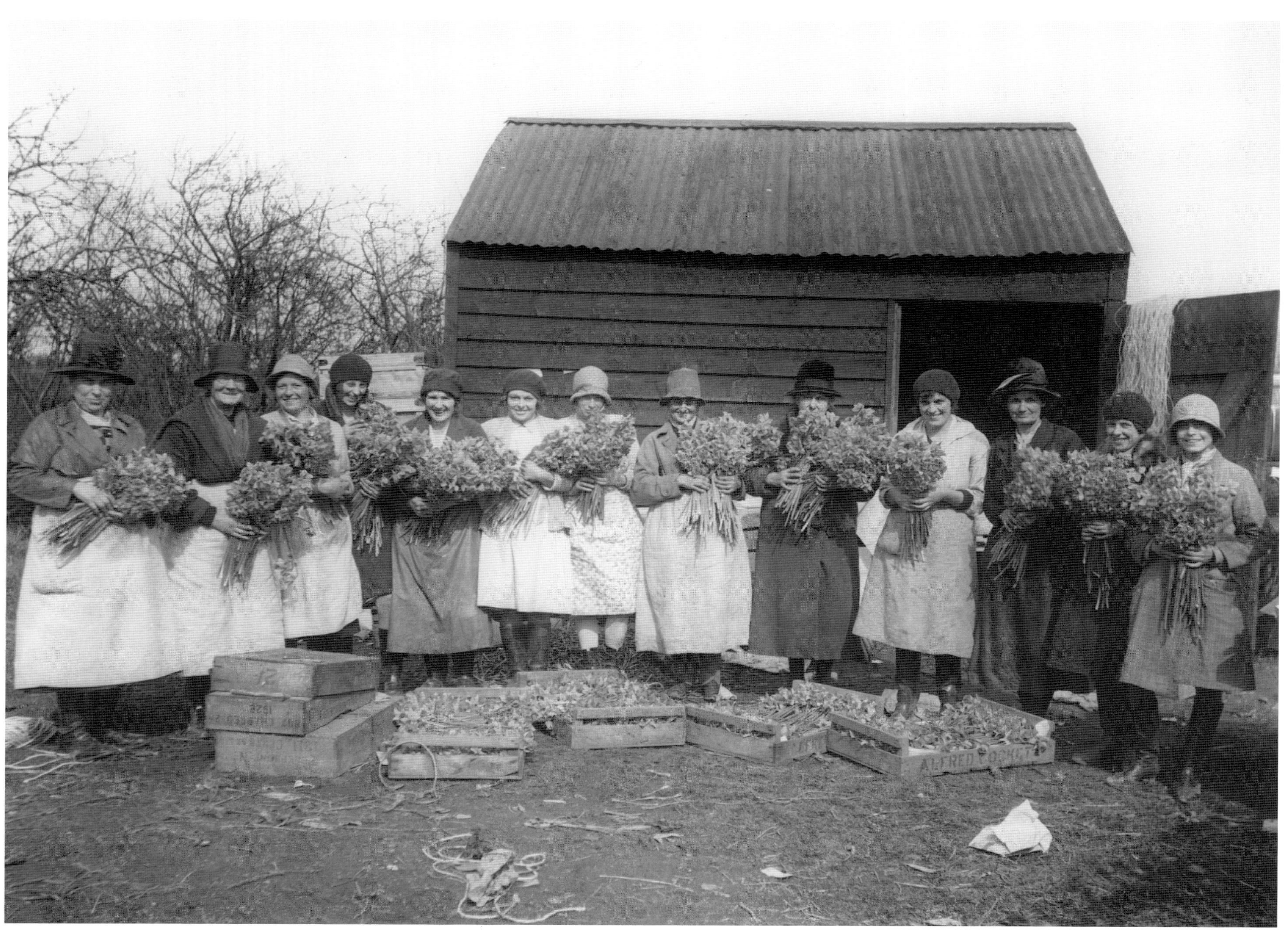

Daffodil pickers employed by Mr Alfred Cockett, with bunches of daffodils that would be sent to markets around the country, 1920s.

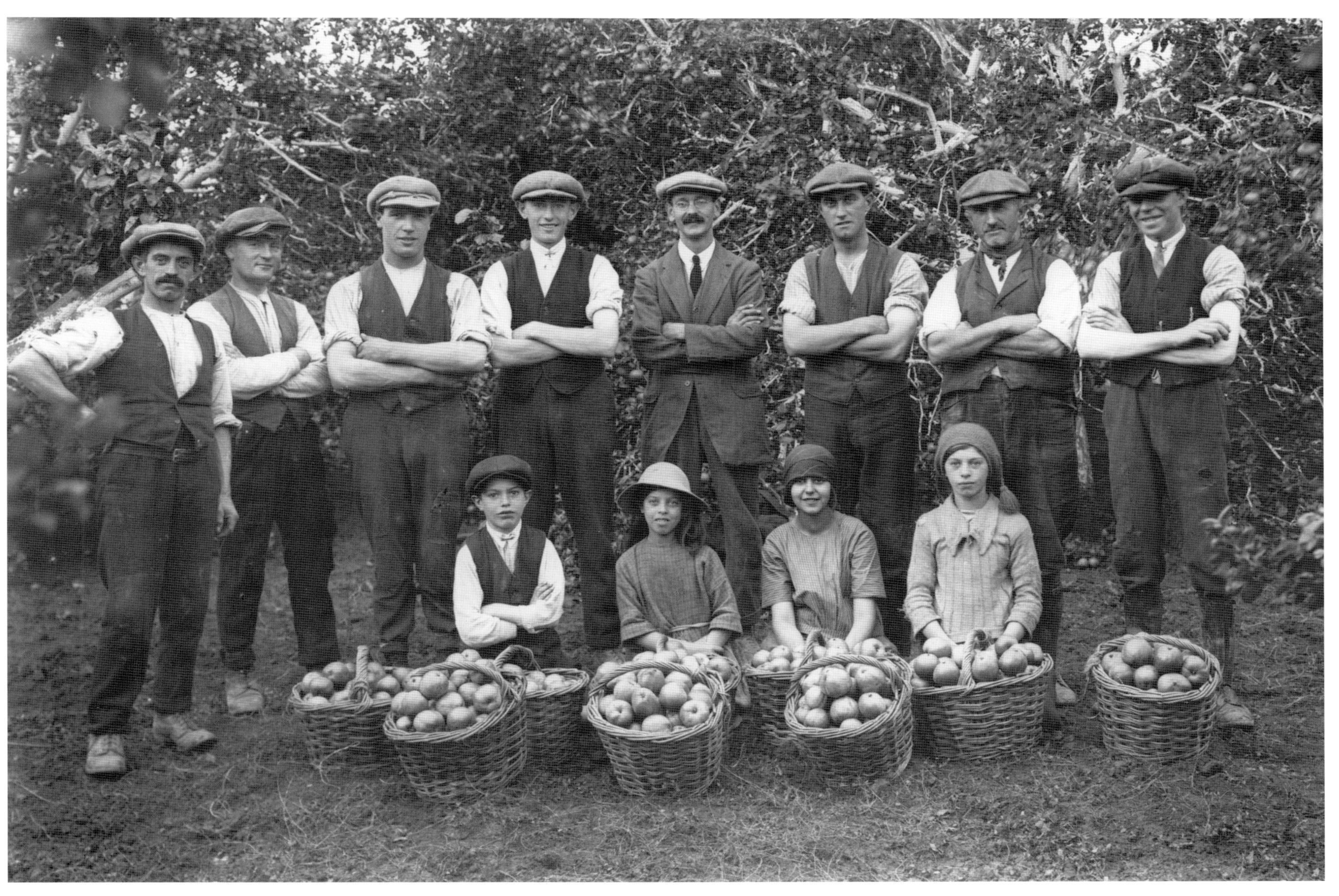

A group of apple pickers proudly displaying the fruits of their labour in the orchards of Alfred Whiting of Leverington, 1930s.

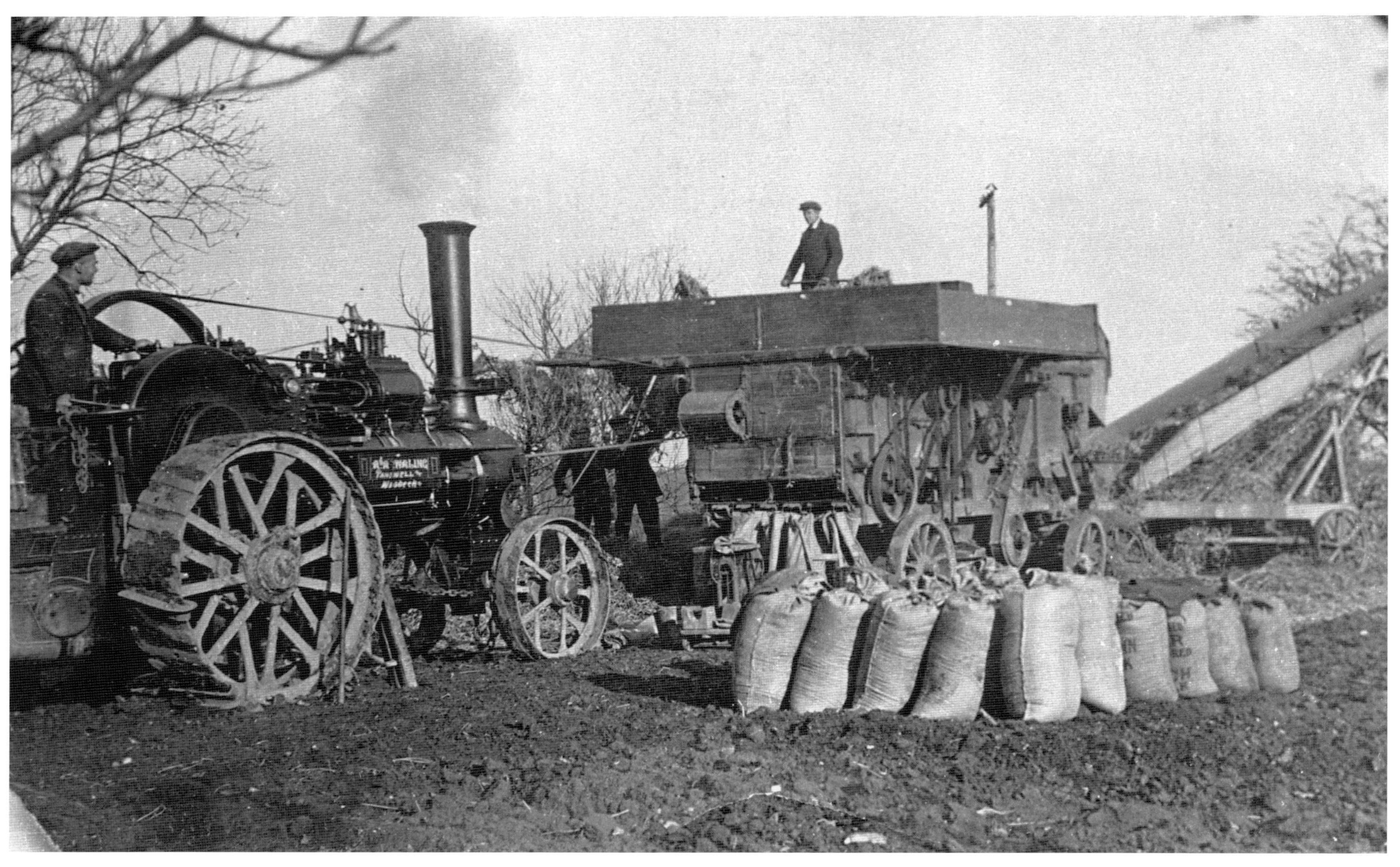

Threshing on Bernard West's farm at Christchurch, c1930. Threshing machines powered by steam traction engines had been replaced by combine harvesters by the mid 20th century.

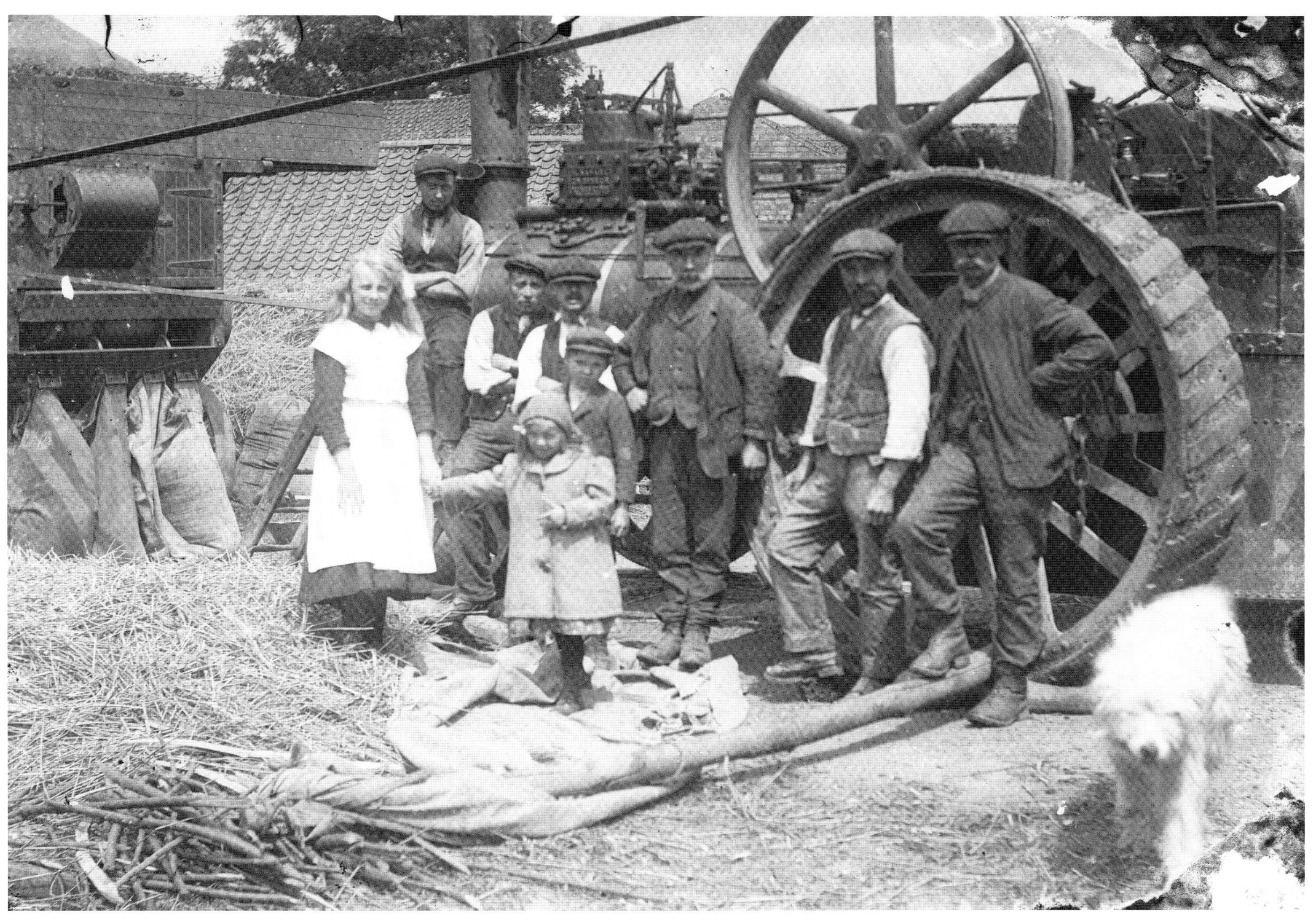

A pause in the work of threshing corn, 1920s. The use of threshing machines, particularly powered by a steam traction engine, revolutionized the process of separating grain which had previously been done by men using flails.

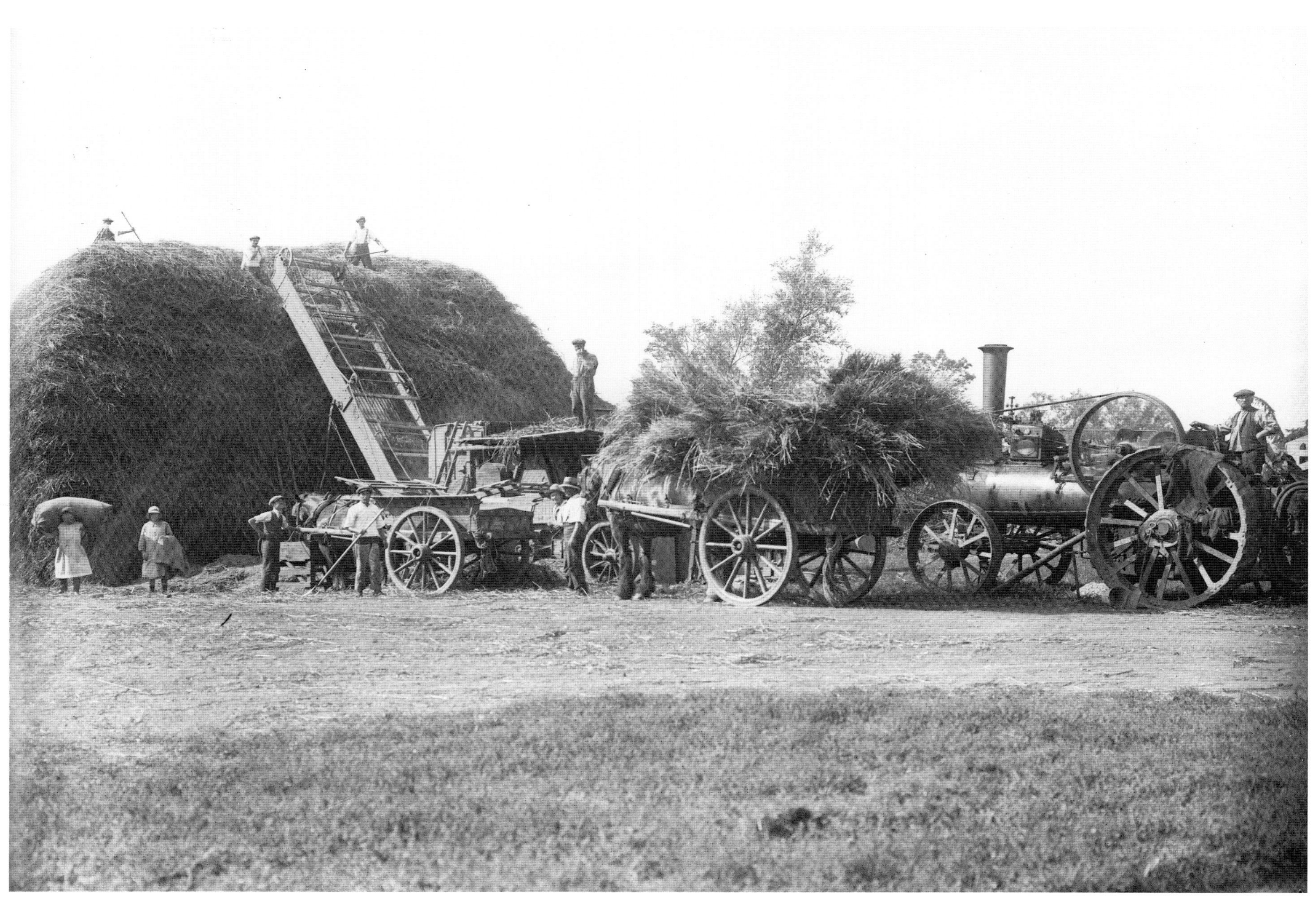

Building a haystack, 1930s. This technique of storing hay has been replaced by the use of square and circular bales, some of which weigh up to a ton.

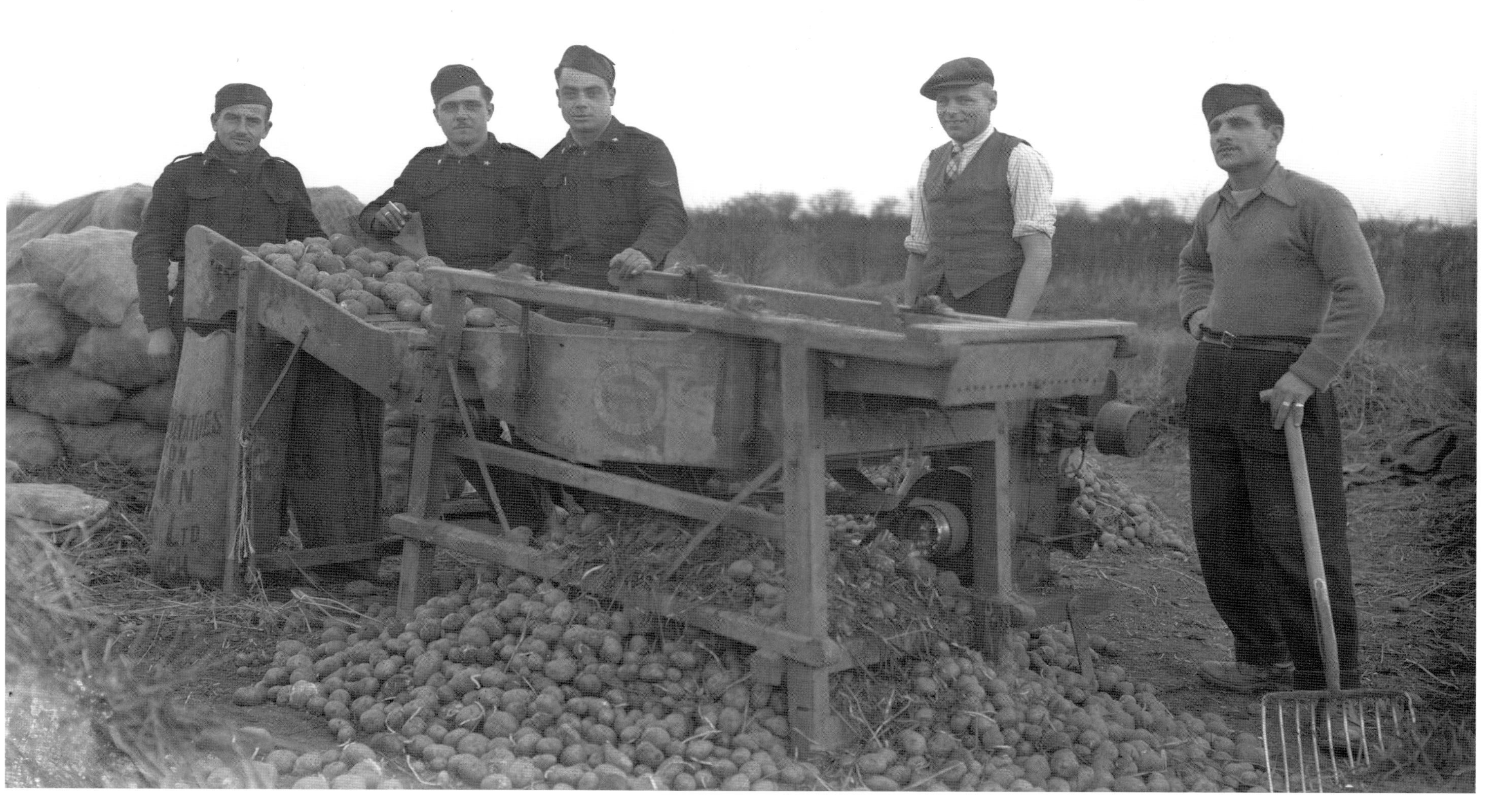

Italian POWs riddling potatoes on Dawson's Farm, Emneth, 1944. As the war progressed, POWs were increasingly used to work on the land around the district.

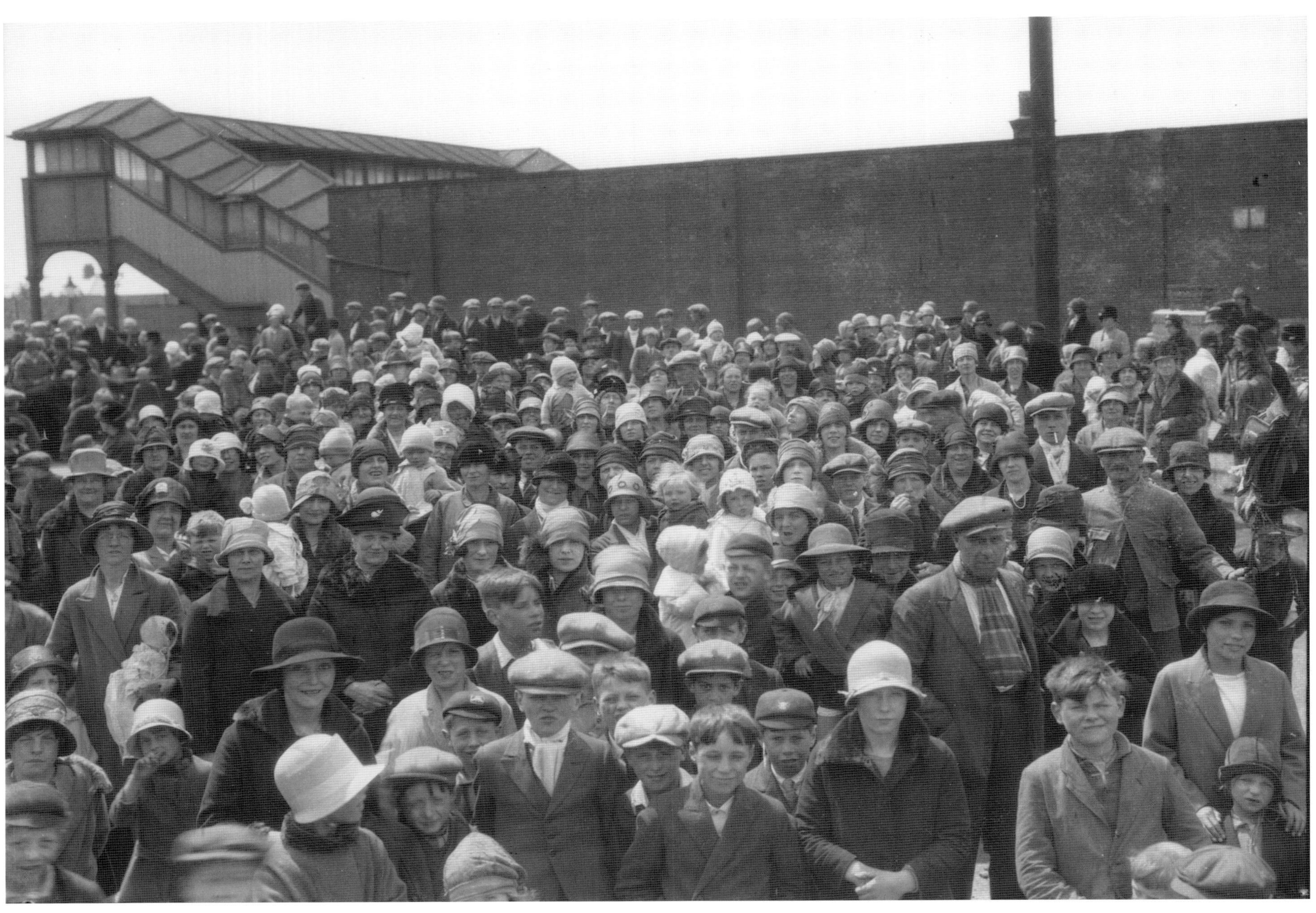

 Fruit pickers from London, newly arrived at Wisbech East Station, 1932.

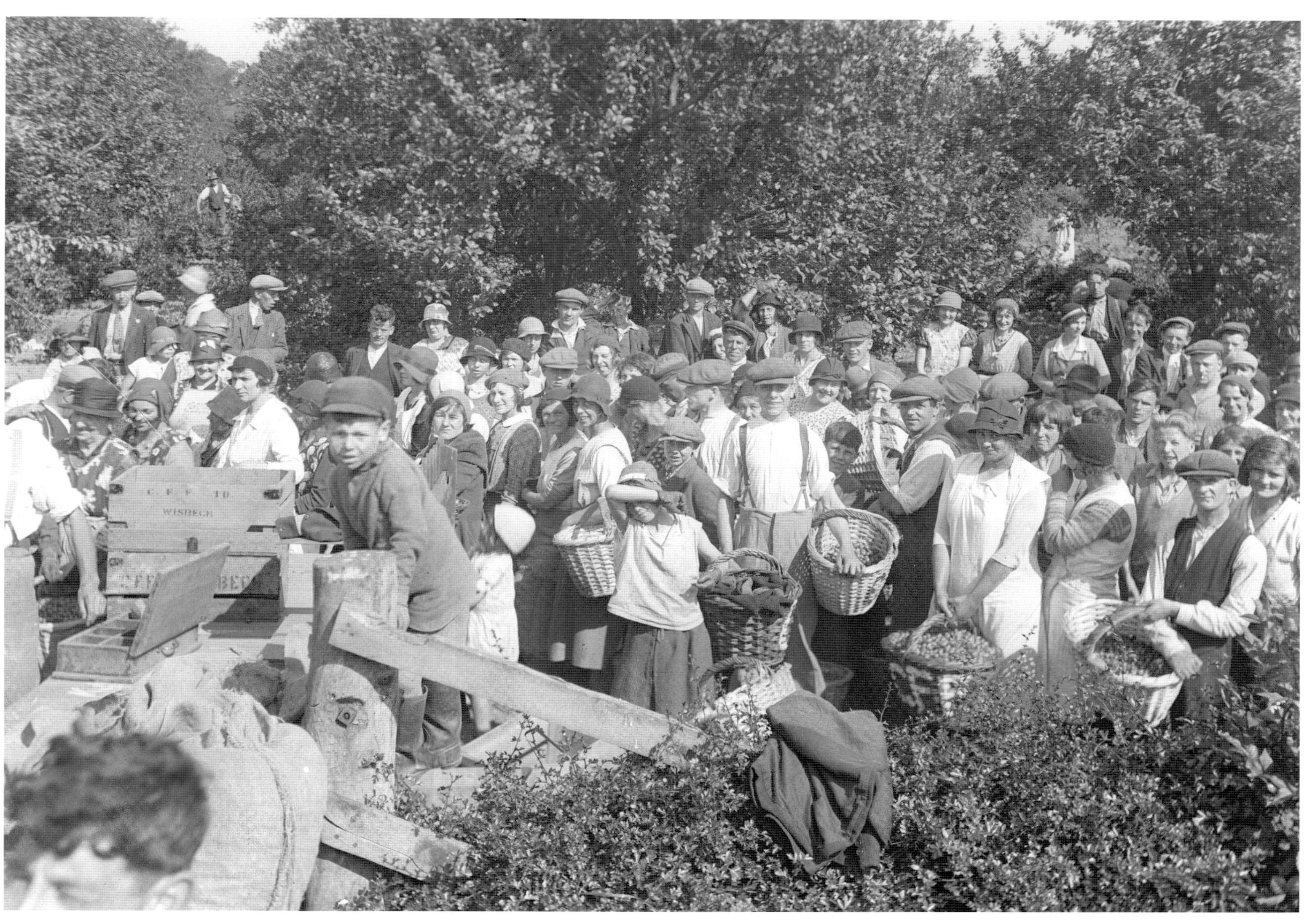

In the 1940s, when these gooseberry pickers were photographed, the gooseberry was already falling out of favour with consumers and jam makers, despite its high pectin content. Gooseberry picking was a family business, with all ages participating as shown by this group at Cockett's Fruit Farm in 1934.

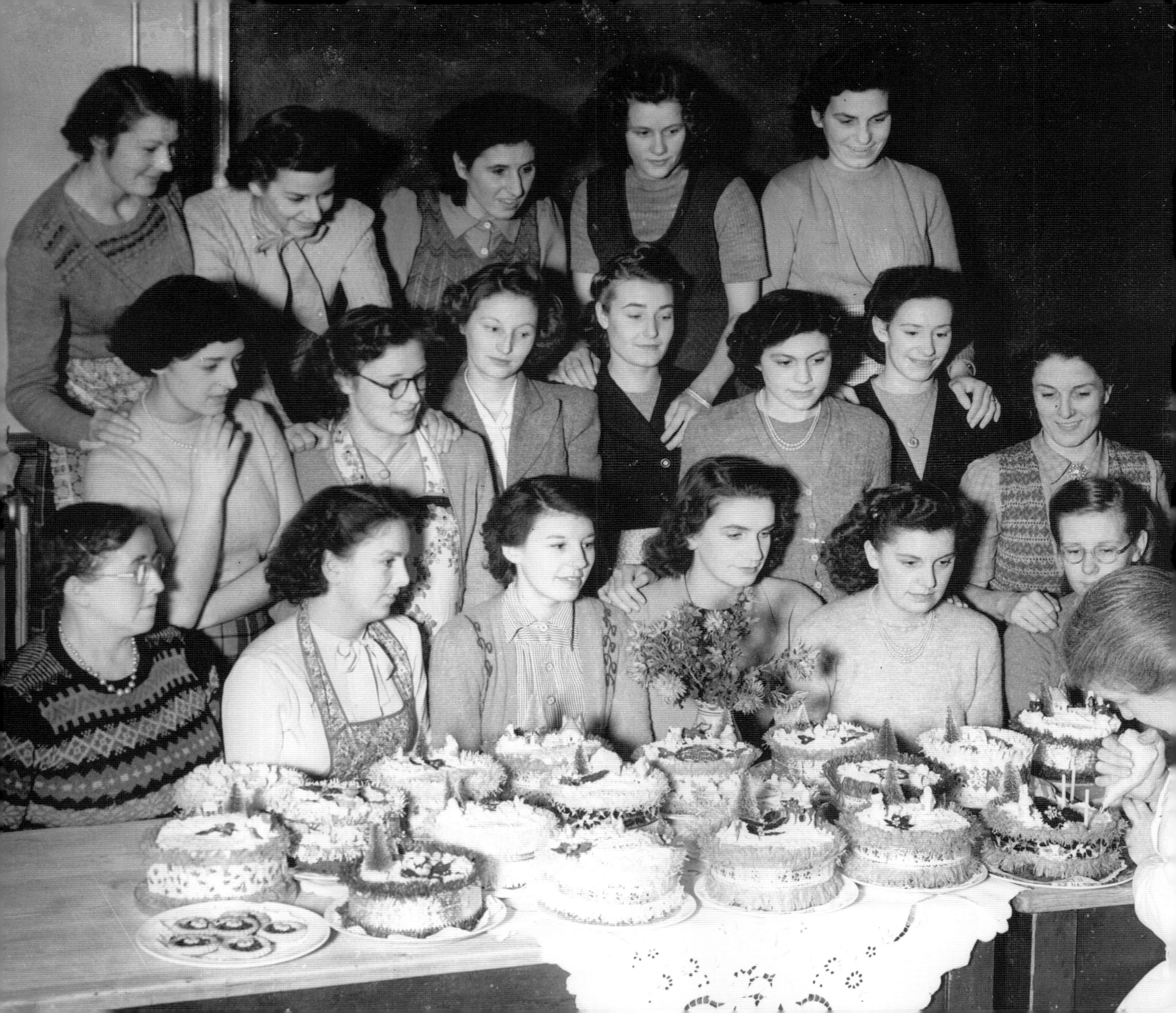

Leisure

Cake decoration display, 1940s.

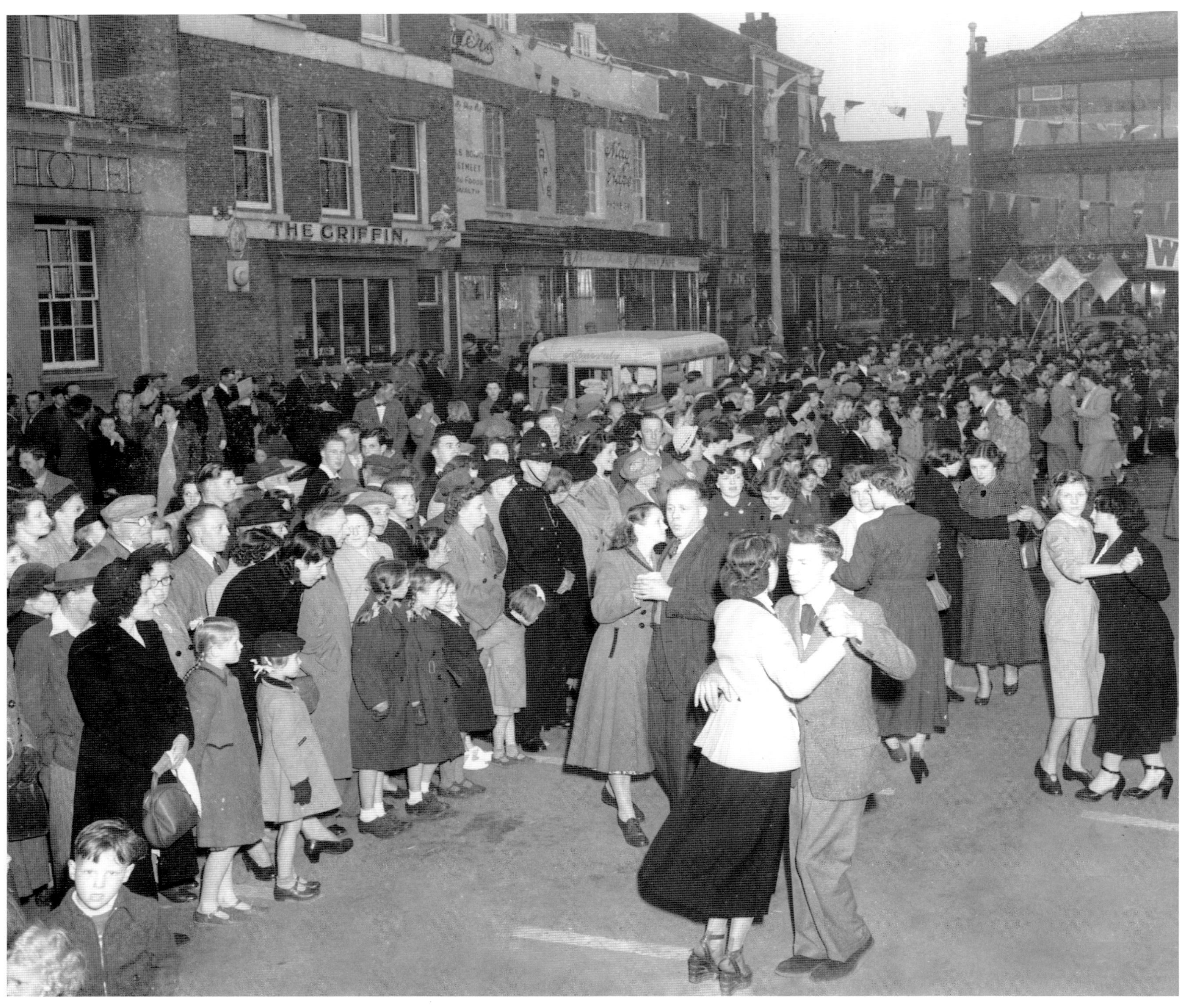

 An open air evening dance on the Market Place as part of Wisbech Shopping Week, early 1950s.

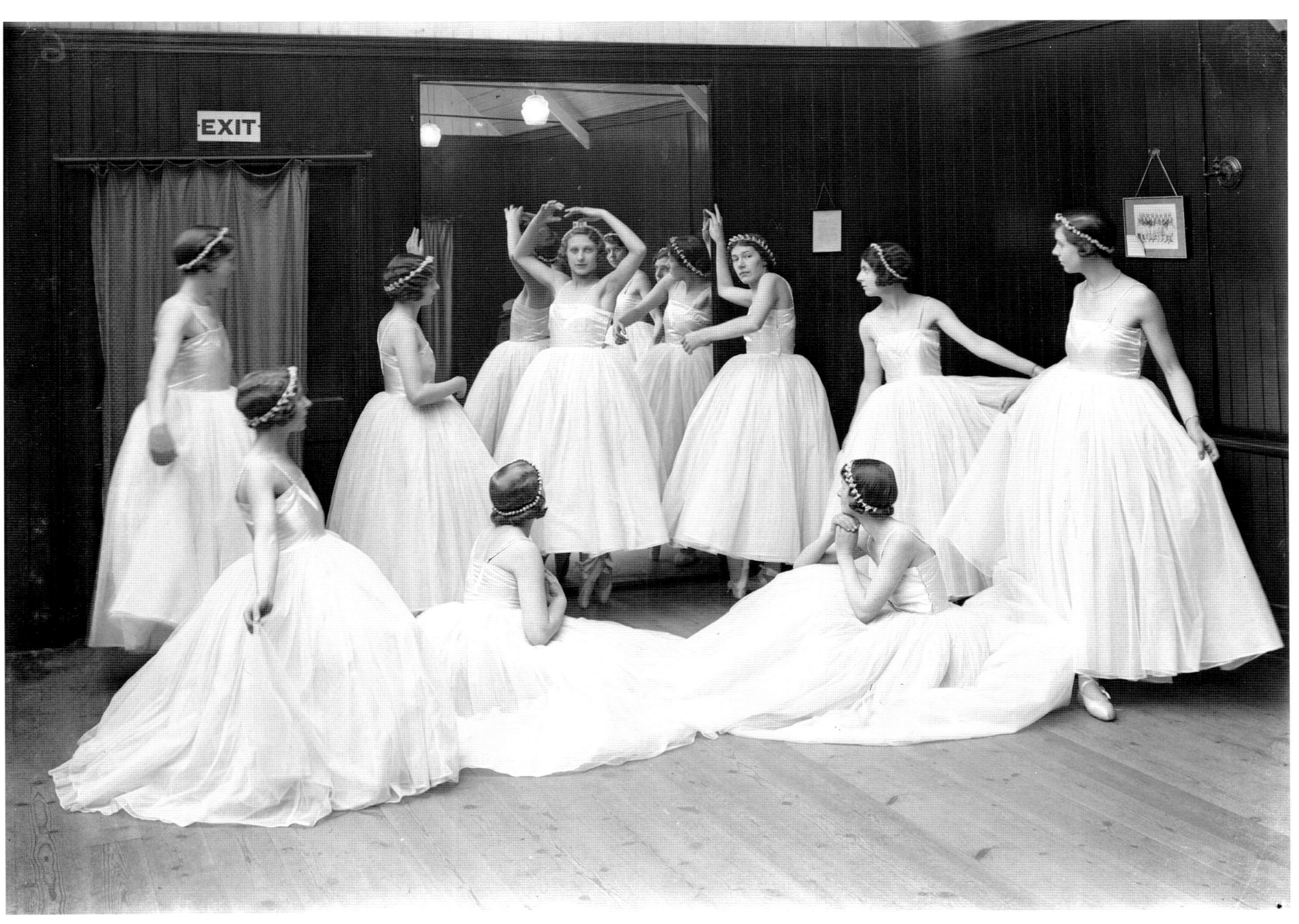

Ballet dancers rehearsing for the Wisbech Amateur Operatic & Dramatic Society's production of *The Quaker Girl* at the Empire theatre, 1933.

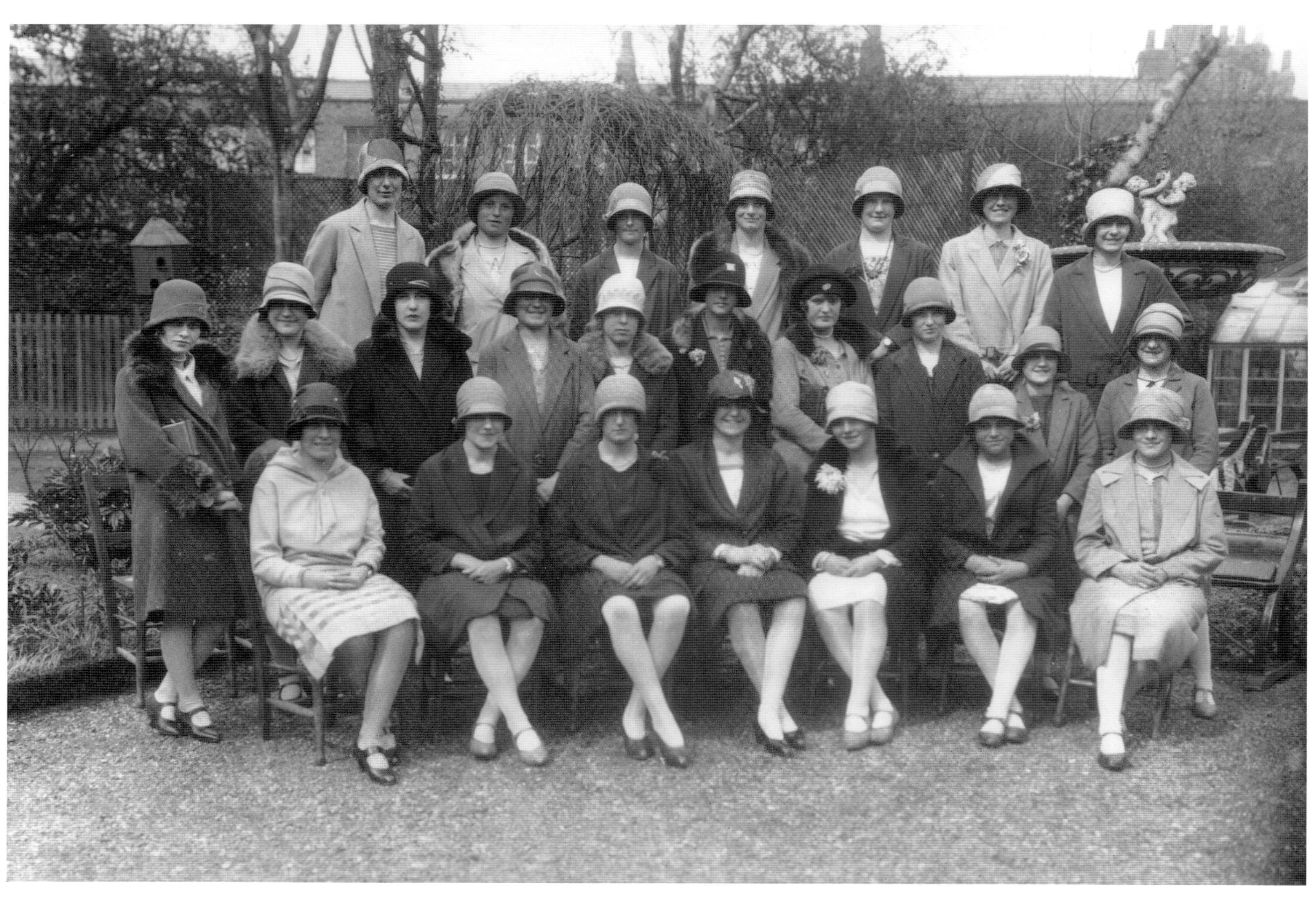

A beauty competition with competitors wearing their iconic cloche hats of the 1920s. Often these hats were embellished by Art Deco designs; by the 1930s, the style had started fall out of fashion.

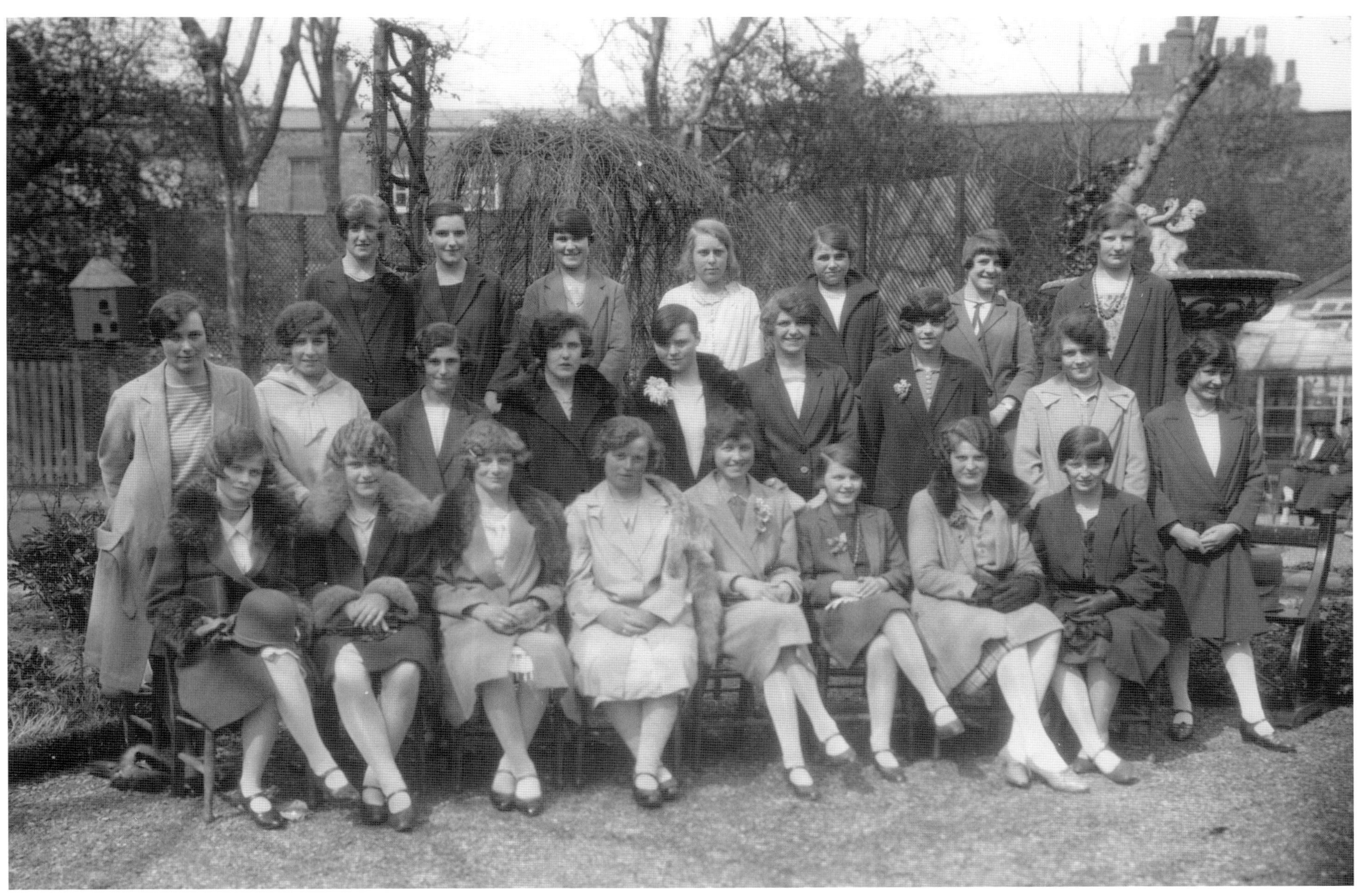

The same group photographed without hats to show off their permanent waves.

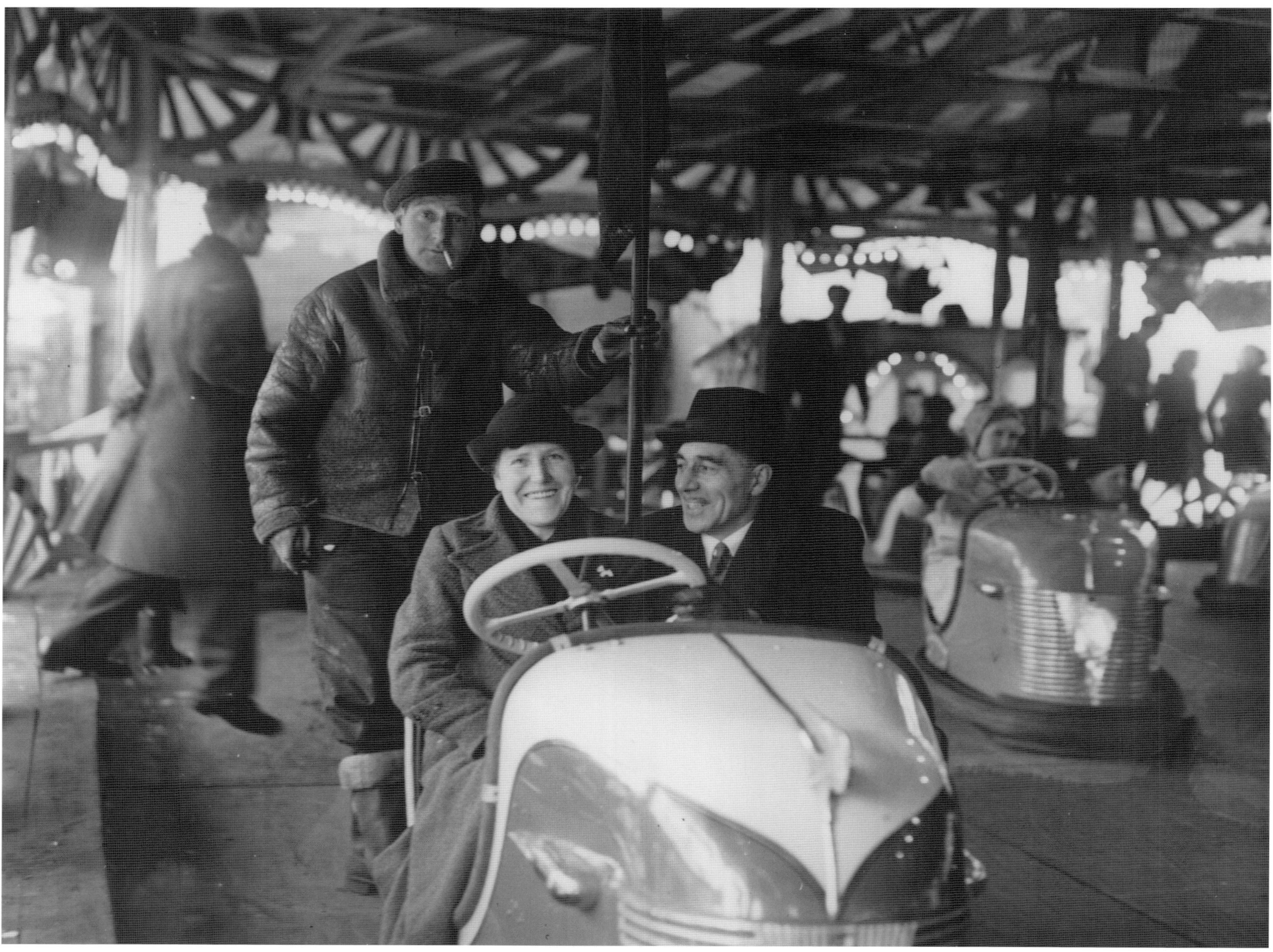

 Dodgems at the Mart, 1950s.

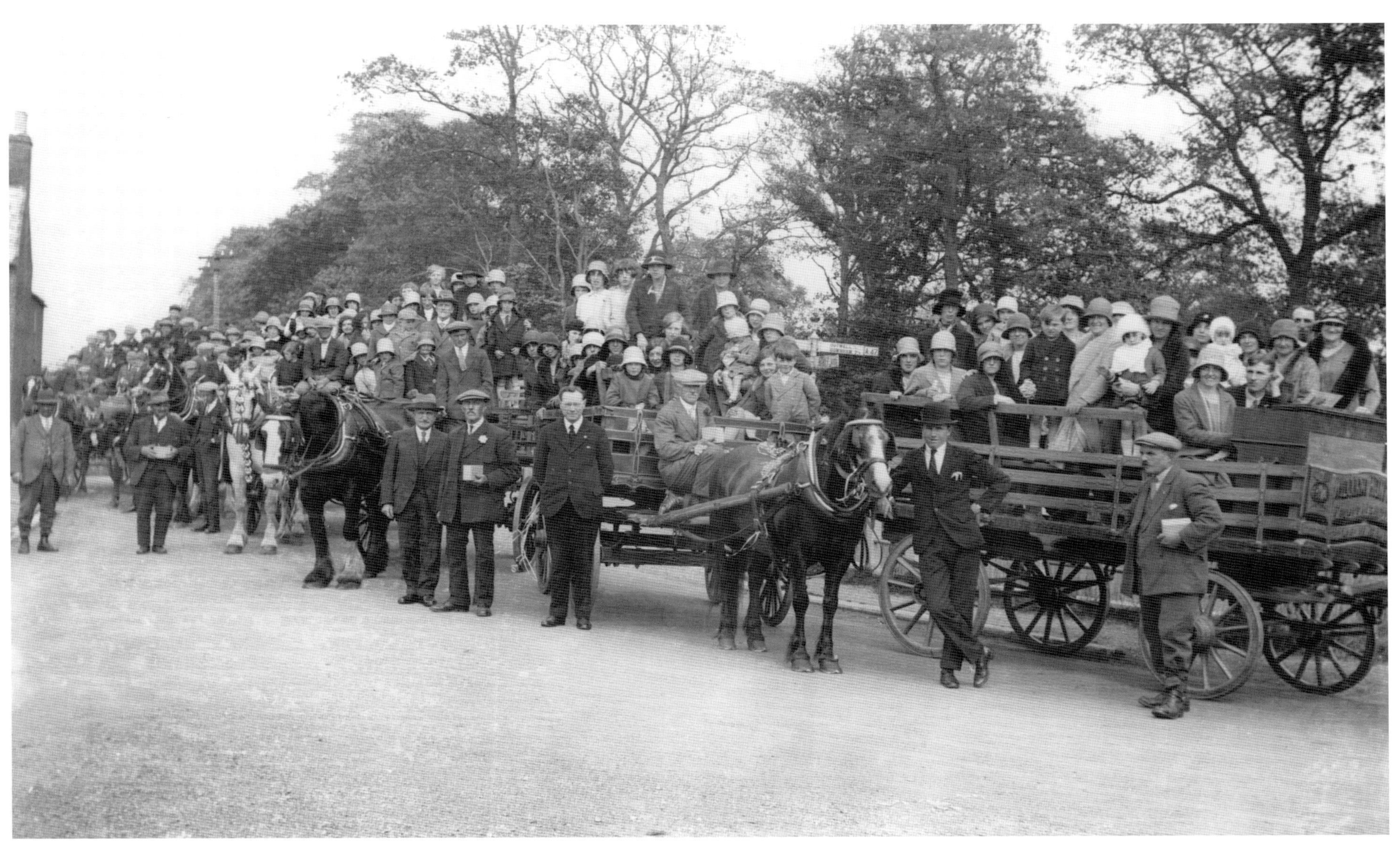

An outing, possibly a church or Hospital Sunday event, at Outwell in the 1930s.

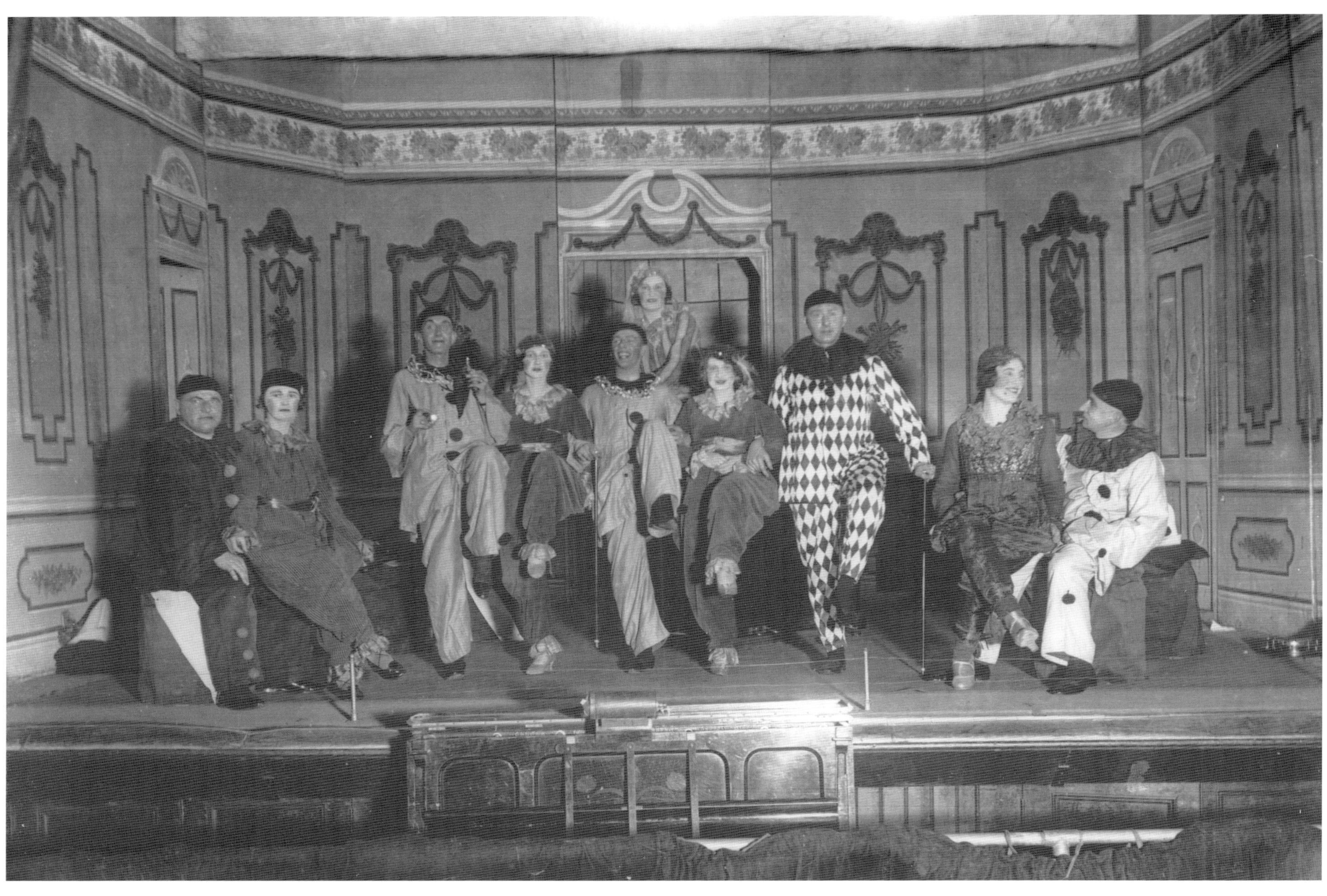

104 A Pierrot Show, possibly in aid of St Augustine's Church, 1920s.

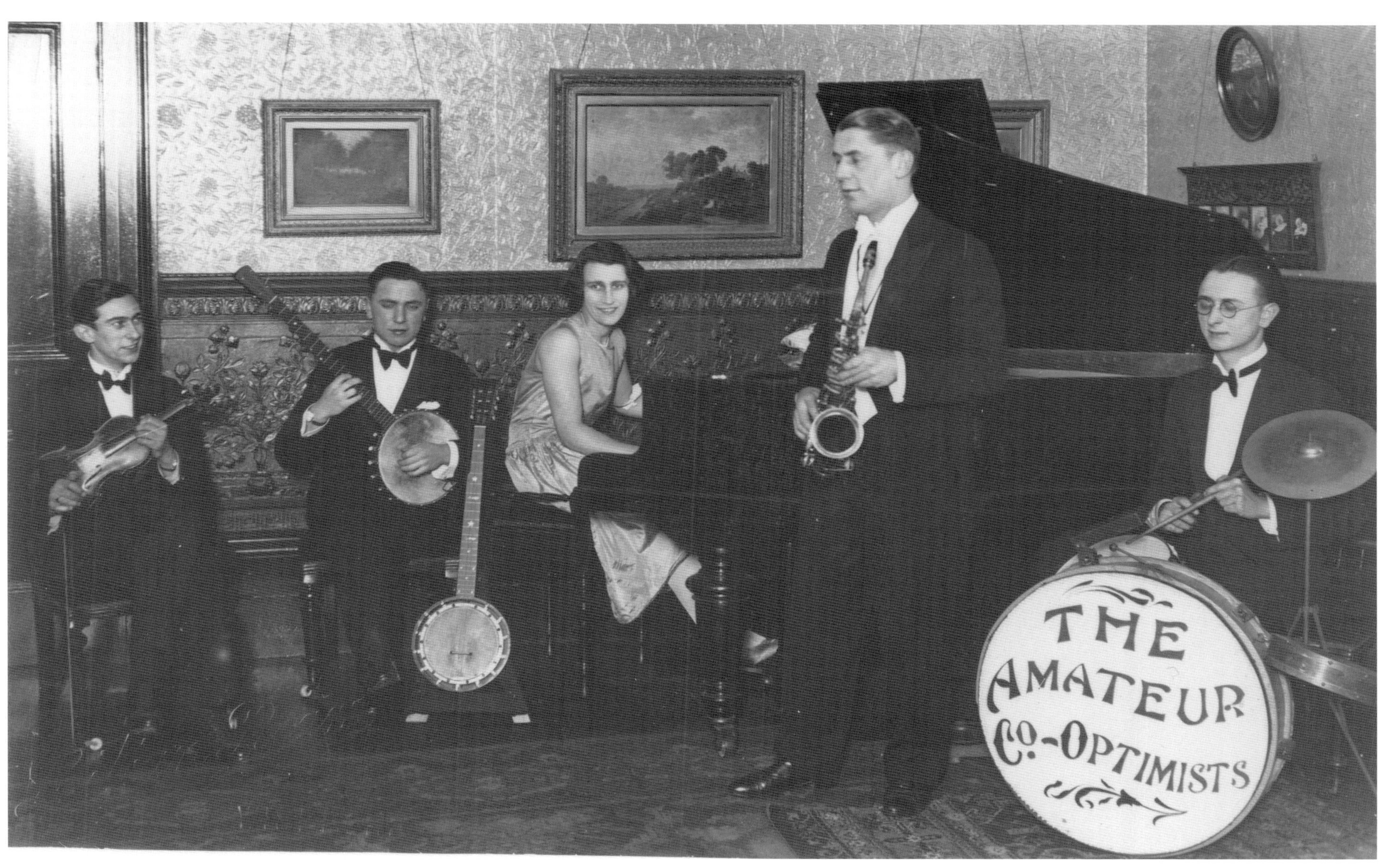

The Amateur Co-Optimists Dance Band, late 1920s.

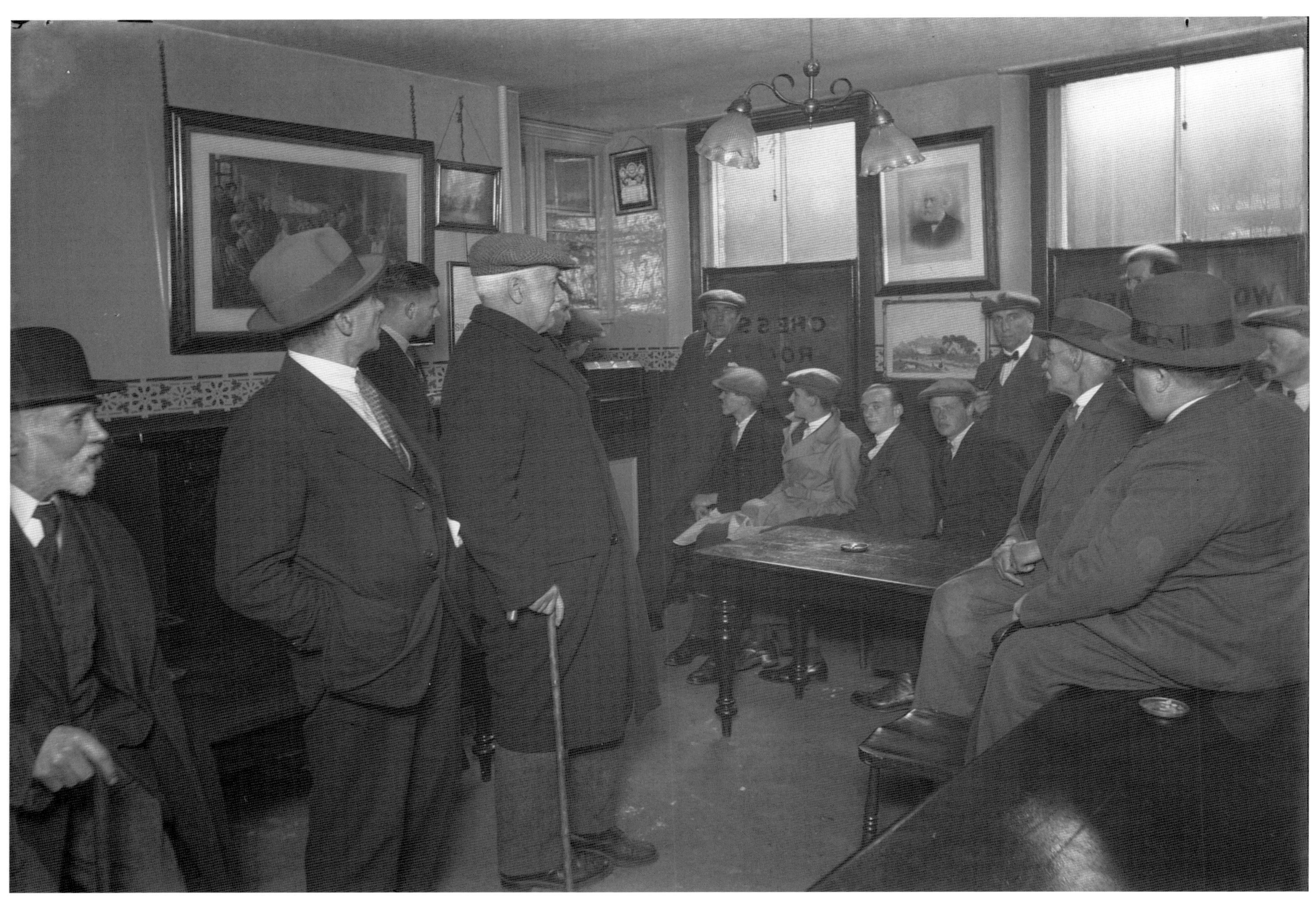

Members of the Wisbech Working Men's Institute & Club listening to the Boat Race in 1930. The Institute was the brainchild of Jonathan Peckover, a member of the prominent Quaker banking family, and provided a non-political and temperance venue, with a substantial library and several self-improving clubs to 'improve' the local working man.

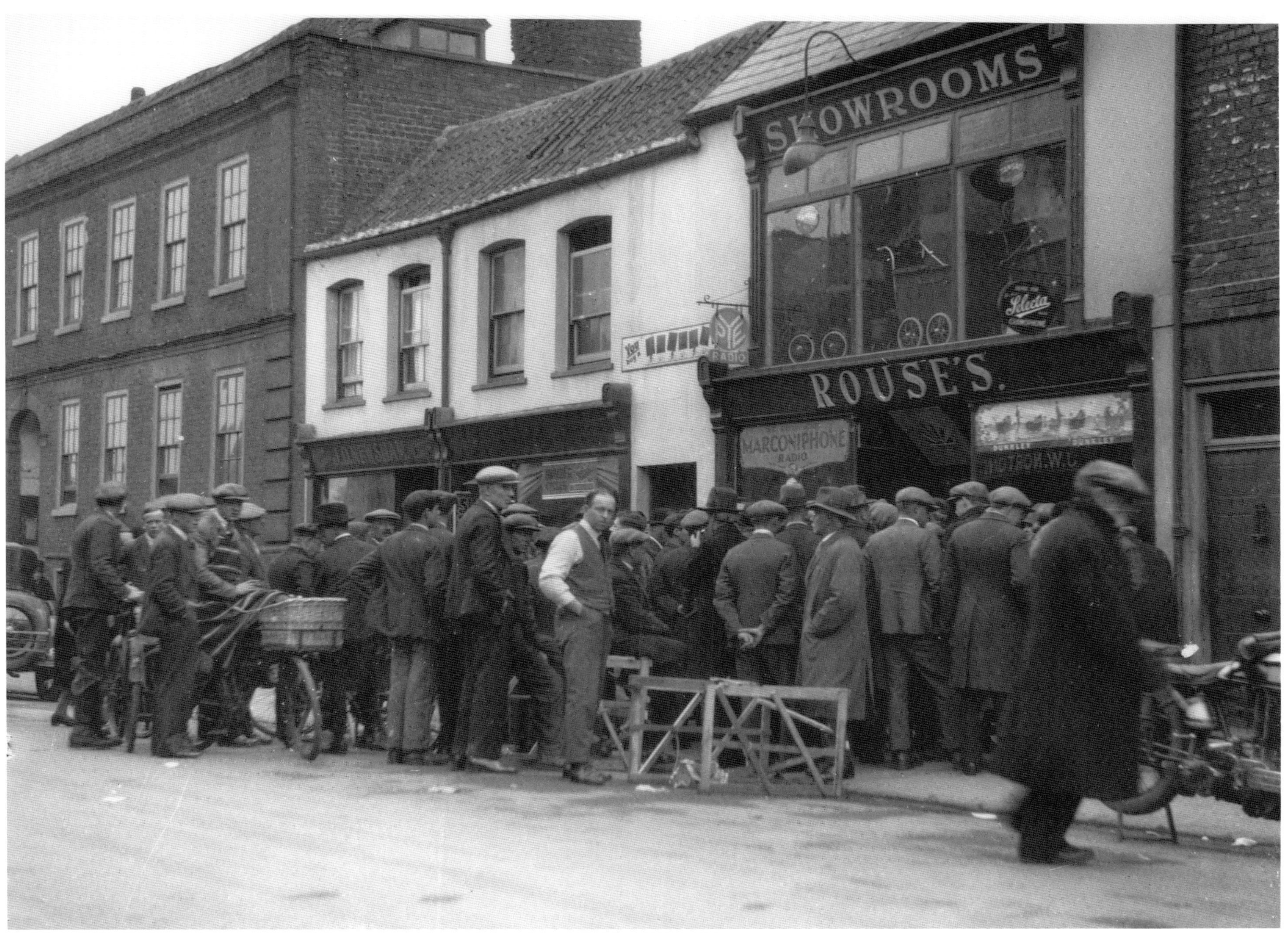

A crowd, gathered outside Rouse's radio shop at 8 & 9 Upper Hill Street, listen to Cambridge win the Boat Race, 21st March 1931.

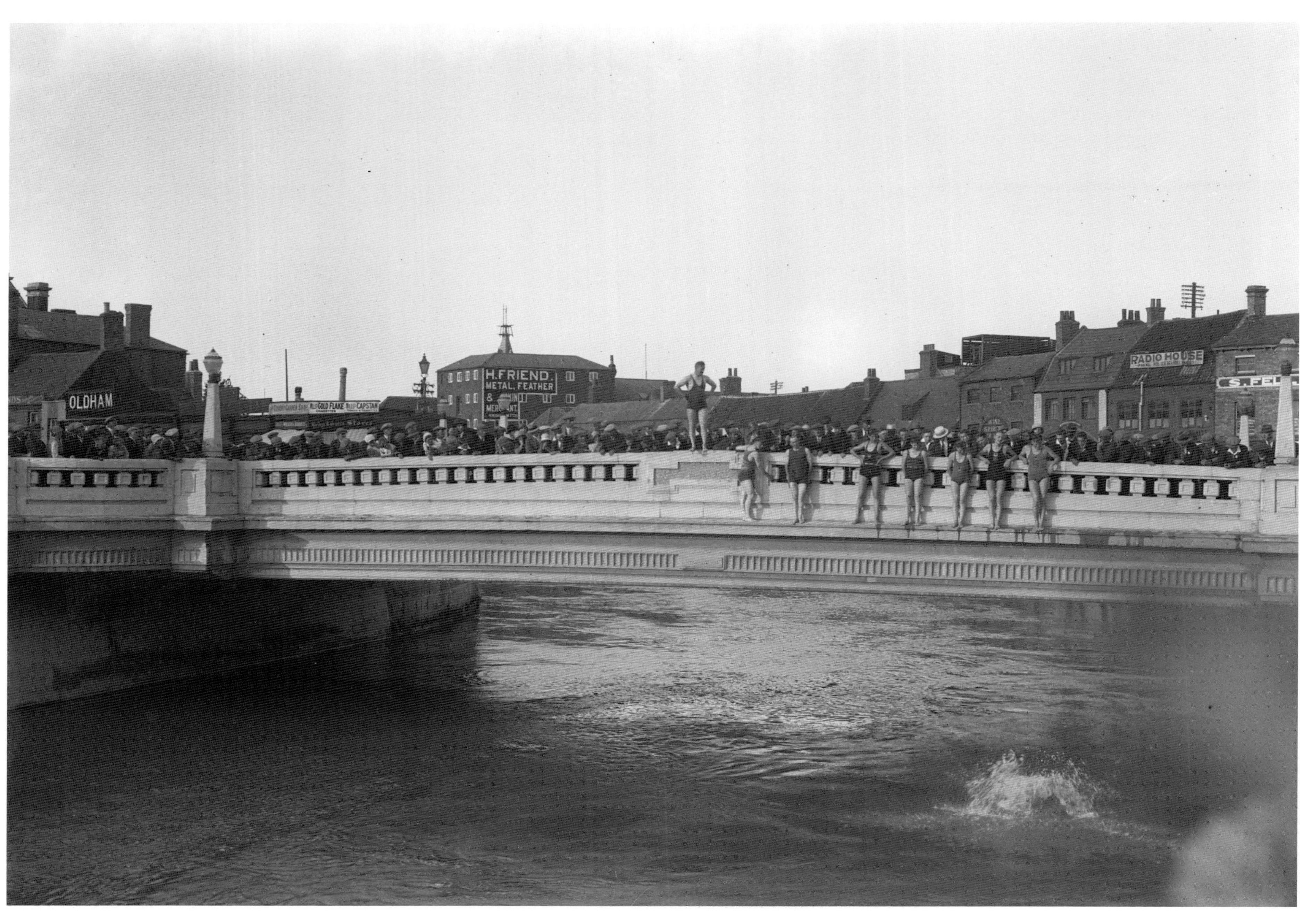

Swimmers diving from Wisbech Town Bridge, 1933. It is hard to imagine this being permitted today or the annual river swim from Sutton Bridge to Wisbech.

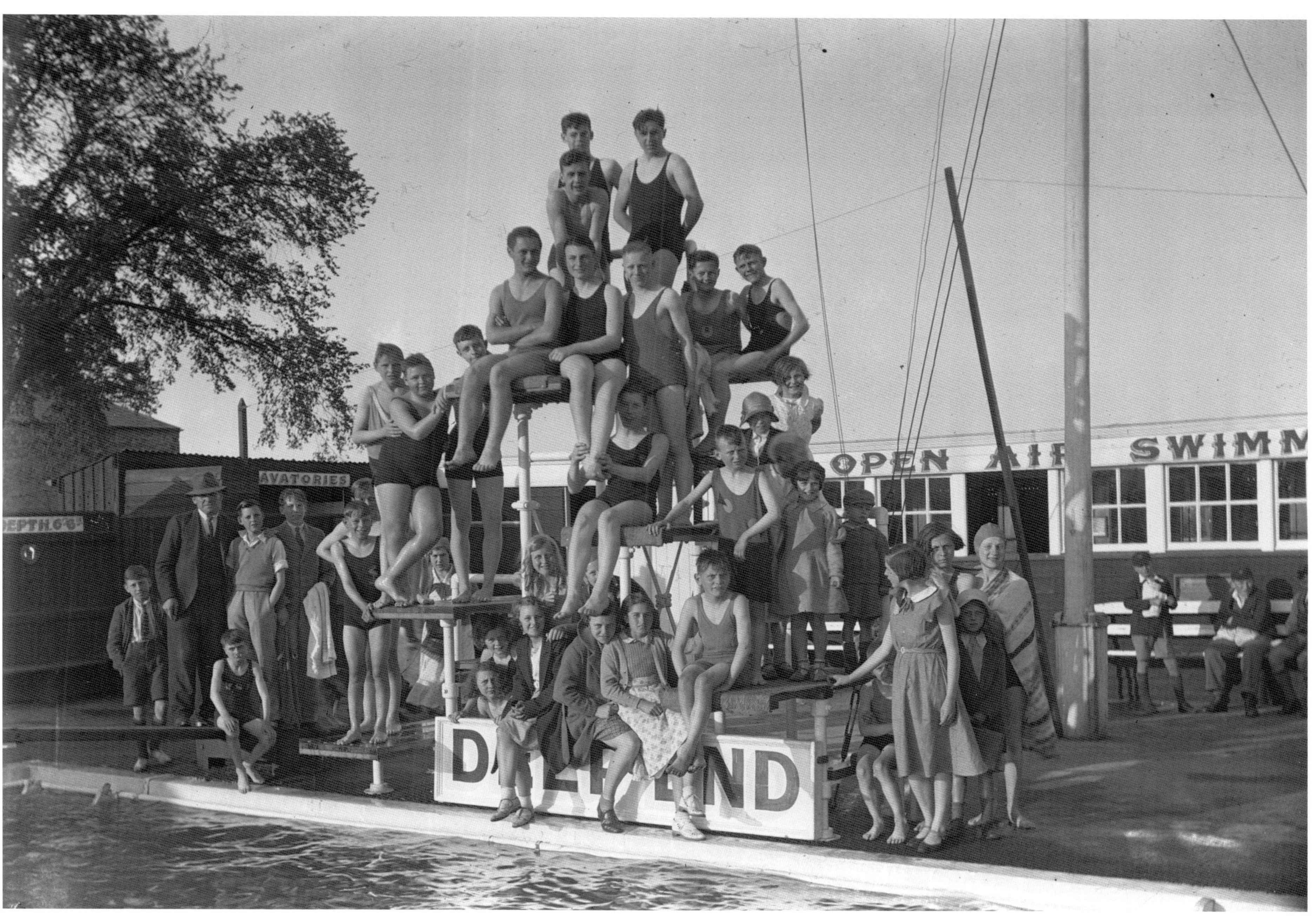

Wisbech Open Air Swimming Bath, 1930s. The baths opened in 1912 and were
located in Crab Marsh near the Swinging Berth. They were built partly as a 109
memorial to Edward VII and partly to commemorate the coronation of George V.

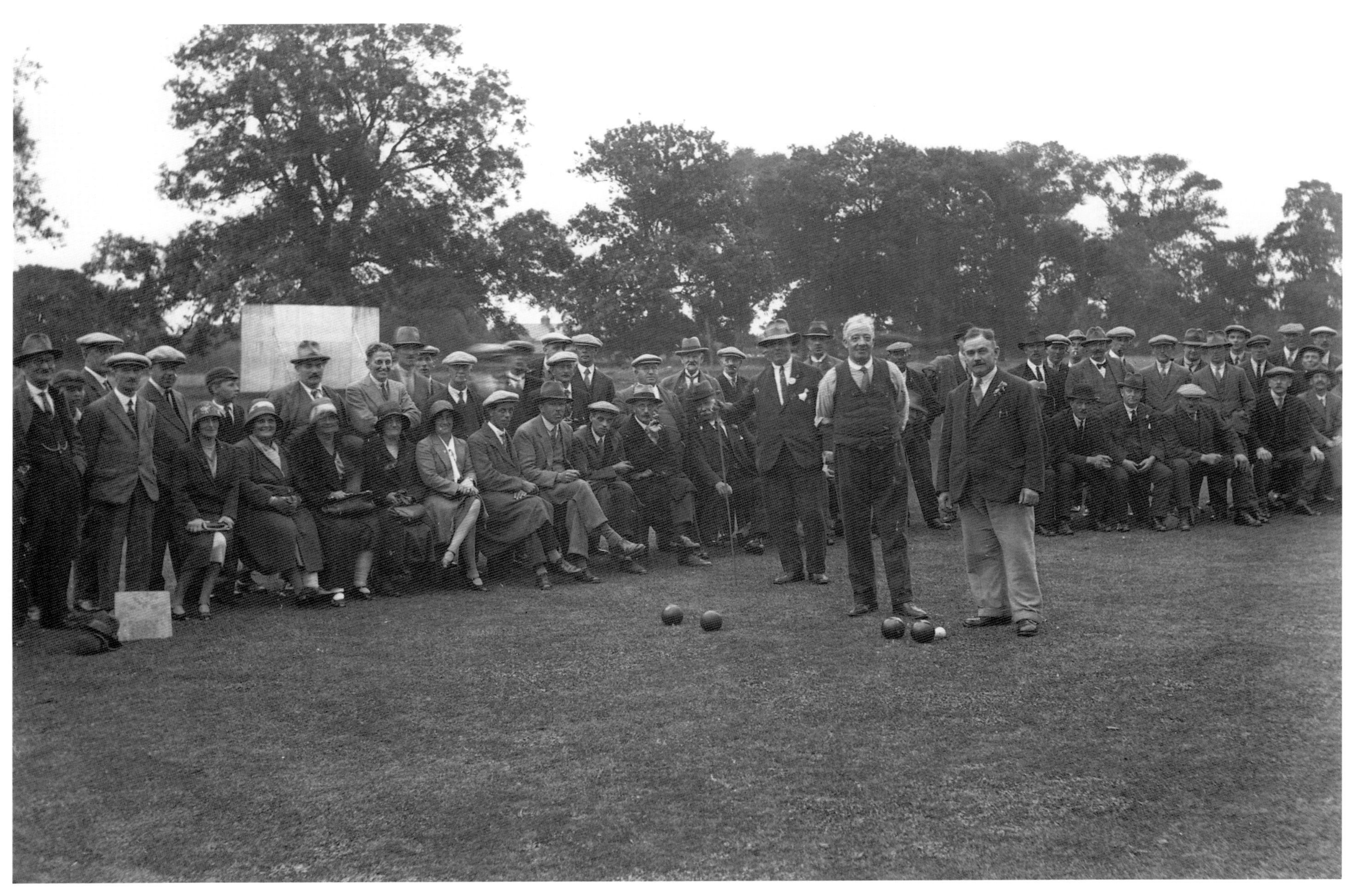

 Bowling match, 1930s.

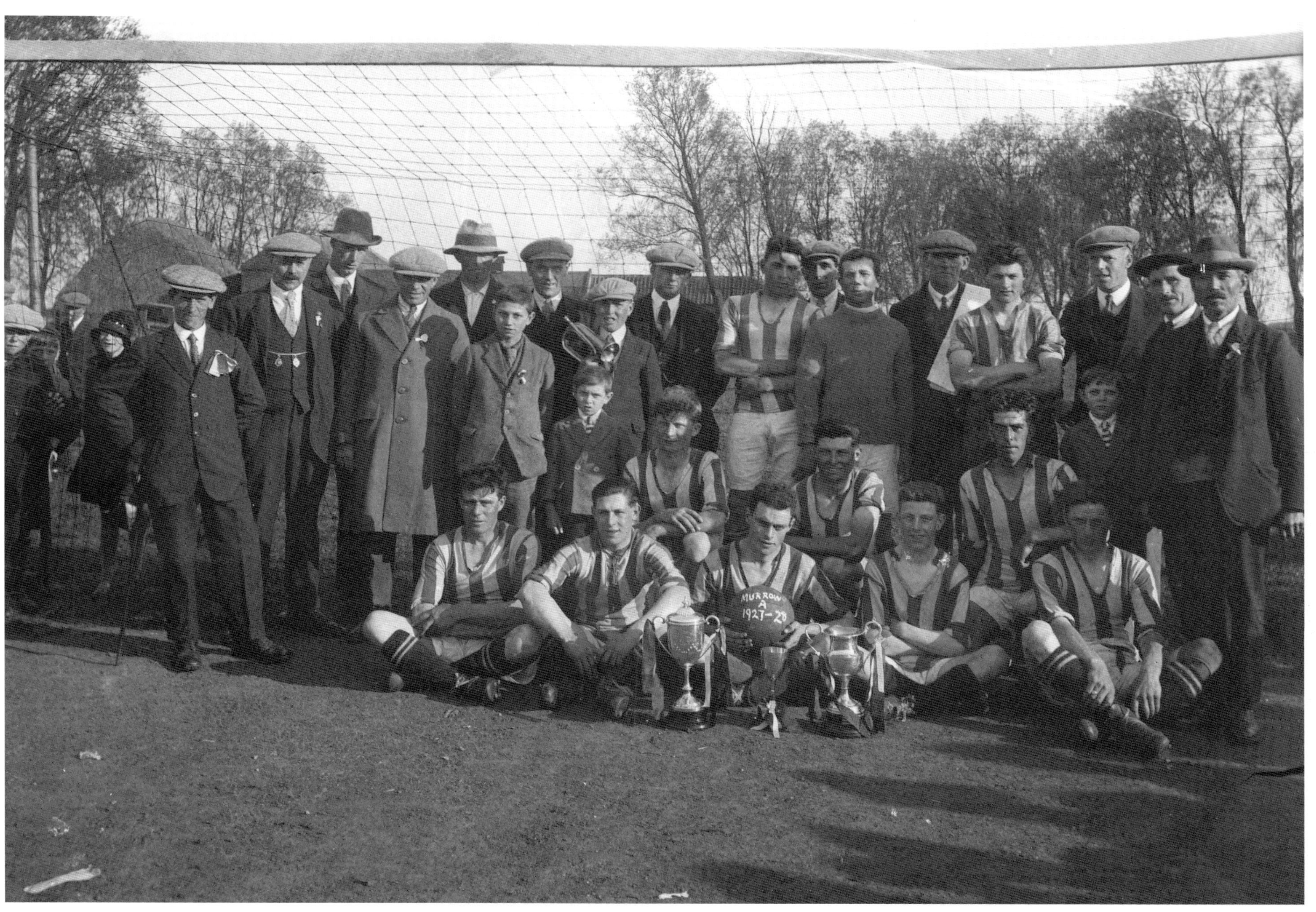

Murrow football team, 1927/28 season.

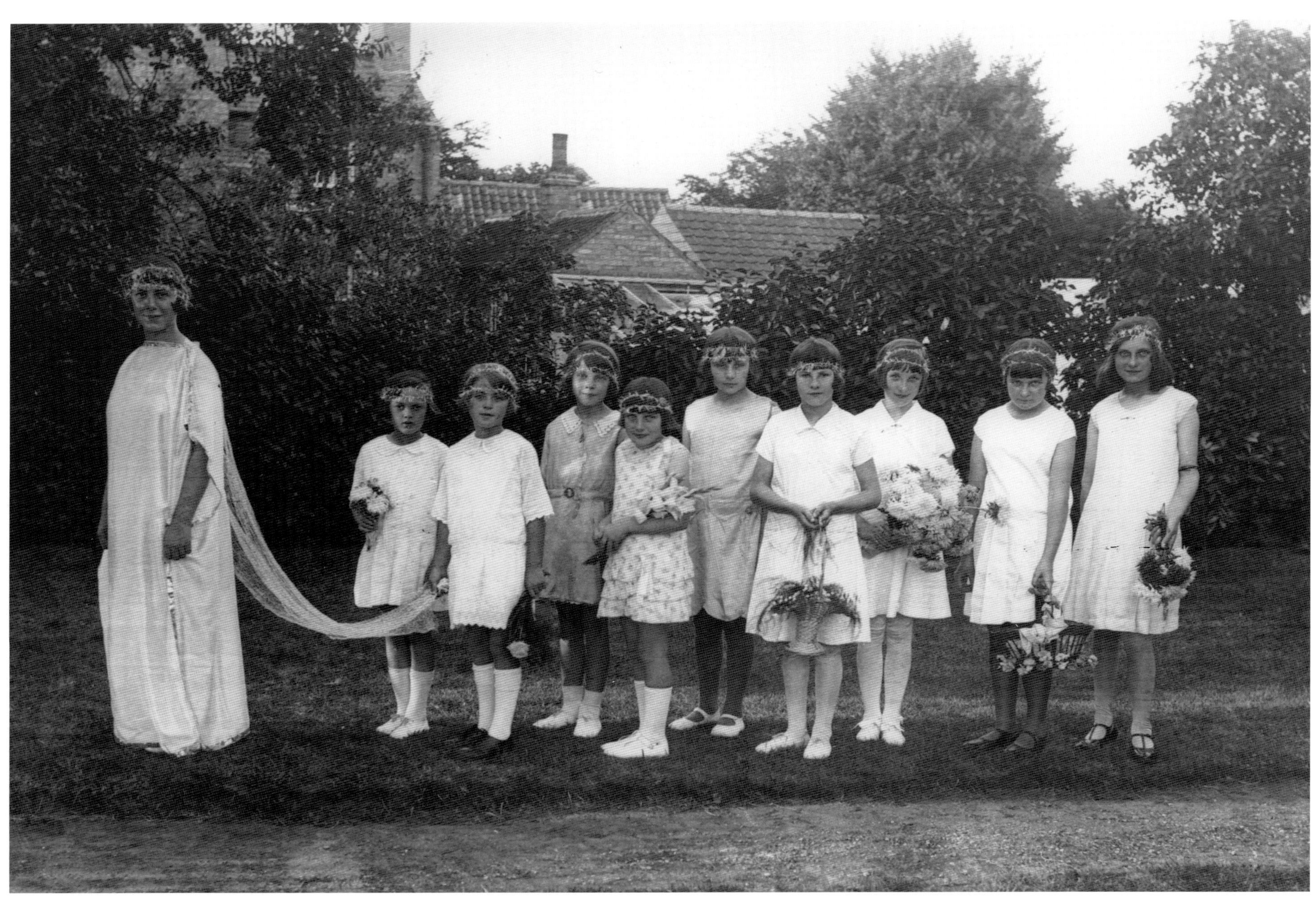

 The Festival Queen and her attendants from Sutton St James School, late 1920s.

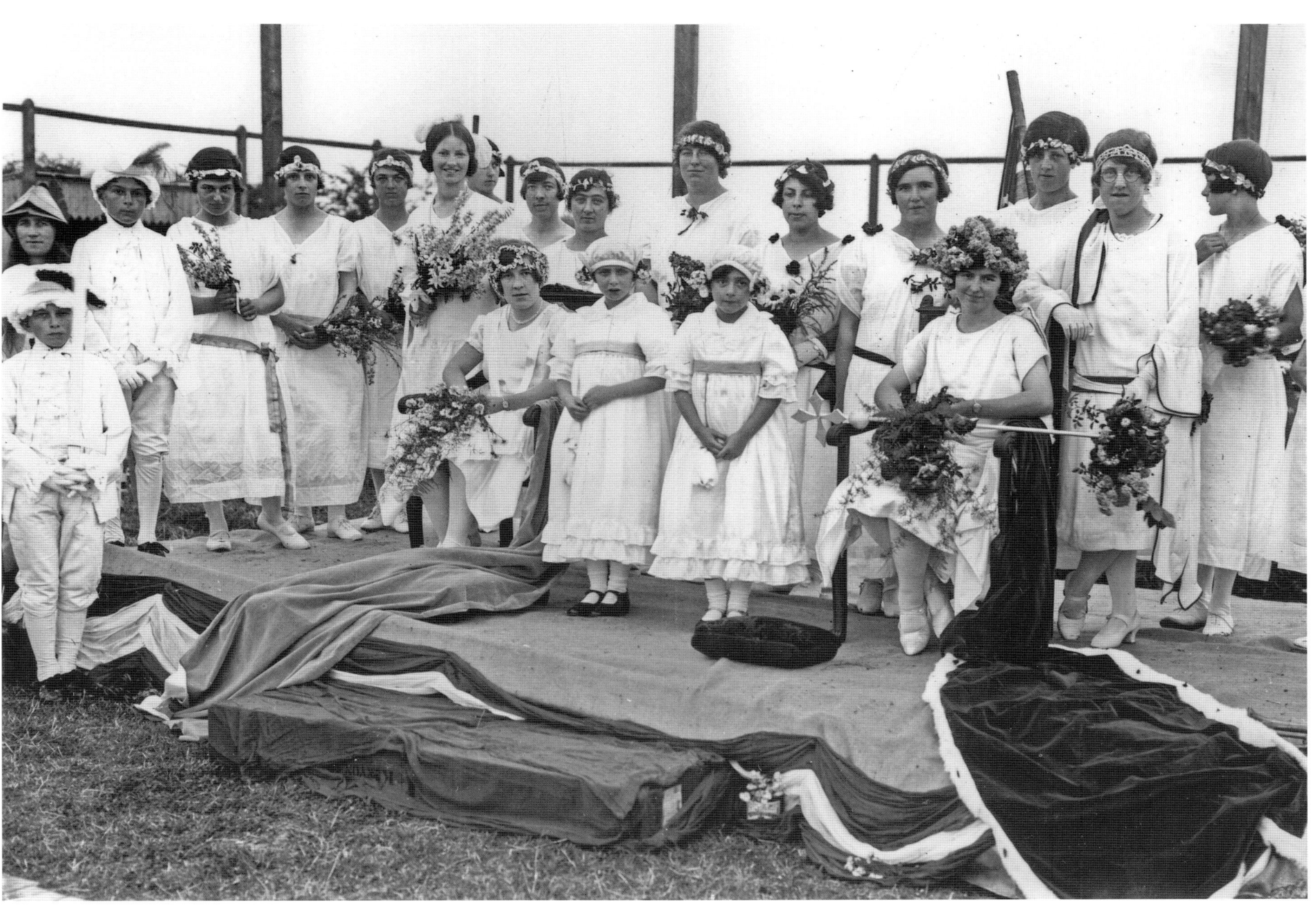

The newly crowned Queen of the Rose Festival at Sutton St James with her attendants, c1931. The festival was started in 1926.

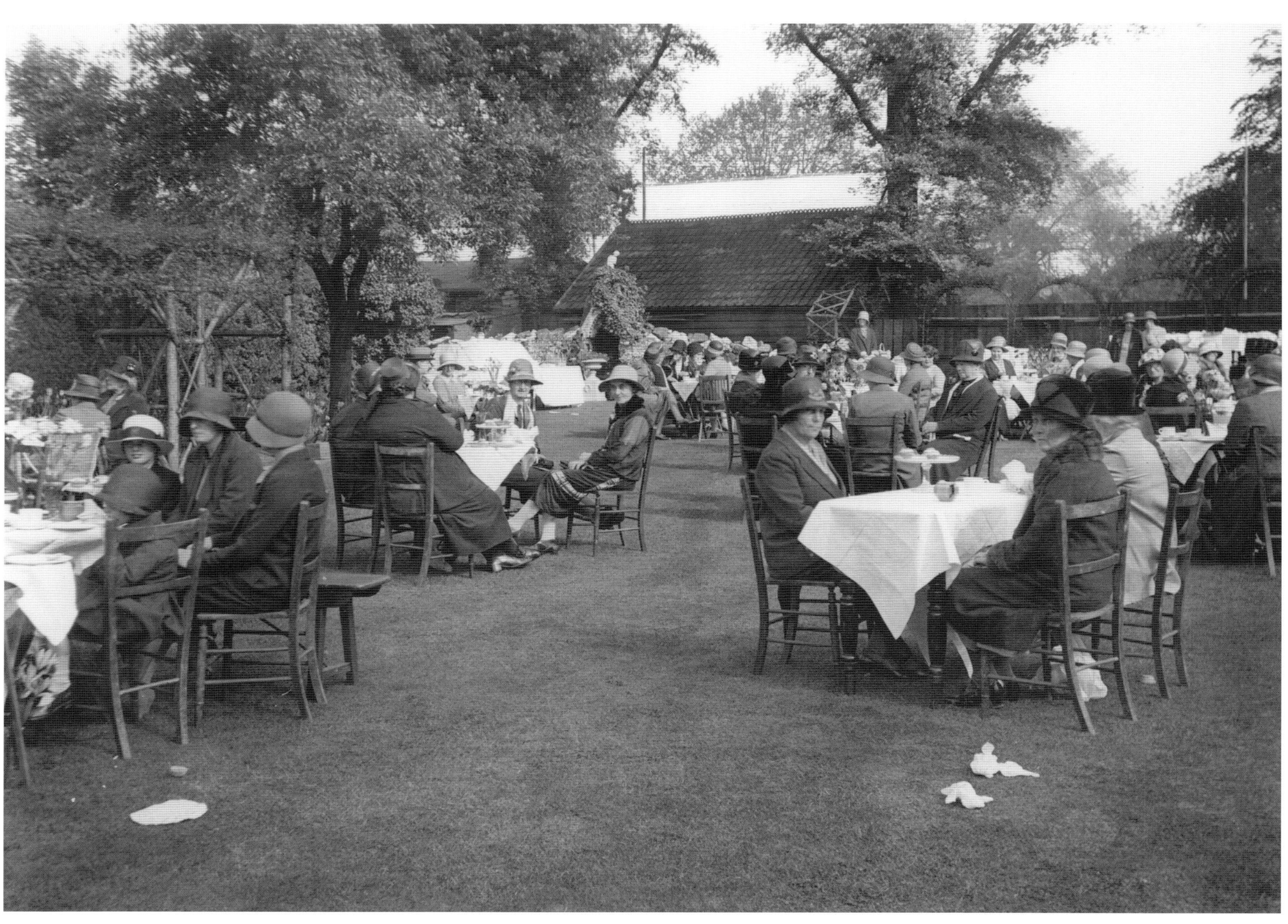

A tea party for the ladies of the Alexandrina Club, 1920s. The Club was formed by Alexandrina Peckover, and was also a base for the Wisbech branch of the Young Women's Christian Association.

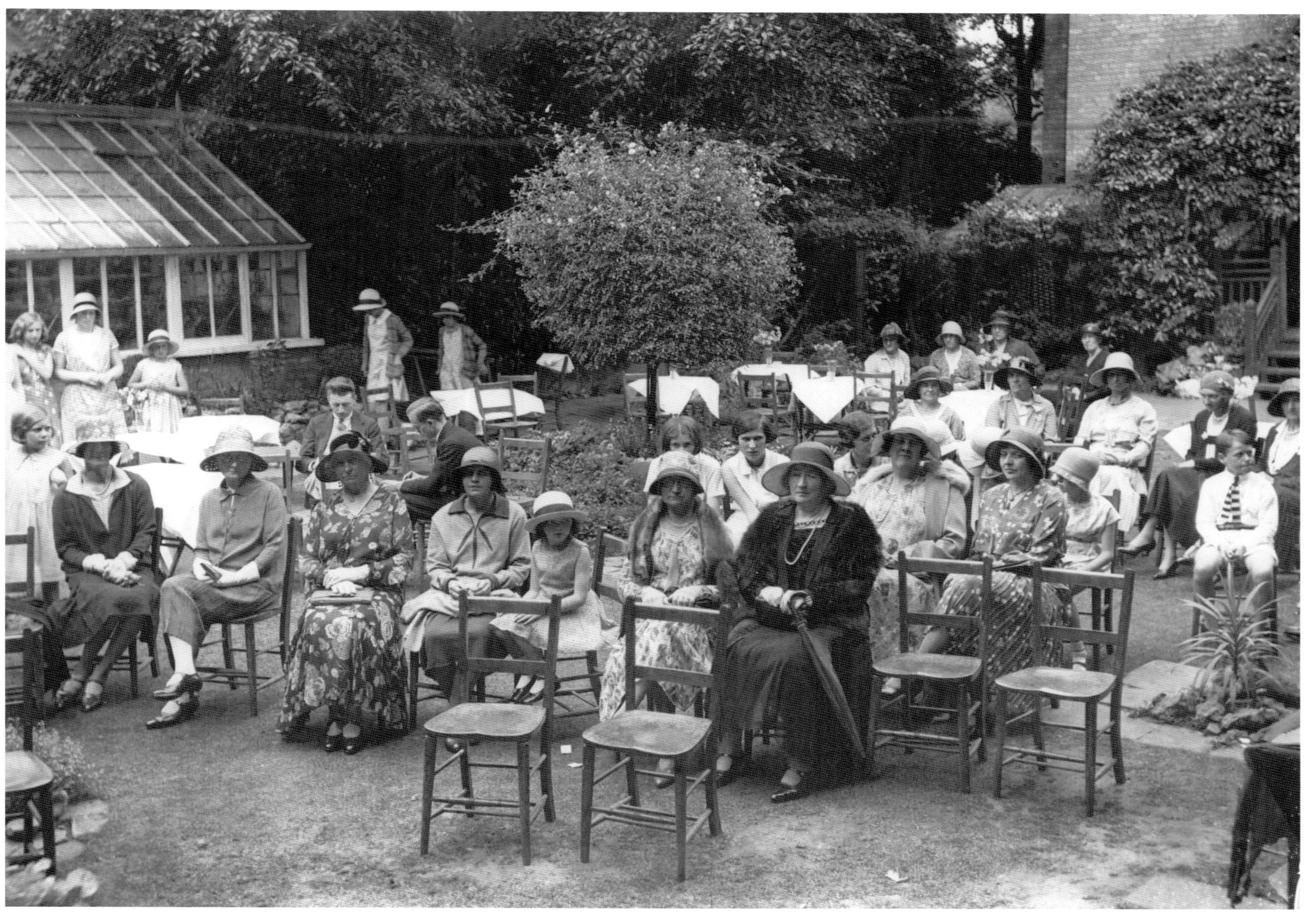

A garden party organised by the League of Pity, 1920s. The League was junior branch of the NSPCC which encouraged children to raise money to support the work of the Society.

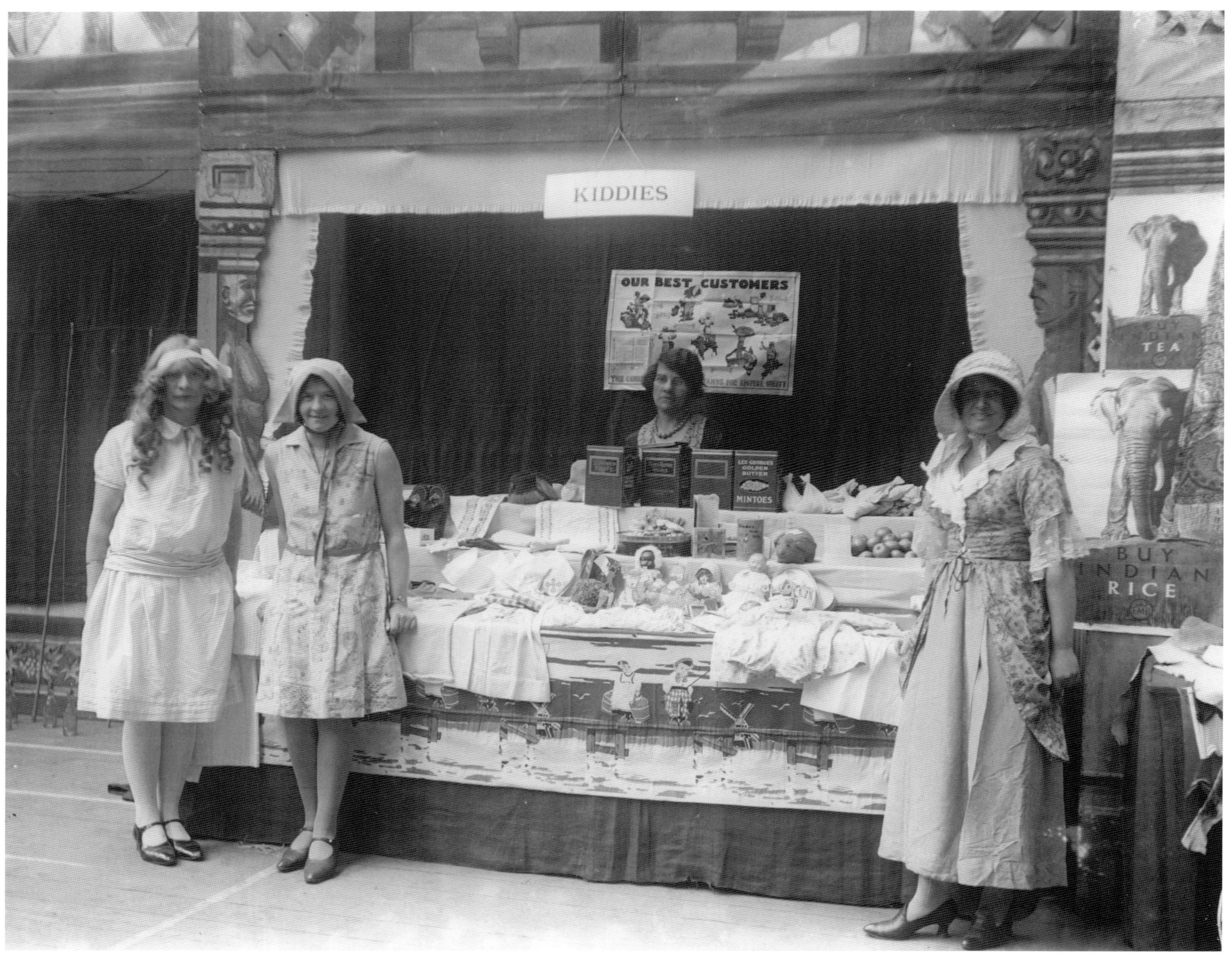

A 'Kiddies' stall at a 1920s fair to celebrate Empire Day, which was held annually on the 24th May. The lady, to the right of the stall, is probably a representation of Little Bo Peep.

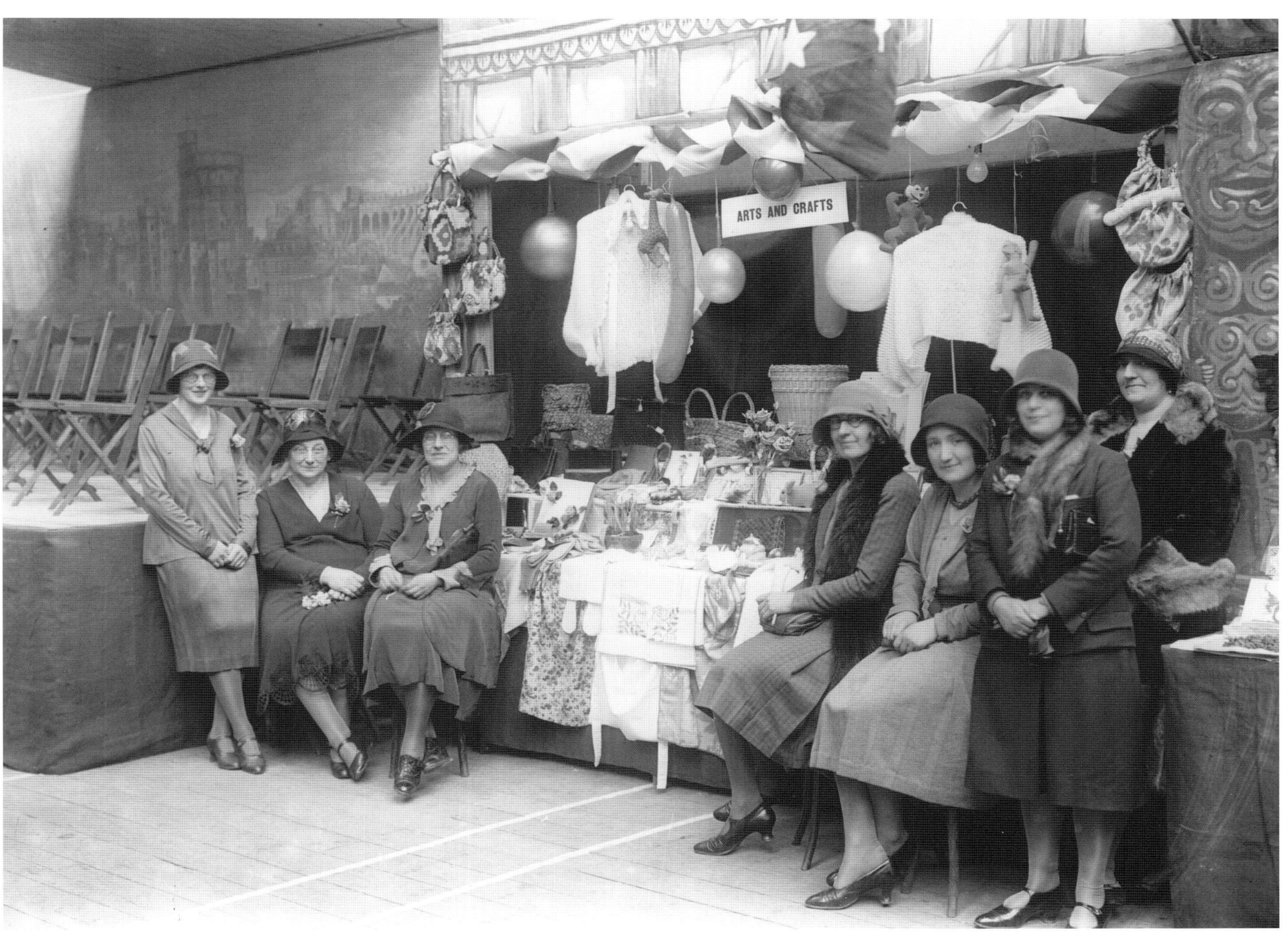

The Arts and Crafts stall at the Empire Day Fair, 1920s.

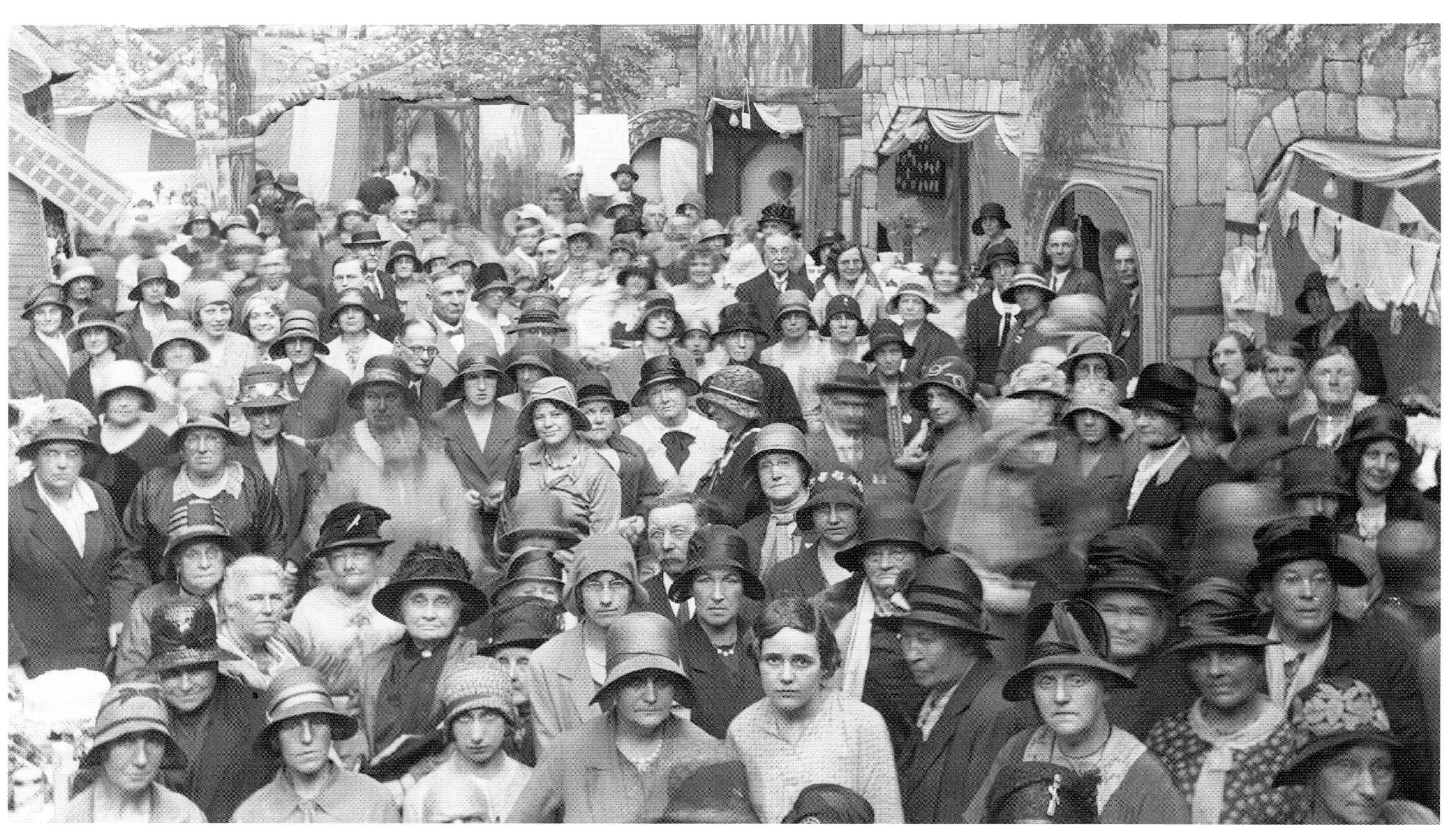

A throng of visitors at a Liberal Bazaar in the 1920s. In the first half of the 20th century, the Liberal Party enjoyed good support in Wisbech and the Isle of Ely.

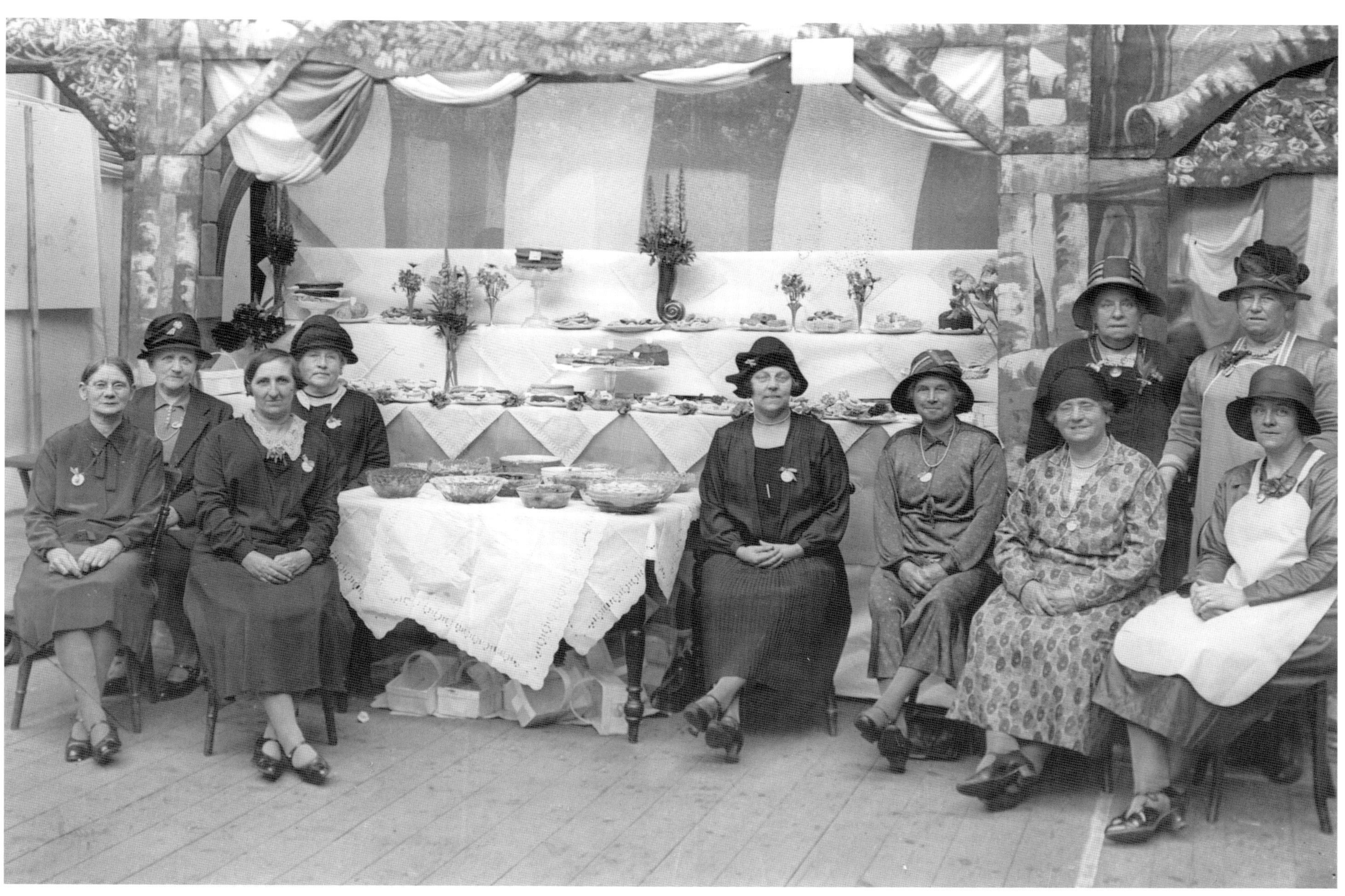

The cake stall at the Liberal Bazaar, 1920s.

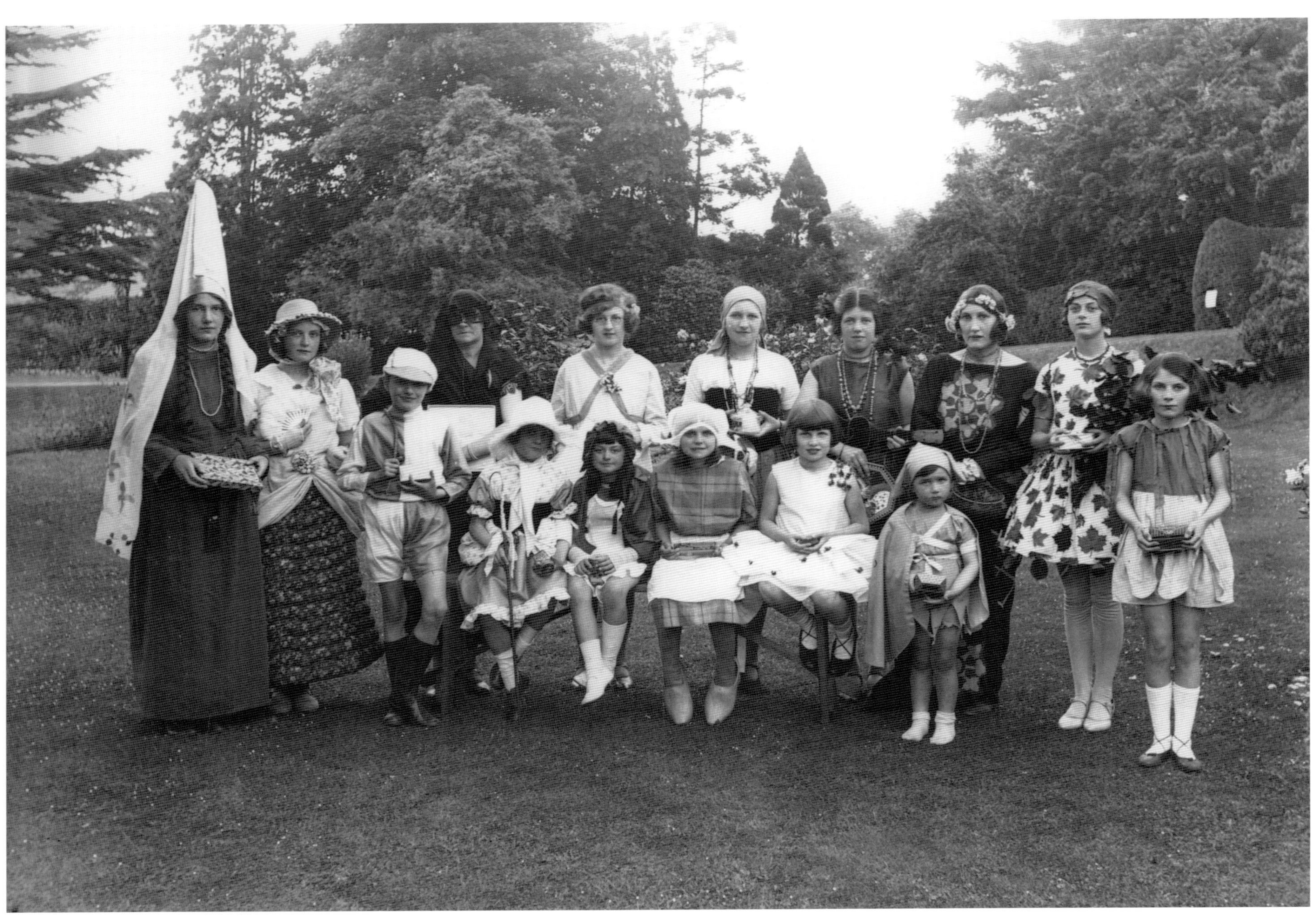

120 A fancy dress competition, 1930s.

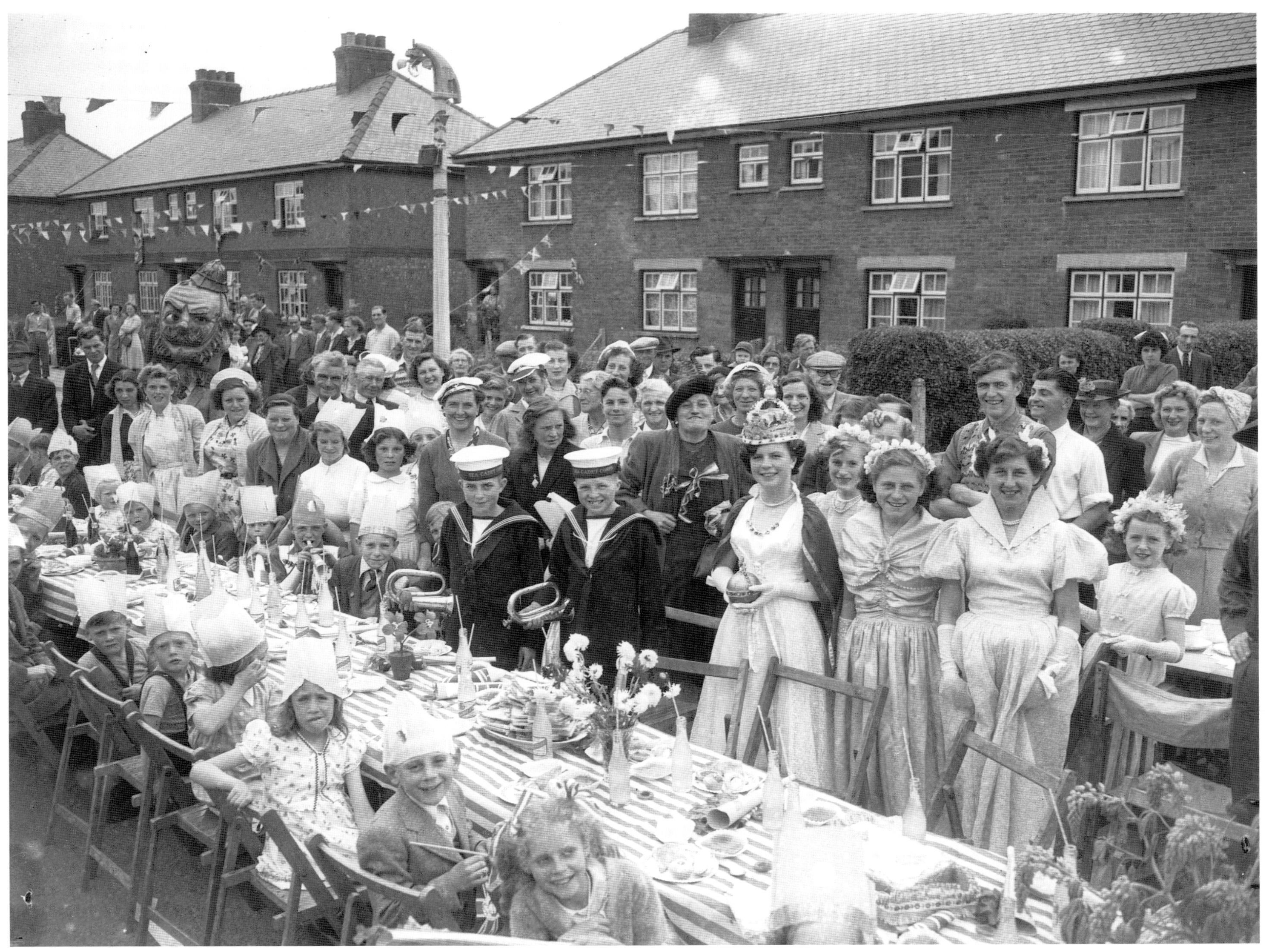

A street party in Southwell Road celebrating the Coronation of Elizabeth II, 1953.

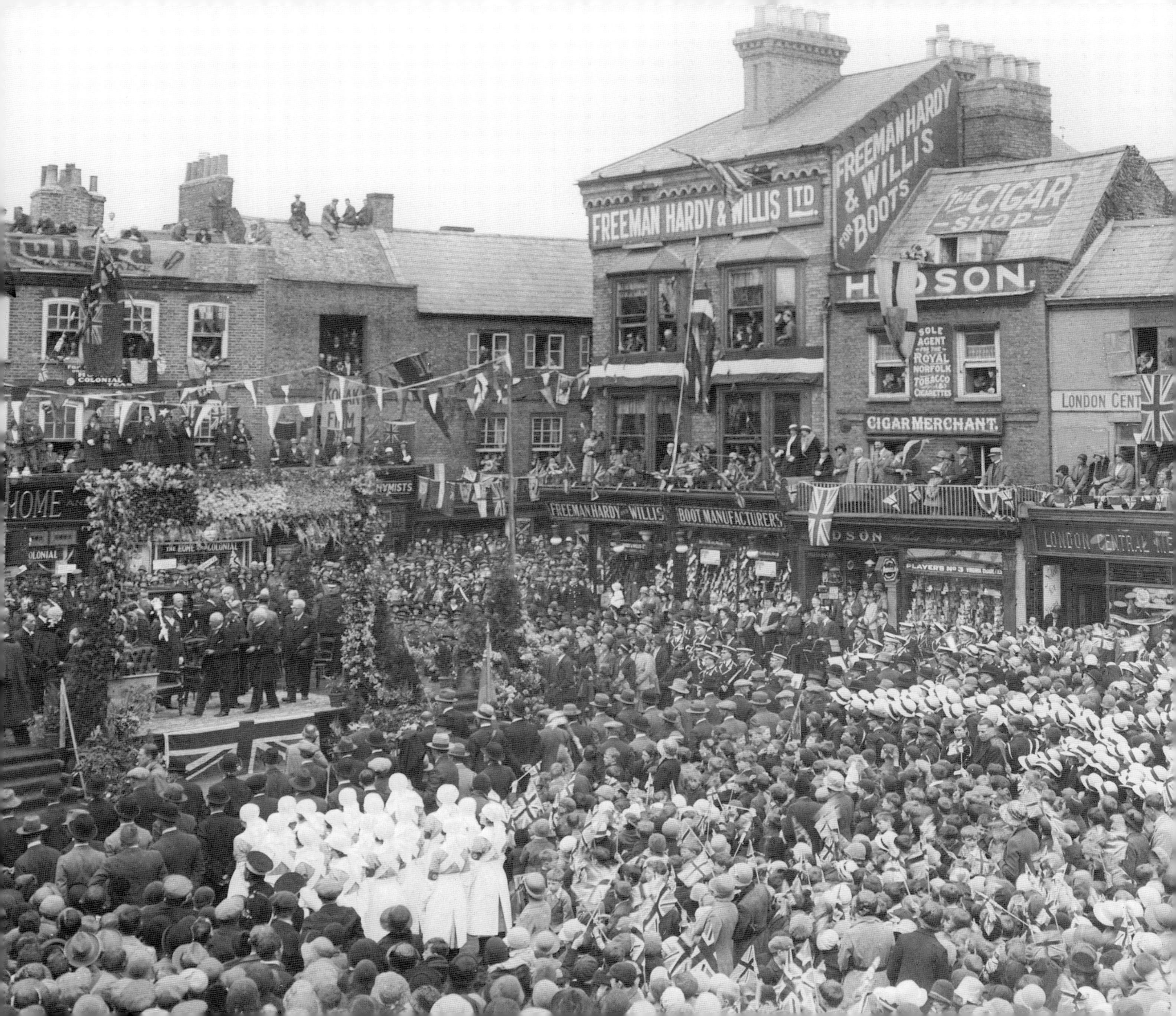
FREEMAN HARDY & WILLIS LTD.
FREEMAN HARDY & WILLIS FOR BOOTS
THE CIGAR SHOP
HUDSON.
SOLE AGENT FOR THE ROYAL NORFOLK TOBACCO & CIGARETTES
LONDON CENT
CIGAR MERCHANT.
HOME
FREEMAN HARDY AND WILLIS
BOOT MANUFACTURERS
LONDON CENTRAL
PLAYERS No 3

Town Life

The civic reception for HRH Prince George, Market Place, 2 June 1932. The Prince later went on to attend the Isle of Ely & Cambridgeshire Agricultural Show at Sibaldsholme Field.

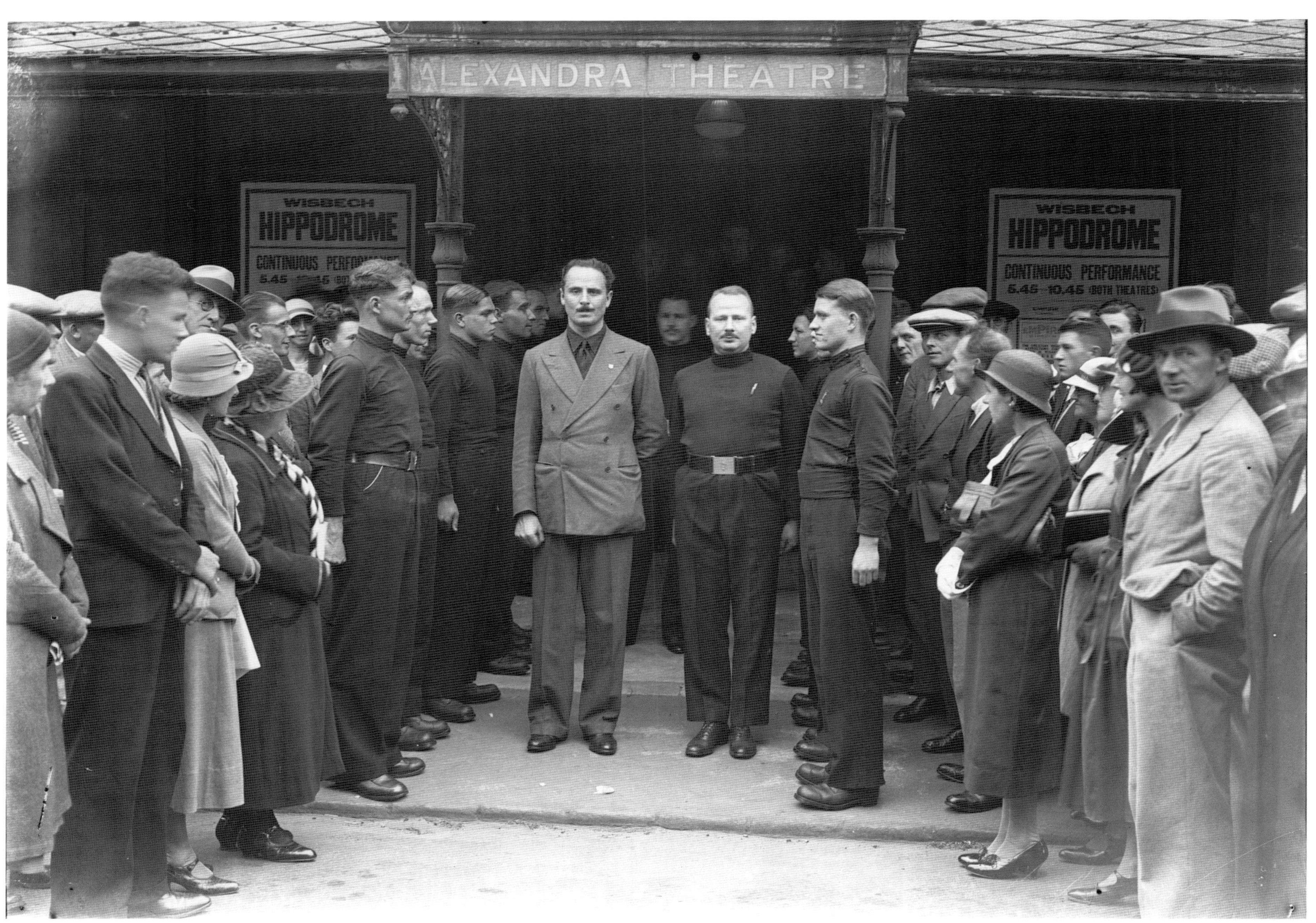

Sir Oswald Mosely, leader of the British Union of Fascists, leaving the Alexandra Theatre, where he had 'explained the Fascist agricultural policy', Saturday 28 July 1934. On Mosely's left is DCH Gunson, the East Anglian Organiser for the Blackshirt movement.

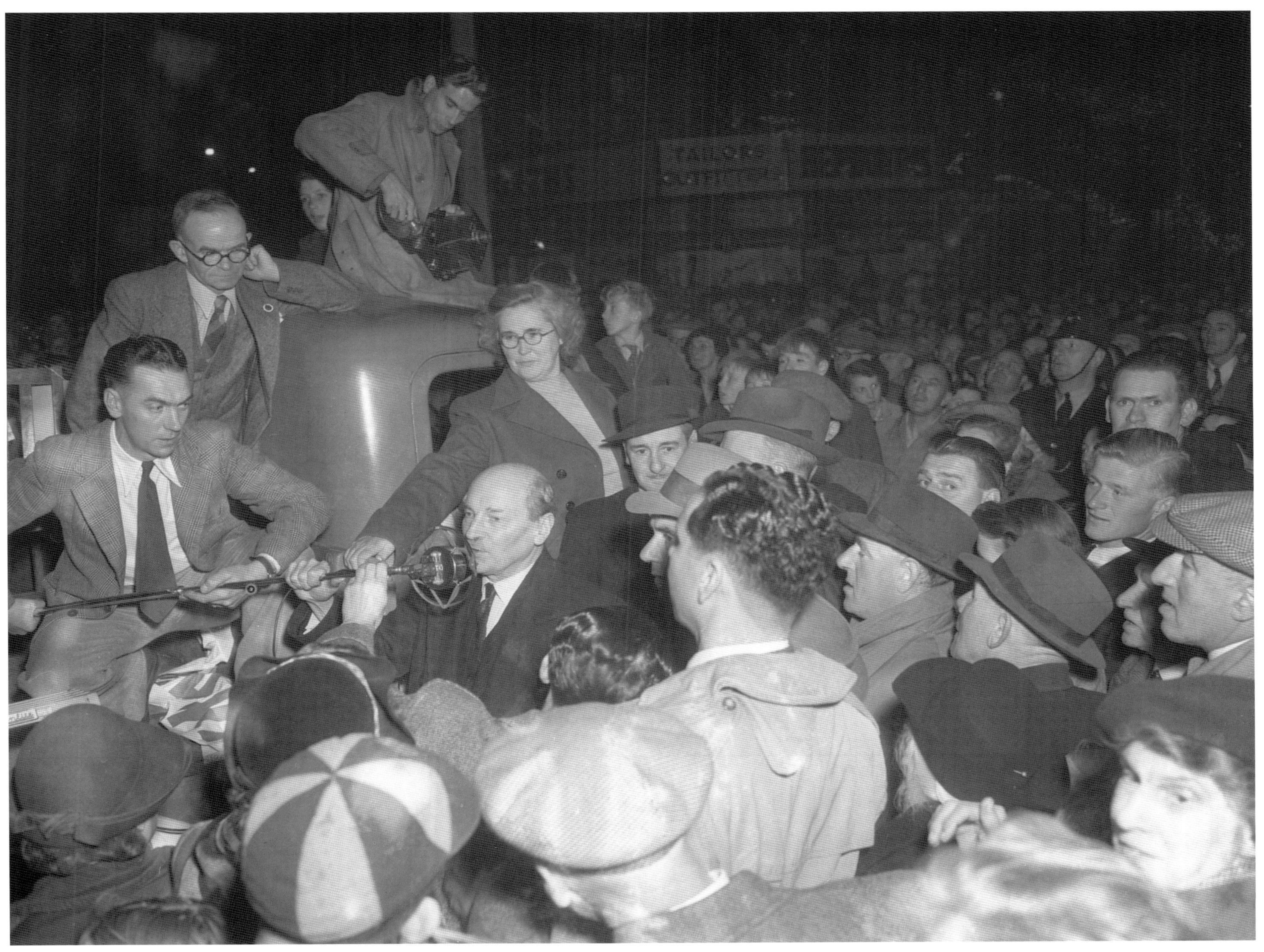

Clement Atlee addressing a large crowd on the Market Place during the General Election campaign of 1951.

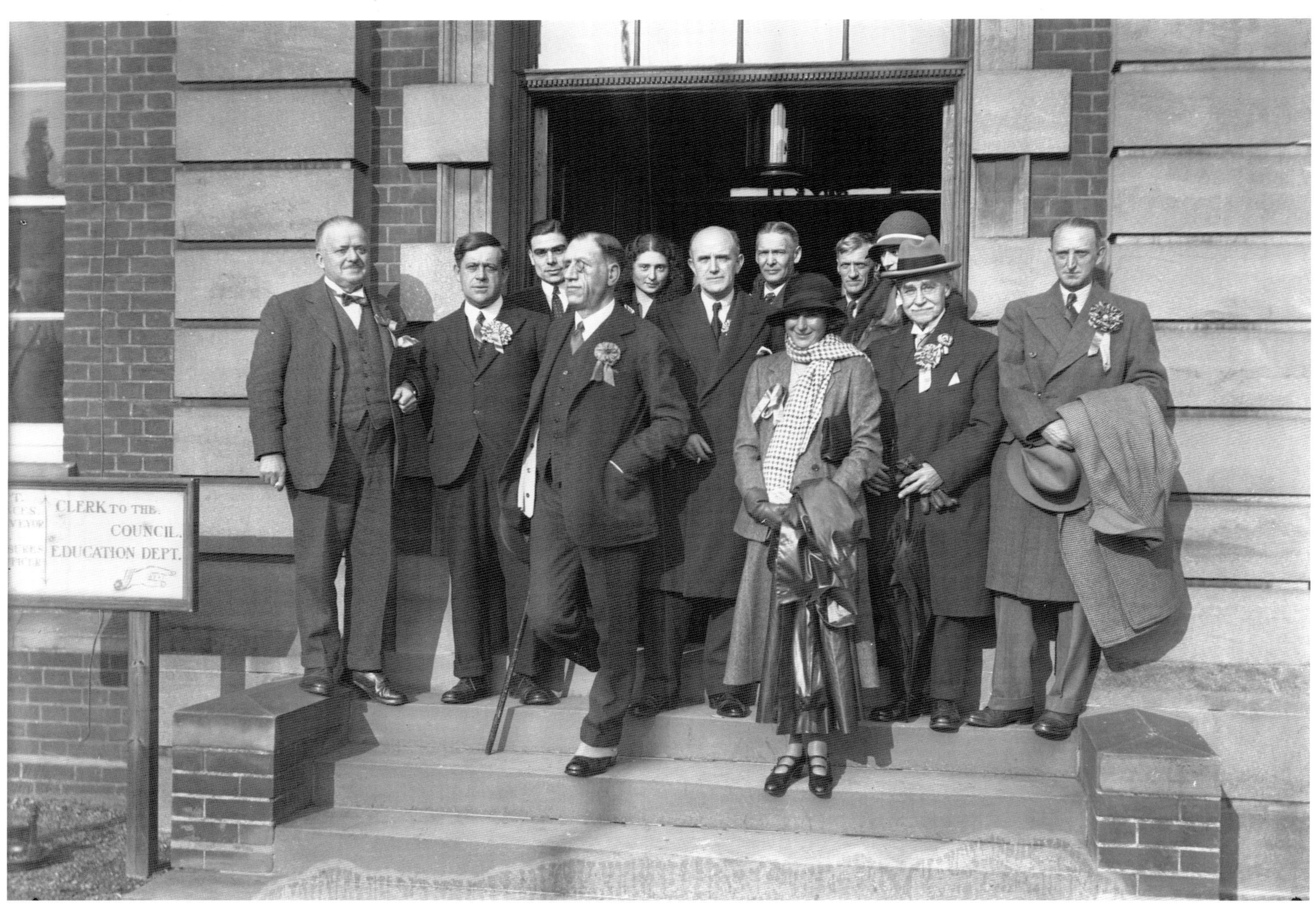

James de Rothschild (in spats) campaigning during the 1929 General Election. He was duly elected MP for the Isle of Ely.

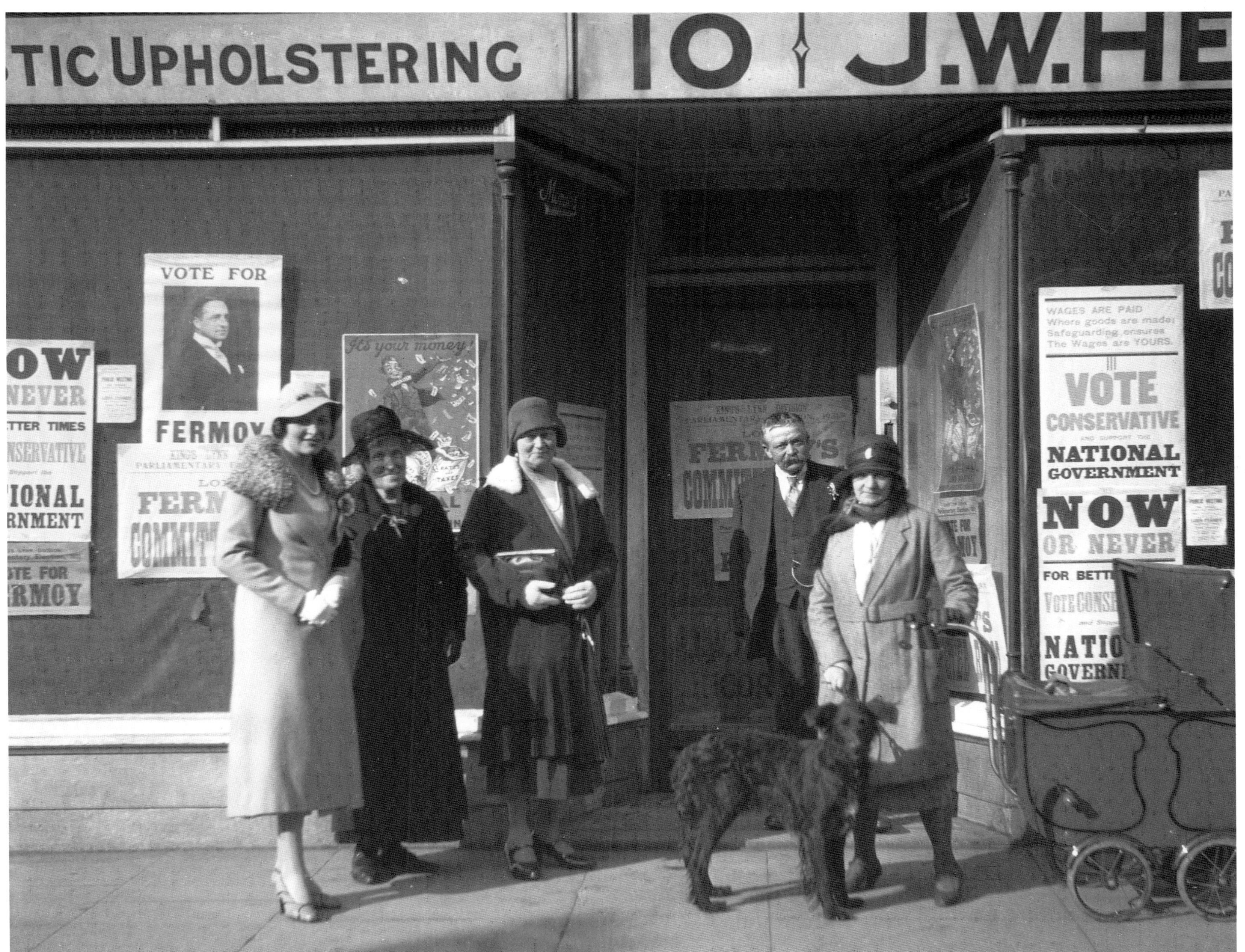

Lady Fermoy, on the left, visiting during the 1931 General Election campaign.
Her husband, Lord Fermoy was returned as MP for King's Lynn division.

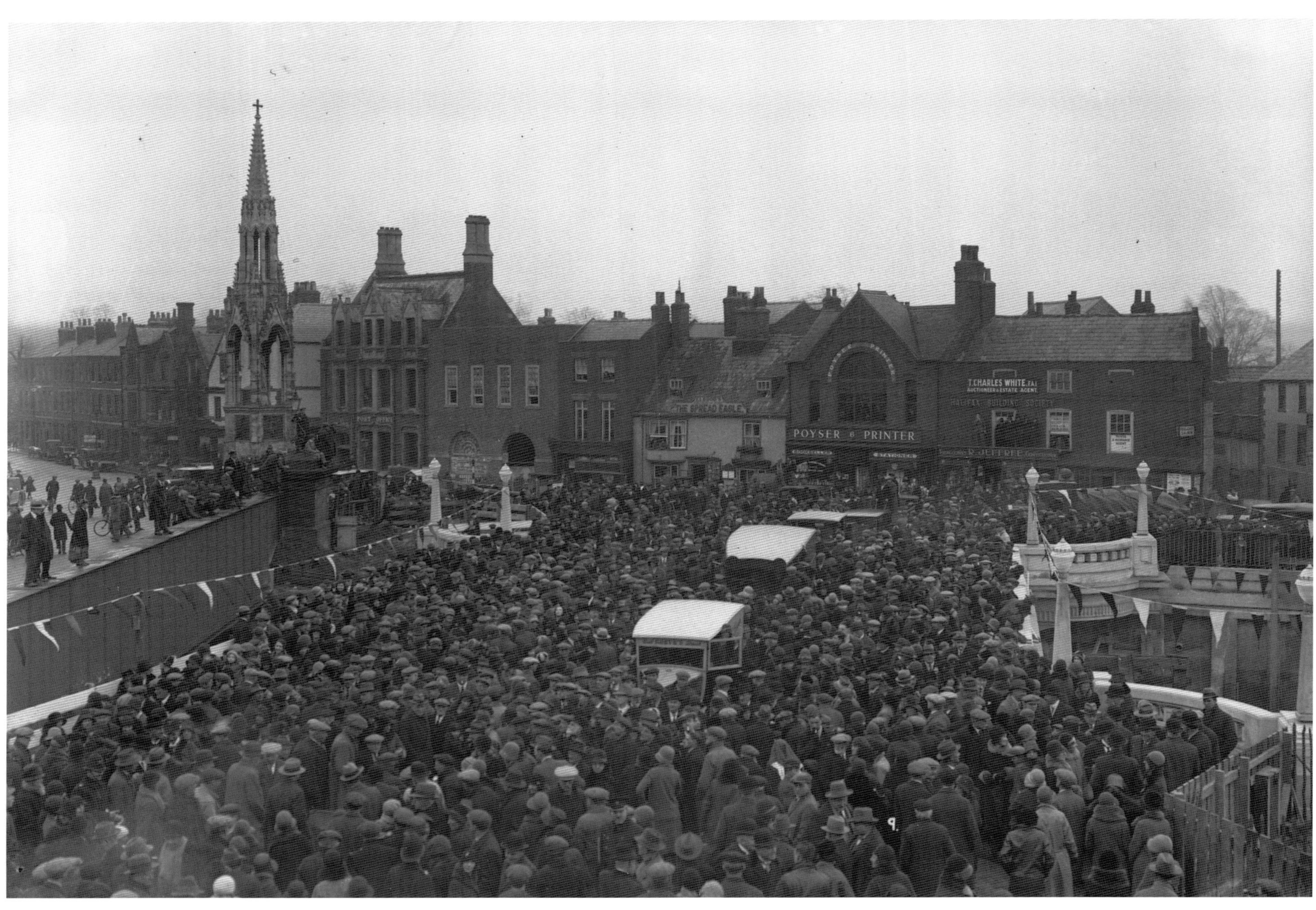

The opening of the new Wisbech Town Bridge on 4 February 1931. The opening was jointly performed by JE Sandall, Mayor of Wisbech, and Alderman HA Whittome, Chairman of the Isle of Ely Highways and Bridges Committee.

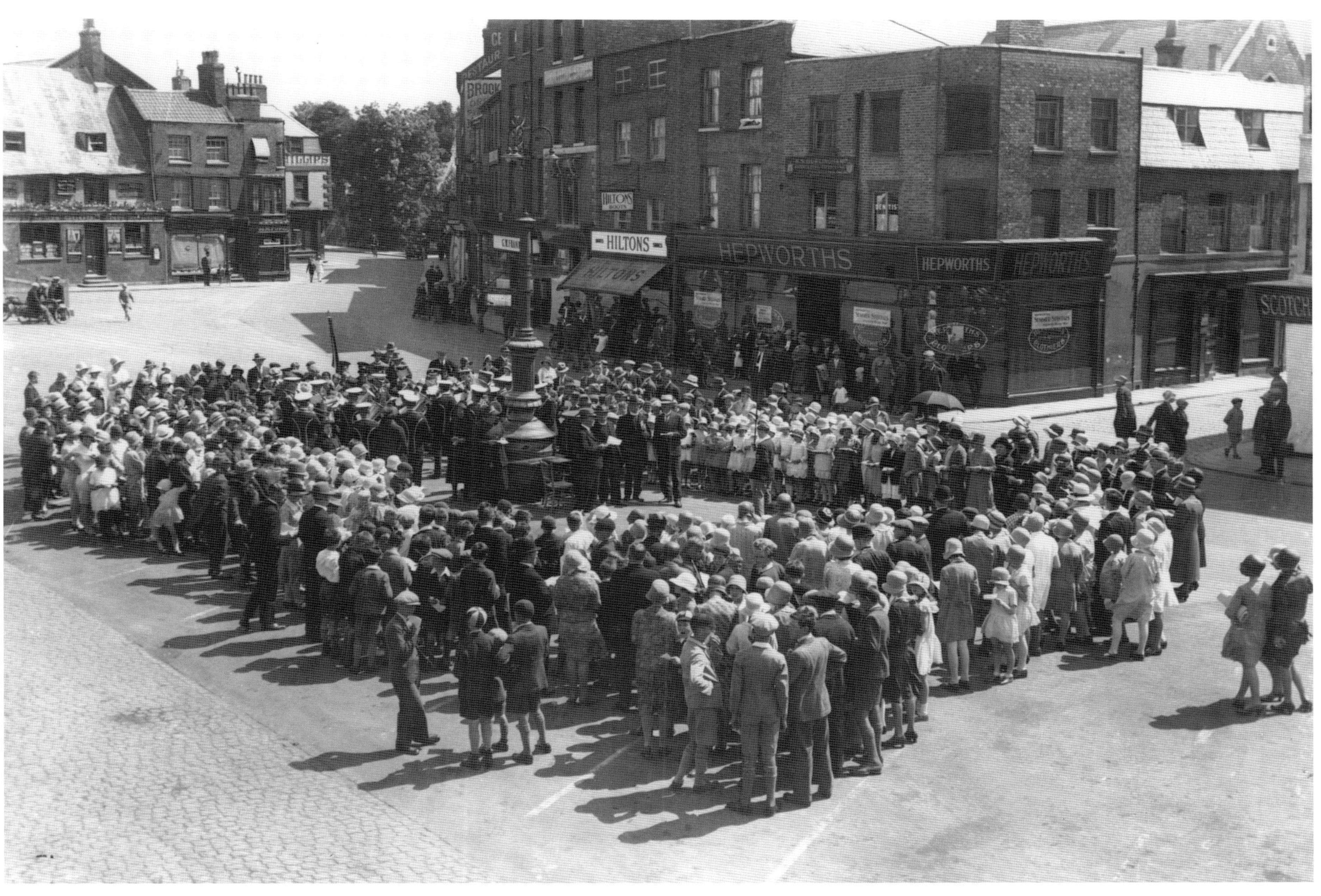

A service on the Market Place as part of a Sunday Schools Parade, 1920s. Of the shop frontages seen in the background only that of GW Franks butcher's shop remains virtually unchanged.

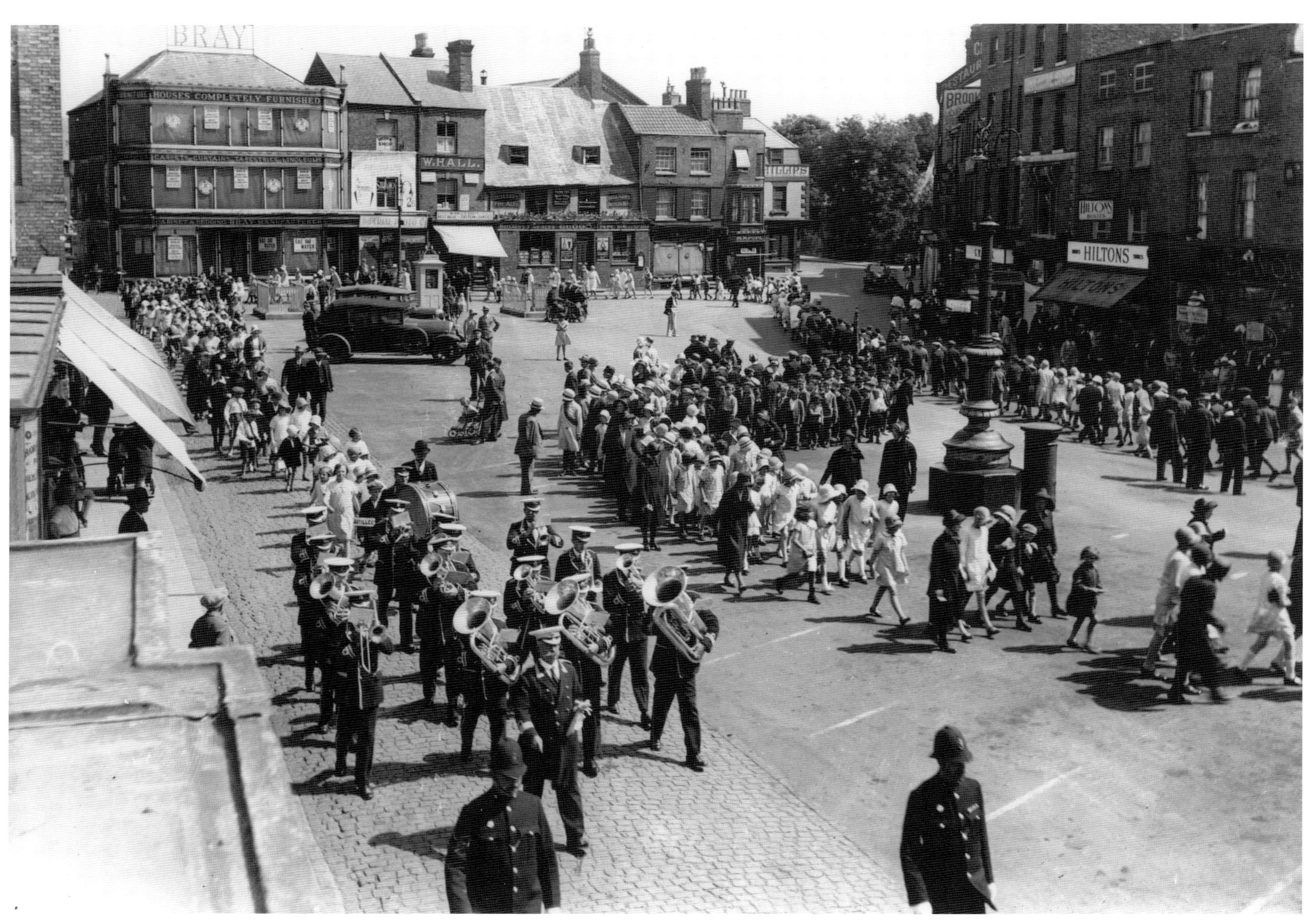

Sunday School Parade, Wisbech Market Place, late 1920s. In the foreground is the Wisbech Town Silver Band, led by its conductor, William Hall.

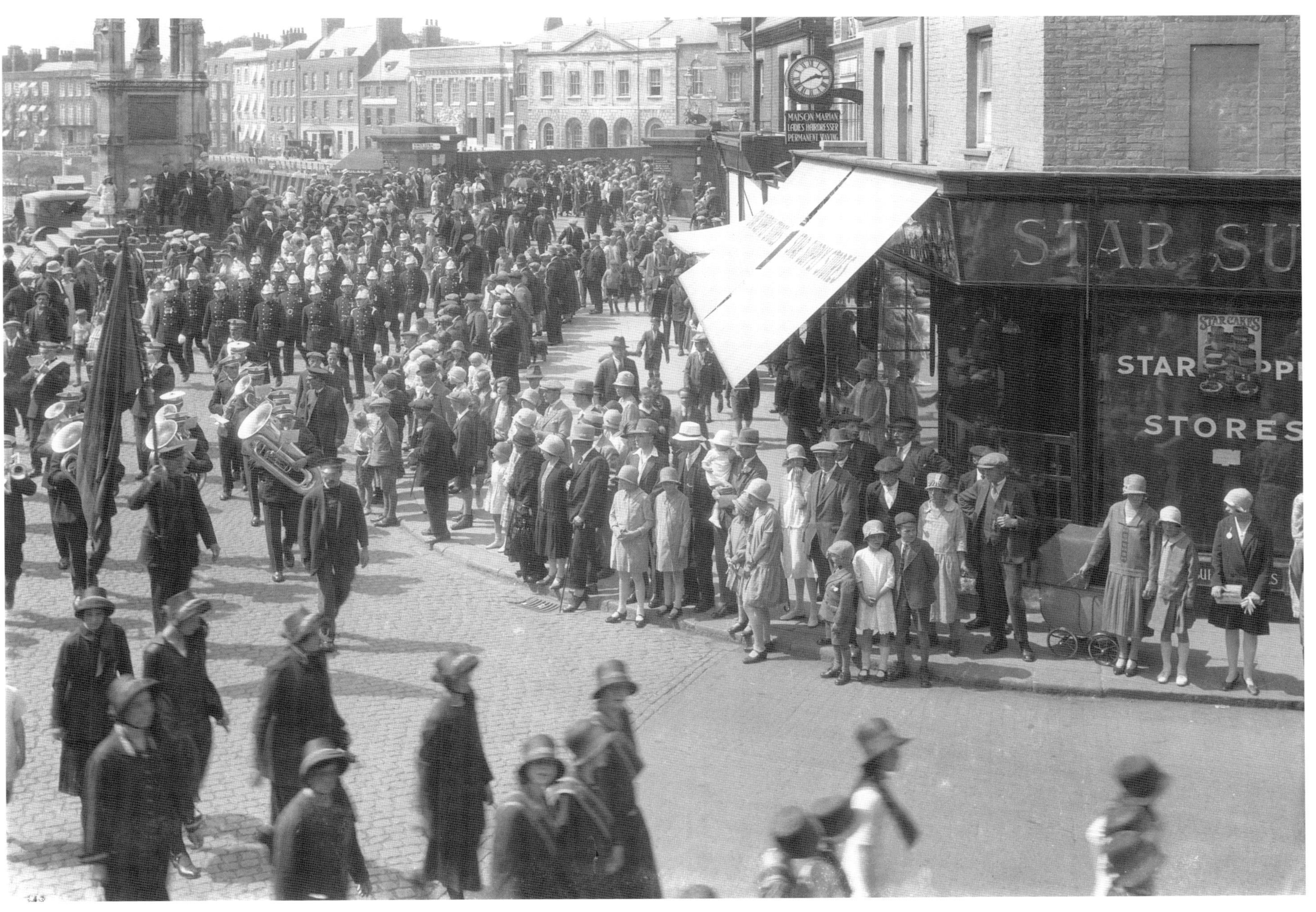

The Hospital Sunday Parade, Bridge Street, 1929. These events originated in the 1700s when funds were raised by a charity Sunday sermon to support local hospitals and later evolved into a fund-raising event to augment the income of the local voluntary hospitals.

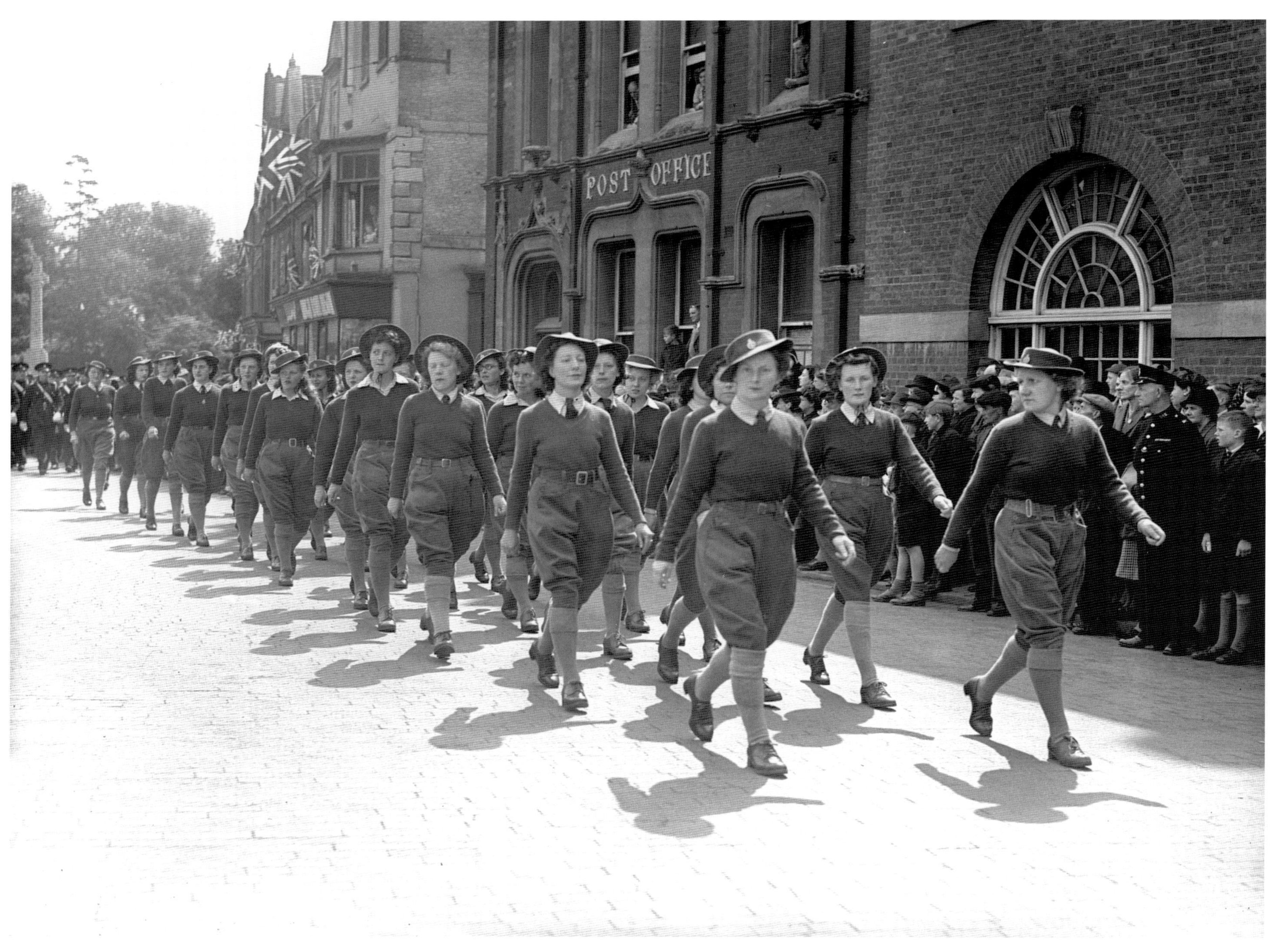

Members of the Women's Land Army marching near the Post Office, in Bridge Street, as part of the parade held to celebrate peace in 1945. Many of the women, who were part of a national force of over 80,000 women, married local men and settled in and around Wisbech.

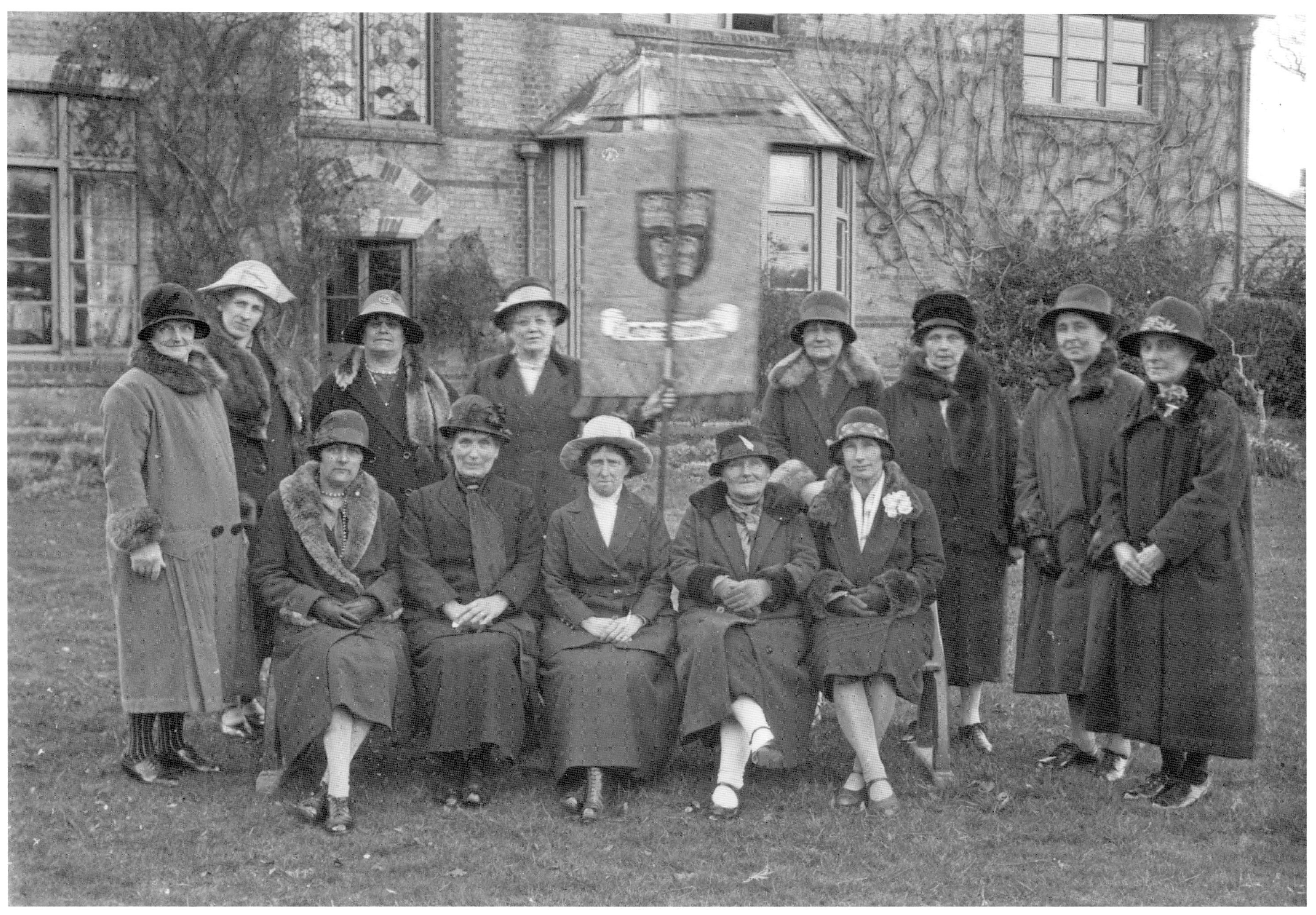

Elm Mothers' Union, 1920s.

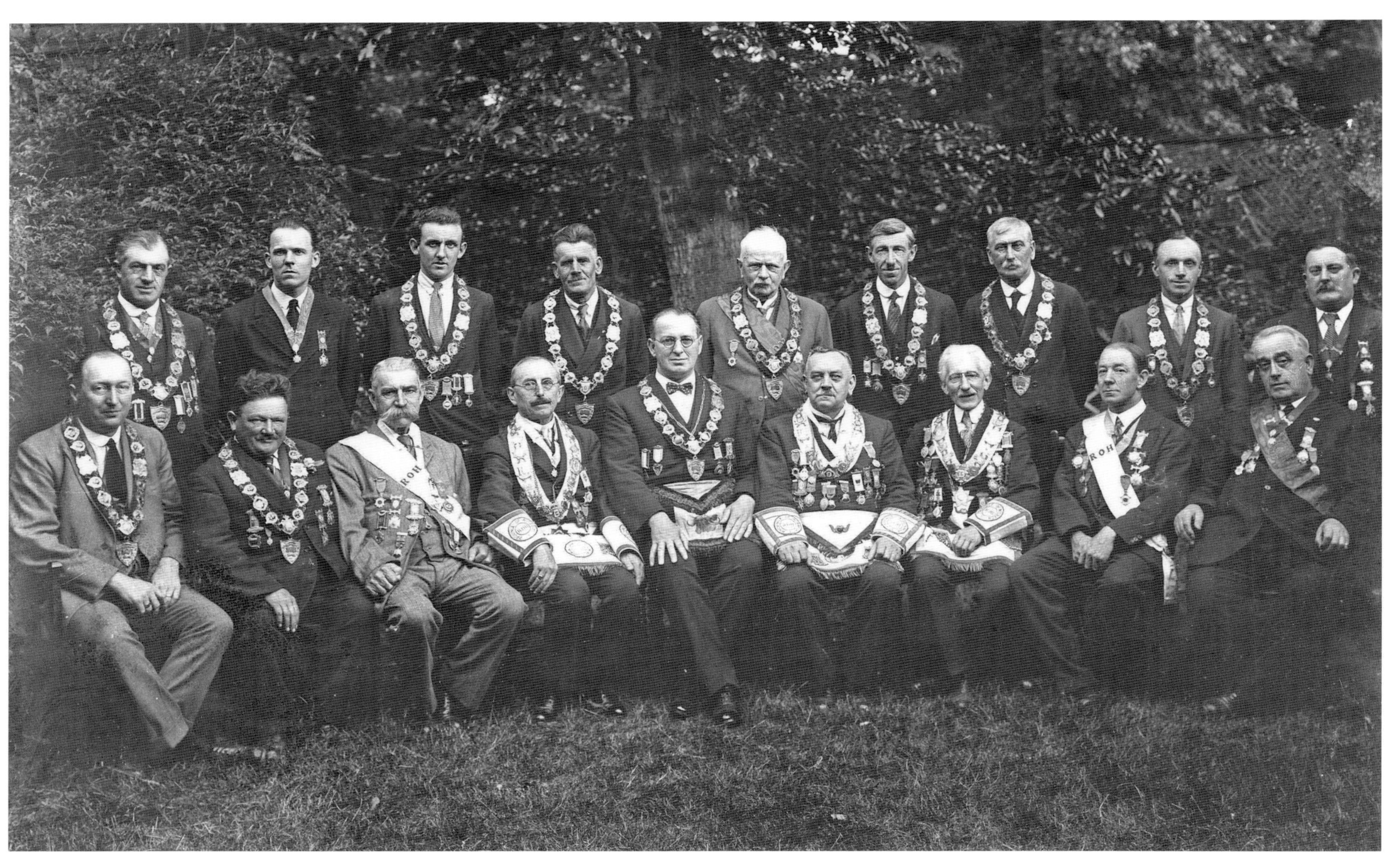

The officers of the Royal Antediluvian Order of Buffaloes, resplendent with their official regalia, 1930s. Wisbech had many different Friendly and Fraternal Societies such as the Oddfellows, Shepherds, Masons and Foresters.

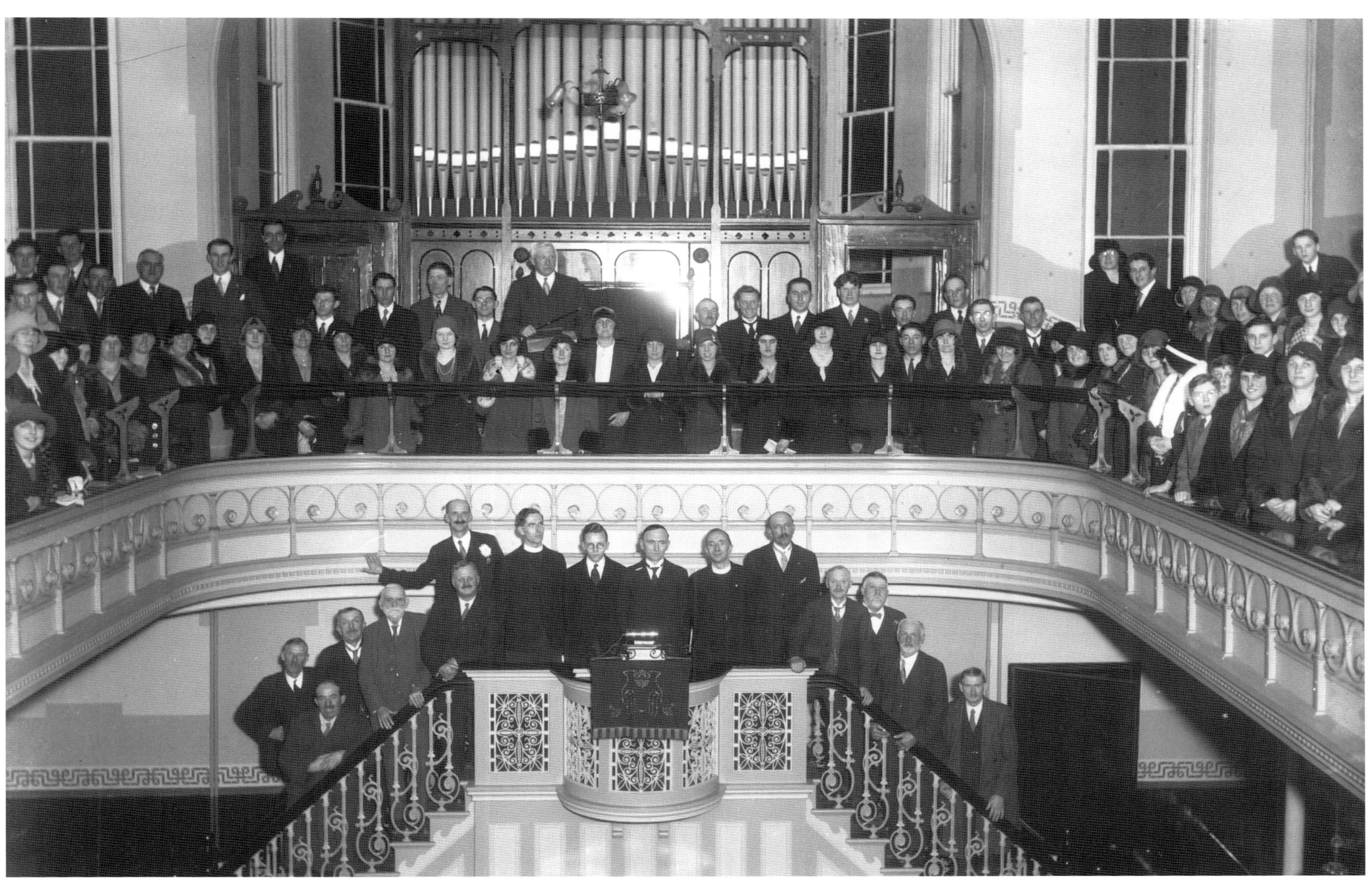

A gathering of the congregation of the Wisbech Primitive Methodists in their chapel in Church Terrace, 1920s. The chapel was replaced by the present Trinity Methodist Chapel in 1969.

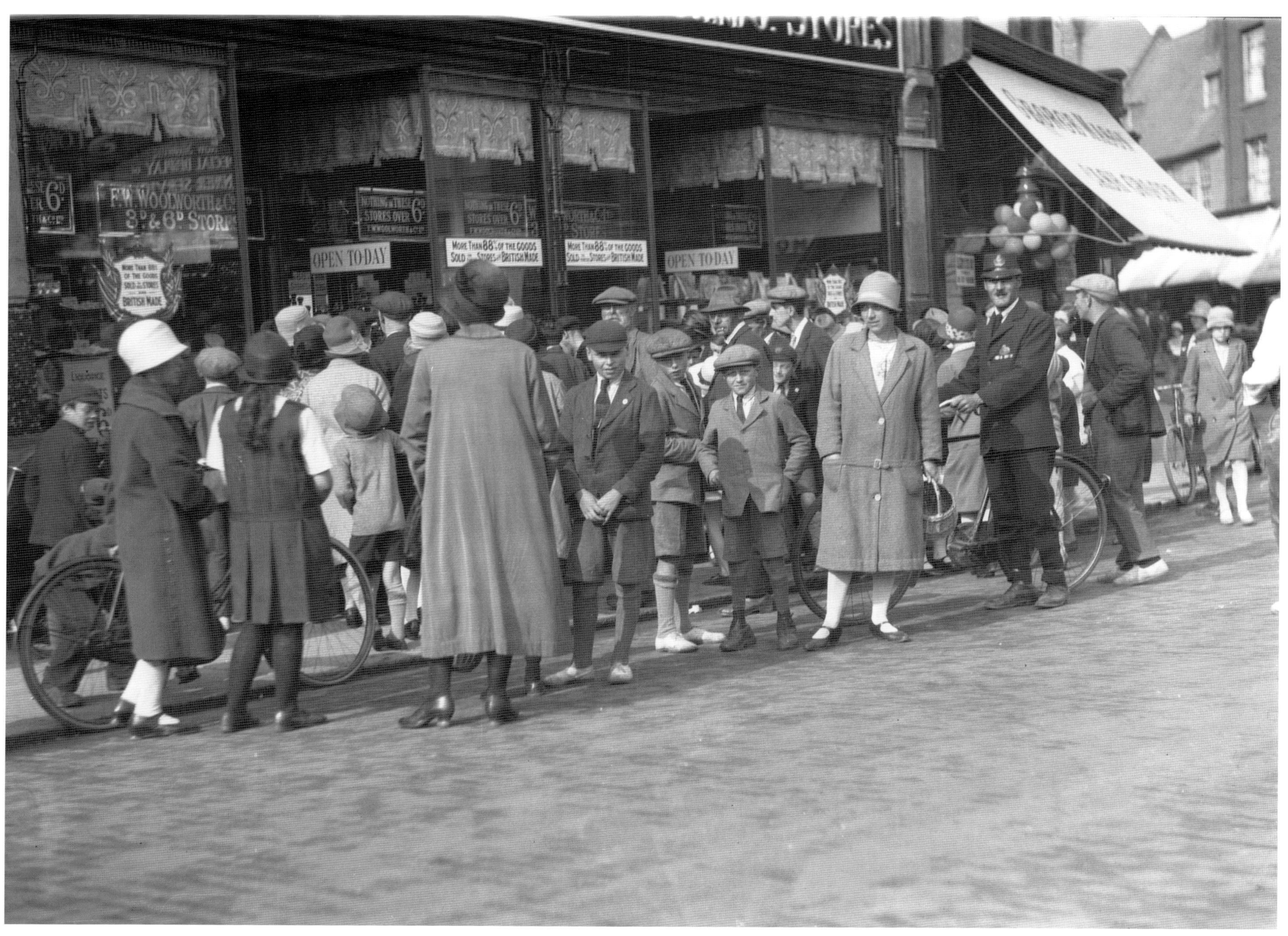

Crowds gather outside the new FW Woolworth store on Market Place for its opening in 1928. The original fixed discount store, Woolworths guaranteed stock which did not cost above 6d and of which 88% was made in Britain.

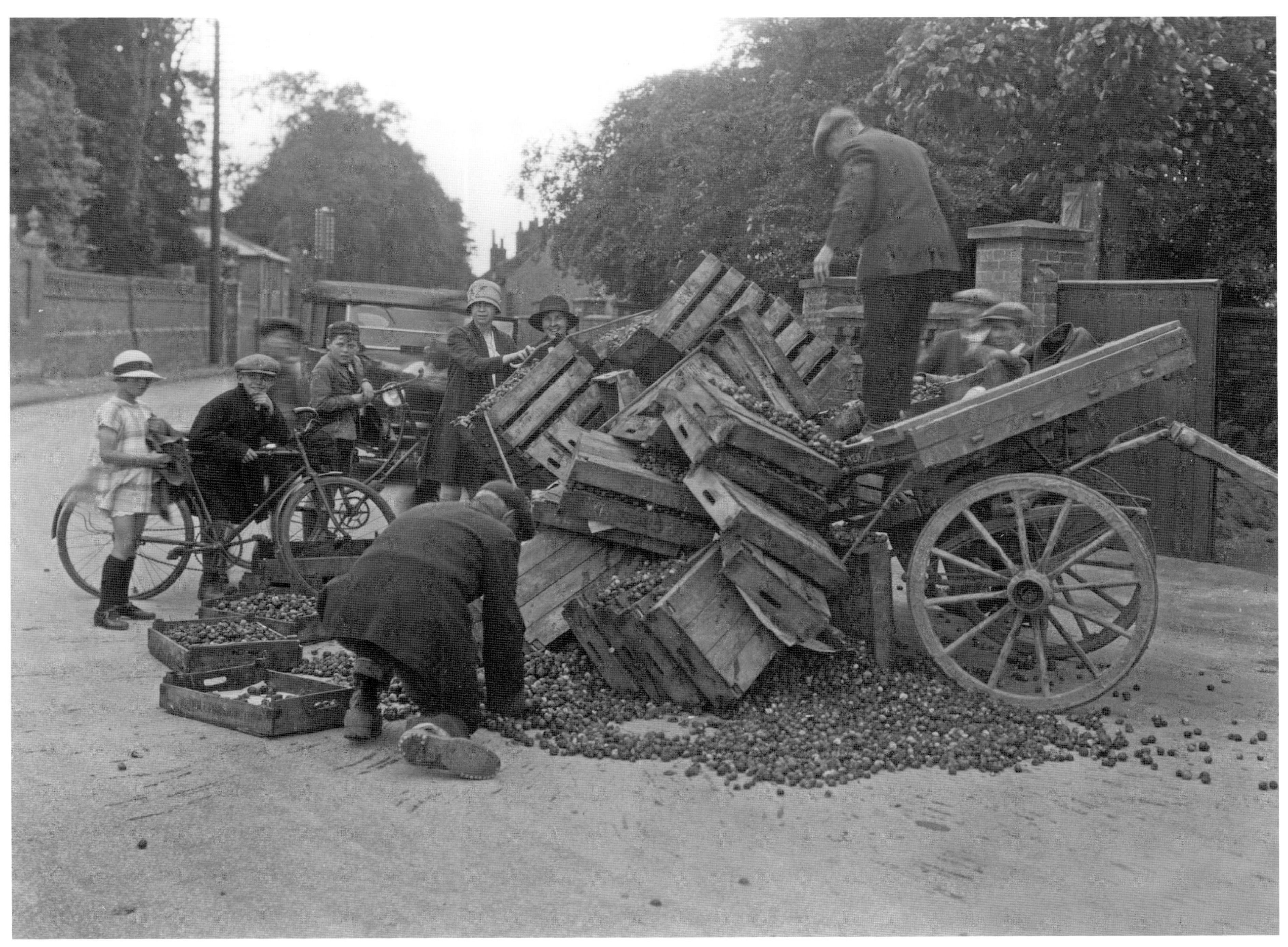

A cart laden with strawberries has collapsed, much to the amusement of the watching children.

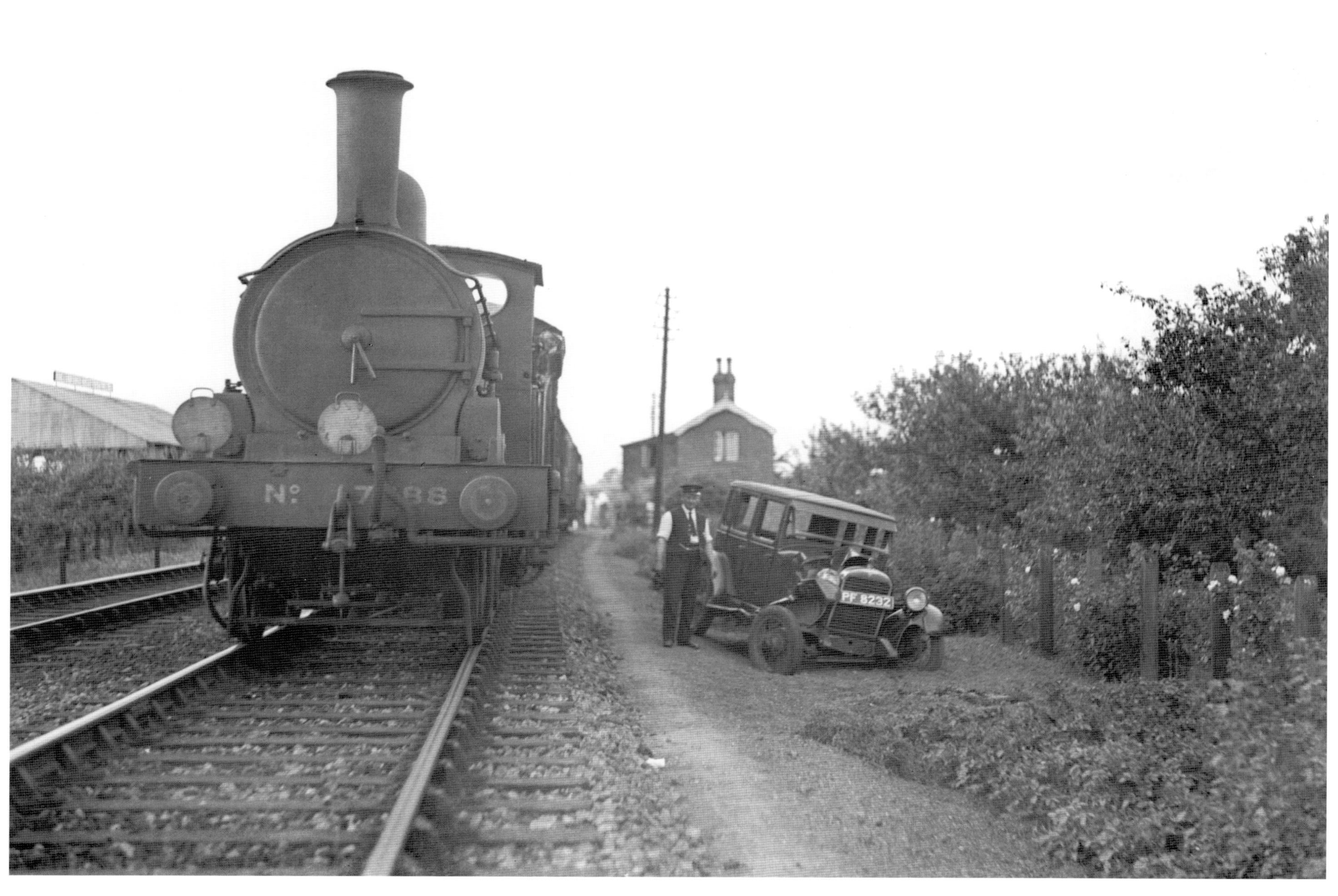

 The aftermath of a crash near the Weasenham Lane railway crossing, 1934.

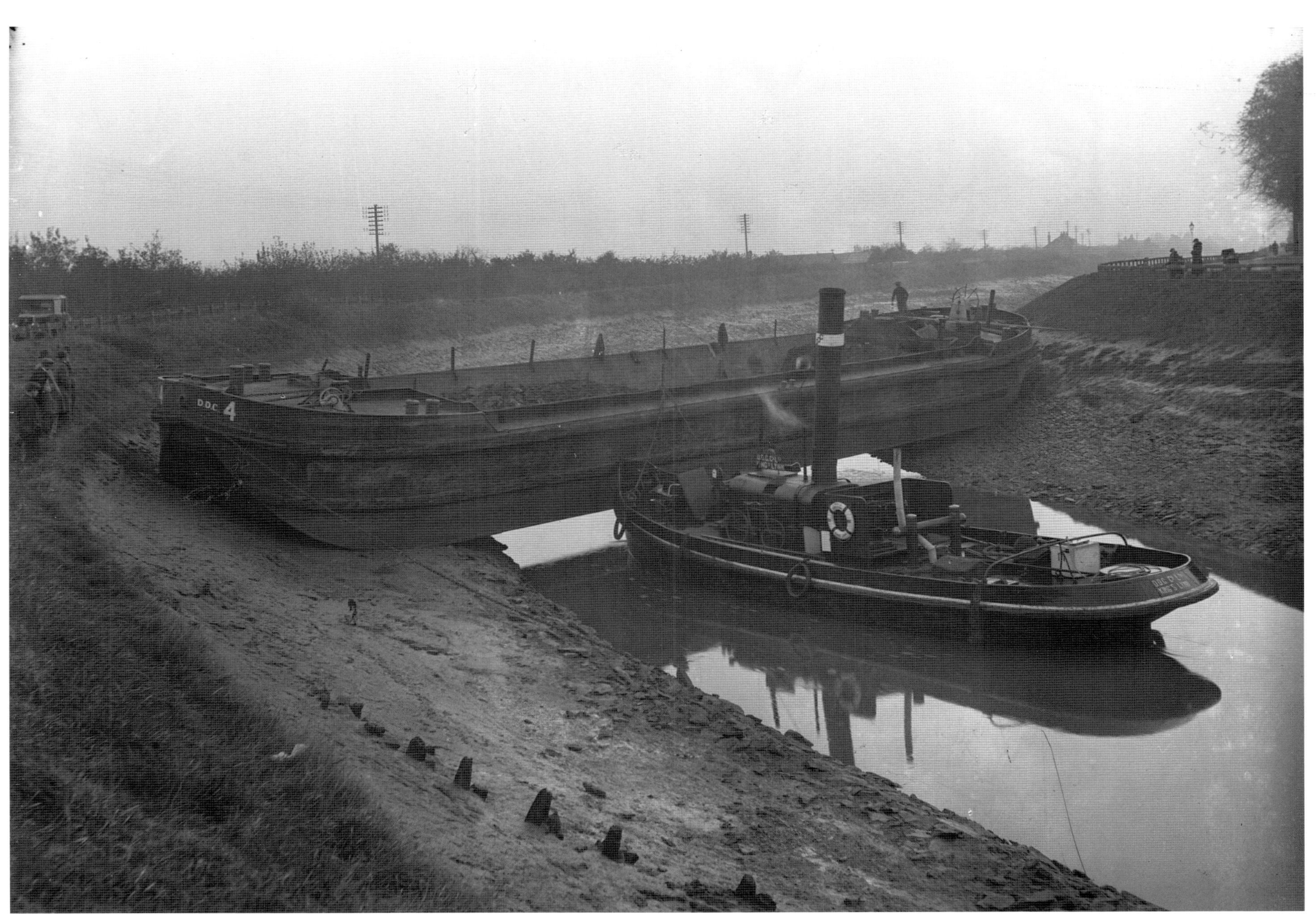

A barge laden with coal stuck across the bend in the River Nene, near Elgoods Brewery, 7 November 1934. The barge had been travelling down the river on an ebb tide when its bow struck the South Brink bank and the fast running tide pushed the stern onto the opposite bank. Despite the efforts of a tug of the Draining, Dredging and Construction Co. of King's Lynn, the barge was not freed until the tide rose in the evening.

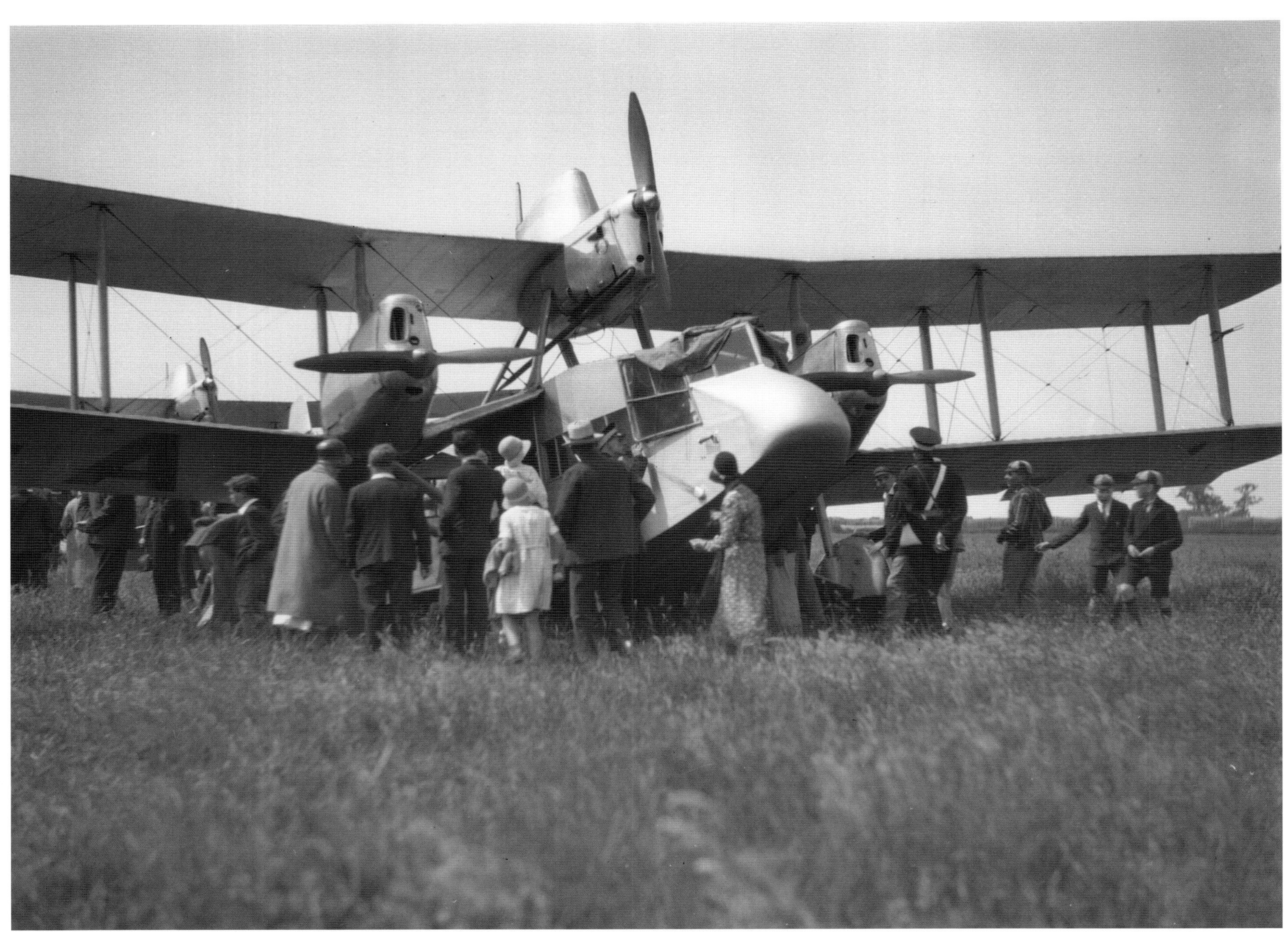

Children and adults examining one of the aeroplanes of Alan Cobham's Flying Circus, Wheatley Bank, Lynn Road, June 1933. The aeroplane is an Airspeed Ferry, G-ABSJ and was used to provide joyrides for the public.

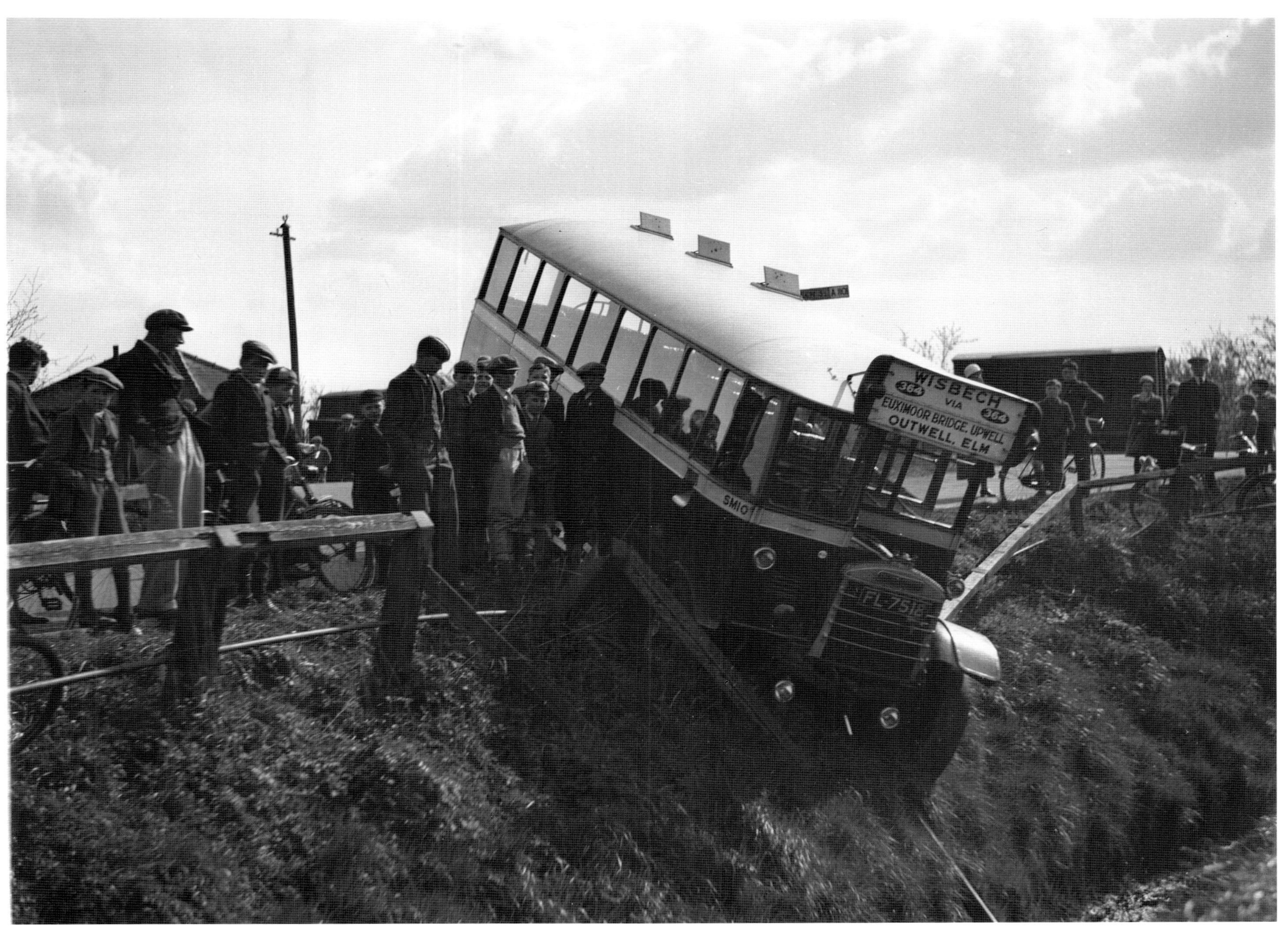

An intrigued crowd viewing the aftermath of an accident, which left an omnibus balanced precariously on the bank of a dyke at Bird's Corner, Emneth, Sunday 22 April 1934. The bus was travelling from Christchurch to Wisbech, when it encountered another bus coming the other way; fortunately, the driver, conductor and solitary passenger escaped unscathed.

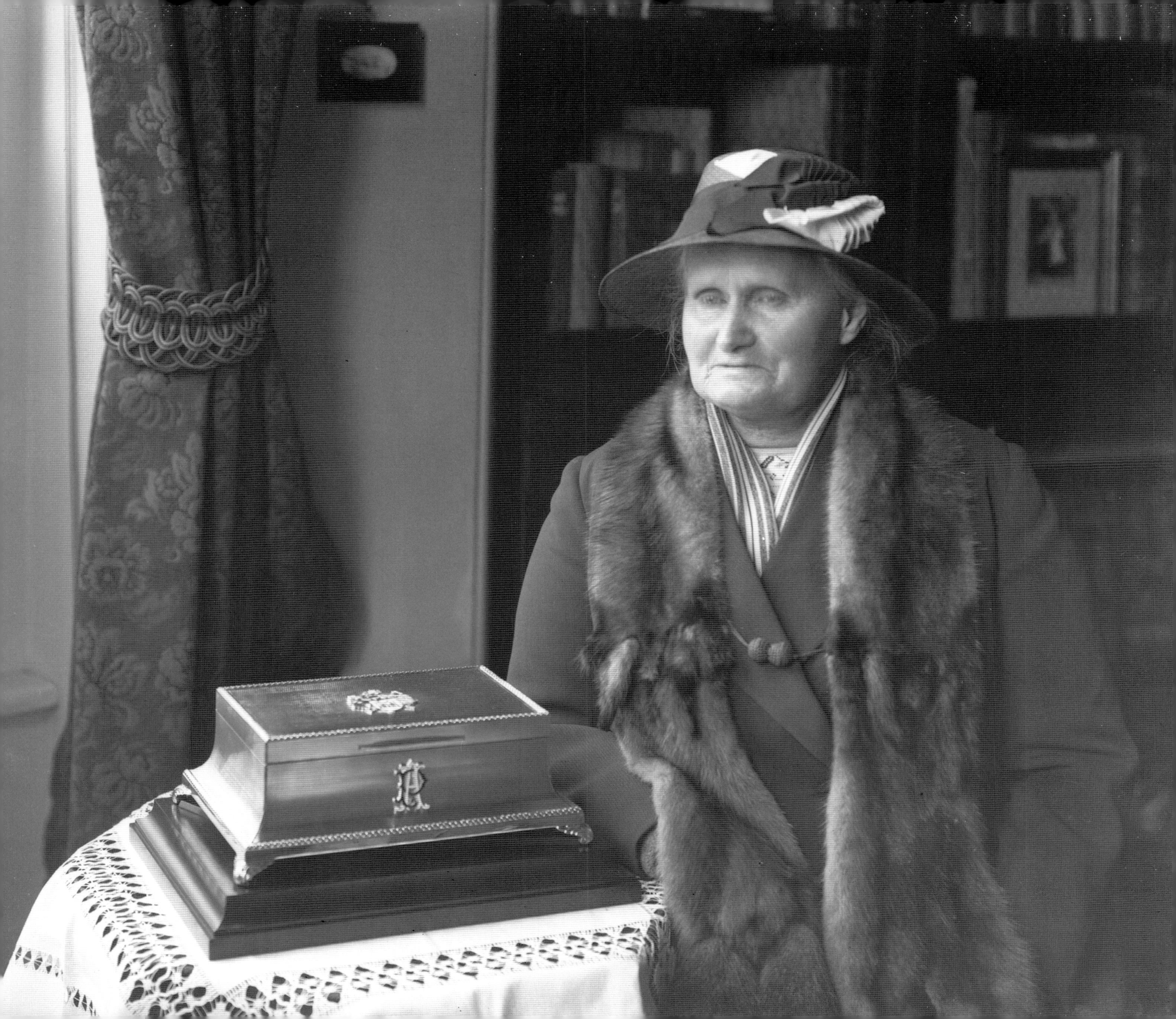

People

The Hon. Alexandrina Peckover, Bank House (later Peckover House), 1934. On the table, is a casket, bearing her initials and the Borough arms, which contains the illuminate resolution presented to her on being made Freeman of the Borough of Wisbech in March, 1934.

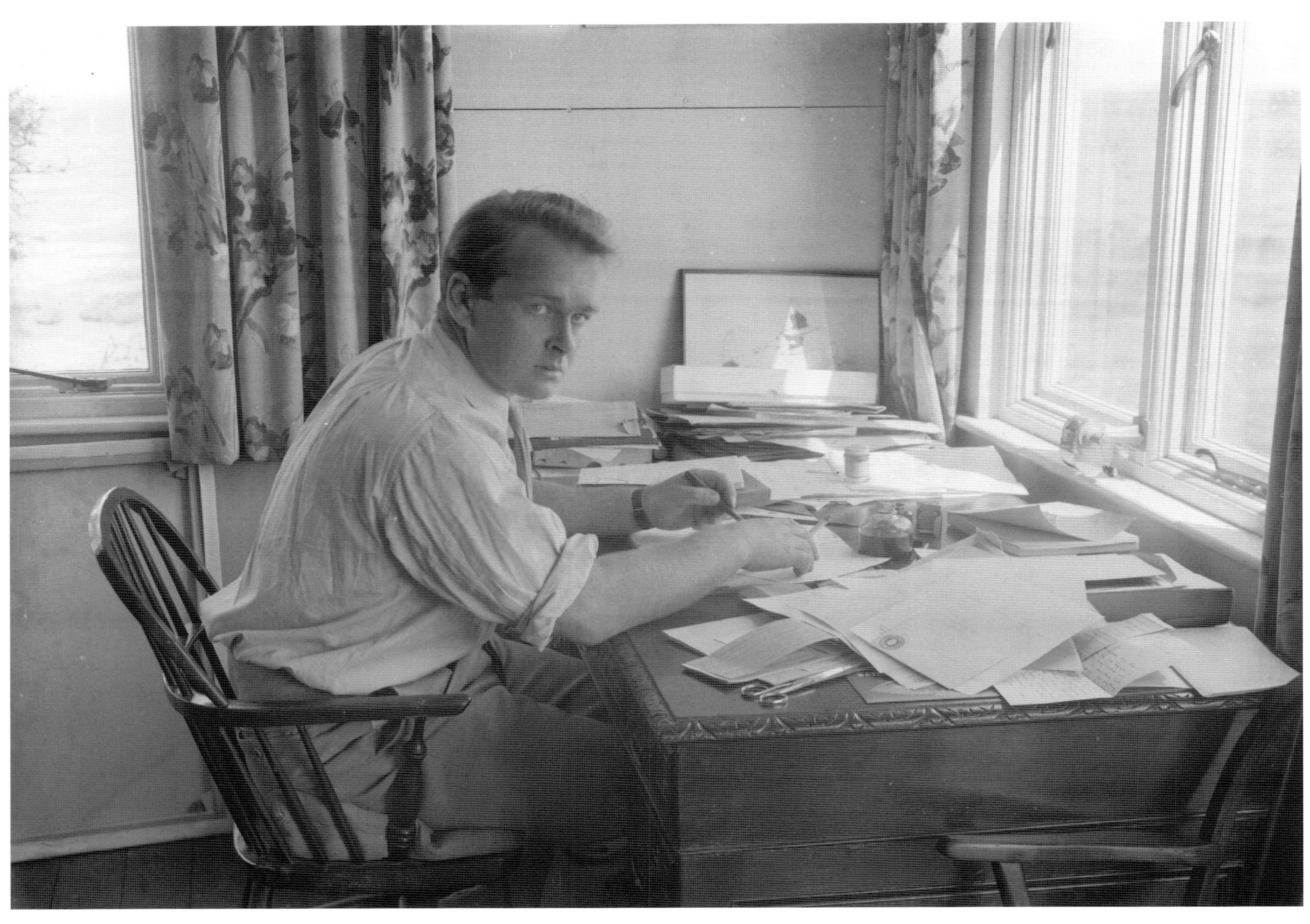

(Sir) Peter Scott, ornithologist, painter and son of Antarctic explorer, Robert Falcon Scott, at Sutton Bridge, 1930s.

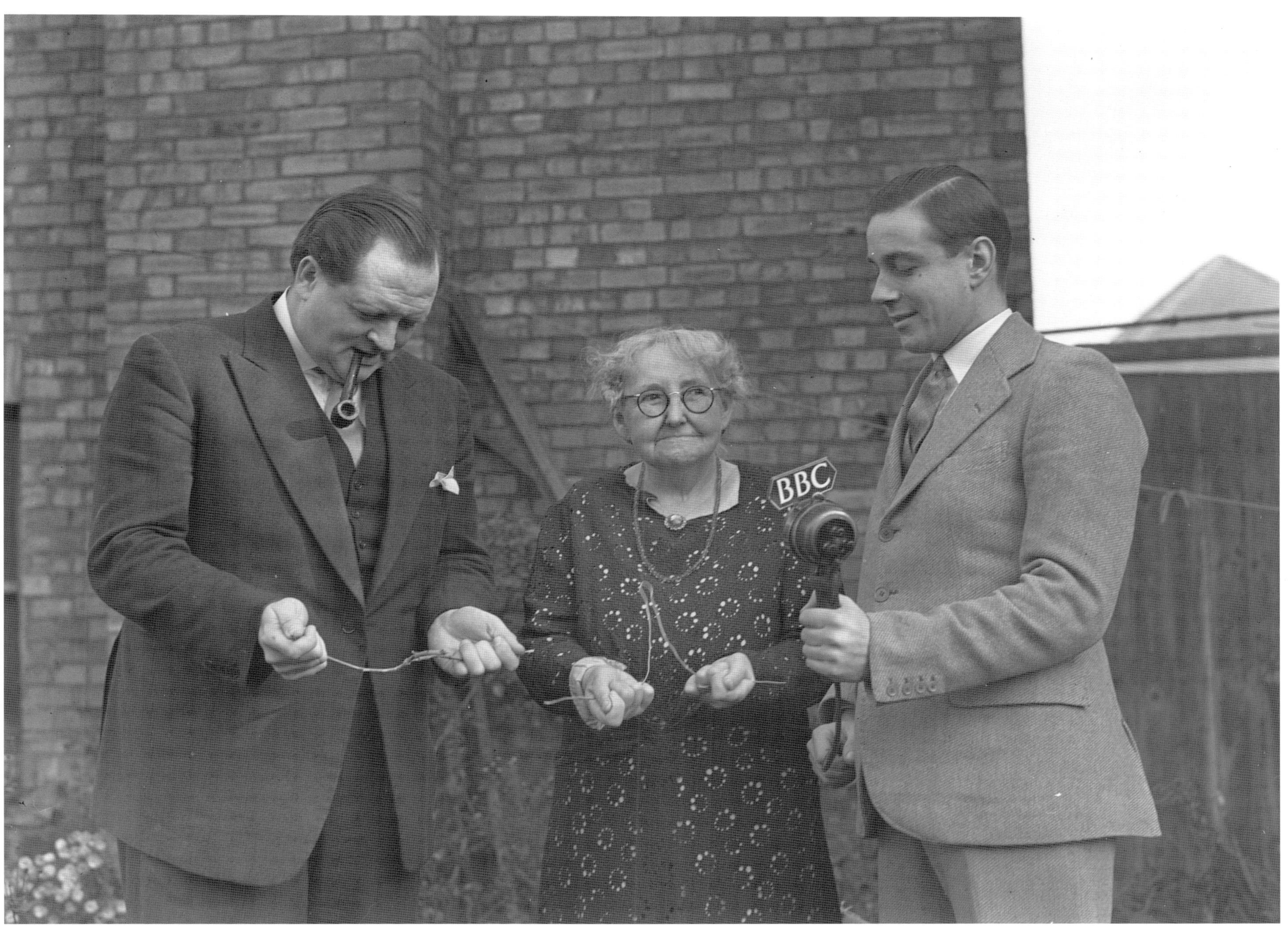

Richard Dimbleby trying his hand at water divining for the radio show, 'Down Your Way', 1949.

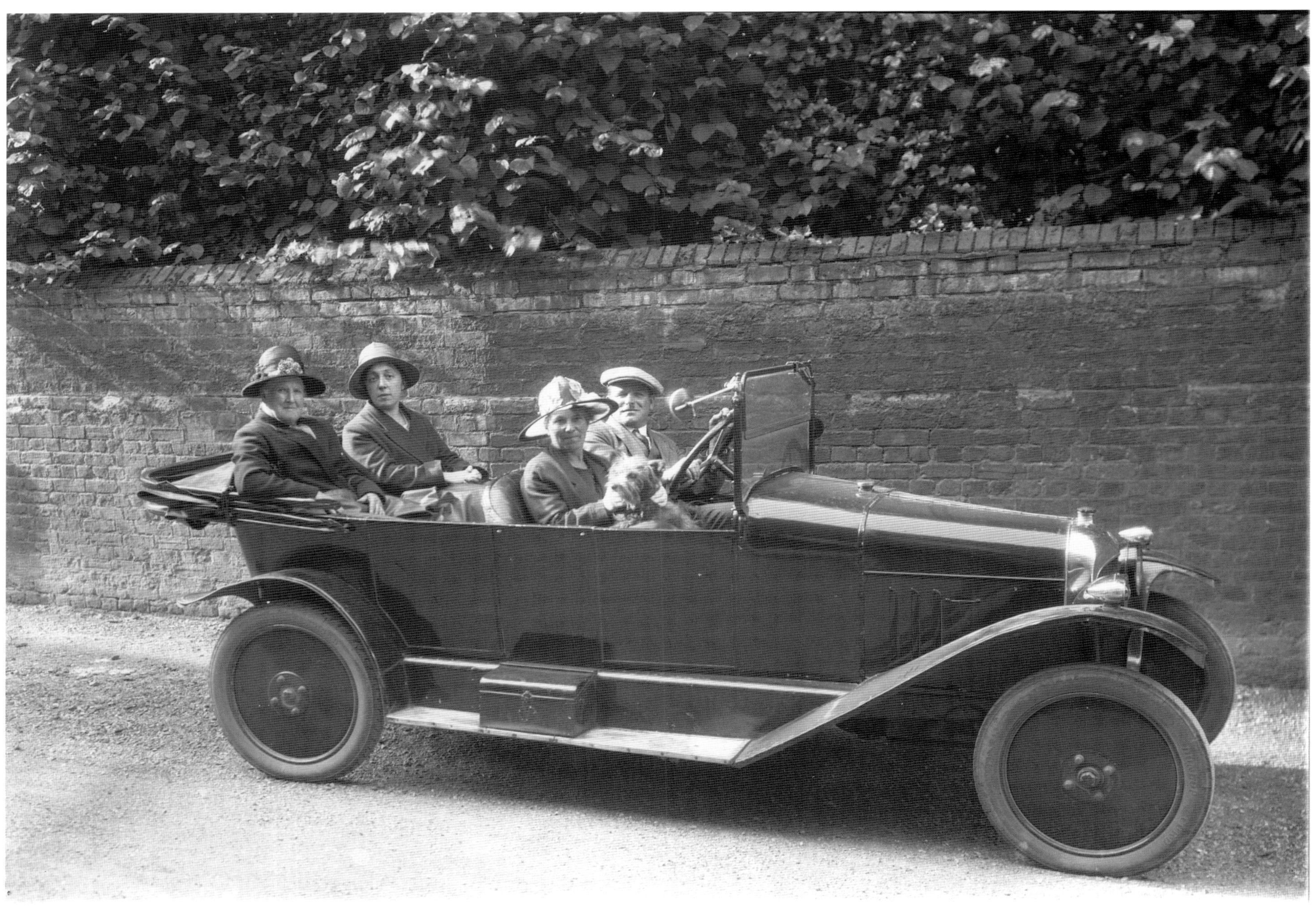

 An outing in a new car is captured for posterity.

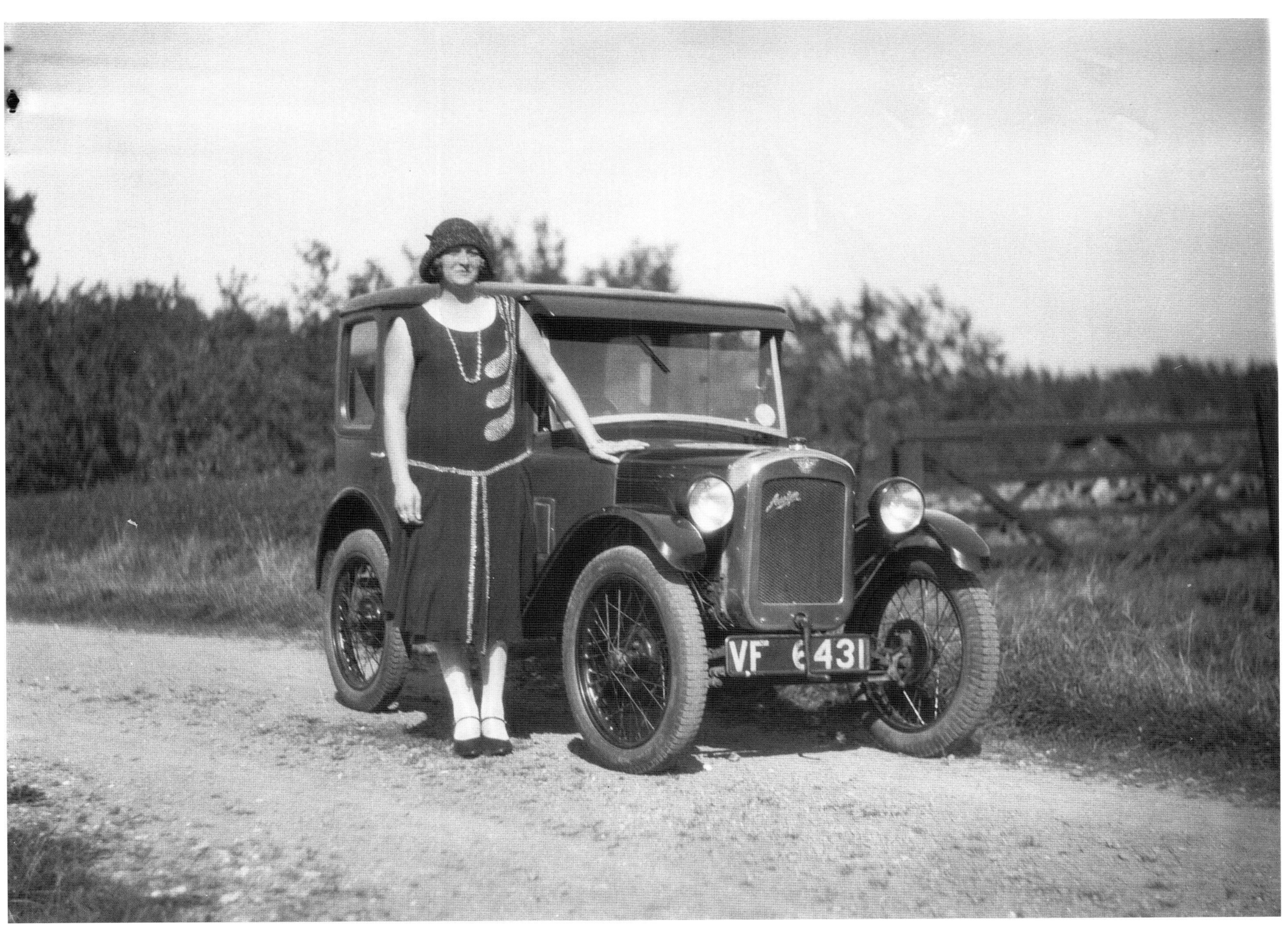

A proud owner standing beside her Austin 7, 1930.

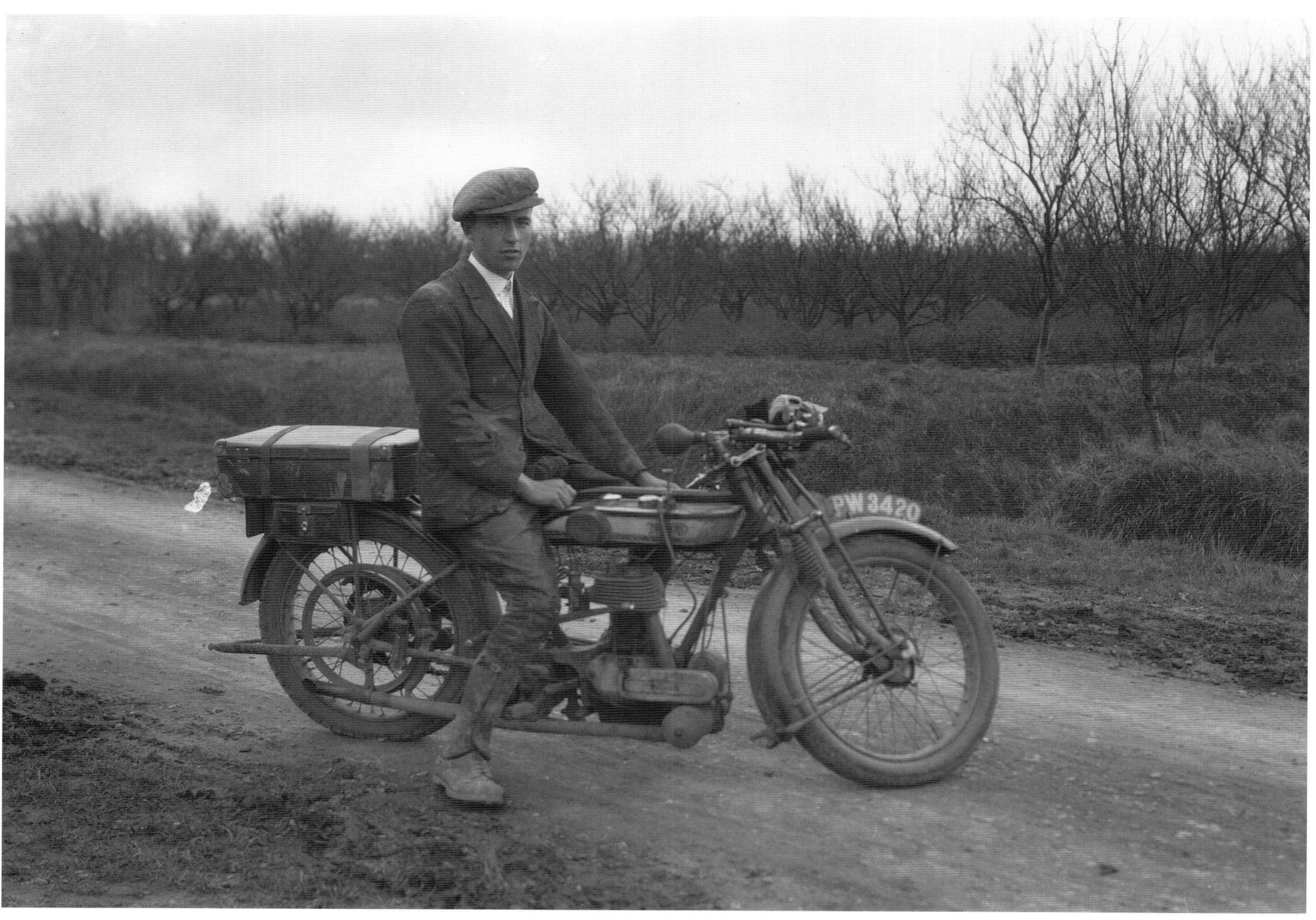

 Mr Spratt on his motorcycle, 1927.

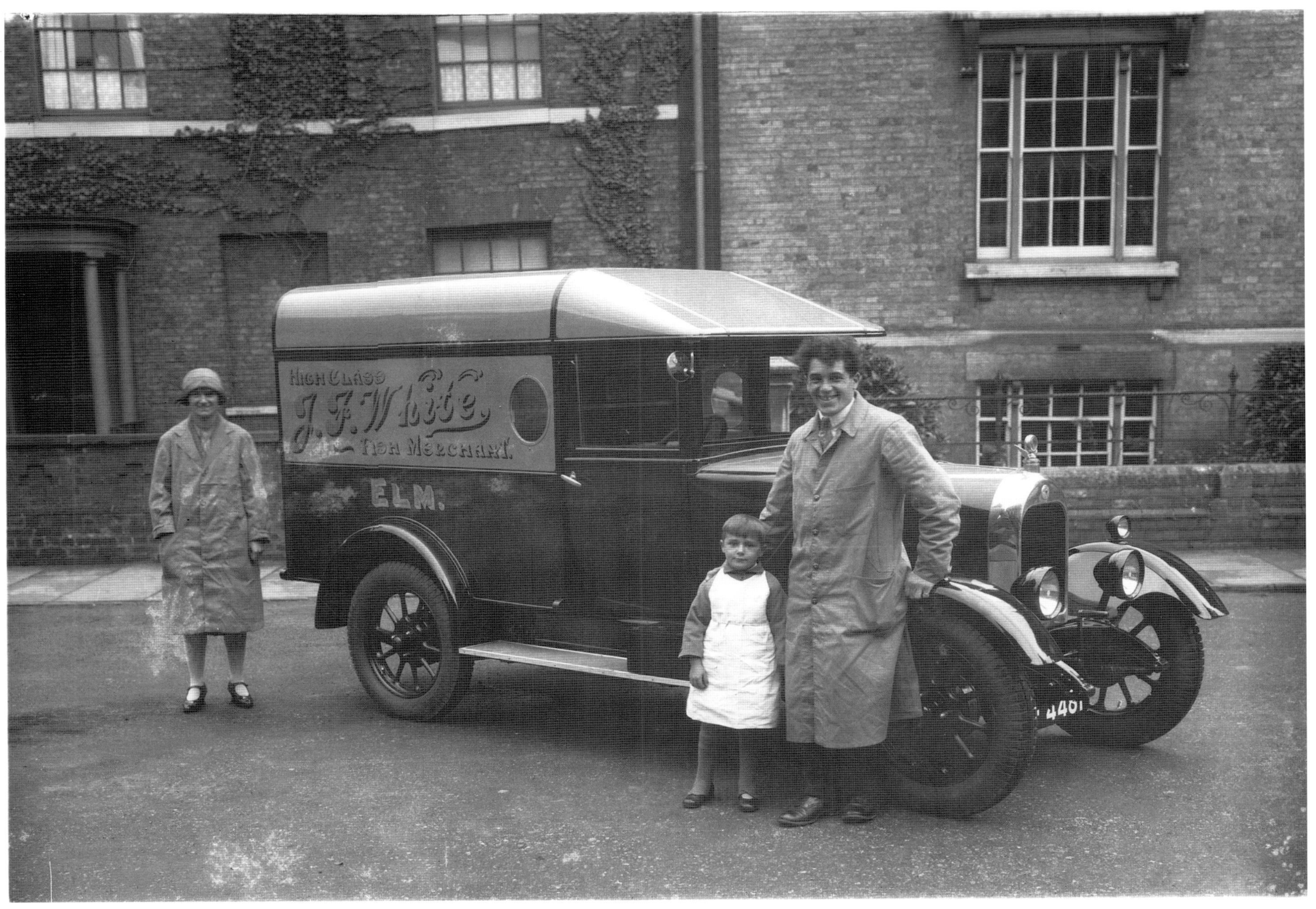

The delivery van of JF White, High Class Fish Merchant, Elm, in Museum Square, 1929.

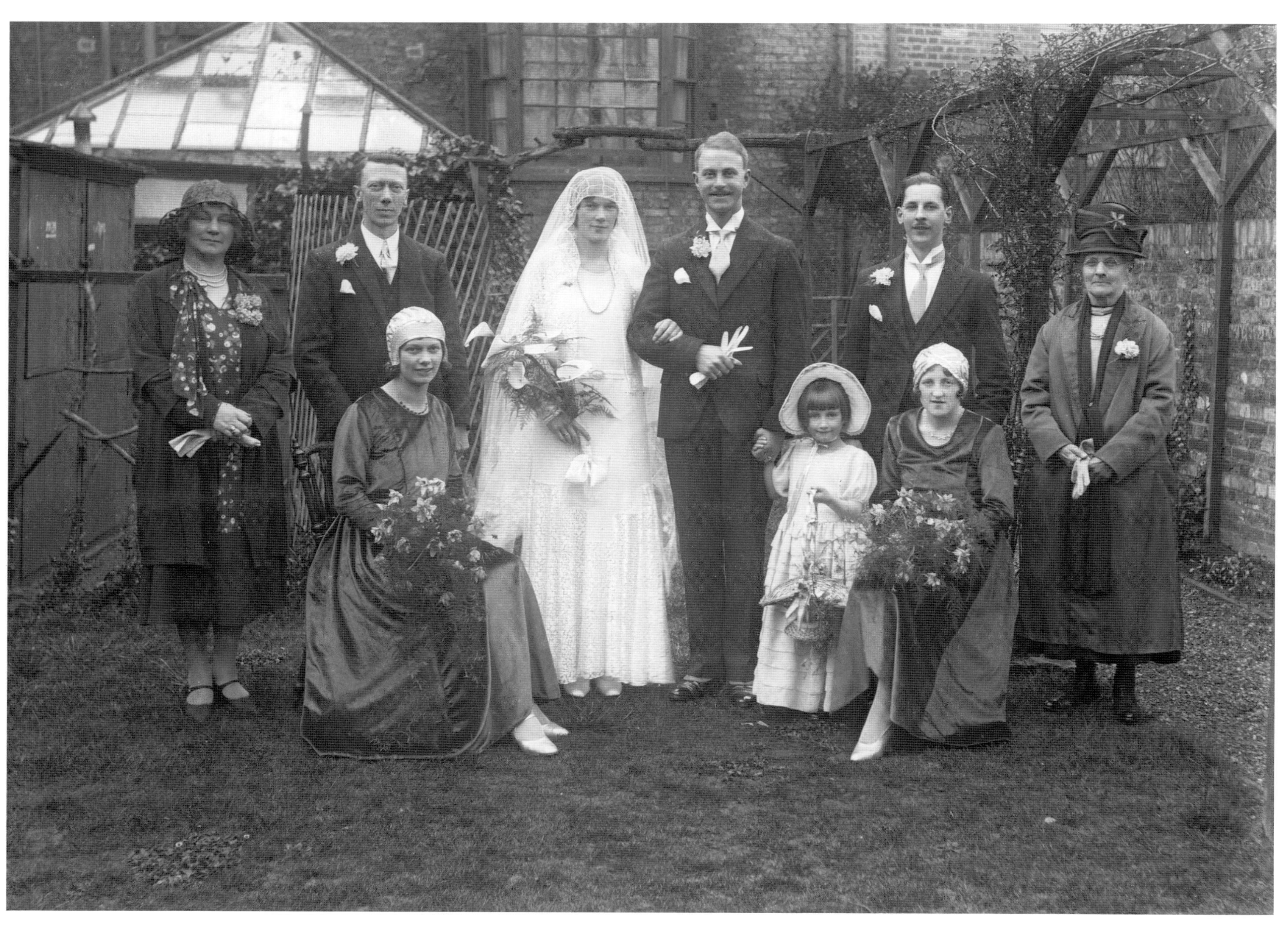

 A group photograph at the wedding of William Fleet Husan, journalist of Spilsby, Lincolnshire, and Florence Muriel Skelton, spinster, of Market Place, Wisbech, 23 April 1930.

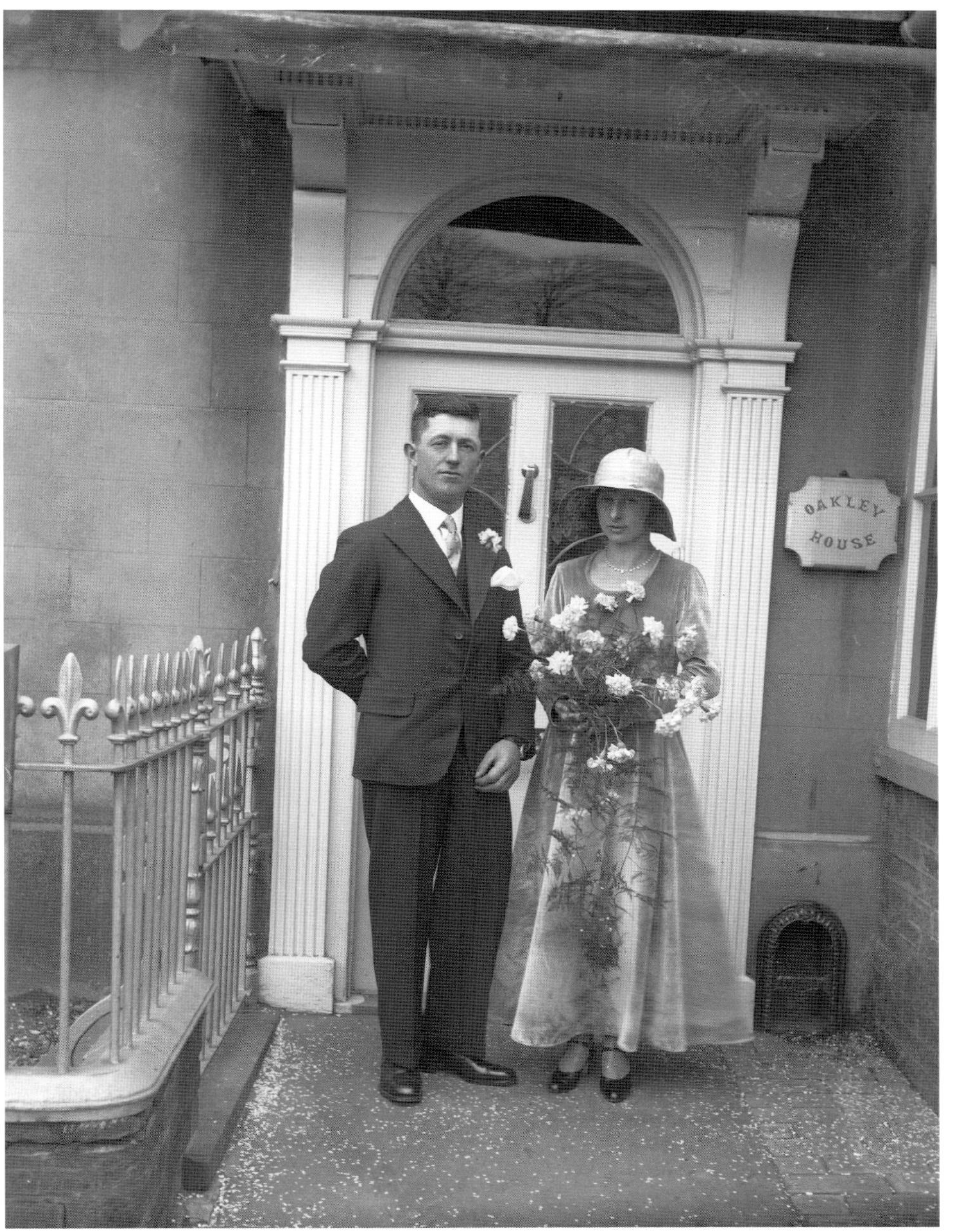

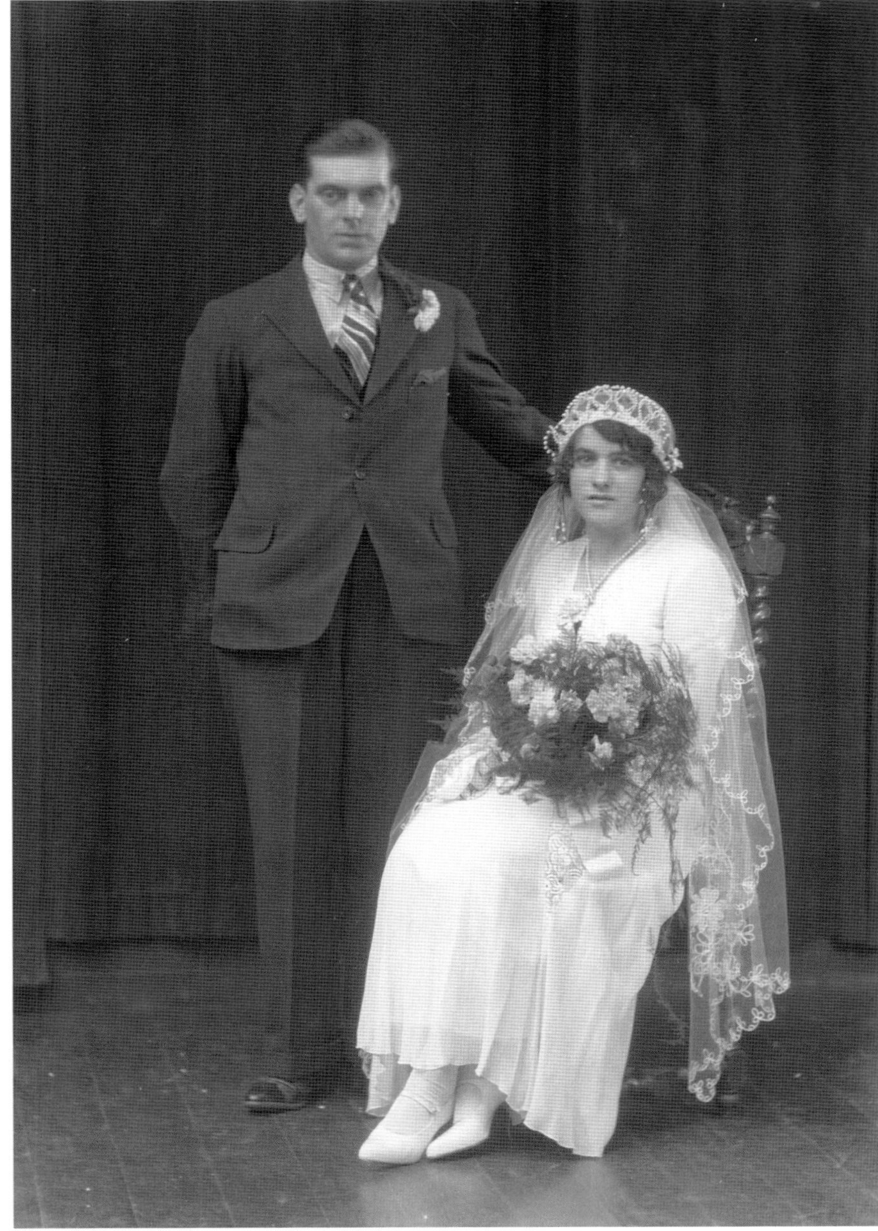

Wedding photographs from the archive.

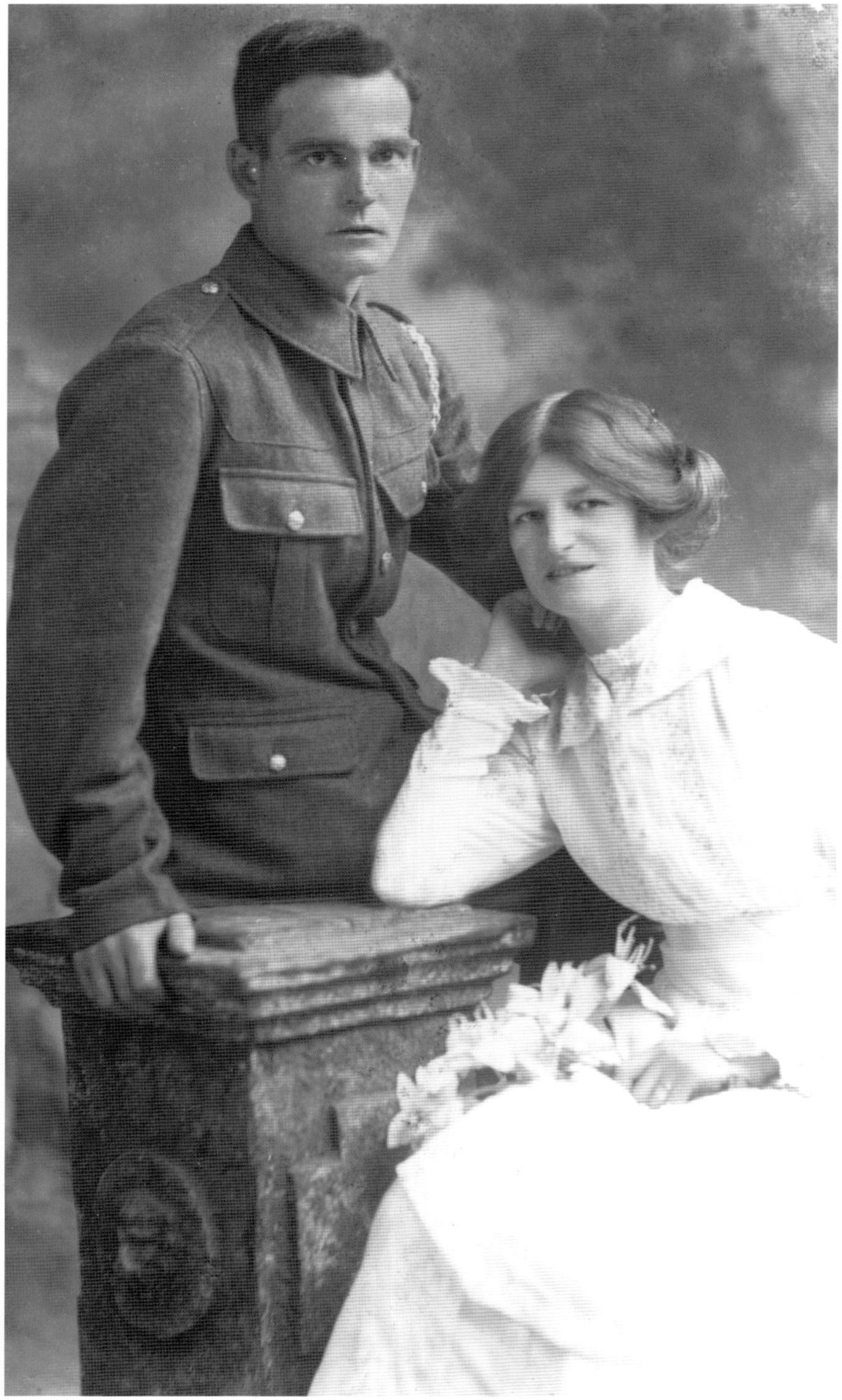

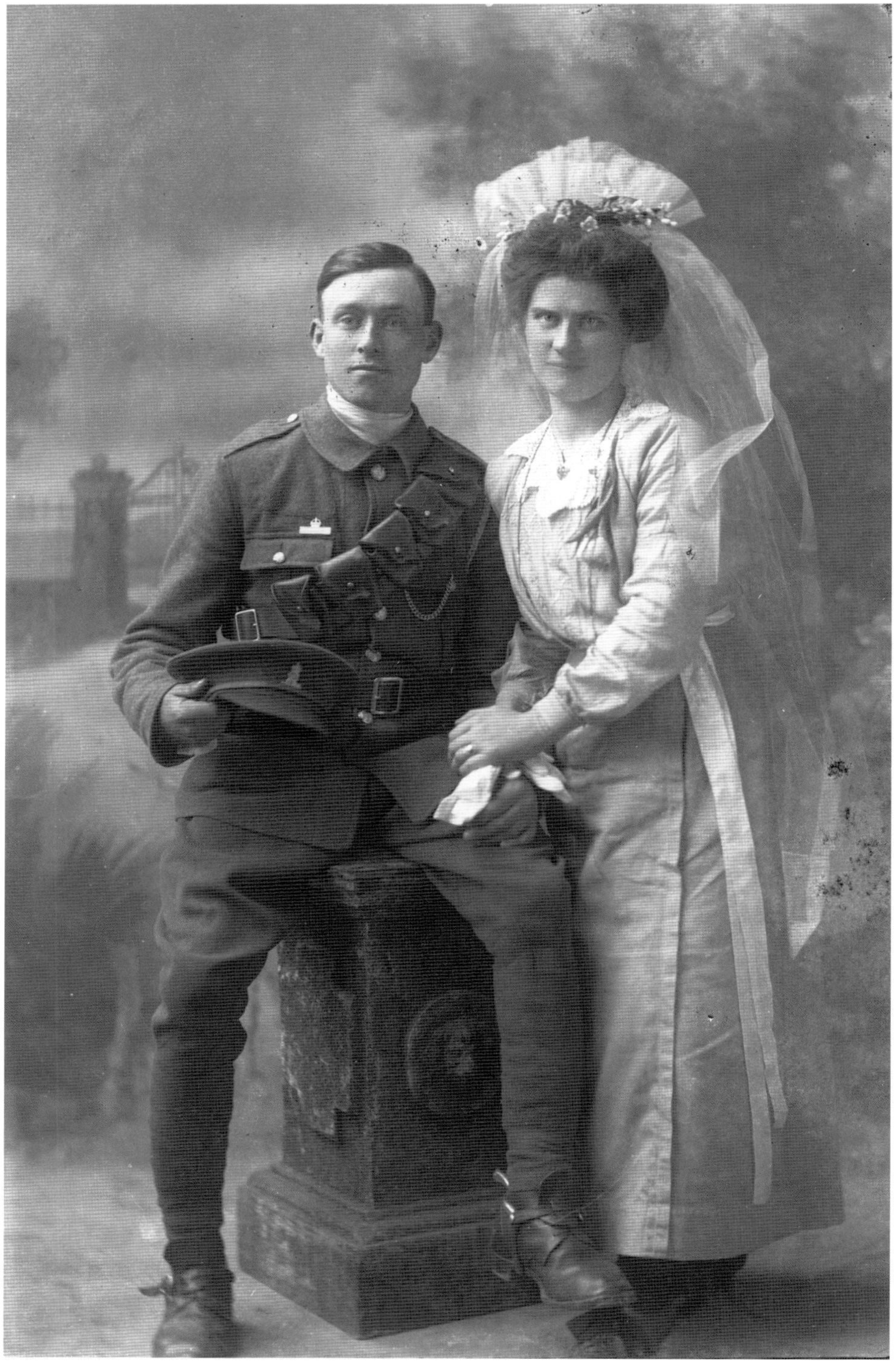

152 Unknown sitters, probably photographed during World War I.

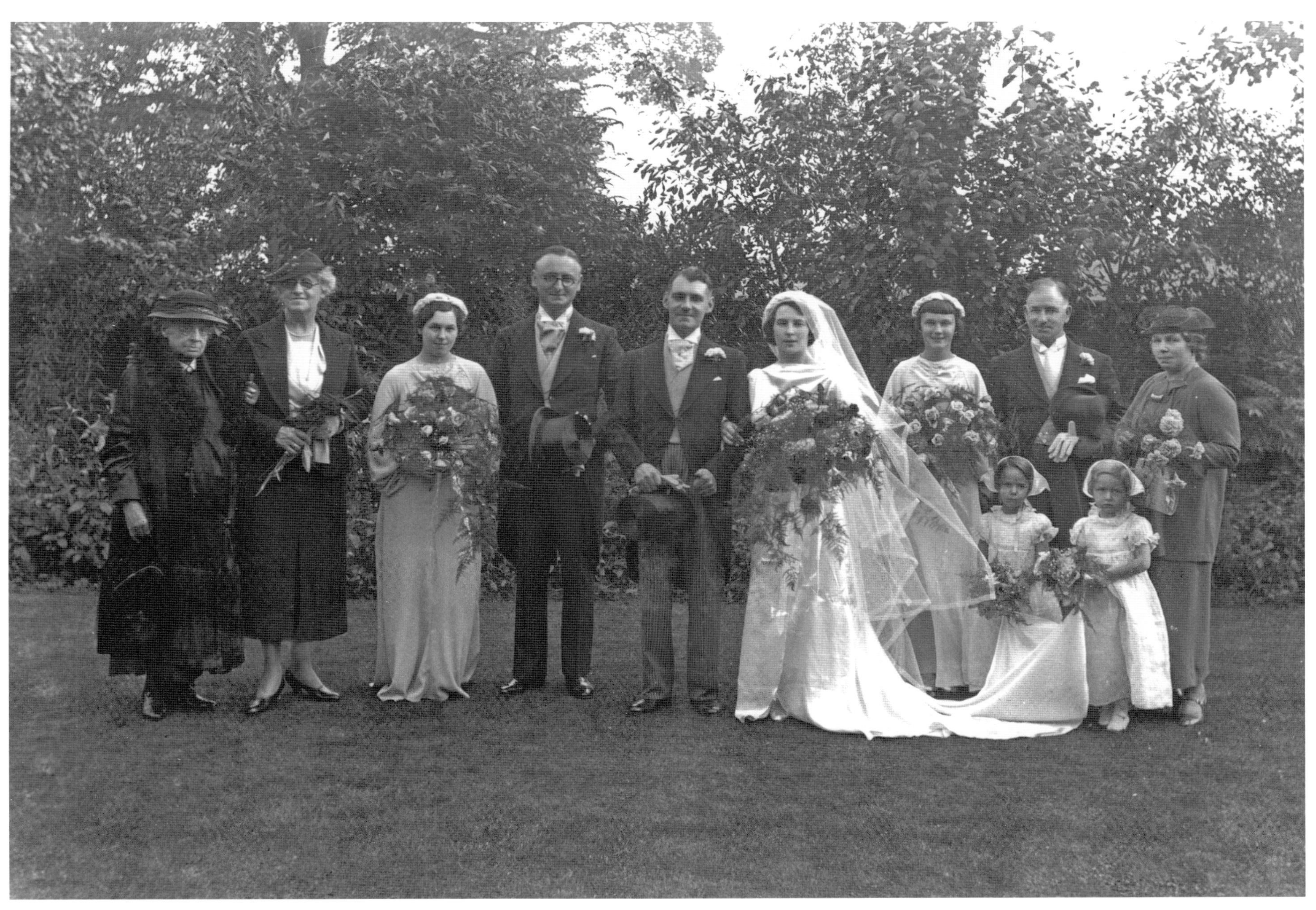

This was a very important wedding photograph for the firm as it was taken at the wedding of Lilian Ream's son, John Roland Fosbrook Ream to Violet May Seaman, who were married at St Peter's Church, Wisbech on 23 September 1936. Lilian Ream, who is second from the left, was one of the witnesses.

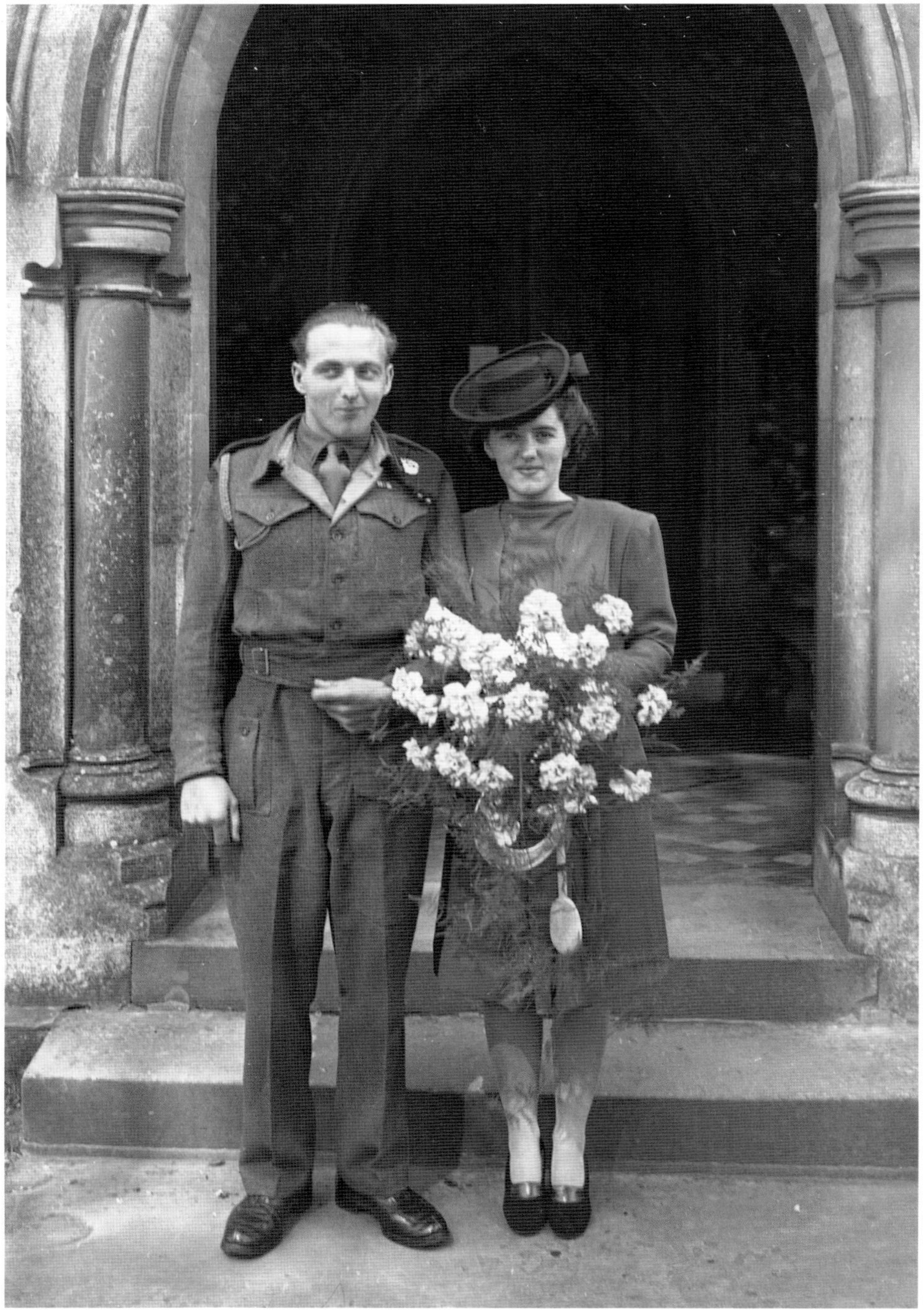

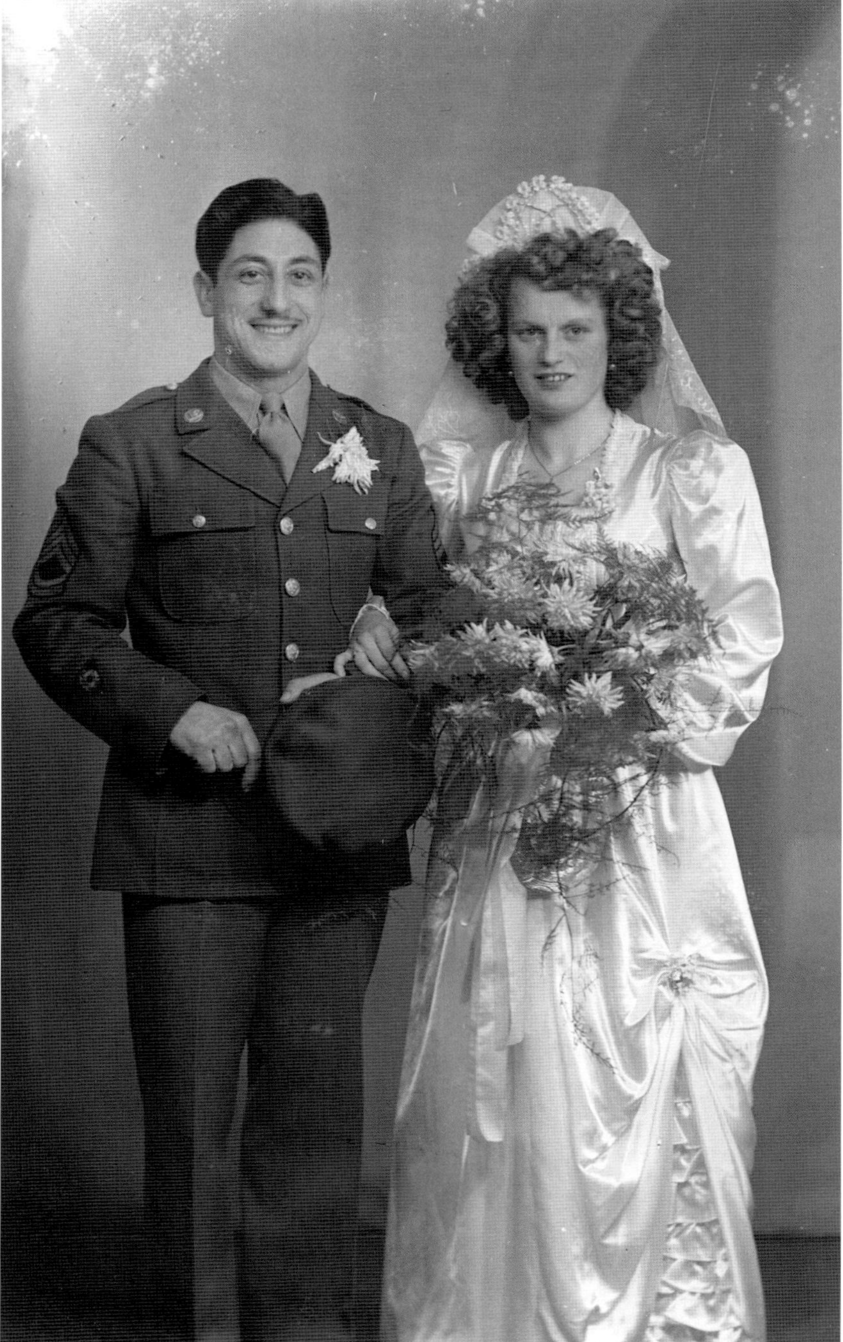

 Unknown sitters, probably photographed during World War II.

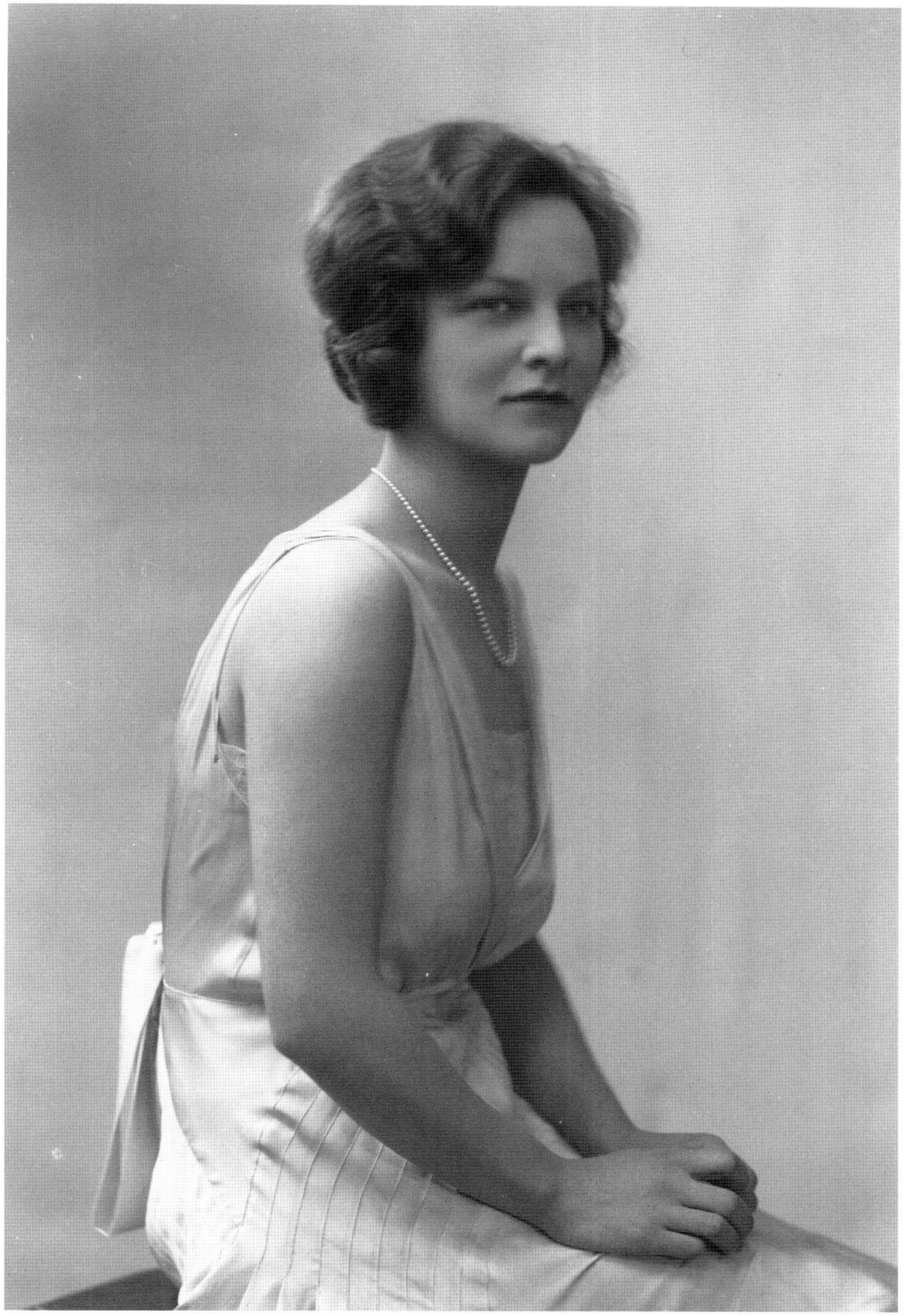

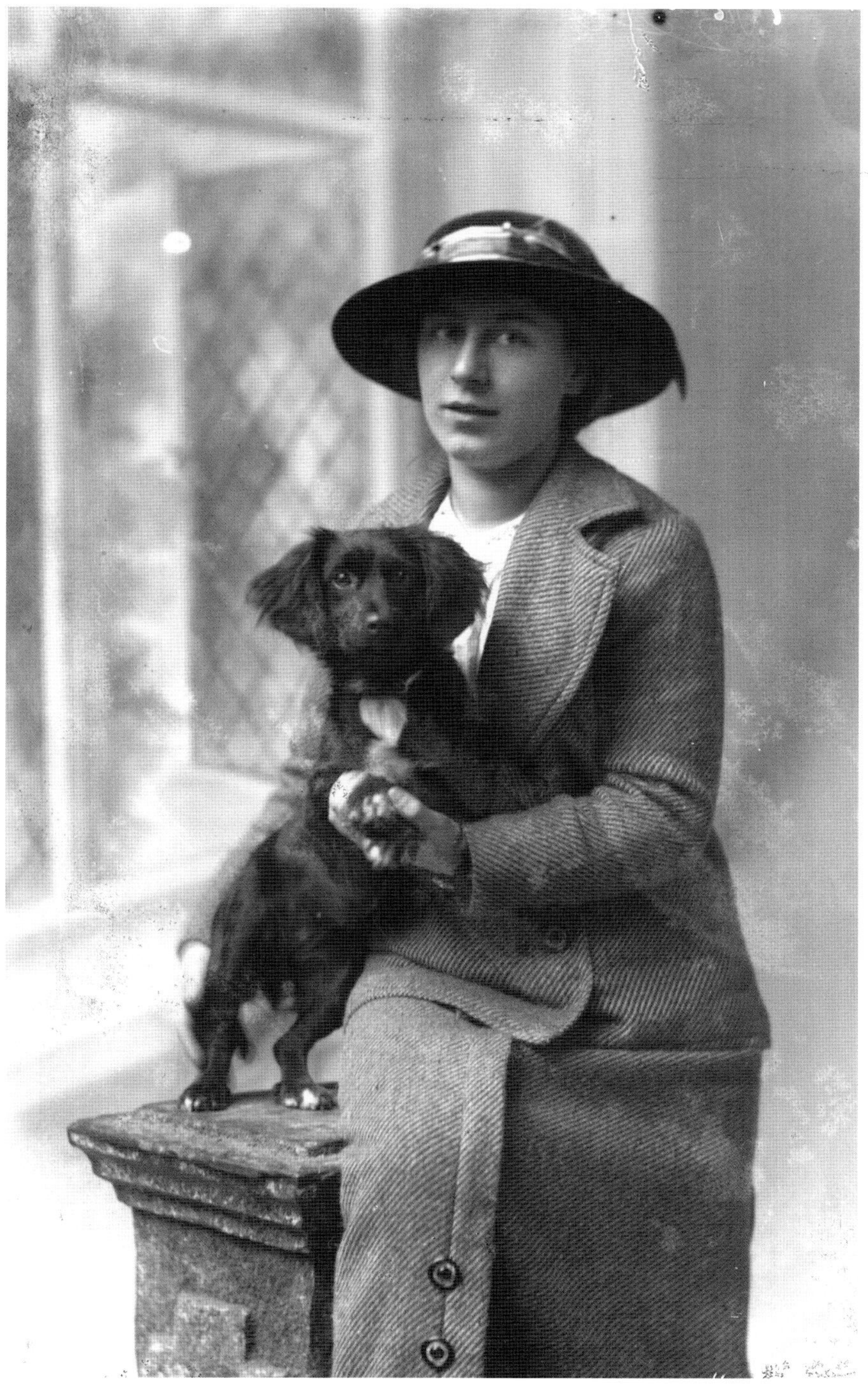

Left. Miss Hickman, 1933.
Right. Miss Beagles.

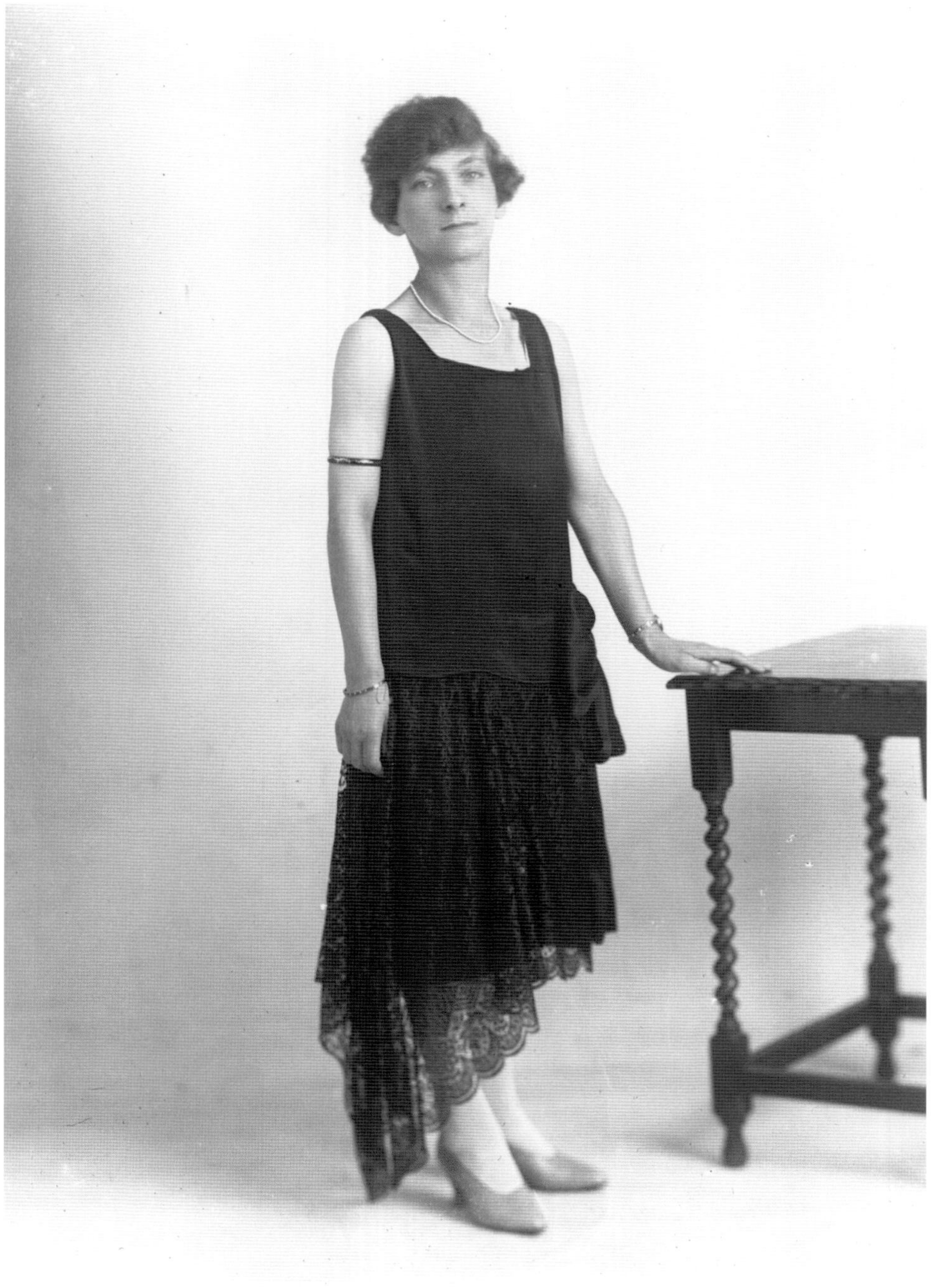

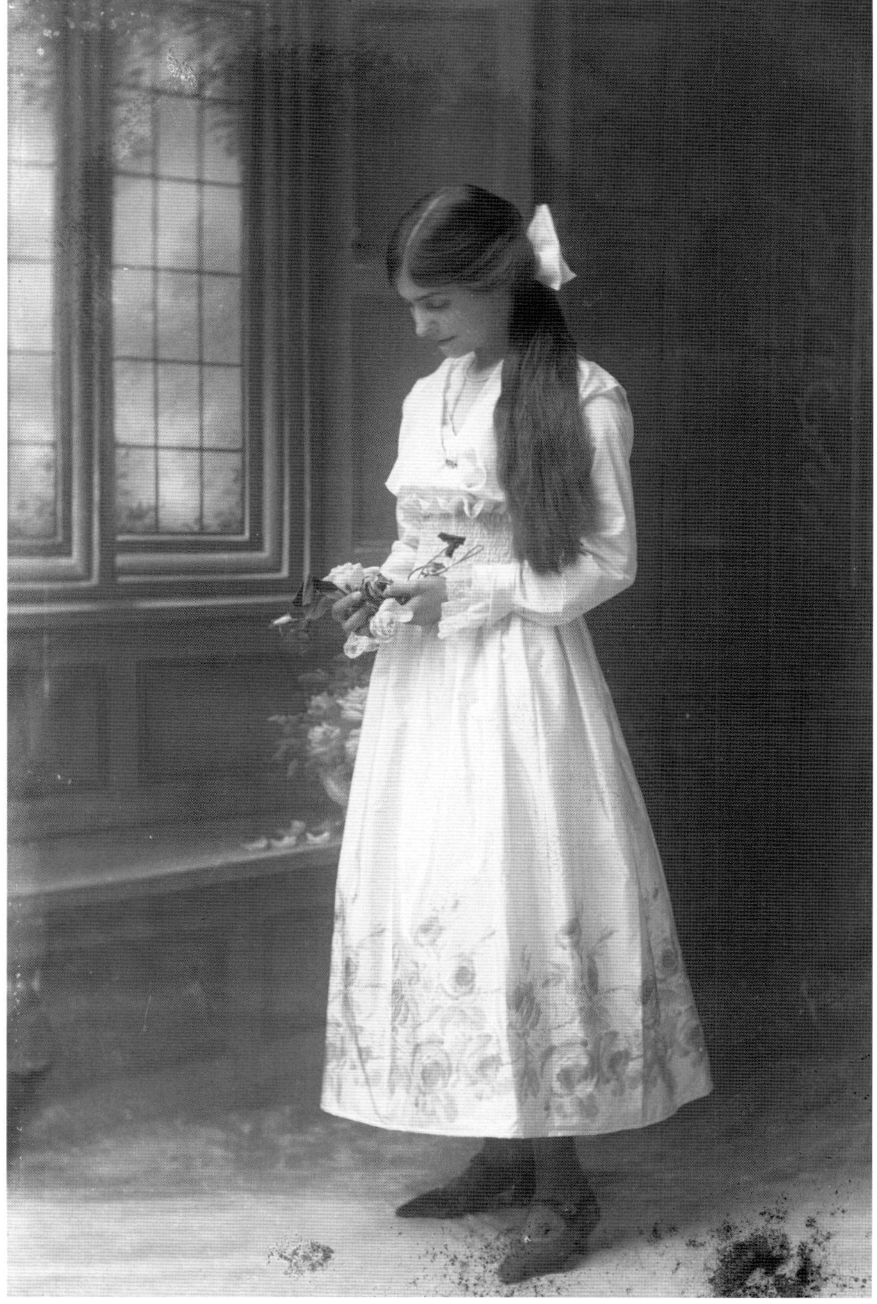

 Unknown sitters.

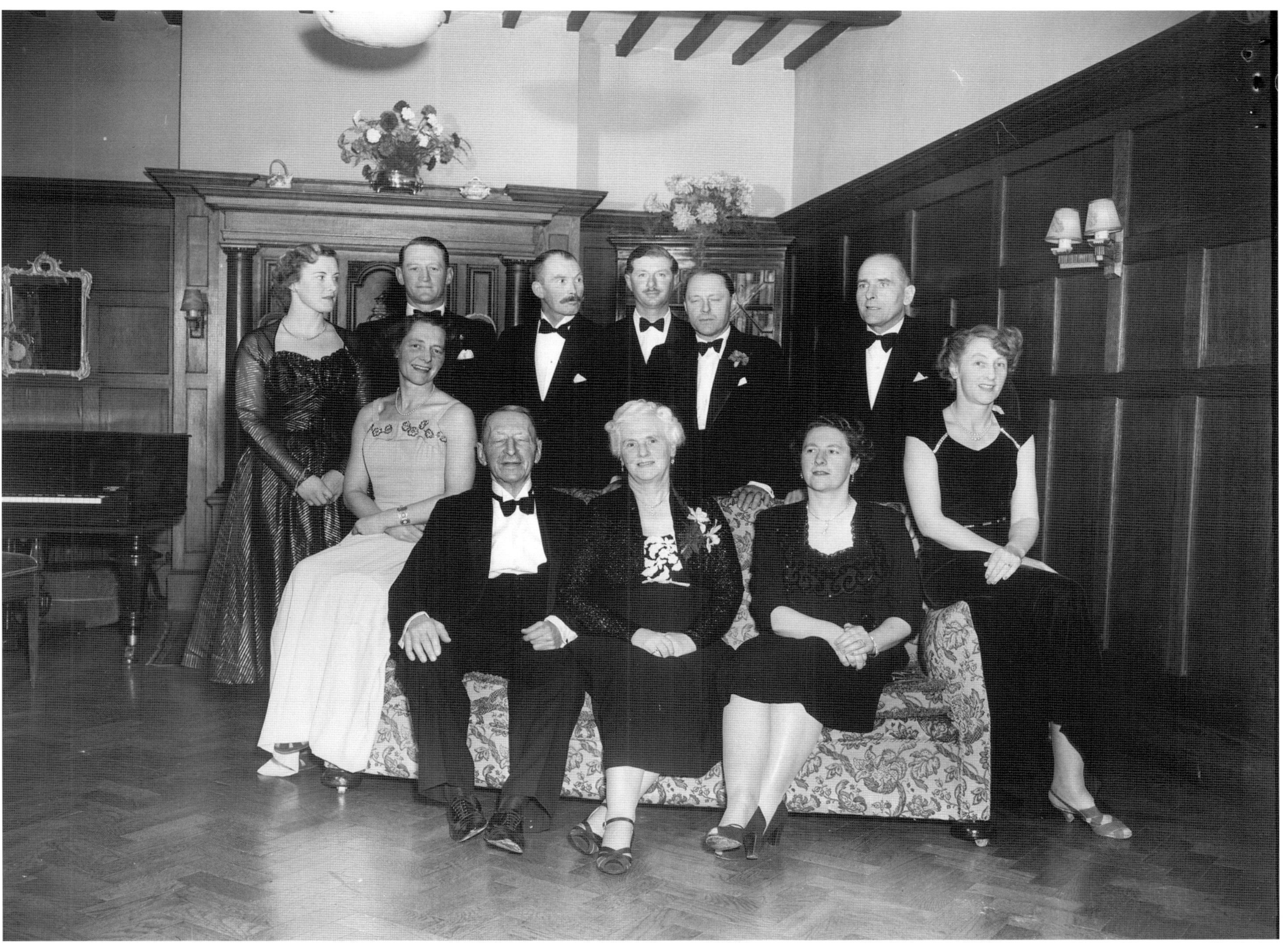

The Image family of Oxburgh Hall, Emneth, 1952.

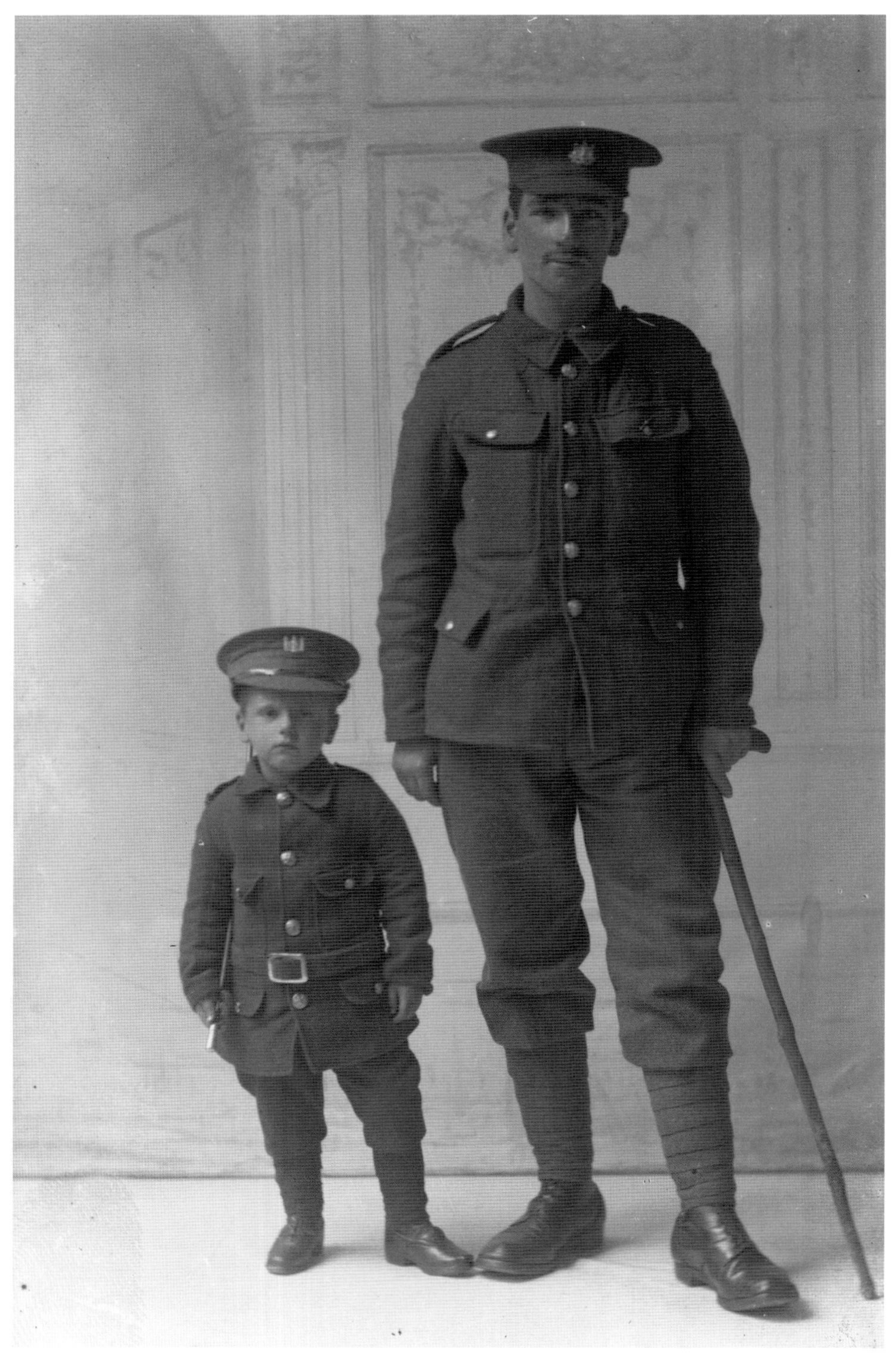

 Father and son, probably photographed during World War I.

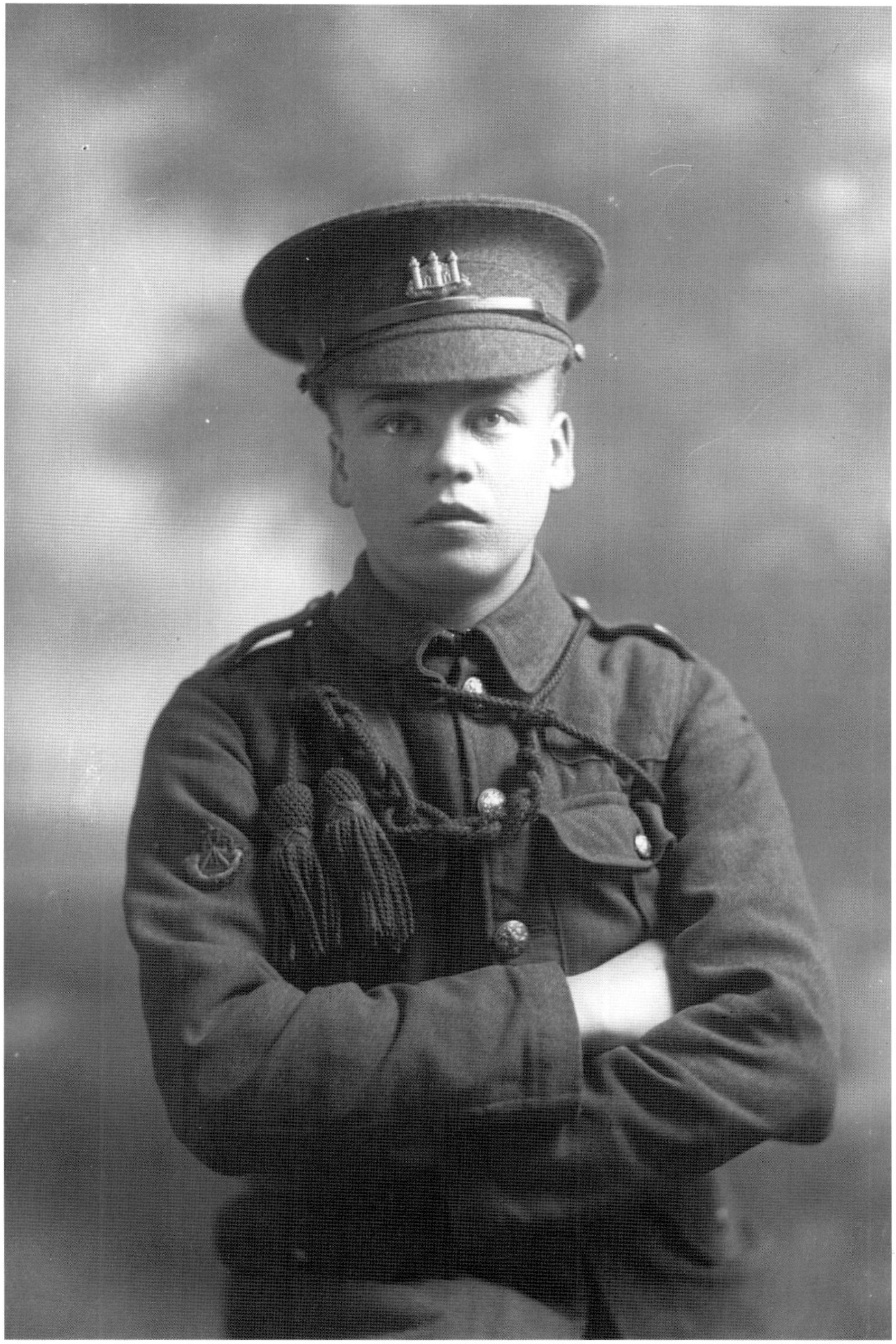

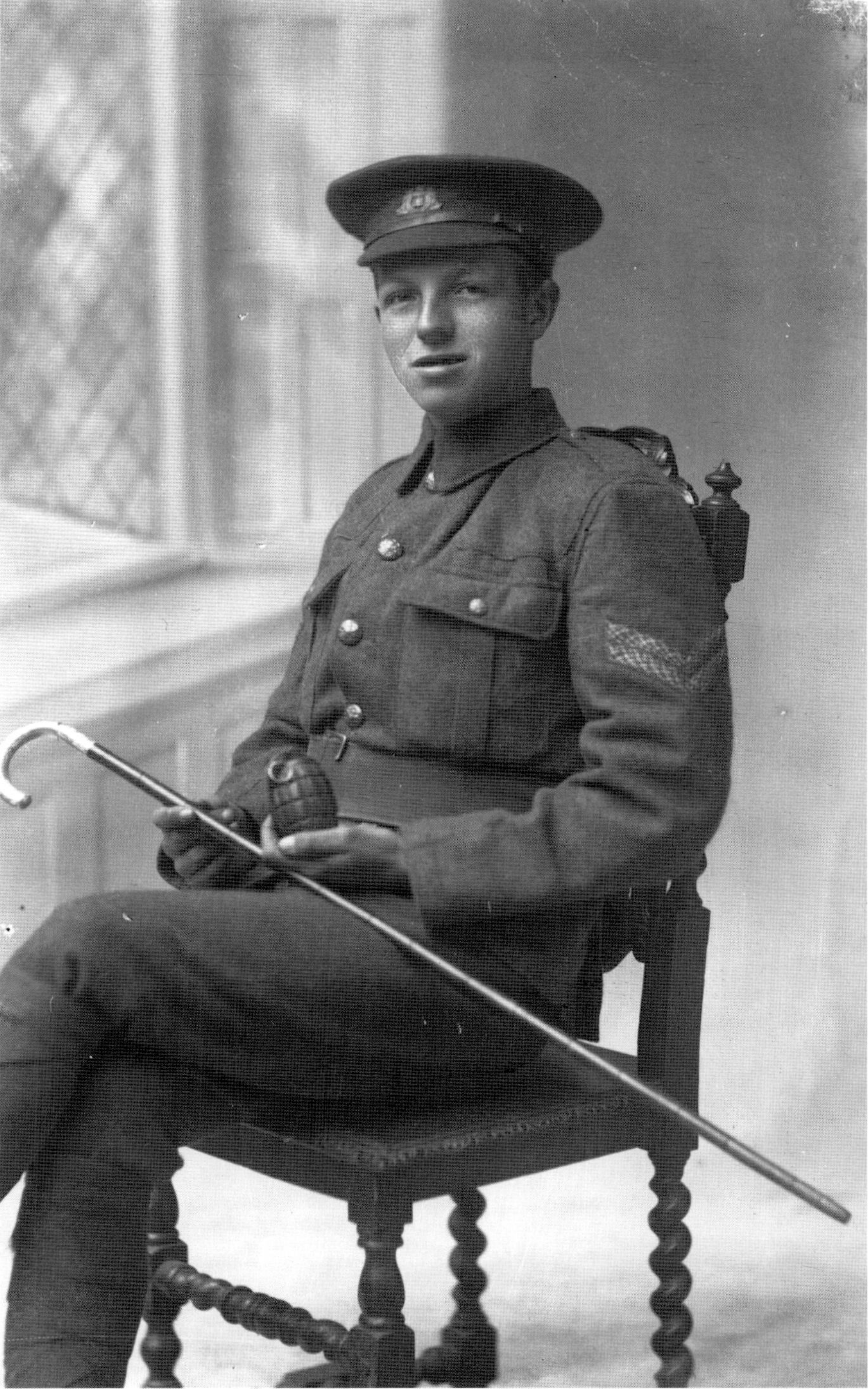

Unknown soldiers, World War I.

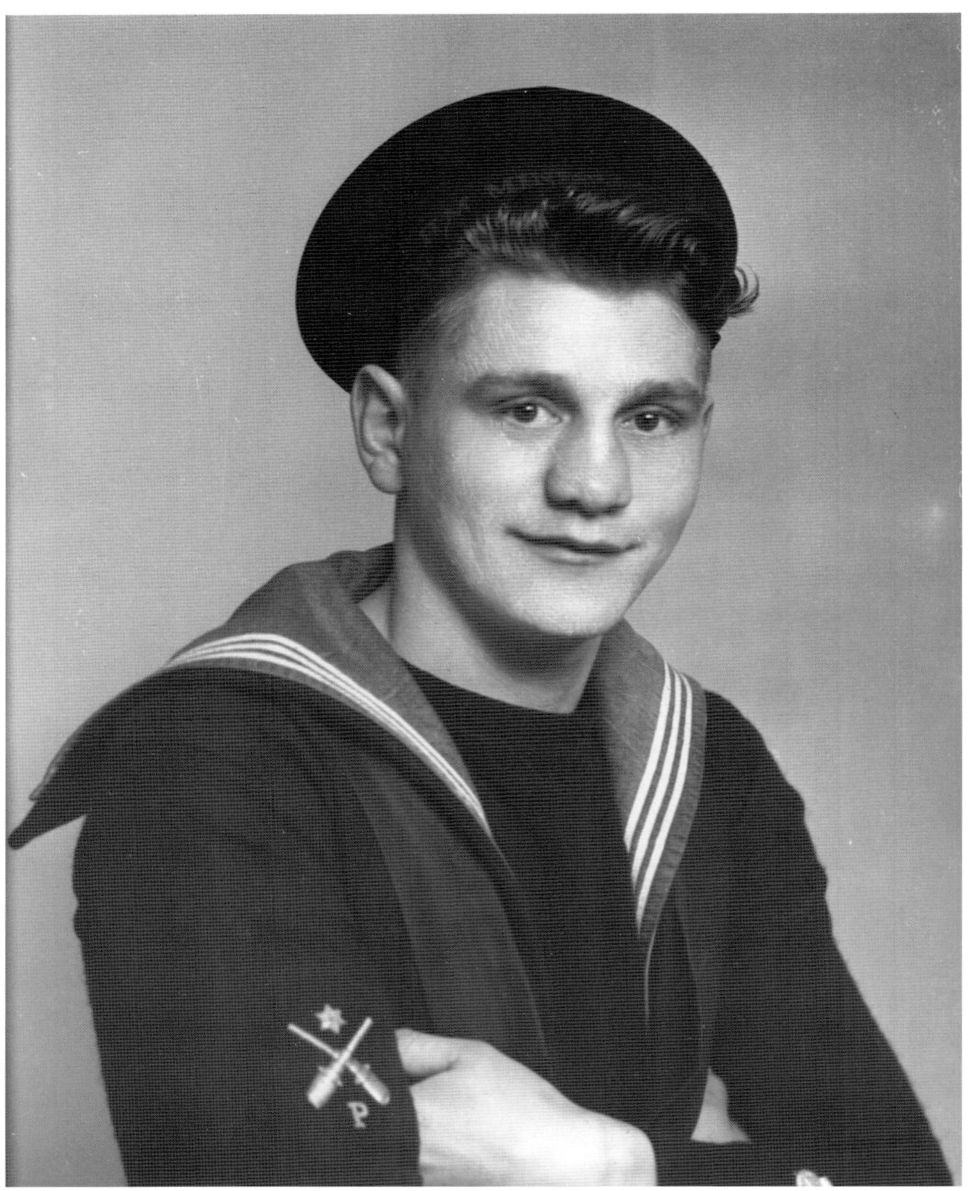

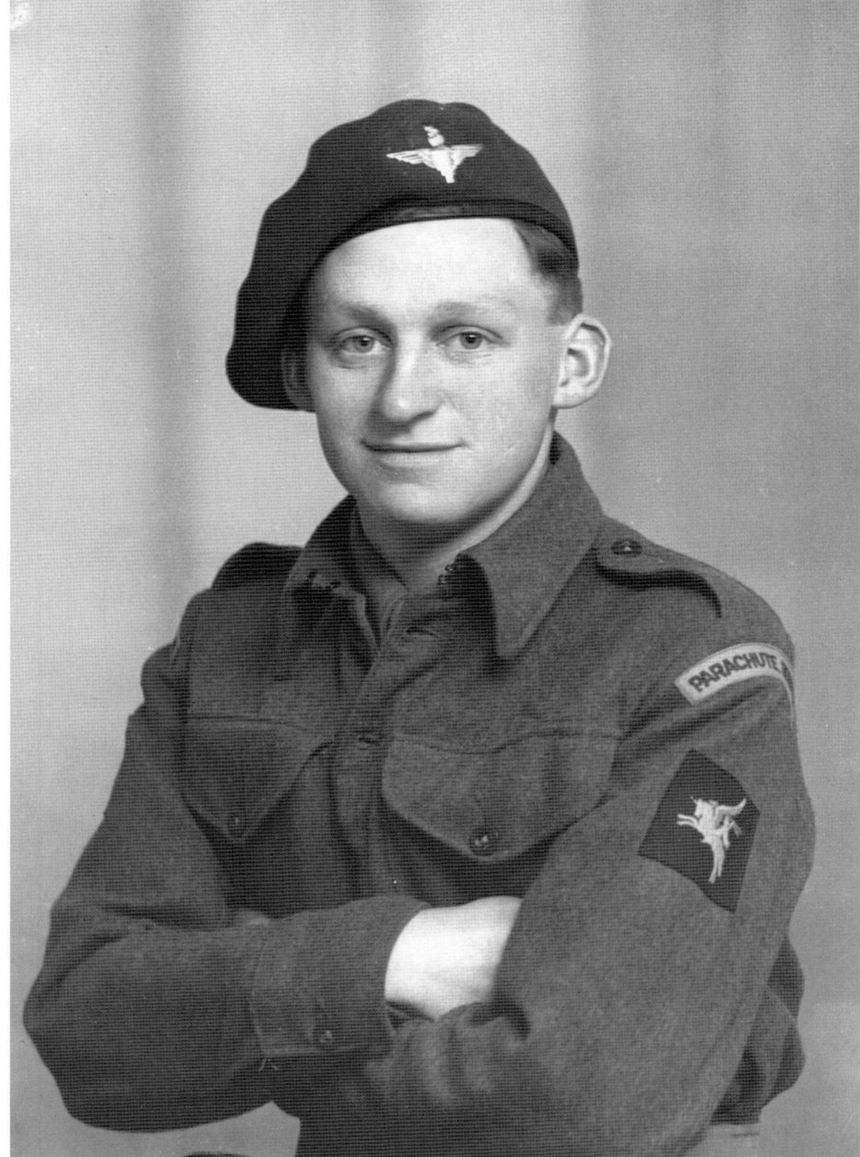

 Unknown servicemen.

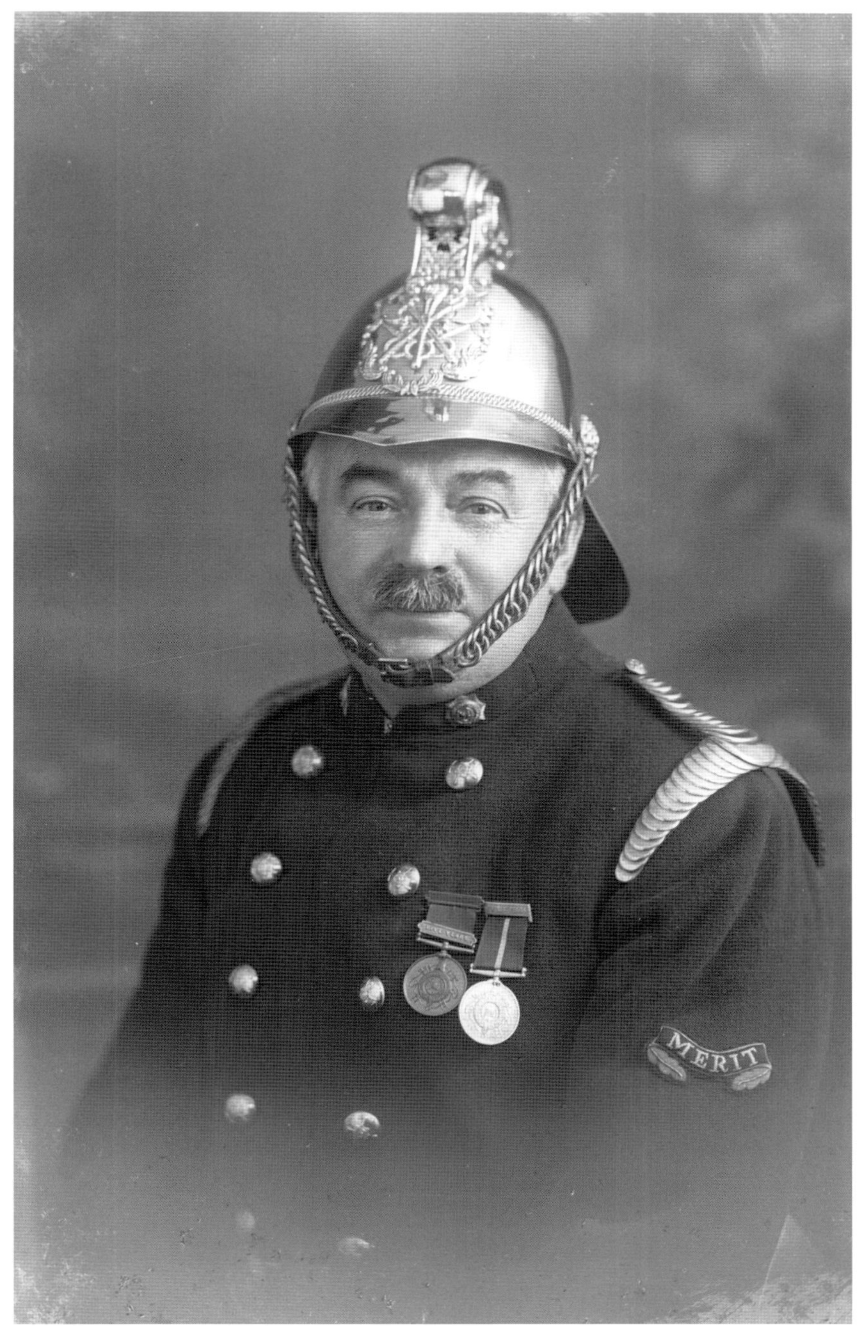

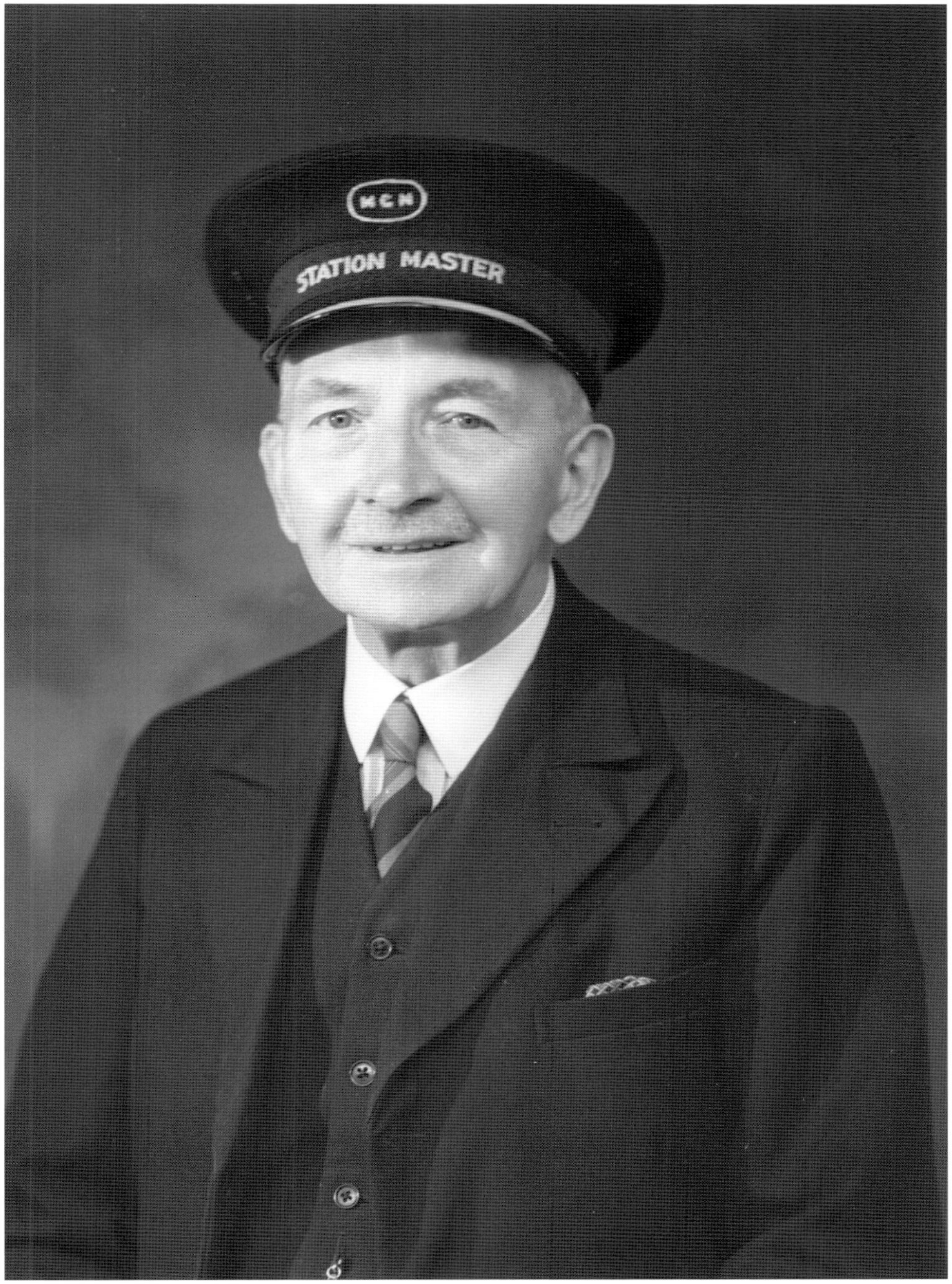

Left. Third Engineer, William 'Bill' Longford, of the Wisbech Fire Brigade, late 1920s. The metal epaulettes denote his status as an engineer.

Right. Mr Lusher, a Station Master for the LNER, 1933.

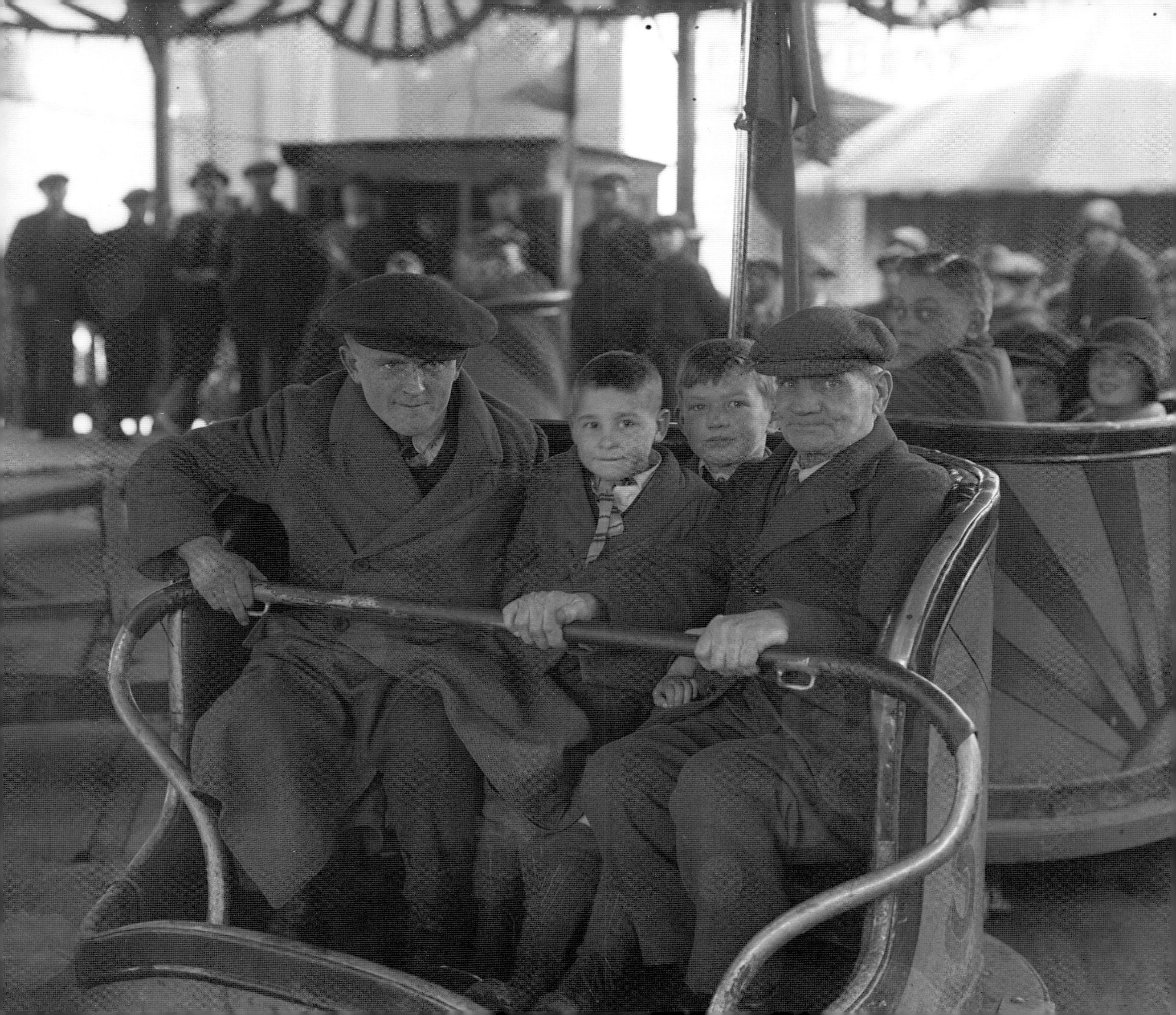

Old Age

On the waltzers at the Mart, 1950s.

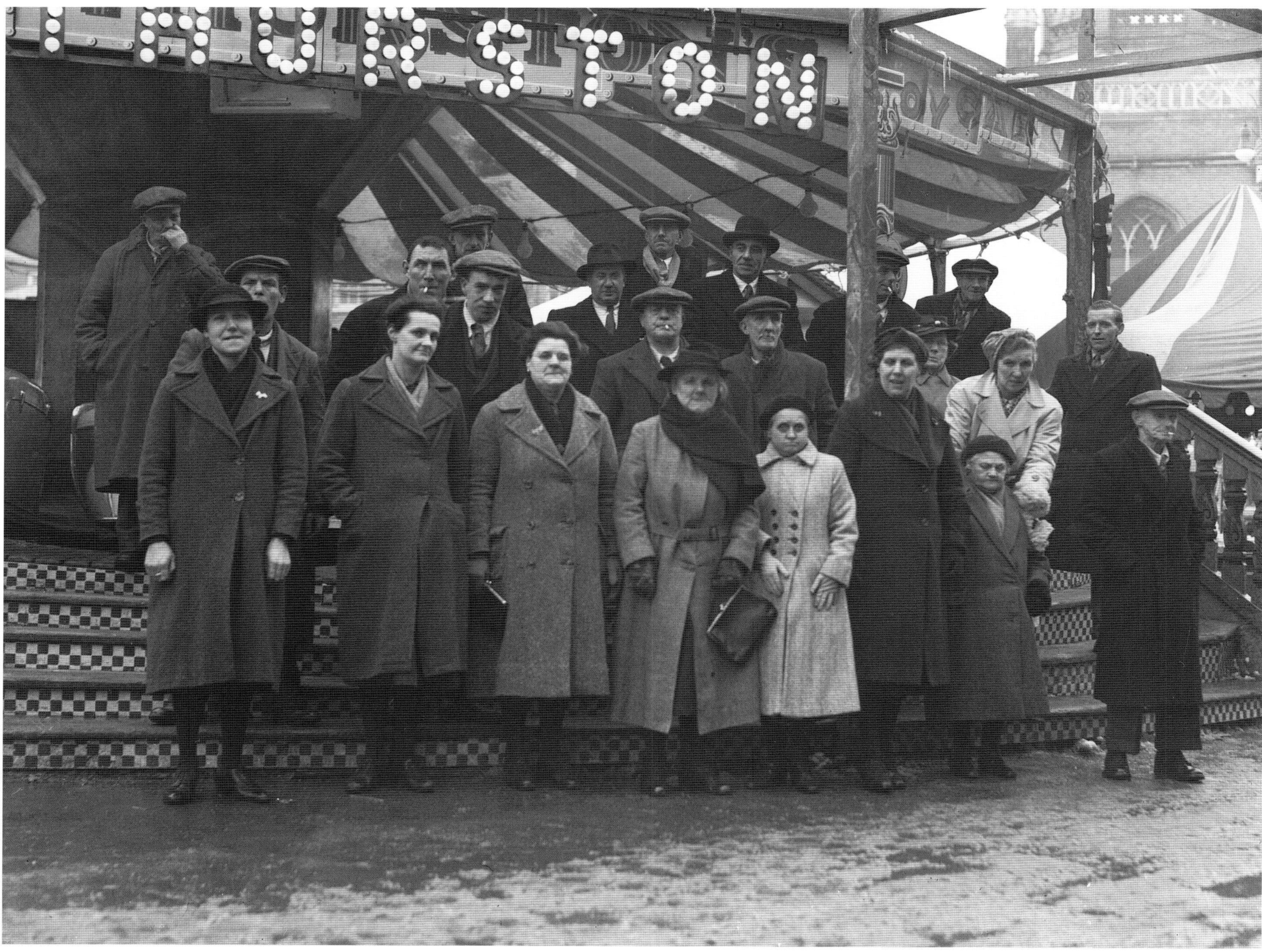

 Pentioners at the Mart, 1950s.

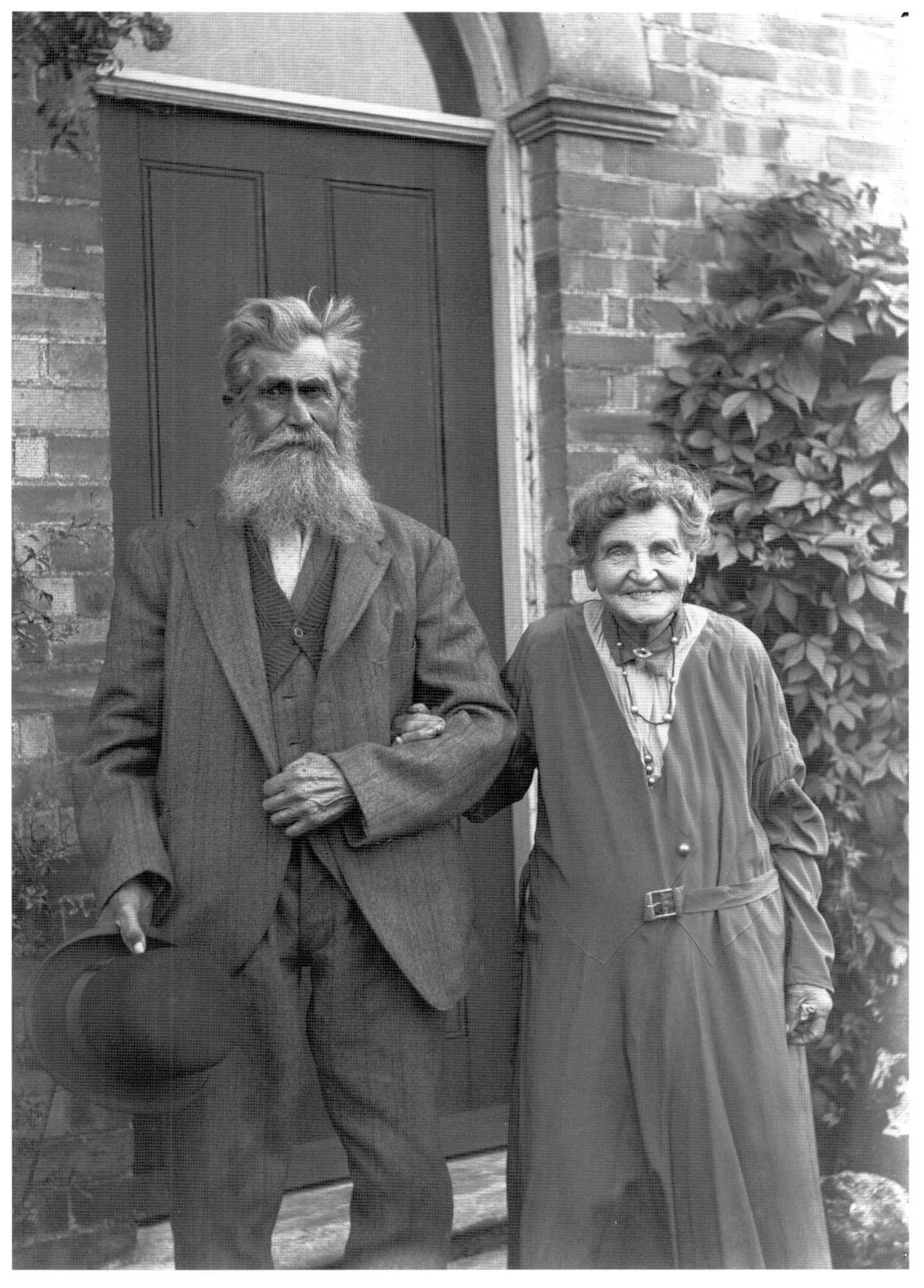

Mr and Mrs Shippey celebrating their diamond wedding anniversary, 1935.

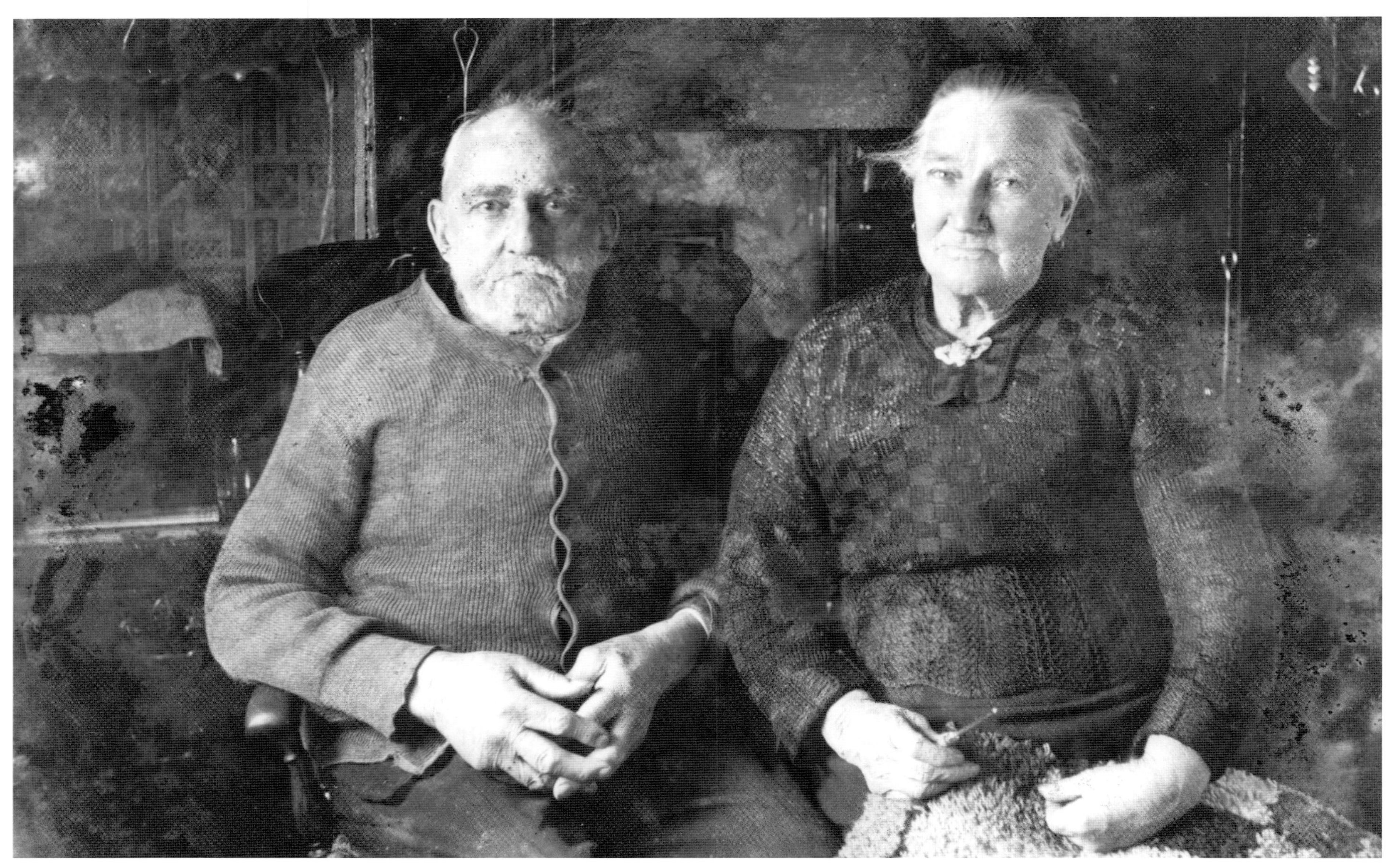

Mr & Mrs Jude, 1935. Possibly a photograph taken for the local newspaper to celebrate their Golden or Diamond wedding anniversary; note that Mrs Jude is making a rag rug.

Opposite. Mrs Corley with her dog, 1958.

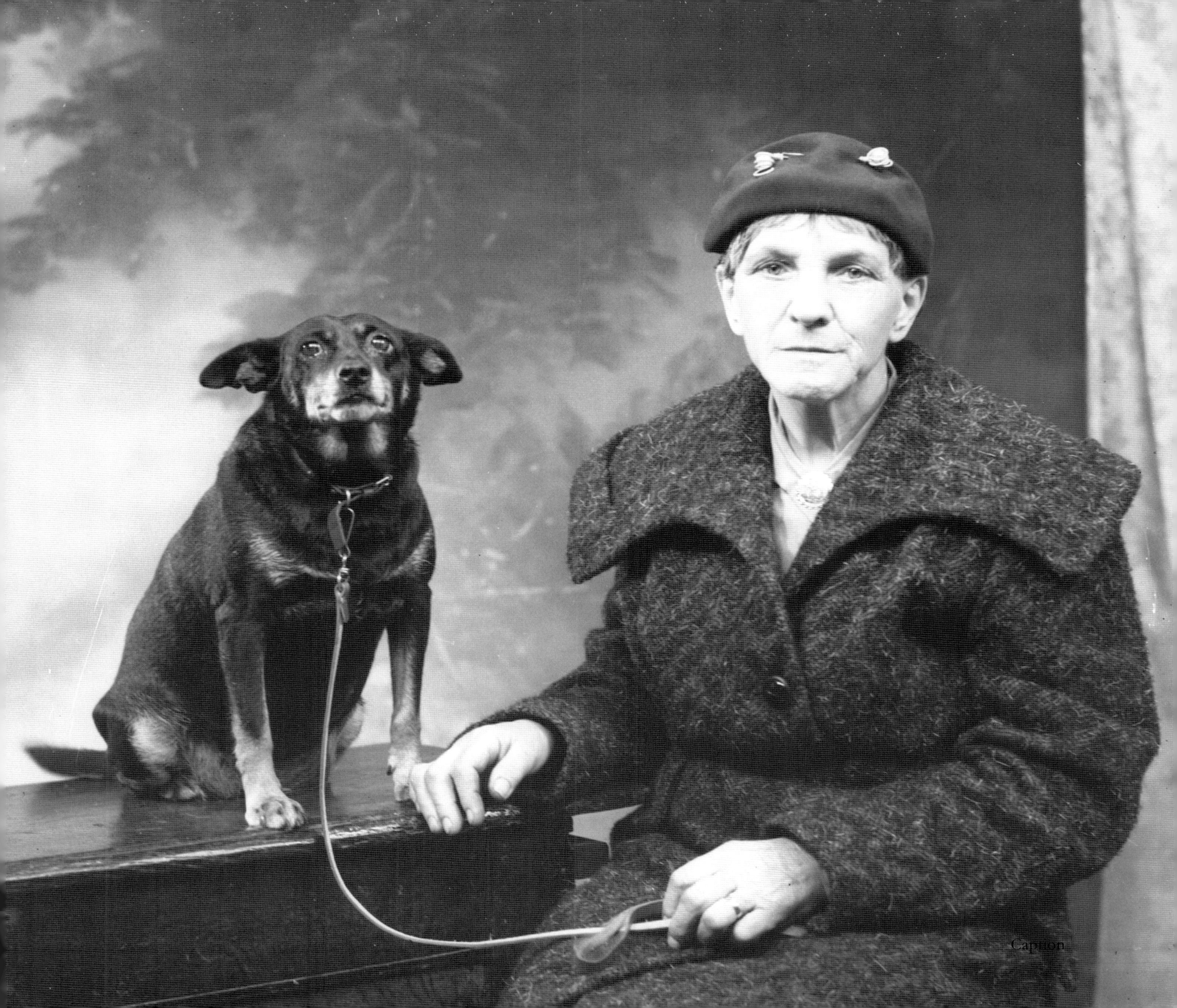

Caption

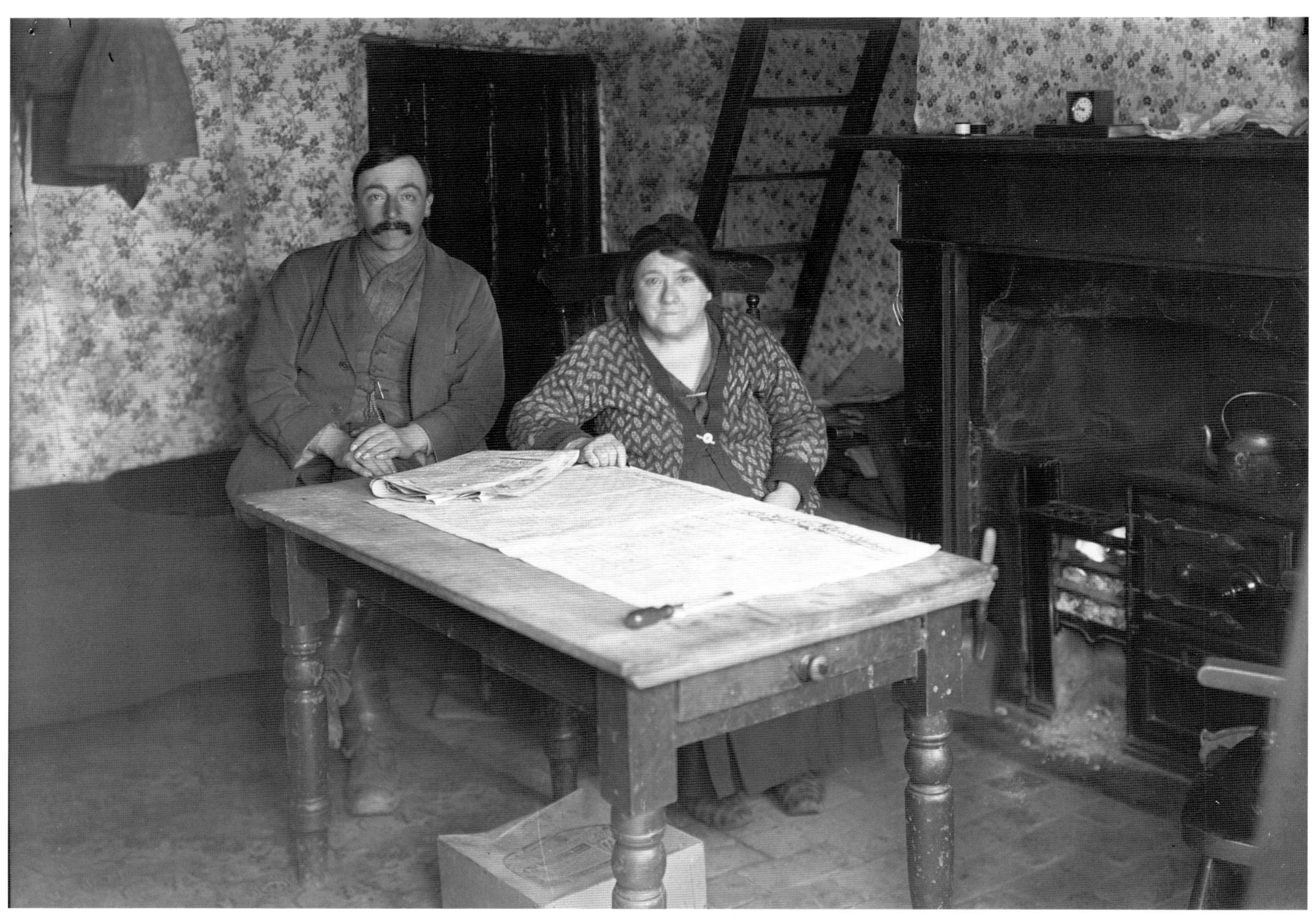

Mrs Piggot and her son, 1934. The Piggots are photographed in their new cottage, which had been purchaced with money from a legacy. Prior to this, the poverty-stricken couple had lived in a small, wooden shed.

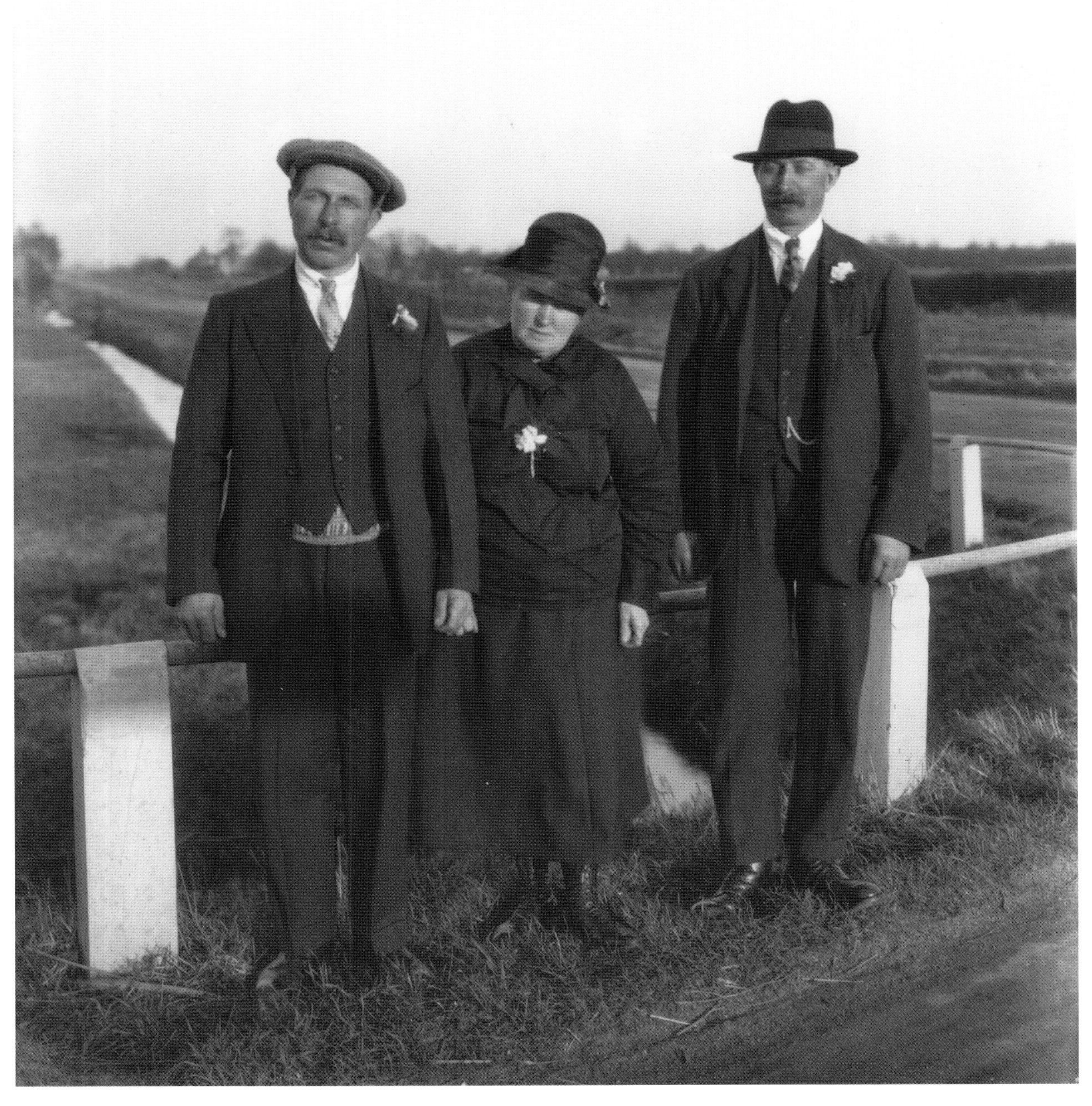

An unknown trio, in their best clothes, pose for a photograph on the road verge, 1930s.

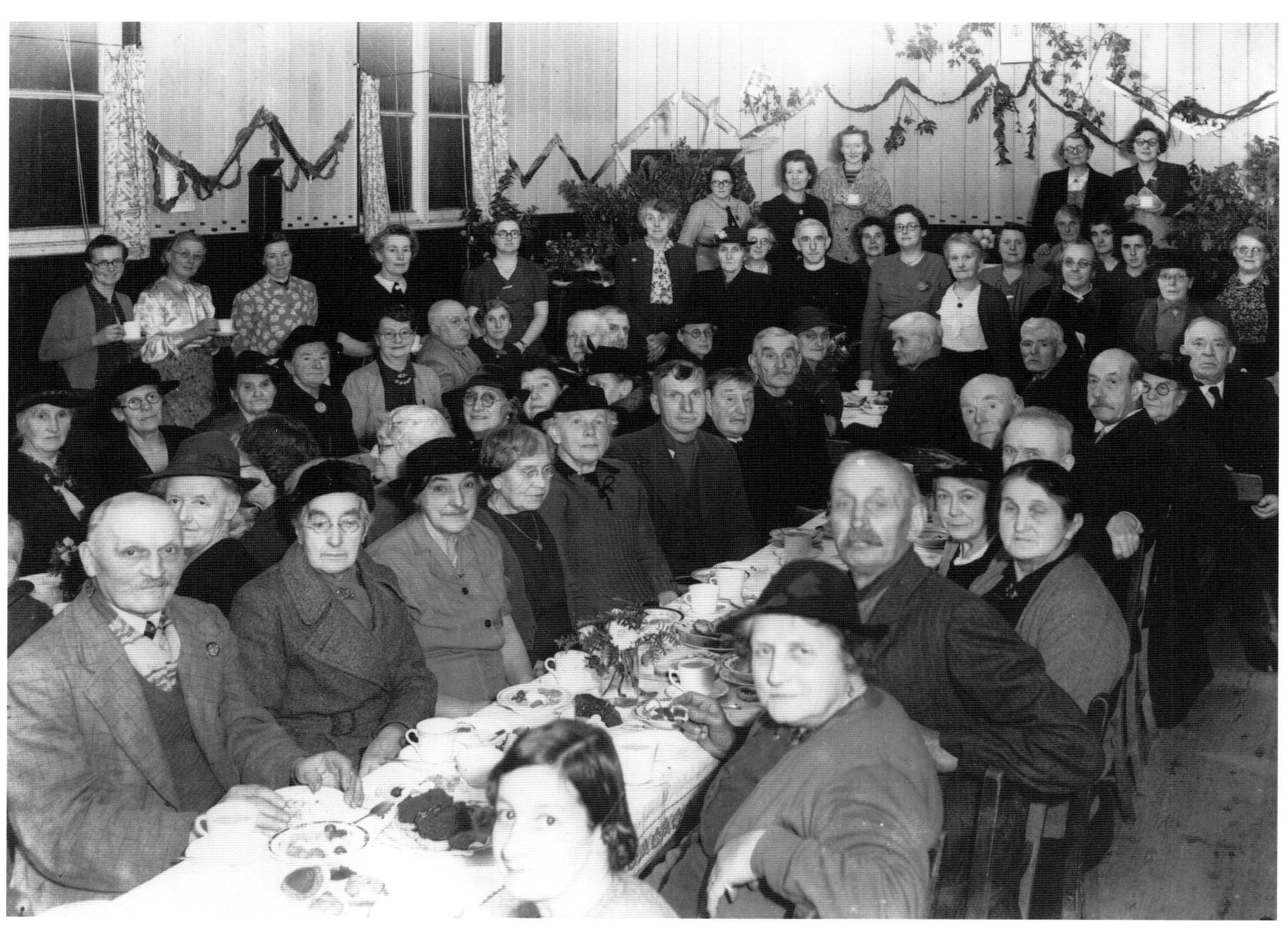

An old people's tea party at Leverington, 1940s. Events such as these were often supported by parish charities.

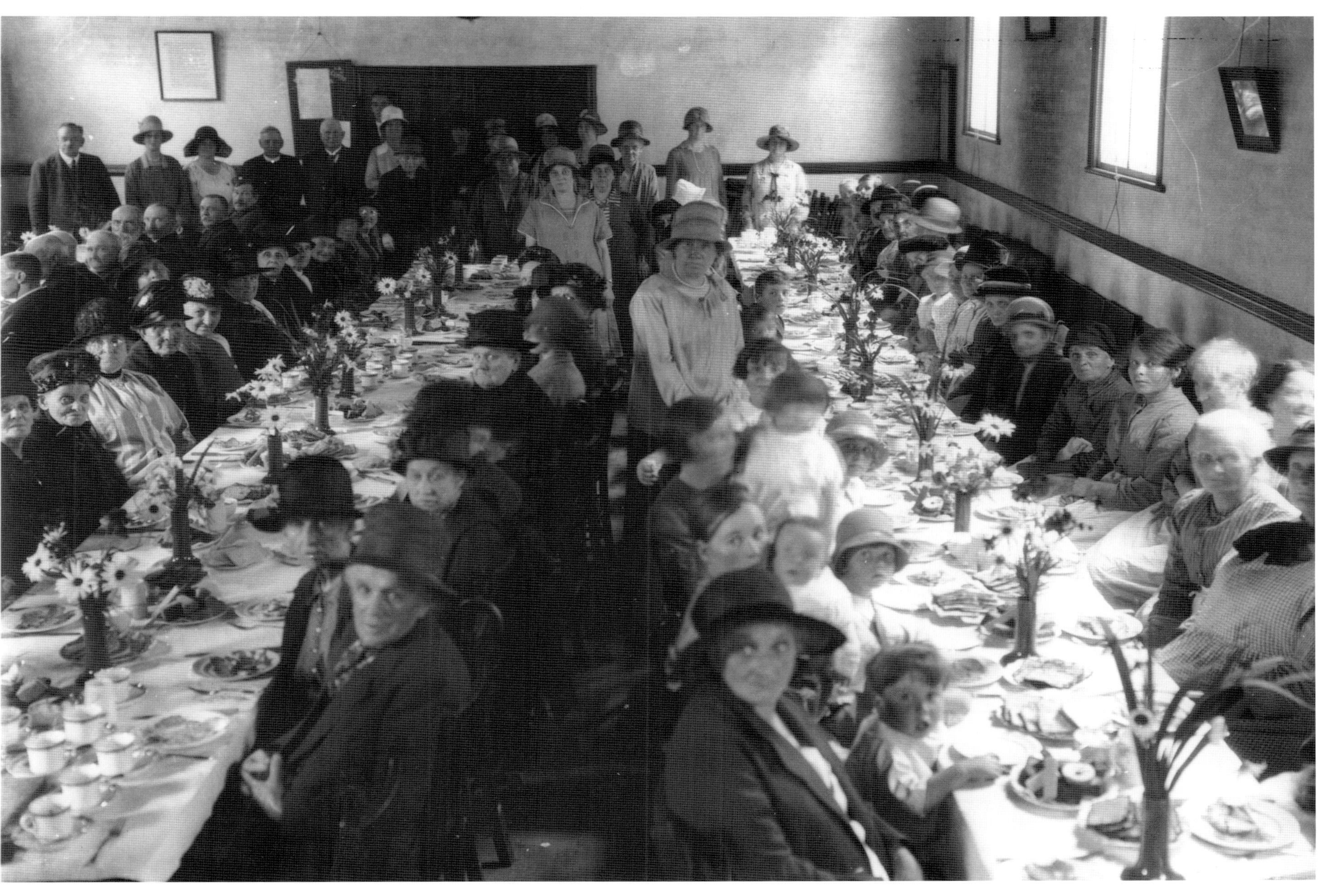

A combined tea for the inmates of the Wisbech Institution (the workhouse) and the town's Almshouses, photographed in the 1920s.

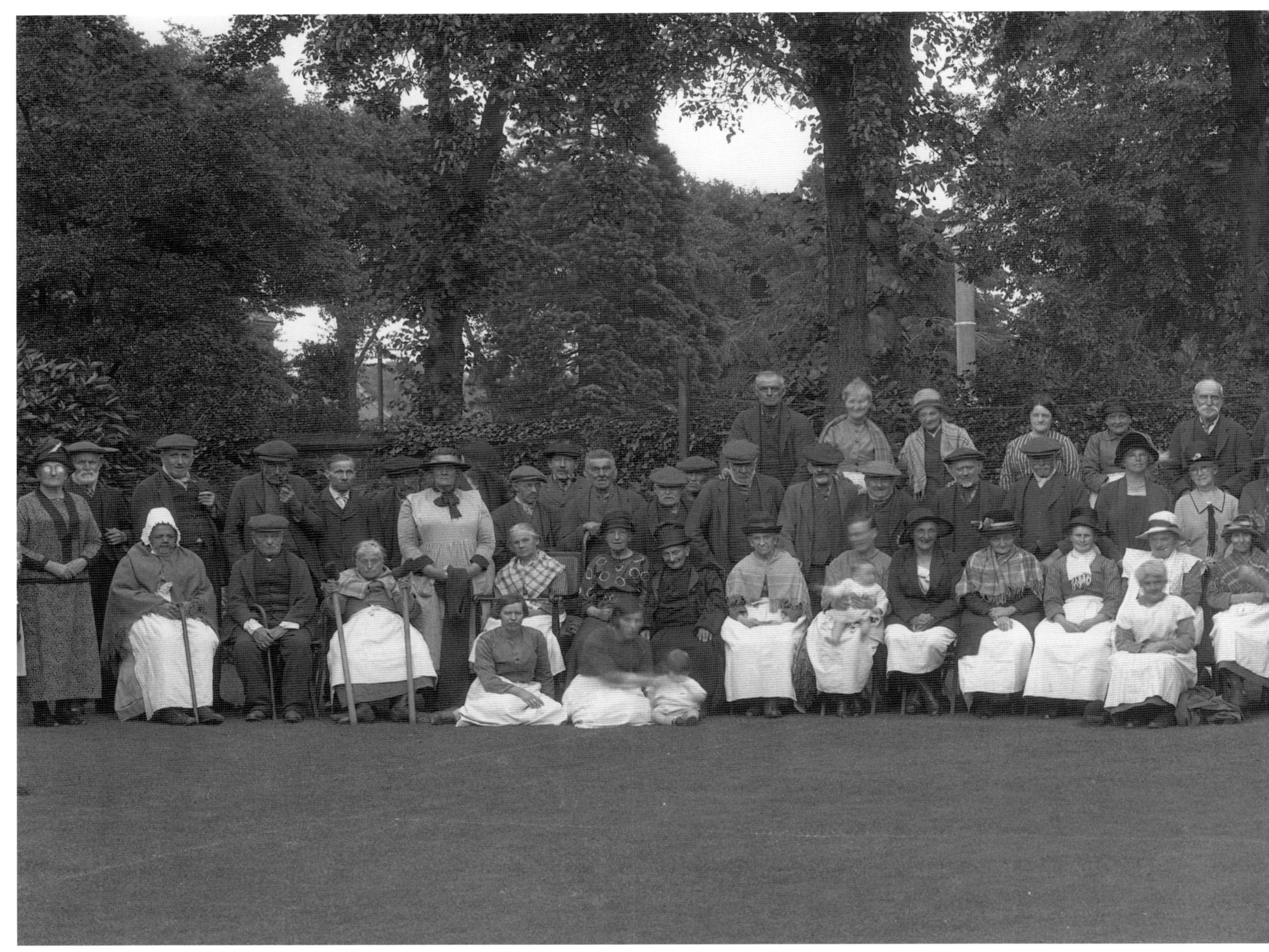

Inmates of the Wisbech Institution and the town's Almshouses, photographed in the 1920s. In the inter-war years, numbers were swelled by influxes of tramps during the summer. It was not until the major welfare reforms of the Labour Government in the late 1940s that the building ceased to be a workhouse.

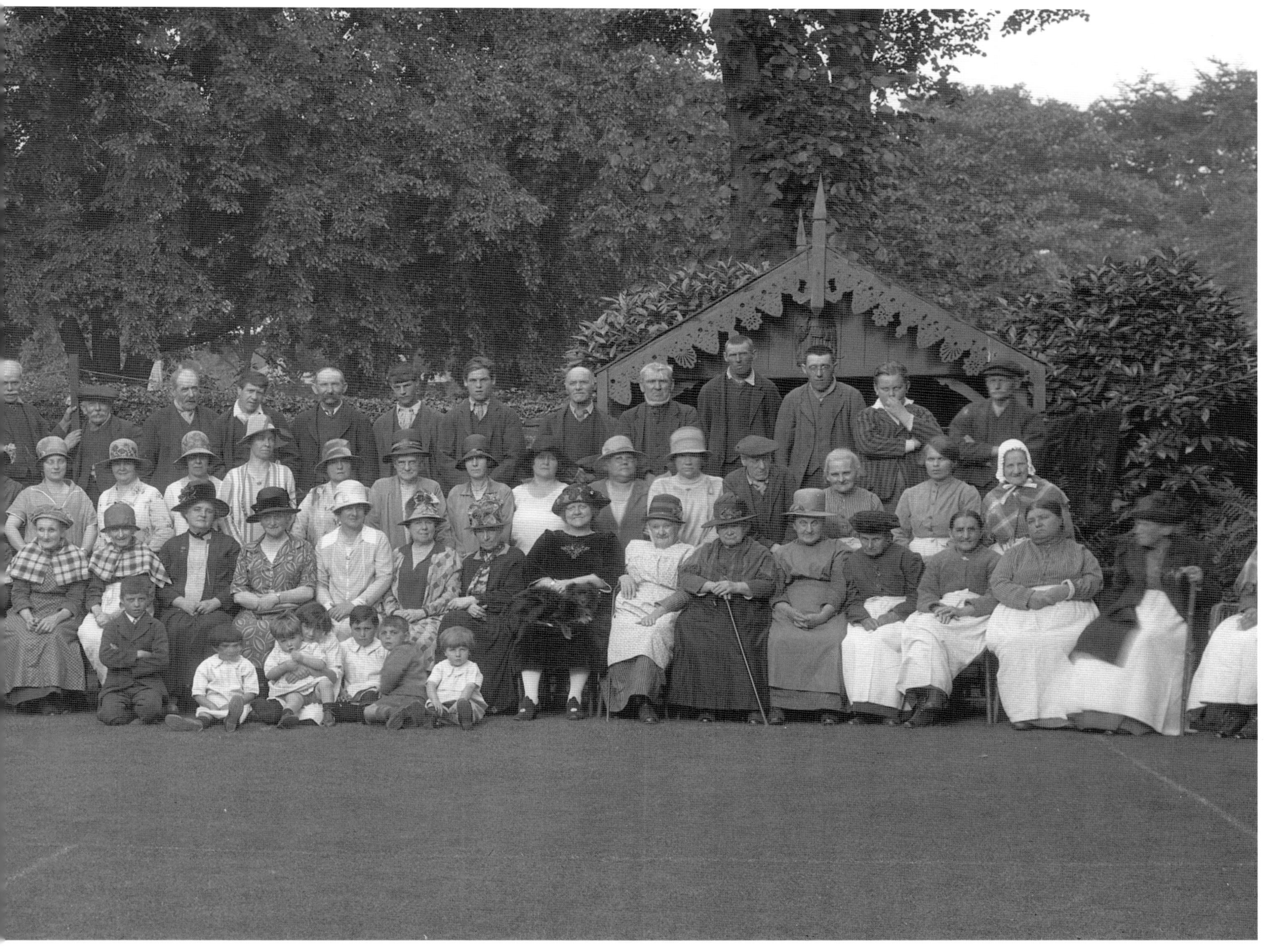

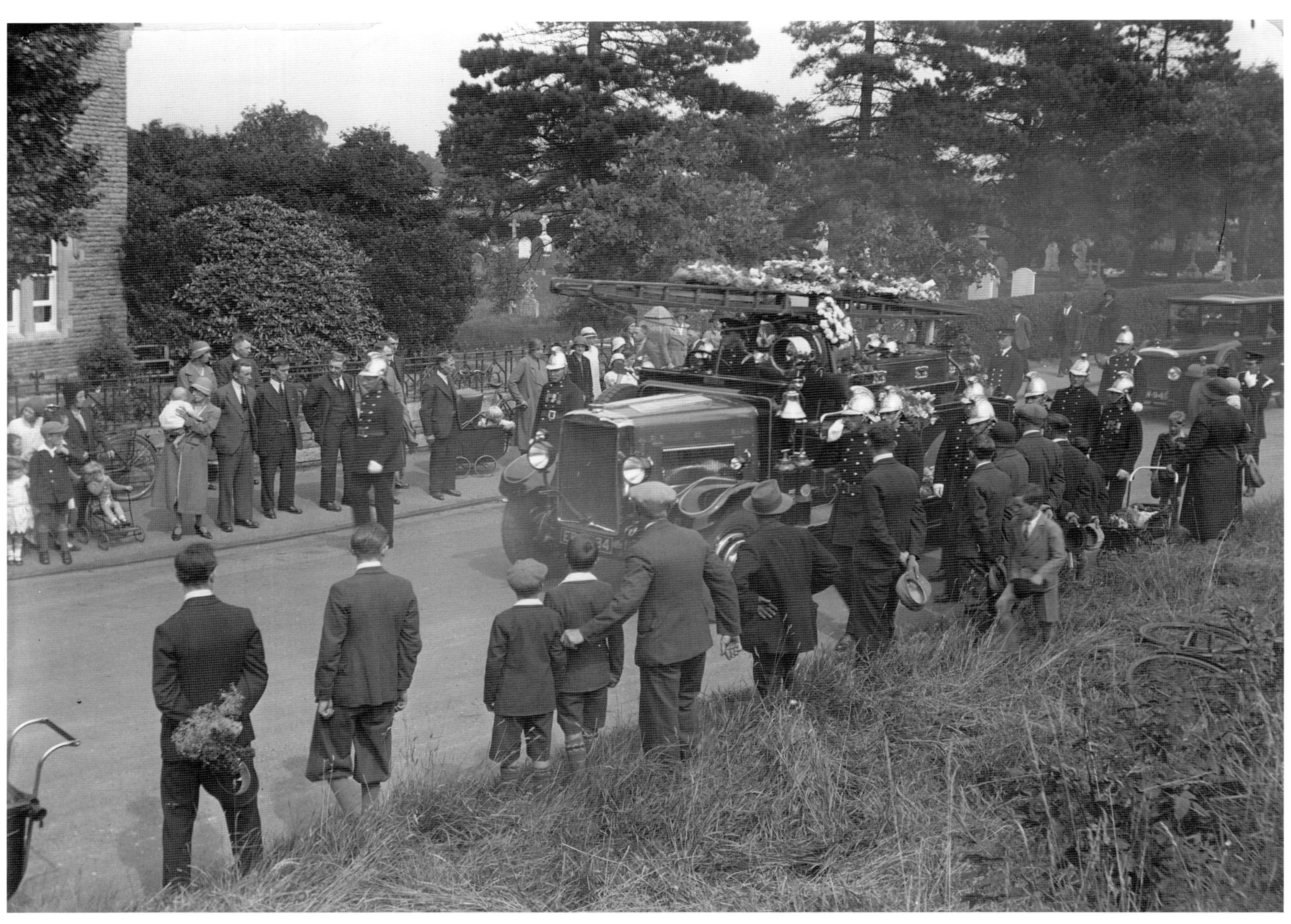

 The funeral procession of Divorah Smith proceeding along Mount Pleasant Road to the Borough Cemetery, 30 July 1933. Mr Smith, whose coffin was carried on the Borough fire engine 'Vivien', had been a member of the Fire Brigade for 32 years.

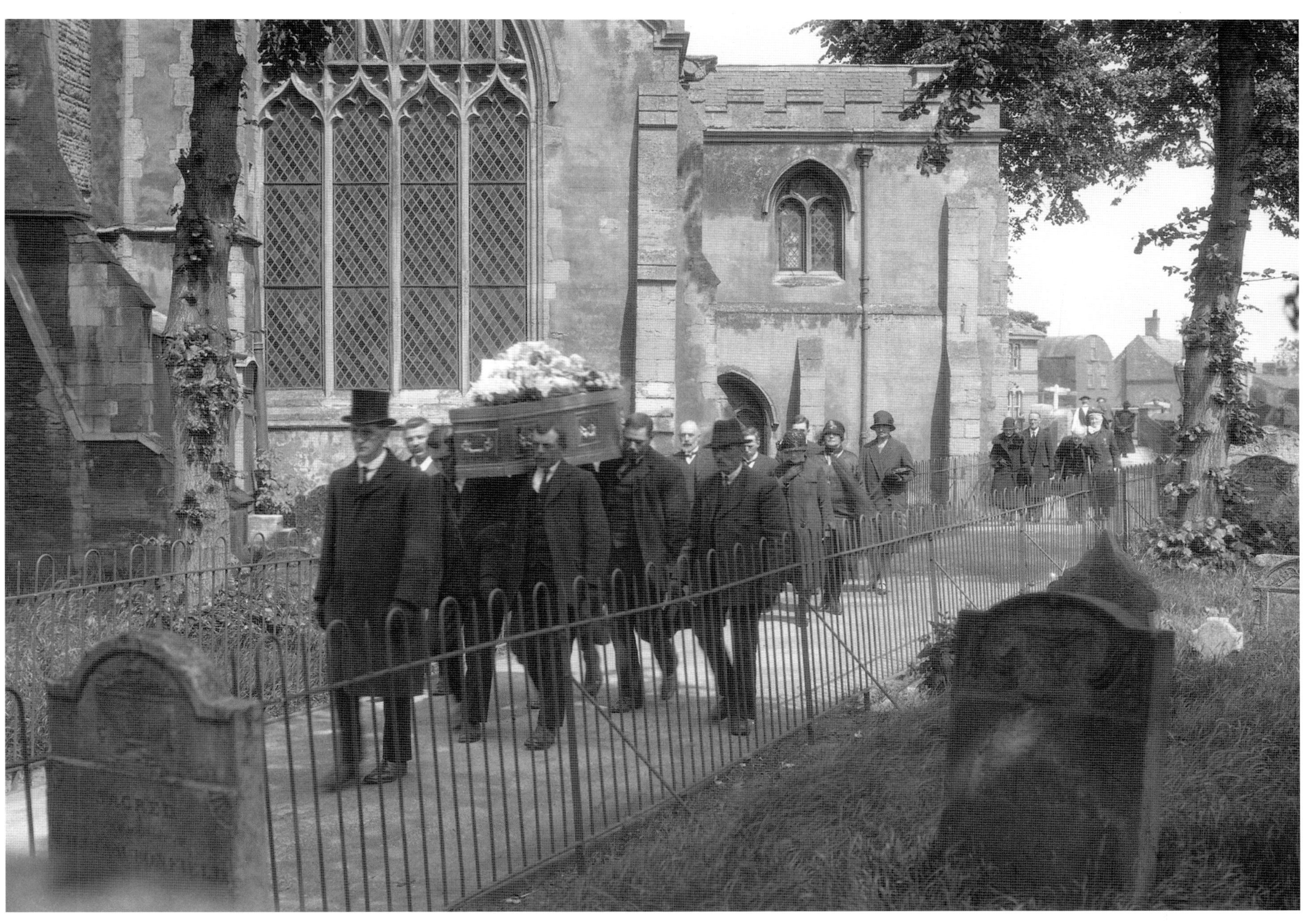

A funeral procession at St Clement's Church, Outwell. The negative envelope bears the reference number and enigmatic note 'Newling-Jones', which suggests this is the burial of Edward Harry Newling on 24 May 1921.

The Lilian Ream Exhibition Gallery Trust

The negatives which form the collection were all either taken by Lilian Ream herself or by members of her staff. The Lilian Ream Studio recorded local people, places, and events.

It was very much a commercial operation and the photographs reflect the variety of customers which ranged from both local newspapers, to shops, factories, sports teams and individuals who wanted to record their family, home or some major happening in their lives.

Portraits were the bread and butter of the business and form about seventy percent of the collection. They illustrate not only changing fashions in clothes but also the way people saw themselves, their families and their place in the world.

No one knows just how many negatives existed when the firm closed down as all the records have disappeared but many were lost before the surviving negatives, numbering between 150-200,000, were acquired by Cambridgeshire Libraries in 1981. The negatives were sorted with the aid of a Manpower Services project sponsored by Fenland District Council and later a number of local exhibitions were held thanks to sponsorship by local businesses.

Unfortunately many of the negatives are in very poor condition and are deteriorating all the time. Cambridgeshire County Council was unable to provide the funds needed to save the collection and, in 1993, handed them over to a newly formed charitable trust in the hope that it would be better able to raise the finance required. The trust has continued to make more of the collection available to the public but progress on conservation is extremely slow.

When refurbishment work began on Wisbech Library in late 2008, the negative collection had to be moved into environmentally controlled storage provided by Cambridgeshire County Council. It was during this transfer that it was found that the collection contained over 20,000 potentially volatile nitrate negatives; these are now housed a separate secure storage facility.

The Lilian Ream Exhibition Gallery was constituted by a Declaration of Trust dated 19th July 1993.

Among the aims of the Trust are:

- To conserve, publish and exhibit photographs and negatives from the Lilian Ream Collection.
- To collect photographs, negatives and documents to enhance the existing collection.
- To promote or undertake research and publish such research.
- To collect oral history depicting the history of Wisbech and the Fens by the use of the existing collection.

LILIAN REAM EXHIBITION GALLERY TRUST
c/o Wisbech Library
5 Ely Place
Wisbech
Cambs., PE13 1EU

www.lilianream.org.uk
Registered Charity No. 1024465

Further reading:

Reams of Wisbech (Cambridgeshire Libraries and Information Service) 1987
Lilian Ream: A Life in Photography (Cambridgeshire Libraries and Information Service) 1992
Wisbech (Chalford) 1996